Airport Warnings: An Airport Policeman Speaks

Airport Warnings: An Airport Policeman Speaks

William R. Herrin

ISBN-13: 9780692953877
ISBN-10: 0692953876

Dedication

To my wife Cindy, with heartfelt thanks for your perseverance during the years I spent on this effort.

I offer a special thank-you to Michael, who is in heaven now. Thank you for your support and your understanding of my efforts; there are few leaders like you. Your support when others failed will be remembered for all my days.

Thank you, Kristen, Ben, Scott, and Karl for your help, advice, and assistance in this endeavor and a special thank you to Paul Dinas for your insightful thoughts.

.........and thank you to the Chapman University students, alumni, and staff that assisted me over many hurdles, your help was greatly appreciated.

Contents

Foreword

———•———

As a current 25-year veteran of the commercial aviation industry, I held airport operational positions including System Manager of Baggage Services, Airport General Manager, International Station Manager and I am currently Senior Airport Services Internal Quality Assurance Auditor of Corporate and Regulatory Compliance for one of the most successful commercial airlines in America today.

During my current career and in the former positions I held, I have worked closely with the local airport authority, Customs and Border Protection (CBP) Transportation Security Administration (TSA) and the local airport Law Enforcement Officers (LEO) to plan for emergencies and much more. It takes many professionals from various agencies to come together with one common goal, and that is to make commercial air travel the safest form of travel in the world.

Earlier in my career, I served as the Manager of System Baggage Services for 52 cities in the U.S. and experienced firsthand the problems air travel consumers faced when airlines delayed, damaged, pilfered or lost customer's luggage. I recognized and understood the once-in-a-lifetime vacation that was ruined, the million-dollar business presentation that was lost, the medication that couldn't be found when you needed it, the wedding ring your grandmother gave you that was stolen from your luggage.

My name is Scott T. Mueller, Aviation Professional & Author of 'The Empty Carousel" a Consumer's Guide to Checked and Carry-on

Luggage. During my career, I sought to improve the airline industry problems in customer service and wrote my book that gave many accounts and facts on the aviation industry and provided potential solutions and education for customers traveling with checked and carry-on luggage. Through education, the customer and the airlines would both benefit.

I met William Herrin when he asked for my advice on the stolen and lost luggage issues that his airport faced. Since then we have talked and networked on his efforts to improve airport security while writing his book "Airport Warnings: An Airport Policeman Speaks." I gave him my thoughts and experiences in the industry and suggestions for improving airport security from a fellow aviation security stakeholder viewpoint.

Now, as a Quality Assurance Auditor and Analyst, I travel throughout the United States, the Caribbean, Mexico and Central and South America where I conduct corporate and regulatory compliance audits. In my accumulated experiences in the aviation industry, I feel changes are necessary to enhance airport security, and the following analogy is an accurate way of describing the state of our airport's security and its much-needed improvements.

Many of the homes in the U.S. are some of the best-built homes in the world. Many have top of the line construction and security systems. Homes are well insulated to protect from the wind, rain, heat, and cold. Builders and homeowners ensure the door, and window seals are extremely tight and energy efficient.

Builders use foam insulation around every pipe, conduit and cable wires entering or exiting the homes, so homeowners are assured their home is well protected from any outside intruders while they go about their daily lives and when they sleep.

In the morning, many homeowners wake up and walk into the kitchen or bathroom in their home and have found an invasion of ants streaming in and out of the home through a small opening, crack or crevice. The attempt to protect the home failed, and the homeowner realizes the ants still find a way to invade their home. You see it is straightforward; ants are opportunists like terrorists, or people who have ill will and these people will use any opportunity to breach the protections of the commercial aviation infrastructure in the United States for many purposes.

From the outside and the inside, our airports in the U.S. appear impenetrable and secure, with the best possible security measures and insulation in the world. But, look closer and think like a criminal or a terrorist and you will begin to see why William Herrin wrote this book and shares his years of law enforcement knowledge, expertise, and concerns with you the reader, the American traveler and aviation professional.

Like William, I have been working in the commercial aviation industry for 25 years. I too share his concerns for the safety of millions of travelers and aviation employees who work or travel in or out of the airports across America.

What William is about to reveal is of vital importance and correct, and there is so much more work to be completed before our airports are truly safe. It is critically important that our Federal, State, and local Governments who own the airports and the security processes, take heed to what William is about to share in the pages that follow.

As an aviation veteran, I thank William for the work and effort he shares. However, it is up to those who can make the changes before our Aviation infrastructure is again savagely attacked. The risks are real, and the potential for loss is great, not only to innocent people but to the American way of life as we know it.

I salute William Herrin for his efforts to share the truth about the vulnerability of airports around the United States. It took courage, resolve, and passion for writing this book. I thank him for his work and his service as a law enforcement officer. I hope his message resonates loud and clear and changes are made soon for the sake of all of us who are a part of best aviation system in the world.

Scott T. Mueller

CHAPTER 1

The Reason

—◆—

"Air travel reminds us who we are. It's the means by which
we recognize ourselves as modern. The process removes us
from the world and sets us apart from each other. We wander
in the ambient noise, checking one more time for the flight
coupon, the boarding pass, the visa. The process convinces
us that at any moment we may have to submit to the force
that is implied in all this, the unknown authority behind it,
behind the categories, the languages we don't understand.
This vast terminal has been erected to examine souls."[1]

— Don DeLillo, 'The Names'

I walked into the airport terminal and looked above me at the massive cathedral ceilings and onto the expansive walkways where thousands
of people scurried to and fro. The last time I was at the airport, I was
one of the thousands of people moving quickly to get through the TSA
screening and onto my flight. During previous airport visits at different
terminals in America, my attention was mostly on what type of food the
place had to eat or to find a comfortable place to sit until it was time to
board my flight. I rarely paused to consider the vast infrastructure of the
airports and only paid attention to the people who were in my way as I
walked through the terminal. However, today was different. Today I was

there to protect the people around me, to safeguard the airport and the extensive infrastructure that I stood in.

The first day of my assignment at the John Wayne Airport in Southern California began, and I was waiting for my fellow supervisor to catch up with me as I walked around viewing my new work location. I smiled as I passed the TSA agent in the exit lane and showed her my identification card. Even in uniform, a law enforcement officer has to provide a particular type of identification to access the secured side of any airport. I continued walking and stopped at the large pane glass windows that afforded me a scenic view of the active runway. I looked down at the airport ramp where aircraft were landing, taking off and were parked next to the terminal as hundreds of workers, looking like ants, crawling over the jets and equipment, running, and walking in every direction. Yes, I was master of all I could see as I suddenly felt a little intimidated by this aspect.

I left my police supervisor assignment a few days before in a busy city where I oversaw law enforcement officers responding to assist people in criminal incidents, family conflicts, medical aid calls and traffic accidents on a daily basis. Now, transferred to the Airport Division and standing in the airport, I realized at this moment in my twenty-seven years of law enforcement, my accumulated knowledge, and specialized training was not sufficient to jump right into this job that I had requested. My partner came up behind me and said; "What do you think?" I turned and smiled and told him I thought it would be interesting and a definite challenge in comparison to my previous duties.

What follows is the extent of my professional experiences and training in airport security that motivated me to address critical airport security issues that formed the reason for this book. To understand a perspective of another person, often one must walk in their shoes. Describing my walk through a law enforcement career that culminated in duties at the John Wayne Airport is an attempt to give you that perspective. I hope through this you will understand my reasoning and conclusions on subjects that are base on my assessments of aviation security successes and failures.

THE FOUNDATION OF AN AIRPORT POLICEMAN PERCEPTION

My new job title was "Airport Division Watch Commander." My new duties were to manage shifts of deputies and sheriff's special officers whose jobs were to enforce Orange County ordinances, State laws, and Federal Laws while providing for the complete security of the commercial airport. My responsibilities included a span of duties ranging from managing airport parking enforcement to a potential control and mitigation of an aircraft hijacking or an active shooter in the terminal. In any airport security incident, everyone from TSA personnel to airline and airport employees would stop and run to safety knowing my law enforcement agency personnel would race to the security event to protect them.

In any major crisis, any outside law enforcement assistance may be five minutes away and when seconds counted, those minutes were an eternity. I was the tip of the spear and was required to act immediately to stop a terrorist attack or major security breach by directing my men and women and all necessary resources to the situation without delay. My defined domain area was the airport property line that reached from the front roadways, parking structures, passenger and private jet terminals to the runways, fuel farm, and aircraft parking zones.

John Wayne Airport consists of 500 acres—the nation's smallest commercial airport by land mass—but daunting in its immense productivity with over nine million souls who annually fly out of this airport. John Wayne Airport surpasses San Jose, Pittsburgh, San Antonio and Sacramento International Airports in the number of yearly passengers. Even with the smallest land mass, John Wayne Airport ranks 40th in the number of passengers out of the 450 airports that are provided screening by the Transportation Security Agency. The weight of responsibility on my shoulders increased with the realization that over a thousand airport employees and an average of 25,000 passengers a day counted on me to provide for their security and safety in this condensed version of a small city.

A newly-assigned airport watch commander is tasked with an enormous responsibility the day he walks into his airport. Trust in this position is required to make the critical decisions that can save lives, or without the proper training, cost lives. His split-second decisions can disrupt flight schedules throughout the nation and delay the lives of countless thousands. For the next six years, I studied the aviation industry and knew my many years in law enforcement were important for me to be successful in my new job, but I also realized it was essential to learn much more. I immersed myself in the history of aviation security ranging from the 1926 Air Commerce Act to the Airport Security Act of 2001. It was important for me to know the role of the Federal Aviation Administration and the Transportation Security Administration requirements and their airport security plan. To understand these agencies, I studied the vast pool of federal protocols to comprehend the complex security matrix that governs airports. I worked with and learned from the FBI, Joint Terrorism Task Force, U.S. State Department, Drug Enforcement Agency, Secret Service Agency, Hazardous Device Unit and the U.S. Customs and Border Patrol teams whose duties encompassed John Wayne Airport. From these agencies, I learned about airport drug smuggling, both foreign and domestic terrorists, enhanced dignitary protection, airport illegal alien smuggling, and bomb response and mitigation.

Every day was a learning experience, and as I progressed, I assumed the additional role of training supervisor. My airport officers situational awareness and homeland security training merited sending my airports 108 officers and deputies to the weeklong 'Incident Response to Terrorist Bombings' course in New Mexico. I also ensured they attended training provided by the Orange County Sheriff's Department's Hazardous Device Squad in their 'Suicide Bomber' three-day course. Using my skills acquired through training and incidents during 15 years as a special weapons and tactics team member, I trained deputies and officers in 'Active Shooter' response and deployment in the airport terminal. My airport civilian training partner and I used table top exercises to teach the TSA, airline employees, and airport employees a wide range of training from screening lane or runway security breach response to an aircraft and airport terminal mass casualties terrorist attack and natural disaster events.

My studies of aviation security accelerated and significantly expanded when I joined and participated in an airport police-networking group organized by Chief Ed Skvarna of the Burbank Airport Police Department. Through his leadership, the 'Airport Police Information Group' (APIG) was created. Within this airport police network, we met, shared and received information and lessons learned with airports from Bakersfield to San Diego, where small regional to large international airport police personnel gathered and learned from each other. The effort of the airport police-networking group is a significant tool that can increase the security of Southern California aviation from criminal and Homeland Security threats. Equally important was a continuous discussion by the group of airport criminal cases and the airport police agencies constructive critiques of the successes, failures, and problems with the TSA, civilian employees, and airlines' management. APIG, (the author of the name smiled when he announced the acronym), is an invaluable aviation security knowledge reservoir filled with many law enforcement professional's years of accumulated training and experiences.

The State of California Peace Officers Standards Training Agency (POST), contacted John Wayne Airport and asked for assistance in the production of a police training telecourse. POST titled the telecourse 'Protecting Our Transportation System.' POST requested a law enforcement aviation subject matter expert from John Wayne Airport and my division commander selected me to assist the State of California in this project. I teamed up with airport watch commanders from Sacramento, San Jose and Oakland International Airports and TSA managers. Collectively, my fellow airport watch commanders and I developed and wrote the aviation security component of the POST telecourse 'Protecting Our Transportation System.' This telecourse was provided to every law enforcement agency in California and any requesting agency from within the United States. Working with these

Northern California airport watch commanders enhanced my aviation security knowledge through networking and collaborative efforts in creating solutions to security issues facing California airports.

Through the years, I received assignments from the Sheriff's Department Airport Division administration to conduct a variety of airport security studies. One study was an airport perimeter security analysis for the John Wayne Airport. To assess my airport from different perspectives, a comparison of other airports perimeter security was necessary. I toured the Dallas/Ft. Worth and Palm Springs International Airports and networked with the Phoenix Sky Harbor International Airport for the perimeter security study. This completed report contained viable recommendations for improving my airport's perimeter security. I completed several other reports on San Jose, Long Beach, and San Diego International airports that included tours and inspections of the airports and review of their airport's critical infrastructure security policies and procedures. I conducted extensive interviews with the airports' watch commanders and other airport employees whose airports were included in the analysis.

Completing one of my final reports in June 2009, titled "Airport Law Enforcement Agencies Comparable Analysis," required me to research 21 airports throughout the United States. Located in the states of North Carolina, Texas, Pennsylvania, Ohio, Indiana, Tennessee, Missouri, Oregon, and California, these various airports resided in many different geographical areas, communities, and cities. Over a period of nine months, I interviewed the airports' police chief, the TSA airport administrator, and the airport administrator or these administrative leaders' designee who were directed to assist me. I acquired information on security problems from a variety of our nation's airports.' Through a considerable number of airport personnel interviews at many airports, I learned effective resolutions of security problems. I gleaned unique perspectives from the 21 airports' law enforcement, Transportation Security Administration, and the administrative airport personnel. Through an array of questions concerning their airport security plan and issues they faced, a database of each airport was compiled and was used in the final analysis report.

Through my studies of airports across America, I learned the John Wayne Airport security problems were systemic throughout the nation's many airports. As I completed years of research, I concluded, that despite all of the airport security work accomplished since 9/11, my airport and virtually every airport in the nation remain in jeopardy of various security threats. From these studies, I sought solutions to prevent or mitigate the security weaknesses at my airport. Some of my efforts as examples were the creation of a 'Terrorism/Criminal Information and Prevention' airport watch program and enhancing our airport's rapid response team with specialized equipment and assets that would aid responding officers in immediately stopping a terrorist attack.

During this long walk through years of problem-solving in my airport security domain, I concluded that today, when you walk into an airport terminal; you are not as safe as you could be. Airport police know the dangers because they know the security systems that surround you and the potential threats we all face. There are airport employees who use illicit drugs and smuggle drugs on passenger aircraft. There are airport employees who steal from passengers, and criminal groups from outside our vast aviation infrastructures who prey on the aviation industry. In our airport terminals, there are serious security failures within the very infrastructures that are supposed to safeguard you and your loved ones. Detailed in the coming chapters are these and many other pressing concerns, but most importantly, recommendations are provided to prevent the systemic criminal and homeland security failures in our nation's airports. Implementation of these recommendations, in my opinion, will make our skies safer for America's aviation industry and our citizens.

As a concerned citizen, and former airport law enforcement watch commander, I feel it is important to share what I've learned regarding the need for security improvements in our airports. My purpose is to sway the focus of airport administrations, federal, state and county law enforcement agencies throughout the nation to prioritize needed security improvements in our airports. For these reasons, we must have an open and transparent conversation with the American public. This book begins that dialogue, inviting all who frequent our airports to join in an open and informed discussion.

As I assembled my years of research and put pen to paper for this book, I reflected on the victims of the September 11 terrorist attacks. I imagine that it was my mom or dad, daughter or son sitting on one of the four 9/11 aircraft, terrified by the assailants and ultimately suffering death at their hands. The thoughts raced through my mind that my loved ones could be at an airport or on an aircraft one day in the future when terrorism again strikes our nation's aviation system. With new resolve on each anniversary of 9/11, my determination grew stronger to find a way to sway the aviation industry to improve the level of airport security so that terrorists never again will use America's airlines to hurt our citizens or the citizens of any other country. Five anniversaries of 9/11 have come and gone since the start of this project, and the warnings are amplified with each new airport security incident I post on airport-warnings.com.

This book is not a textbook for aviation students, rather just a straightforward viewpoint from a former airport watch commander who feels much more can be done to strengthen the core components of our aviation security. It will not cover every facet of the vast fields of airport security, but it will cover vital areas of concern for the traveling population. My findings are fact-based and supported by historical events and present-day events that continue to occur at our nation's airports. To achieve improved airport security, we must understand just how vulnerable our airports are.

Many will agree with me and many will not; thoughts and questions about where we went wrong and why we did not solve many of our simplest aviation security problems will occur. The answers will come when we ask the questions generated by these thoughts and reason prevails.

AN ACTIVIST RECOMMENDATION

Your vote for the right candidate and your potential activism can create change in your community airports, change that those of us in the law enforcement field has not been able to make on our own. From the President of the United States, Congress, States and county leaders, elected law enforcement officials and airport directors, they all work for you. You have the right to inform these public servants collectively that your security is first and foremost, and they will act. You hold power, and you should exercise that power to improve the safety and security of our nation's vital aviation infrastructure.

In my years of working in the aviation security field, I took Captain A.G. Lamplugh aviation quote and applied it to my aviation security duties:

> "Aviation in itself is not inherently dangerous. But
> to an even greater degree than the sea, it is terribly
> unforgiving of any carelessness, incapacity or neglect."[2]

— CAPTAIN A. G. LAMPLUGH

I used Lamplugh thoughts that aviation is terribly unforgiving of any carelessness, incapacity or neglect in the context of our nation's aviation security. As a society, we know the threats posed by the Islamic State of Iraq and the Levant (ISIL) and al-Qaeda within our very borders. Complacency or carelessness or neglect has crept up, and we are failing to improve the security of our aviation infrastructures vital components. An airport director, police chief or homeland security administrator who does not strengthen their airport security that would stop a future aviation catastrophe, would have to reconcile the outcome of that event to the victims and their families. The mother of twin daughters died at the Brussels Airport Terrorist Bombing, her daughters survived. Will the head of Brussels airport security and the airport director pause and consider what they could have done to have prevented this attack or at the least mitigate it? Will airport directors around the world think about the victims both dead and alive and take steps to prevent this from happening at their airport? I pose these questions and present these thoughts for debate and hopefully, the creation of new solutions to our aviation security weaknesses.

CHAPTER 2

Why Our Airports Are Significant Targets

———————

"The Wrights created one of the greatest cultural forces since
the development of writing, for their invention effectively
became the World Wide Web of that era, bringing people,
languages, ideas, and values together. It also ushered in an
age of globalization, as the world's flight paths became the
superhighways of an emerging international economy. Those
superhighways of the sky not only revolutionized international
business; they also opened up isolated economies, carried the
cause of democracy around the world and broke down every
kind of political barrier. And they set travelers on a path
that would eventually lead beyond Earth's atmosphere."[3]

BILL GATES

THE DECLARATION THAT AMERICA'S AIRPORTS are significant targets of
terrorist and criminals is a serious statement. The purpose of this statement is not to alarm a society, but rather to inform them of the threats
facing our aviation industry. Once equipped with this knowledge, citizens will be empowered to ask for reasonable remedies that will mitigate
or eliminate the security problems facing our aviation industry. For this
purpose, I present the reasons why our airports are vulnerable to terrorist and criminal threats. These judgments of our airports' vulnerabilities

serve as a prelude to a series of events that depict our nation's airport security weaknesses.

Airports Are Targets for Economic Objectives

"The American economy can't function without the ability to travel; travel can't happen unless it's safe...."

U.S. Travel Association President and CEO
Roger Dow in response to the LAX shooting
and TSA report; March 27, 2014[4]

On September 11, 2001, our nation was thrust back in time to November 6, 1910, the day before the first aircraft cargo shipment took off from Dayton and landed in Columbus, Ohio.[5] For six days after 9/11, our country was forced to live in a world that we had not seen for 89 years. Products usually shipped by air now could only be moved by ground or sea. In today's aviation commerce, virtually everything, except volatile and dangerous items, is shipped in passenger and cargo aircraft. During the six days, our society suddenly could not immediately gratify its needs by obtaining goods from one coastline to another within 24 hours. A vast number of businesses who relied on immediate delivery of their goods throughout our nation and the world stopped delivering their products.

Today, the world's economies are global and expanding with the daily worldwide production of goods. Globalization of economies and the 21st-century transportation revolution feed off each other continually and whose future is limited only by the imagination and ingenuity of people. With this globalization comes fluid movement of people, products, and services worldwide. In 15 hours, you can fly from New York to China non-stop. In 16 hours, you can fly from San Francisco to Dubai.[6] The world sends its visitors and immigrants through more than 80 United States airports—points of entry with more than 10,000 air transport companies using 15,500 passenger airliners to assist them into our country. Our airports are the Ellis Island of the 21st Century.

In 2016, airlines flew 3.6 billion passengers throughout the world, obtaining revenue of over 701 billion dollars. In 2015, more than 895.5 million passengers flew out of America's airports, culminating in 7 percent of the U.S. Gross Domestic Product (GDP).[7] The Federal Aviation Administration 2016 projected America's passenger numbers on airline flights will grow at 2.1 percent every year from 2016 to 2036.[8]

Civil air transport industries are crucial to promoting trade anywhere in the world with ease and speed. Cargo freight flights reaped $55 billion in revenue ton-miles through U.S. airports in 2014, resulting in $564 billion in cargo transported domestically or to other countries. Private, non-military parts, airplane engines, and equipment parts also contributed approximately $80 billion for the U.S. trade balance, reaching the top net export for the past decade.[9]

The Federal Aviation Administration spent more than $15 billion in 2014 on air traffic operations, facilities, and grants that supported additional spending in the economy, totaling over $27 billion while producing 218,000 jobs that earned $8.5 billion.

The U.S. travel and tourism industry generated nearly $1.6 trillion in economic output in 2015, supporting 7.6 million U.S. jobs. Travel and tourism exports accounted for 11 percent of all U.S. exports and nearly a third (33 percent) of all U.S. services exports, positioning travel and tourism as the nation's largest services export. One out of every 18 Americans is employed, either directly or indirectly, in a travel or tourism-related industry. In 2015, U.S. travel and tourism output represented 2.6 percent of gross domestic product.

While the majority of activity in the industry is domestic, expenditures by international visitors in the United States totaled $246.2 billion in 2015, yielding a $97.9 billion trade surplus for the year. According to U.S. Department of Commerce projections, international travel to the United States should grow by 3 percent annually through 2021. The United States leads the world in international travel and tourism exports and ranks second in terms of total visitation.[10]

Daniel Yergin, an author and Pulitzer Prize winner, said the airline industry drives the daily "economic takeoff of our nation." Yergin went on to say the aviation industry enables America's economy by bringing every corner of the country together by moving our citizens and products. It's the "backbone of economic growth."[11] The airports in America alone employ 1.2 million people and support over 9.6 million jobs. The total number of people who work at airports are second only to the largest employer in America; Wal-Mart, who employs 1.3 million workers.[12]

My airport serves as an example of how a midsize airport business affects the local economy. At the conclusion of John Wayne Airport's expansion in 2013, the County Business Council conducted an analysis of the expansion and its economic impact. The Council stated the airport's new construction would produce nearly 1.2 billion dollars of economic benefit for the Orange County area and that for every $1 invested, more than $2 will be put back into the economy.[13] The aviation industry will continue to grow, for not only America's economy but also the world as a whole. Aviation transportation is indispensable to the future of the United States economy strength and success.

Because of the vast importance of the aviation industry to our economy, our airports will continue to be a high-value target for terrorism. The National Intelligence Estimates (NIEs), is the authoritative assessments of the Director of National Intelligence and provides a view of a quasi-military terrorist group's goals. According to the Director of the NIE, al-Qaida will continue to target and attack America's prominent political, economic and infrastructure strengths. In this particular assessment on national security, the NIE stated al-Qaida's goals are to produce "mass casualties, visually dramatic destruction, significant economic aftershocks, and fear among the U.S. population."[14]

Never in the history of America has any single terrorist attack been more successful regarding the loss of life, economic loss, visually dramatic destruction and instilling fear in our citizens than the attack on September 11, 2001. Osama Bin Laden's words in 2004 gave one core reason behind the 9/11 attack:

> "America is a superpower, with enormous military strength and vast economic power, but all this is built on foundations of straw. So it is possible to target those foundations and focus on their weakest points, which, even if you strike only one-tenth of them, then the whole edifice will totter and sway.... We were patient fighting the Soviet Union with small humble arms for ten years, we depleted their economy till they vanished, all grace be to Allah. You should take a lesson from that, we will be patient fighting you, Allah's willing till either one of us dies."[15]

The best security for the safe operation of the air transportation industry is essential to our nation. The inspired men and women in the early aviation revolution operated with an appropriate level of trust in humankind that we were safe in the air in the context of the times in which they lived. These aviation pioneers could not have imagined the silver birds that carry our nation's citizens to our cities and the world, would one day be used as weapons against not only our people but also the very fabric of our nation's strength—the economy.

In February 2017, Adam Rose of the University of Southern California Center for Risk and Economic Analysis of Terrorism Events (CREATE), released a study of what the economic impact would be of an attack on our aviation industry. In summary, Rose said an attack on an airline or airport could cost the economy billions in losses. Rose based $10 Billion in economic losses would happen if there were two terrorists' attacks on the LAX Airport Terminal and on an airliner taking off from Los Angeles.[16]

Yale University, on their YaleGlobal online publication, cited author Gabriel Weimann findings. Weimann studied Jihadist discussions online websites and said: "There is another type of Jihad being used, and it's called Econo-Jihad and states al Qaeda is 'fine tuning' its selection of targets to harm the Western economy." The March 2013 issue of al Qaeda magazine *AZAN* praised the 9/11 attacks and subsequent wars as a method to destroy our economy:

"19 gallant young men did to America what it could never have imagined...America would never even dream of peace until peace became a reality in Muslim lands...America was dragged into a war it could never win and inevitably, its economy collapsed and it now stands on the brink of destruction as it plans its humiliating withdrawal from the lands of the Muslims."[17]

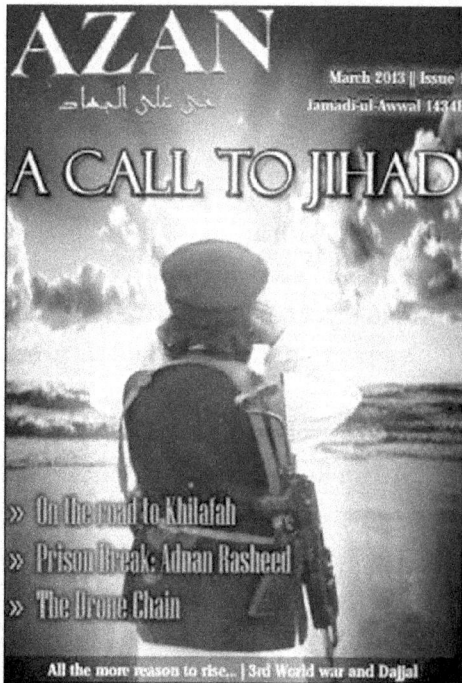

March 2013 AZAN, courtesy of AZAN Magazine

Robert Taber noted in his book, 'The War of the Flea: Guerrilla Warfare Theory and Practice' that the terrorist has time on his side in the field of the "politico-economic arena." He emphasized that a prolonged campaign against a group of terrorists affects a country's typical investor who will not put his money in an unsafe institution that sways with the uncertainty of a campaign by insurgents wishing to topple a government.

In the year 2000, Gerald Dillingham of the United States General Accounting Office (GAO), testified before the Senate that the aviation security system was weak in several critical areas of airport security. Dillingham gave the example of the 1995 Bojinka plot as he sat in front of Congress and said terrorist had planned to use 11 American passenger airliners and emphasized how civil aviation is a desirable target. He gave this chilling premonition of what an attack on America's passenger airline industry and its economy would do just one year before the catastrophic attack on America on September 11, 2001:

"...the threat of terrorism against the United States is an ever-present danger and, coupled with the fact that aviation is an attractive target for terrorists, indicate that the security of the air transport system remains at risk. Protecting this [aviation] system demands the highest level of vigilance because a single lapse in aviation security can result in hundreds of deaths, destroy equipment worth hundreds of millions of dollars, and have immeasurable negative impacts on the economy and the public's confidence in air travel."[18]

<u>Airports Are Targets for Political Objectives</u>

Terrorists conceptually believe the destruction of American economic and civilian targets will force the U.S. and its allies to withdraw their support of Israel and their military presences in the Middle East. The outcome the Islamic terrorist extremists hope for and believe in is the

United Middle East, free from the Western "Crusaders," will bring about a final cleansing of Israel from the Middle East. The first World Trade Center bombing mastermind, Ramzi Ahmed Yousef, confirmed the terrorist political objective to the FBI:

> "Yousef talked at length about Israel being an illegal state and that Israel is committing criminal acts against Muslims. Yousef stated that the American people would need to convince Washington of changing Israeli policy and this would happen by bombing various locations in the U.S."[19]

A major goal of the terrorist methods is to sway our citizens to oppose America's commitment to its allies and support of the Middle East secular democracies. The terrorist methods to accomplish this goal will result in the death and injuries of many Americans. Al-Rimi, the Al Qaeda in the Arabian Peninsula (AQAP) senior military commander, warned America in 2013:

> "Your security is achieved by stopping the foolish, who rule you, from oppression and aggression. Know that oppression and aggression rebound on the throats of the perpetrators. Your leaders are assaultive, oppressive and tyrannical, and you stand behind them cheering, supporting and voting for them."[20]

Death, Propaganda and World War III

Al Qaeda launched its version of World War III on September 11, 2001. They took American citizens and American aircraft by force and did not negotiate or make any demands. Without mercy, Al Qaeda's militaristic operational plan used a civilian aircraft as a weapon of mass destruction and launched it into the impenetrable might of our nation's military power, the Pentagon. Al Qaeda used two other civilian aircraft to destroy the symbol of American economic strength—the World Trade

Center buildings and killed 3,000 innocent American citizens. If not for the brave souls on United Airlines Flight 93, hundreds or even a thousand more Americans would have died in Washington, D.C.

The terrorist achievement of 9/11 created extreme anxiety and fear that gripped the American population. It was the first time America suffered such a massive attack on its soil, and it shook the foundations of our country with its aftershocks echoing to this very day. We now live with the reality that there isn't much that can invoke more mass fear in our citizens than an incident or threat aimed at America's airline industry and its principal base of operation, the airport.

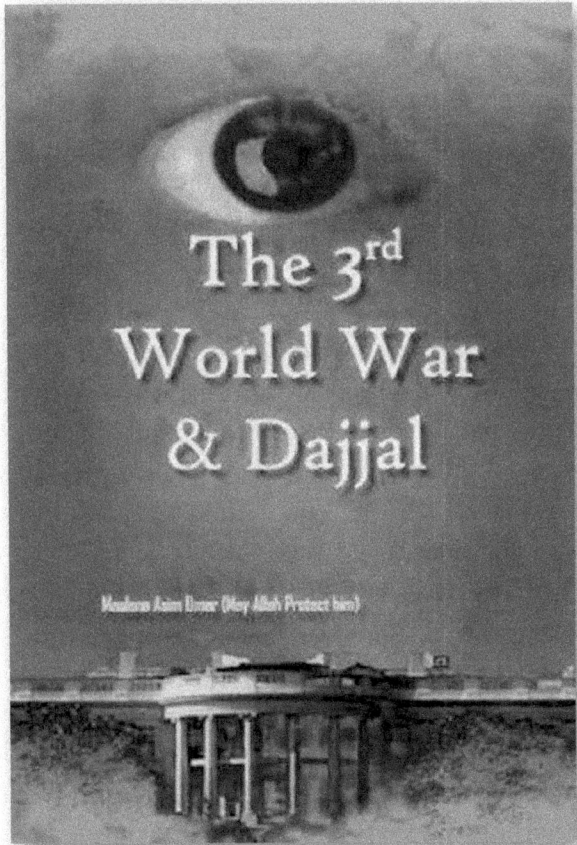

AZAN Magazine: Dajjal, Courtesy of AZAN Magazine

The Rand Corporation highlighted the terrorist choice of airports as targets through historical data that reveals aviation attacks resulted in more than 5,500 deaths worldwide since 1980 including the 9/11 fatalities.[21] Reaction to the terrorist attacks in the Istanbul, Brussels, and Moscow International Airports reveal the world's attention is drawn to attacks at airports and on the aviation industry. Death and destruction capture the publicity the terrorist seek for their terrorist strategy propaganda component.

The 9/11 attacks gave al Qaeda a huge propaganda platform. In a research paper for the North Atlantic Alliance Organization (NATO), Maurice Tugwell defined propaganda "as any information, ideas, doctrines, or special appeals disseminated to influence the opinion, emotions, attitudes, or behavior of any specified group to benefit the sponsor directly or indirectly." Maurice Tugwell further said, "Propaganda and terrorism are identical insofar as they both seek to influence a mass audience in a way that is intended to benefit the sponsor." Tugwell described the nexus of propaganda and terrorism with the analogy of a boxer's two fists and without both; a terrorist is fighting with one hand tied behind his back.[22]

In 2007, a terrorist was arrested for plotting the JFK Airport attack. Terrorist Russell Defreitas told an informant that "Anytime you hit Kennedy, it is the most hurtful thing to the United States. To hit John F. Kennedy, wow... They love JFK—he's like the man. If you hit that [airport], the whole country will be in mourning. It's like you can kill the man twice." Defreitas stated a secondary effect his plan would have: "Even the Twin Towers can't touch this;" (regarding blowing up JFK) "This can destroy the economy of America for some time."[23]

This statement by Defreitas gave me pause as I thought of the actor icon 'John Wayne,' who is one of America's classic heroes and whose name is on my airport. Wayne portrayed America's fighting soldier image in many movies, from the Alamo, Sands of Iwo Jima, to the Green Berets. General MacArthur told Wayne: "You represent the American serviceman better than the American serviceman himself." Jimmy Carter said

Wayne was a "national asset," and stated Wayne was a symbol of the basic qualities that made America great.[24] I thought many times while walking the John Wayne Airport terminal, what mentally ill person or lame terrorist might want to kill John Wayne symbolically by attacking my airport similar to the JFK terrorist plot.

One of the driving factors of these attacks is the symbolic significance, and media attention garnered throughout the world when terrorists attack airports. Instant communication occurs through the technology as the media make breaking news available across the world. Within seconds, at the scene of a terrorist attack, come cell phone videos/pictures, texting, tweeting, uploads to Facebook and a myriad of social websites activity. The obsessive 24/7 coverage by the media lends a valuable propaganda tool that terrorists use quite well in making their message known throughout the world.

With the significance of the economic standing of airports throughout the world comes the realization that terrorists have taken notice, and airports are now the subject and a tool of terrorism. An example of an airport terrorist incident whose byproduct was a massive propaganda tool was the 1985 TWA Boeing 727 airliner Flight 847 hijacking. The incident resulted in nearly two weeks of uninterrupted television broadcasts on every major television network in America. Hijacked Flight 847 left Athens Greece, and for three days, it flew back and forth between Algiers and Beirut. The dynamic hijacking scene culminated in the killing of U.S. Navy seaman Robert Stethem on the runway. Israel held 700 terrorist prisoners from previous criminal and terrorist incident arrests; release of these prisoners occurred to secure the release of Israeli passengers that were held captive on the hijacked flight.

As a direct result of this hijacking, 850,000 Americans declined to fly overseas for fear of terrorism, with over 50 American tours to Italy and 30 tours to Greece canceled. The TWA hijacking not only affected the economy but also served as a psychological attack and a new propaganda tool for terrorists. Imagine if this terrorist incident occurred in our current age of social media and technology. A profound impact on the world would occur simply from the amplified coverage. Tugwell argues, "Media coverage of terrorism is closely linked to propaganda."

WHY AIRPORTS ARE HIGHER VALUE TARGETS THAN OTHER VULNERABLE TARGETS

Why are terrorist organizations so fixated on the American aviation industry when there are passenger rail transportation, shopping malls, sports stadiums, and many other densely populated and less guarded targets?

Would an attack on a subway or railroad passenger car have the ability to increase the external collateral damage beyond the rail car or train station? Let's look at a terrorist attack on a passenger train system and compare for an answer. Terrorists attacked the passenger railroad system in Madrid Spain on March 11, 2004, and comparing the two targeted passenger modes of transportation reveals a stark difference in outcomes. Terrorist groups analyze the results of their efforts and weigh their future investments of assets and personnel when planning future attacks based on the most destructive model:

MADRID SPAIN, PASSENGER RAIL TERRORIST ATTACK COMPARISON

* America's 9/11 – Four Passenger Aircraft, Spain's March 3, 2004 – Four Passenger Rail Trains
* Spain suffered $220 million in economic loss compared to America's two Trillion dollars.[25]
* Spain's human loss was 191 killed and 2,000 injured; America's human loss was 2,999 killed and 6,293 injured.

In a passenger train or subway rail attack, the external economic losses would never be as large as 9/11 nor have the external effect on the USA or world economies. The financial markets suffered fewer damages in the Madrid Rail terrorist attacks as noted by the International Monetary Fund working paper titled, "The Impact of Terrorism on Financial Markets in 2005" by Barry Johnston and Oana Nedelescu, which states:

"In comparison with the impact of the 2001 terrorist attacks on the United States, the effects of the March 11, 2004, terrorist attacks on Spain were felt much less by the capital markets, and by the financial markets in general (Figures 2 and 3). In the euro area, the Dow Jones EURO STOXX fell by about 3 percent on March 11, and continued to drop during the following days but recovered almost completely by the end of the month. Similarly, after a small decline, the Standard and Poor's 500 returned to the pre-March 11 levels in less than a month."[26]

However, what if a large metropolitan U.S. city like New York's subway rail system was the target of a terrorist attack and the attack succeeded in stopping all passenger rail system movement for a 30-day period? The results would greatly impact the local New York economy and related businesses. Susan Berfield of *Bloomberg Business* News wrote an article on the effects of the destruction of the New York subway system by Hurricane Sandy. The article provides an insight into the effects on the economy of New York if this were to happen. Berfield cited a report written by researchers and led by Klaus Jacob of Columbia University, who provided estimates on the failure of transportation infrastructure systems in the entire New York metropolitan region. The report cited the economic loss could span $48 billion to $68 billion with 90 percent of the service restored in less than a month and a 100 percent of the system restored within two years.[27] This type of loss would be terrible for the city of New York, but its external economic cost effects on the rest of the nation or the world would not come close to an aviation passenger disaster on the scale of or greater than 9/11.

The Domino Effect of Attacks on the Aviation Industry

The composition of the passenger aviation flight system are cities called hubs with flight paths of passenger aircraft described as spokes going to other cities. The airlines developed the hub and spoke system to save costs and increase the number of airline company flights. One of the major problems of the hub spoke aviation flight system is the cascading effects if a hub experiences delayed or stopped flights. Not only is the entire nation's spoke and hub system affected, but also so are the external businesses that rely on the airlines and passengers as customers.[28] The external economic losses of aviation related businesses were compounding factors that significantly enhanced the economic loss to America and the world on 9/11.

The 9/11 Twin Towers firms and occupants are examples of the external effects of an attack on our aviation industry regarding the further loss of life and additional damage to our economy. When a security incident occurs in an airport, the airport loses revenue, and then an external loss of income occurs at other airports and interconnected airline businesses. The November 2013 Los Angeles Airport shooting in a small non-hub passenger terminal affected 1,550 scheduled airline flights and 167,050 passengers.[29] Additional significant losses of revenues occurred in the aviation connected businesses such as the cargo transport companies, the hotel/lodging industry, food/restaurants, car rental/transportation, entertainment venues and other hospitality businesses that depend on airports travelers in their communities.

Many of America's populated targets are enticing and viable targets of terror. Al-Qaeda, and the Islamic State of Iraq and the Levant, continue to plot methodically and precisely to fulfill their promise to destroy America. Strong airport security will prevent or mitigate the external collateral damage that would supersede far more than just an airport or airplane destroyed. Airport security benefits extend to the occupants of high-rise buildings, nuclear power plants, sports stadiums and government buildings where an aircraft could do extensive damage and kill a large number of innocents.

TERRORIST ARE STILL FIXATED ON AVIATION AROUND THE WORLD

In the years researching and analyzing the terrorist threat to America, what became evident is the fixation by terrorists with using aviation as a tool of death, destruction, and propaganda to serve their cause more than any other method. *The Guardian* reporter Jon Boone's article on June 8, 2014, described how the Karachi Airport terrorist attack in Pakistan was a blow to Pakistan's economy:

> "The attack could also deal a major blow to business confidence, which had begun to perk up following the election of industri-alist Nawaz Sharif as prime minister. Sharif's factions of the Pakistan Muslim League are anxious to attract foreign inves-tors back to Pakistan, many of whom were scared away from the country by a sharp deterioration in internal security. Karachi, the home of key industries including finance, is particularly important for the economic growth he vowed to bring to the country. Sharif has long wanted to attract foreign airlines back to Pakistan, including British Airways, which cut its services fol-lowing major terrorist attacks."[30]

SOME EXPERTS LAST THOUGHTS ON THE VALUE OF THE AVIATION INDUSTRY

Former U.S. Air Force Secretary Michael Wynne said:

> "Our country's vastness and its economy depend upon commercial aviation as the backbone of national and international commerce... Global trade undergirds America's strength and allows the United

States to project its economic power. In my opinion, the commercial aviation industry and the Airport Associations are a crucial component of America's economic strength. This has been true for decades, and will remain true into the foreseeable future."[31]

In August 2008, Moody's Economy.com chief economist Mark Zandi remarked in the 'NextGen: The Future of Flying,' that:

"Aviation is the glue that keeps the global economy together. Without widely accessible and well-priced air travel, the global economy will quickly become less global."[32]

Are we safe in this current configuration of security networks that overlap and sometimes counter each other at our nation's airports? Sheldon H. Jacobson of the University of Illinois has researched aviation security operations since 1996, and he suggests that we must "define, implement, change, and continually update the available layers of airport security proactively to prevent future attacks." In his 2011 report, he notes that:

"I posit that as we look into the future and evaluate the trajectory of aviation security, based on the decisions of the past decade, the air system is at the riskiest point that it has been since 9/11." Watching through the "I"s of aviation security, June 16, 2011.[33]

CHAPTER 3

The Terrorist Threat and Reasons to Strengthen Airport Security

———————

"Terrorist groups, in general, have always seen aviation
as a big target. They will continue to try because aviation
is such a big fat target that attracts global attention."[34]

*RAFFAELLO PANTUCCI, DIRECTOR OF SECURITY, DEFENSE THINK
TANK, ROYAL UNITED SERVICES INSTITUTE*

I RECEIVED A RADIO CALL of a bomb threat at the north terminal. I ran
with my officers to the pre-designated incident command post to meet
the TSA supervisor, the Deputy Director of Airport Operations, and
the airline managers. We arrived at the pre-determined location virtually at the same time, and I received the bomb threat information from
my officer. I repeated the bomb threat information to my fellow security
managers and told them an evacuation of the terminal was necessary. I
then ordered a search of the public area with K-9s and our personnel.
The airline managers dropped their heads as they knew flights would be
delayed even as the deputy airport director asked me to get this done as
soon as possible.

An evacuation announcement on the terminal speaker system
reached over a thousand passengers who, like deer in the headlights,
looked up and just stood there. A skirmish line of officers, TSA and

airport personnel, started herding the passengers to the outer roadway. Before the last passenger was out the door, the K-9 teams had
already deployed, and sector searches began. I heard the question
asking if we could hurry up as the deputy airport director and airline
managers walked up from behind me. I looked into their strained
eyes and said we were close to completion. Airplanes that were supposed to be taking off were still at the gates waiting for the passengers. Aircraft that had landed were parking down the taxiway
with passengers eager to get off the plane. The roadway was backed
up for miles with cars waiting to drop off passengers. Just a single
bomb threat created chaos at my airport. However, the impact didn't
stop here. Within hours, at airports throughout the country, aircraft
would be taking off without passengers from my airport that would
miss their connecting flights. The gates opened as we finished our
search and passengers streamed in, some angry some with faces of
concern. It took my airport four hours to return to normal because
of a 45-minute terminal evacuation.

The identity of the person who made the threat that a bomb was
in my airport is unknown. Speculation by law enforcement pointed to
someone who lives in the nearby community as the one who disrupted
the airport operations with the false bomb threat. An airport watch
commander jurisdiction lies within the perimeter of a passenger airport. But around his airport, in the very community that he lives and
works, lies potential threats to the aviation industry. Terrorism studies have revealed that half of terrorist attacks were planned, rehearsed,
and implemented on targets within 30 miles of the terrorist cell or lone
wolf's abode.[35] The airport watch commander builds his security parameters and matrix based on his education, training, acquired skills, and
real life experiences, but it also must include a working knowledge of the
local people and communities that fall within the threat environment
that the airport resides.

Since 9/11, domestic and foreign terrorists have used "leaderless
resistance" principles that make it very hard for law enforcement to

infiltrate or discover their plans to target our nation's aviation industry and other critical infrastructure.[36] These loosely affiliated people with extreme ideologies are unpredictable as they operate on the fringe of foreign and domestic terrorist groups. Texas Senator John Cornyn said Islam's small minority defiles its religious creeds and tenets to accomplish what they feel are righteous causes. He said, "The enemy is not just terrorism. It is the threat posed specifically by Islamist terrorism, by Bin Laden and others who draw on a long tradition of extreme intolerance within a minority strain of Islam that does not distinguish politics from religion, and distorts both."[37]

An airport threat matrix consists of, in part on assessments by local, county, state, regional law enforcement, and federal task forces. An essential component in threat assessment reports for my airport security advancements and recommendations were evaluations of the local populace and the capable threats that they may have posed in the past and may pose in the future. Many examples can be used to show what shapes my airport's security matrix and the many security domains of our nation's airports. One particular area of concern that brings trepidation to an airport watch commander is people on the terrorist watch lists in and around our nation's airports. These types of contacts may occur more frequently than one imagines. Insight into this world provides examples of encounters at airports with subjects whose names reside in a database called the Terrorist Watchlist.

The United States Secretary of State amended the designation of al-Qaida in Iraq with an alias of the Islamic State of Iraq and the Levant (ISIL) as its primary name. ISIL also is mentioned in news accounts in another term as the Islamic State of Iraq and al-Sham (ISIS).[38] The worldwide al-Qaida organization and the Islamic State of Iraq and the Levant are the predominant threat to America, but other terrorist groups pose significant threats as well. These terrorist groups membership range from foreign and U.S. citizens and are active in America.

In 2015, ISIL made threats against the United States of America in this statement:

"We have 71 trained soldiers in 15 different states ready at our word to attack any target we desire. Out of the 71-trained soldiers, 23 have signed up for missions like Sunday, We are increasing in number bithnillah [if God wills]. Of the 15 states, 5 we will name, Virginia, Maryland, Illinois, California, and Michigan."[39]

To make matters much worse, on February 26, 2017, the Iranian Revolutionary Guards Commander Abbassi said he had terrorist cells within the United States when he said:

"I'll be brief. We have two million Iranians there [America]. Be certain that I will raise a guerilla army from amongst them against you. You know this well. Look how vulnerable you were on 9-11 when four Arabs who don't know how to fight managed to endanger your foundations. Yet with us, you face a nation that's even stronger. You forget we have 7000 Ph.D. holders in the U.S. If only eleven people created 9/11, do you realize what we can do? We have people from all Islamic Countries [in America], deport them all. But we are working on the Mexicans too and the Argentinians too. We will guide anyone who has problems with the U.S." [40]

A Terrorist Watch List Suspect at an American Airport

The following discovery of a terrorist watchlist subject by an airport watch commander directly impacted an American airport security procedure and resulted in changes to security protocols. This incident amplified the critical needs for airport police officers' throughout America to remain vigilant in the airport community they protect.

The airport watch commander was patrolling the airport roadways at this American airport on the main terminal outer loop road. He merged with traffic and pulled up behind a commercial vehicle that was arriving at his airport. The vehicle was obeying the speed limit, so it didn't concern him at the moment. The watch commander looked at the driver's eyes through his rear window, and at the same time, the driver turned toward his rearview mirror. As the driver of the commercial vehicle suddenly realized a black and white police unit was behind him, he quickly sat straight up, placed both hands on the steering wheel, and continued to flick his gaze back at the police vehicle following him.

Now, most people get nervous when a police car is behind them. In fact, after 33 years in law enforcement, I still get a little bit nervous when a city police unit is hugging my car's rear end. I immediately start retracing in my mind my last mile or so of driving to see if I did anything wrong, such as did I forget to flip on my turn signal, exceed the speed limit, or use my cell phone? For the most part, the police officer is just patrolling, and you're the lucky stiff that by happenstance becomes his lane buddy.

The driver's body language in the commercial vehicle immediately told the watch commander he was nervous, and his constant, furtive eye-movement made the seasoned police watch commander's intuitive senses tingle. The watch commander changed lanes and slowly approached the side of the vehicle, holding back just enough so the driver couldn't see the watch commander observing him. A white male sat in the driver's seat, with a full bushy beard but relatively short hair. The immediate thought "white supremacist biker guy," but the watch commander dismissed that as he continued to stare at him. There was something else going on here; his instincts insisted that something wasn't quite right.

He proceeded to the front of the airport terminal, and the commercial vehicle approached the inner loop of the airport roadway. The watch commander watched the subject park where other commercial vehicles usually stopped, so he passed him and parked his police unit on the curb nearest his office. The watch commander's uneasiness grew, but he kept telling himself, "Don't be such a paranoid freak!" His gut was telling him that something wasn't right with this guy, and he wanted to know who he was and what he was doing at the airport—at his airport.

He watched in his rearview mirror as the subject parked his vehicle where the watch commander thought he would park, with the variety of other commercial service vehicles that come to the airport. He called a police officer to meet him in the control center and had the control center officer place a camera on the vehicle. When the police officer arrived, he pointed to the vehicle on the monitor and told him he wanted to know everything about the driver, including his firstborn's name. Under Homeland Security protocols, everything that enters airport property is scrutinized, including regular walk-through inspections at the airport of commercial vehicles that park in front of the airport terminal. The officer was instructed to obtain information on every commercial vehicle on the curb to prevent the driver of the subject vehicle from knowing he was the center of attention.

Approximately 45 minutes later, the officer returned with the subject's driver license information and vehicle permit numbers. The vehicle and drivers information passed to the Control Center officers, and they ran him through the police databases. An immediate notification that the subject was on the Terrorist Watchlist in a northern part of the state came up in the data search.

The airport police called the investigative authorities, who instructed them to maintain video camera surveillance of the subject's movements, and the investigator affirmed to the watch commander that the subject in the service vehicle was on the Terrorist Watchlist. Their instructions were not to contact the subject; as his status level was "observe but do not contact."

The investigator arrived an hour later and said the situation had become a little more complicated. The watch commander's subject was driving a commercial vehicle that belonged to another subject who wasn't in the car this day. This other person who owns the service vehicle was coincidently also on the Terrorist Watchlist under the jurisdiction of the County in which the watch commander's airport resided. But the driver of the service vehicle today was from another county well north of the watch commander's County and was listed on the Terrorist Watchlist under that County's jurisdiction.

The airport watch commander was bothered by the discovery that the investigative unit already knew but did not inform his airport police that one terrorist watch list suspect was driving daily into and around his airport. But even more so, he was greatly troubled by his discovery of another terrorist watchlist suspect who joined the local suspect and were tag teaming his airport. The watch commander felt the investigation units should share confidential information with the airport police of any terrorist watchlist suspect who was visiting his airport.

It was a possibility that these two terrorist watchlist subjects were gathering intelligence on this airport for any number of reasons to include pre-operational planning for a criminal or a terrorist event. Terrorist pre-operational periods typically spanned years when they selected targets in the past, but due to technology, terrorist groups have more secured networks by use of encrypted applications that have streamlined their communications with each other. Now, terrorist groups have organized and planned their attacks in shorter time periods. They then can execute their terrorist attacks quickly without fear of discovery by intelligence groups or police.[41]

Terrorists will collect information on potential targets during visits and document the infrastructure with a variety of means to include photographs, sketches, and diagrams. Terrorists will not choose just one target for consideration. Terrorist selects multiple targets when they plan operations. They analyze the selected targets and then store the data for selection when their predetermined time or an immediate opportunity presents itself.

Fragmented stories like this are many and are another example of a first line police encounter that quickly disappeared into the black hole of the Federal Intelligence Centers. For months, this airport continually monitored the suspect. When all was said and done, and the suspect disappeared from the airport police radar, was another piece added to the intelligence puzzle board? Intelligence personnel investigations of these contacts have a primary purpose: to find the mastermind and the extent of any criminal or terrorist plans that may be local, national, or worldwide. Law enforcement starts with the front line foot soldier of the terrorist cell or their operating groups and hopefully, through time, the appropriate agency will arrest or terminate the key players at the top of the terrorist group organization chart.

On July 2, 2014, FBI agents encountered Fadi Dandach at the Orange County (John Wayne) Airport, Santa Ana, California, attempting to board a flight to Istanbul, Turkey.[42] Dandach went to El Modena High School, nine miles from my airport. At age 22, Dandach pled guilty to attempting to support ISIL and sentenced to 15 years in prison. Dandach serves as an example of a terrorist recruit who attempted to fly from my airport. The unknown terrorist who may work in the shadows near my airport or who lives in nearby communities is a threat to any airport.

"Has ISIS reached O.C.? Arrest here intensifies questions."

"Federal authorities allege that the 20-year-old, also known as Fadi Dandach, was planning to join ISIS, just like Douglas McAuthur McCain, a San Diego man identified as having died last weekend on the killing fields of Syria's civil war. Dandach declared he would, "assist ISIS with anything ISIS asked him to do.""[43]

What Is The Terrorist Watchlist?

In this particular incident, the suspected terrorist was identified because his name came up on a terrorist watch list. The making of this watch list starts with the Terrorist Identities Datamart Environment (TIDE), a highly classified database governed by the National Counterterrorism Center in McLean, Virginia. TIDE searches daily and obtains thousands of birthdates, names, aliases, and critical data described as a variety of terrorist parts and pieces that they use to try to match with submitted Central Intelligence Agency, State Department, FBI, and many other U.S. agencies' names, faces, and biometric data. TIDE is not a watch list but the mother lode repository of information that supplies the watch lists. [44]

Every day, TIDE sends a flood of new names that is estimated to average 10,000 a day to the Terrorism Screening Center managed by the FBI, where they combine TIDE's names with their domestic terrorism list to create the master terrorist watch list called the Terrorism Screening

Database (TSDB). A TSDB database containing watchlist subjects' information passes to four U.S. agencies whose job is to sort out this maze of possible terrorists and then add it to their separate watch lists.

TSA maintains three passenger screening lists called "no fly," "selectee," and "secure flight." The no-fly list is for those selected as possible terrorists who are not allowed to ride on any U.S. designated flight. If you are on the 'no fly' list, it means you were nominated because you are a known or suspected terrorist who either participated in activity such as engaging, preparing, or planning an attack, gathering information on targets, and other non-public criteria. The 'selectee' list allows a person on this particular list to fly, but they face extra scrutiny before boarding a flight. The 'Secure Flight' is a passenger prescreening program that is risk-based, which strengthens security by identifying high-risk and low-risk passengers before their arrival at the airport. Identifying high-risk passengers occurs by matching their names against trusted traveler lists and watchlist. Secure Flight prevents individuals from boarding an aircraft who are on the No Fly List and Centers for Disease Control and Prevention Do Not Board List. [45]

TIDE had grown to 875,000 people and the TSDB to 520,000 and is an asset for the frontline screening personnel at America's points of entry and the federal, state, and local law enforcement agencies. These databases continue to grow on a daily basis.[46]

What will be missing from the TIDE data banks will be the number of terrorists who have passed quietly over our nation's borders from 2014 to 2016. The weakening of the Border Patrol and the implementation of the 'Catch & Release' policy has opened the front door to terrorist crossing our borders undetected. According to the Center for Immigration Studies (CIS), in 2014 and 2015, the illegal, undocumented, unscreened, no background or whatever politically correct title you wish to apply to the number of foreigners, these people totaled 1.7 million. The actual number is larger as the CIS factors in an annual death rate of 250,000 illegals already in the U.S. and a percentage that returns to their country. It is safe to say, based on the CIS formula, well over two million illegals have crossed our border within the last two years, and the numbers increase each month. The terrorist secreted in these numbers will not be added to TIDE until their arrest, or they come under surveillance by the anti-terrorist forces inside the U.S. Compounding this problem is the number of immigrants arriving in the U.S., has accelerated from 30.2 million in 2000, to 42.1 million in 2015.[47]

In May 2017, the U.S. Border Patrol reported illegal crossings into America had dropped 76% after President Trump increased enforcement and added enforcement manpower. Additional resources and efforts by the new administration also targeted the illegal MS13 Gang members inside the U.S. for prosecution and extradition back to their countries of origin. Let us hope for the security of the United States, that this trend continues.

The following illustration layout depicts the complexity of the nomination process;

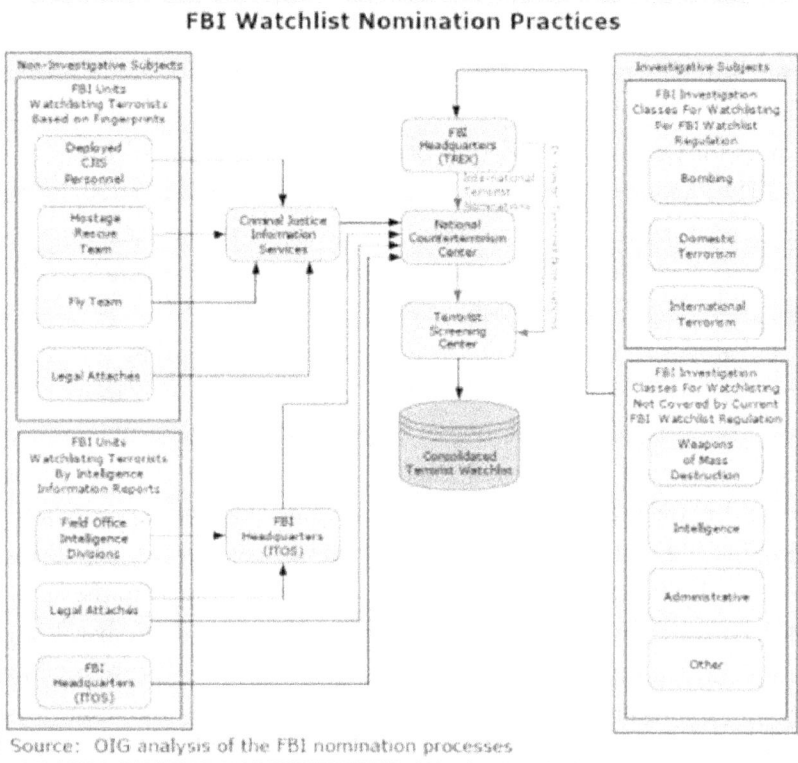

FBI Watchlist Nomination Practices

Source: OIG analysis of the FBI nomination processes

According to the FBI, " these watchlists contain various types of data:

Biographical such as the name and date of birth
Passport number, any known aliases, etc.
Criminal history like warrants, arrests, etc.
Biometric data including fingerprints, etc.
Immigration data about visa type, travel dates, departure country, destination country, a country visited arrival dates, departure dates, the purpose of travel, etc.
Financial data (large currency transactions, etc.)"[48]

A Conversation with a Terrorist Watchlist Suspect

At an airport in the Central United States, an airport watch commander's was in the police conference room sitting across from a man who was on the National Terrorist Watchlist. The watch commander and the terrorist watchlist suspect were waiting for a team of investigators as they engaged each other in conversation. The subject casually told the watch commander that in his travels, he is sometimes queried as to his business. He said he had nothing to hide and would talk until the investigation was satisfied. The watch commander smiled and continued to make small talk while the investigators were driving to the airport.

This conference room had seemed large to the watch commander when he attended previous administrative and staff meetings here, but that night, the room seemed exceedingly small, with only him and this possible enabler of terrorism occupying the room. During the conversation, the subject told of his fundraising activities and his goals of helping Palestinian families with their daily sustenance and educational needs. In turn, the watch commander shared with him his past fundraising efforts for homeless and abused children. They agreed that helping other people was a worthwhile and necessary cause.

How did a suspected terrorist and an airport watch commander come to be in this room discussing charity work? Rewind to a few hours earlier when the airport police received a call from the dispatcher who told the watch commander an airliner was an hour away from their airport, and there was a problem onboard. The watch commander went to the control center to retrieve the information firsthand. The dispatcher told him an airline company called and said one of their inbound passenger jets called the departure airport airline to report a problem. The airline said, passengers, onboard their flight overheard a man talking on his cell phone, saying something suspicious before the plane departed. The airline stated the man was Middle Eastern and was talking about "a large number of people who were going to die because of Israel and America" and similar statements that scared the two passengers sitting adjacent to the subject.

During the flight, the frighten passengers told the flight attendant their concerns. The flight attendant reported the passengers' concerns to the pilot, who then radioed the information to their departure airport. Notification to the airline management chain of command occurred and, in turn, they contacted the departure airport airline. A significant amount of time had elapsed until the airline management in control notified law enforcement that possible Homeland Security implications were onboard the aircraft. They decided to keep the plane in route to the destination airport rather than turn it around to the departure airport. As a result, they notified the arrival airport, and the investigative responsibility fell on the shoulders of the watch commander at the destination airport.

While in the airport's control center, they ran the name of the passenger on the flight manifest through a criminal and terrorist database. Without going into the intricacies of the intelligence alert system, the name of the passenger who made the concerning statements raised enough red flags to circle Tiananmen Square. The watch commander called the investigator and told him a passenger on an inbound aircraft created safety concerns for the aircraft crew. The watch commander told the investigator the passenger name was on the Terrorist Watchlist. The investigator accessed the passenger name records in his database and told the watch commander he wanted to interview the passenger and to have him stay there until he arrives. These special investigators' duties take them all over the state and their Homeland Security responsibilities, and caseloads are immense. The urgency in the investigator's voice meant they would drop what they were doing and get there as soon as possible.

The watch commander anxiously waited at the passenger aircraft-boarding ramp that connects the commercial passenger aircraft to the terminal. Before the plane scheduled landing, the watch commander arrived 30 minutes early to the Jetway. He didn't want to risk the passenger in question slipping past the airport police security in the crowds at the airport. The watch commander learned from other emergency incidents onboard passenger jets in flight, the nervous pilots step on the gas so they can get rid of the problem as soon as possible.

The police dispatch alerted the backup police officers to assist the watch commander when they were told the aircraft was five minutes out. The police stood there as the aircraft landed and taxied to the jet-way. A well-dressed man with a professional persona walked off the plane, with an airline attendant standing silently behind the passenger of interest, pointing a finger at him with a panicked expression on her face. The police approached him and told him who they were and asked if he would talk with them concerning an incident aboard the flight. The watch commander expected his answer to be "no," and thought he would keep walking. But he looked at the watch commander and agreed to go with him. The watch commander breathed a sigh of relief and knew he wouldn't have to detain him or arrest him. Law enforcement tries to use the least amount of authority with citizen contacts, and by using the right words, body language, and tone of voice, an officer can create a consensual encounter situation instead of a legal detainment.

Together, they walked to the baggage claim area. The watch commander stood next to him while waiting for his luggage and said he needed to ask him a series of questions. He said he would not mind, as he picked up his luggage and walked with the watch commander to the secured police administrative area. They entered into a conference room where he was offered a beverage as they sat down. The watch commander told him some passengers on his flight overheard his cell phone conversations. They were concerned when they heard him say 'a large number of people would die.' The watch commander asked if he would like to clear this up. The subject smiled again, but the smile did not reach his eyes. He said the Israeli Nation, with America supplying Israel with arms, brings death to many Palestinians in the conflict to free Palestine. He said he was on a fund-raising mission to keep the money, food, and materials flowing to the Palestinian people in Gaza. The watch commander listened to him intently, watching his body language, looking for deception or any indicators that he was misleading. He went on to say how he traveled throughout the world in his quest to secure money for his charities and felt his mission was one that would reward him well in the afterlife.

The watch commander excused himself for a moment and left the room to call the investigators to determine their updated arrival time. The investigators said they were approaching the airport that very moment. True to their word, they walked through the front door a few minutes later and talked to the watch commander. The investigator that handles the airport told the watch commander this person participates in direct funding of terrorist groups, but he couldn't tell me anything else.

He and his partner entered the conference room and conducted their interview. An hour later, they walked out of the office and drove away with the subject. Following the standard operating procedure for Homeland Security field incidents, the investigators left the airport with the subject, and as an unfinished book with no end, the airport police were left to wonder about the outcome. The frontline of law enforcement personnel are the first responders who secure a subject, hand them off to the proper authorities, and never hear the outcome of the investigators' continuing homeland security scrutiny.

My airport resides in a county where pertinent airport security intelligence data is available, that, when used by an airport security force, will determine the airport's security needs that are consummate with the threat level in their areas. The report of the National Consortium for the Study of Terrorism and Responses to Terrorism (START) presents many threat factors that an airport security matrix should consider. This report specifically highlights the criteria of potential terrorist hotspots that many of our nation's airports lie in. The START report stated some factors place a region as most likely to suffer a terrorist attack. These factors are:

- areas with high population density
- a high percentage of foreign-born residents
- a great amount of language diversity
- a high percentage of non-citizens

START utilized data from the Global Terrorism Database (GTD) to analyze terrorist attacks from 1970 through 2008. Since the 1970s, Manhattan, New York, San Francisco County, California, Washington D.C., Los Angeles County, California, Miami-Dade County, Florida, and Orange County, California are designated as nexuses of terrorism by the START report.

When I read the START Report, it concerned me, as it should any law enforcement officer whose community has similar existing threat criteria. Any airport security administrator must look beyond the airport roadway fence line and see the potential threats that lie in the community around the airport. My airport averages nine million passengers a year, and its acreage is quite small; it's one of the smallest commercial airports regarding land size in the United States, even though it's in densely-populated Orange County, California. Orange County is the smallest county in square miles in California, but it is third in population in the state and sixth in population in the United States with well over three million people. An average of four-thousand people occupies each square mile in Orange County. Orange County is affluent and mostly conservative in views and lifestyle, well known for its tourism and is incredibly diverse, teeming with people from all walks of life.

One component of the elevation of risk for cities in the START report is the correlation between terrorist attacks and areas with dense population. The report states an elevation of the risk occurs when high percentages of foreign-born residents, non-citizen foreign-born residents and a significant amount of language diversity are present in a given area. Every airport police official must consider foreign-born residents and their susceptibility to conversion into an extremist state whose ideology supports terrorism.

On a visit to Colorado in August 2014, James Comey, the former director of the FBI expressed grave concerns about his agency findings that the ISIL is recruiting Americans through the world wide web. He cited Shannon Conley, a 19-year-old suburban Denver woman, recruited into radical extremist Islam because of propaganda on the internet. [49]

Shannon Maureen Conley was a nurse's aide who lives in Colorado. In April 2014, she was arrested by Homeland Security at the Denver International Airport preparing to board an aircraft for a flight to Turkey. The federal charges cited supporting and providing material and resources to a designated terrorist organization. Conley previously converted to Islam and became a radicalized extremist, and when her parents found out, they notified the Federal authorities. The FBI interviewed her, warned her of the charges that could be brought against her if she supported terrorist organizations. Conley told the FBI she needed three elements for her to conduct terrorist operations: means, opportunity, and intent. The intent was there but the right moment and resources were not. Conley said fulfilling her plans might have allowed her to be able to wage Jihad in a year. Conley also stated that if civilians, women or children were on a military base, they would be acceptable collateral damage for terrorist attacks. Conley prepared herself for involvement with ISIL by joining the U.S. Army Explorers where she learned tactics and military operations and used the online internet to meet an ISIL operative and make travel arrangements to Iraq.[50]

In assessing the terrorist threat to my airport, I discovered my state has more Islamic mosques and centers than any other state. There are 30 mosques in California, with seven of them located in Orange County. These religious centers' leaders adamantly disapprove of their followers becoming involved in extremist ideologies but these centers, like many throughout the world; have to be considered recruiting grounds for the terrorist threat. ISIL recruitment of Dandach and his arrest at my airport gave me pause for great concern, but I had an even greater concern for Adam Gadahn, who lived merely a few miles from my airport.

ADAM GADAHN: A HOMEGROWN EXAMPLE OF POTENTIAL THREATS TO AMERICA'S AIRPORTS

I watched a young man named Adam Gadahn talking to the world on television, and his words bothered me greatly. Having faced many dangers in my life, I knew the unknown danger lurking in the shadows were to fear the most. Adam Gadahn was an American from near my hometown. Gadahn was just a kid when he moved with his parents, Phil and Julie Gadahn, from Oregon to the unincorporated area of Winchester in Riverside County, California. Gadahn mother and father raised him in the Christian faith, and at 15, Gadahn moved into his Jewish grandparents' home in a residential area just seven miles from the John Wayne Airport. While with his grandparents, Gadahn searched on the internet for religious sites and blogs in his quest for what he termed was fulfillment. Gadahn found Islamic websites and Islam appealed to him. Gadahn went to the local Islamic Society in Orange County and told a teacher he wanted to convert to Islam. Gadahn read the conversion literature provided to him, and a week later, he took the Shahada (to accept the creed of Islam) in front of a packed mosque.

Gadahn became very involved with the center and even served as a security guard. Sixteen-year-old Gadahn met Deek, a Palestinian-born

American citizen, and Diab, an Egyptian National. Deek and Diab held Islamic extremist views that the Islamic Center leader would later use to expel them from the mosque. But nevertheless, they were able to recruit Gadahn into their ideology and put him to work for the nonprofit group called, "Charity Without Borders." The federal government intelligence agencies investigation determined the Charity Without Borders organization was a conduit for illicit money transfers to al-Qaeda causes from within the United States.

Gadahn made his way to Pakistan and joined a group of radicalized Islamist terrorists who killed thousands of our fellow Americans. As a homegrown terrorist radicalized by al Qaeda, Adam Gadahn received a new name: Azzam al-Amriki, interpreted as "Azzam the American." Gadahn quickly became the media spokesperson and propagandist for al-Qaeda. For over 15 years he appeared in internationally televised videos giving warnings and threats to countries espousing the destruction of America and Israel.[51]

Adam Gadahn was one of my local community members who knew my airport and my community. I can only imagine how many times Gadahn visited my airport when he lived in my town. I'm even more concerned about what Gadahn could have shared with al-Qaeda concerning Orange County while al Qaeda and their affiliate terrorist groups planned their short-term and long-term strategies. A person like Gadahn should be every airport's greatest concern of a potential threat near their airport. The radicalization of all races: Caucasian, Hispanic, Black or Asian members of the community give rise to the fears of possible extremists of both genders, and all races may gain employment in American airports and the community in which they reside.

Communications were retrieved inside the Pakistani home of Osama bin Laden addressed from Gadahn to Osama bin Laden in the form of letters. Gadahn letters were practically lectures to the infamous leader of al-Qaeda. The letters revealed the extent that a California farm boy, death metal music fan, whose father was a Jewish Christian, had risen to the inner circle of the notorious al-Qaeda terrorist group.

By happenstance, Gadahn was in the wrong place at the wrong time in January 2015, when a drone missile strike killed him and some other terrorists who were holding a number of American hostages on the Pakistani-Afghanistan border.[52]

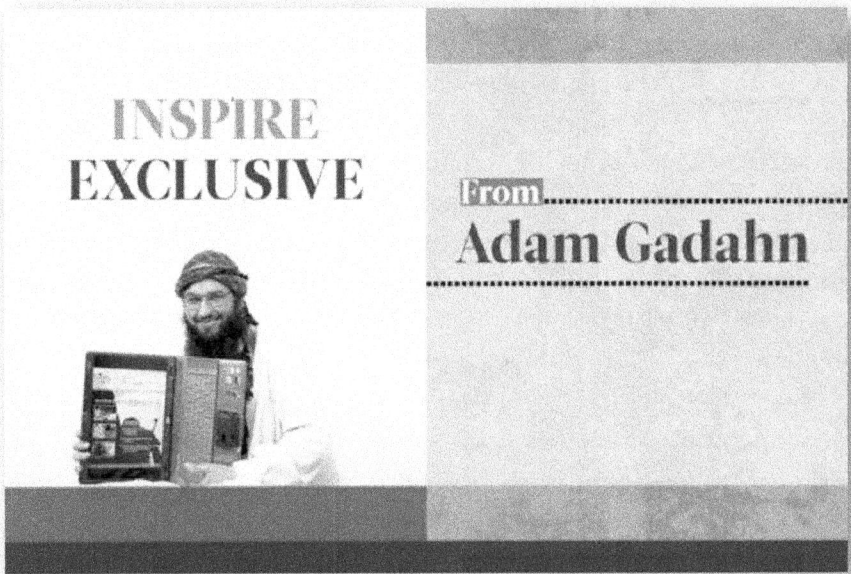

Inspire Magazine, 10th issue, March 2013,
Photo courtesy of Inspire Magazine

Are there other Adam Gadahn's who pose a real threat to the security of the airport in your community? How can we know the number of people in my county and our nation who are willing to support or commit terrorist acts? In February of 2012, the Hartford Institute for Religion Research and the Council on American-Islamic Relations conducted a national count of mosques in the United States and found that the number of mosques has doubled since 9/11. Within ten years, the number of mosques in America has increased. In the survey, 2,106 mosques are in the U.S. and identified. In the year 2000, an audit showed a total of 1,209 mosques and 962 mosques in 1994." California is second with 246 mosques, close to New York, who had the largest number of mosques at 257.[53]

In the "American Mosque 2011" Report Number 1, Ihsan Bagby stated, "mosque leaders were asked to estimate the total number of attendees in a recent Eid Prayer or to determine the total number of Muslims associated with the mosque." The count submitted numbers revealed approximately 2.6 million Muslims participated in the prayer. Based on that number, the estimated Islamic population in the United States was elevated to approximately seven million.[54] The most important question asked of the mosque leaders in the "American Mosque 2011" report was; "whether they agreed with the following statement: Radicalism and extremism are increasing among Muslim youth—in their experience in their area." One percent strongly agreed, six percent agreed, and seven percent were neutral regarding whether or not radicalism is increasing among Muslim youth.

Internationally, intelligence agencies theorize that a certain percentage of the Muslim population are radicalized and are supportive of terrorist groups like al Qaeda, but a Gallup Poll found seven percent of the Islamic population was radicalized in the number surveyed.[55] Using my region as an example, in 2003, CAIR estimated that 450,000 Muslims lived in the Southern California area. Now, hypothetically speaking, let's say that one percent of Southern California's Islamic population was won over to the radicalized al Qaeda or ISIL way of thinking. Using one percent equates to 4,500 likely people in the Southern California Islamic population, who surround my airport and whose predisposition is to hate our way of life. Is this a stagnant number? Unfortunately, no, as the math tells us when we divide 4,500 radicalized people into teams of two, like Diab and Deek, then the potential for growth can be endless? If each two-person team were able to convert another person, like Diab and Deek won over Adam Gadahn, then we would now have to worry about 6,700 possible Diabs, Deeks, and Gadahn's running around our local communities, hating our way of life and supporting terrorist groups. However, this math formula keeps on multiplying, doesn't it? They would theoretically continue to grow in numbers as they continued to convert American youth and spreading radicalized Islam within our nation.

A fact supporting this theory is the San Berndindino mass murderers, Syed Rizwan Farook and Tashfeen Malik, who persuaded their neighbor, Enrique Marquez Jr., to convert to Islam. Marquez supplied Farook the assault weapons that killed innocents in the 2nd largest mass shooting in California.

Guns used in the San Bernardino shooting, Photo: San Bernardino County Sheriff's Department

Disturbing news for our nation's airports security administrators concerns the Hezbollah terrorist group whose members live in communities near our nation's airports. Only 25 miles from my airport and just miles from Los Angeles International and Burbank Airport, Southern California gang members affiliated with the Mexican Mafia joined the fight in Syria for the Syrian government and Hezbollah against the al Qaeda and affiliated forces attempting to overthrow the Syrian government. The U.S. Justice Department in July 2014 investigated over a hundred American citizens who traveled to fight in Syria or Iraq.[56] Forty of these fighters have returned to the U.S.; with the FBI tracking them as of October 2014.[57]

The FBI stated that dozens of more Americans were fighting on the side of al Qaeda in the same conflict in Syria. The Mexican Mafia in 2007 was running businesses in Los Angeles whose sole purpose was a front for Hezbollah to raise funds for terrorist activity. The FBI raided and closed down the businesses.[58] On May 28, 2014, Robert Windrem and Pete Williams of NBC News reported an American citizen carried out an al-Qaeda planned suicide bombing in Syria. The news account said it was the first suicide bombing by an American citizen in the Syrian civil war.[59]

How Great is the Threat to Our Nation's Airports?

Airport law enforcement evaluates and learns from criminal incidents and investigations and information from public sources to include the media, that shape law enforcement planning and operations. President Obama on May 28, 2014, said to the graduating class at West Point that terrorism is the greatest national security threat to America as reported by Phil Mattingly and Margaret Talev of the *Bloomberg News*. Foreign correspondent Lara Logan has a vast amount of experience in reporting on the terrorist threat and understands the problem the world faces. During a report on October 8, 2012, on *CBS 60 Minutes*, she stated:

> "They still hate us, now more than ever. The Taliban and al-Qaida have not been vanquished, they're coming back... The recent terrorist killings of Christopher Stevens, the U.S. ambassador to Libya and three other officials are a harbinger of our vulnerability, the Taliban and al-Qaida are teaming up and recruiting new terrorists to do us deadly harm."

One Airport Example of a Perceived Threat

One of the most critical components of airport security throughout our nation is a trained vigilant populace in and around an airport who can identify and report criminal and terrorist indicators exhibited by suspicious subjects. Well-trained and educated airport employees and the airports neighboring populace increase the airport's layered protection that our nation's aviation industry must have. The cost of implementing a program like this is negligible, but the value is priceless.

An airport in America created such a program called an Airport Business Watch program. Airport law enforcement created and initiated the program by visiting the business offices around the airport, explaining the program and asking for their support by partnering with the airport police. The airport police watch commander went to a business that was very near the airport's fence to talk to the owner of the company. While explaining the details of the program to the business owner, an employee in the next room overheard the airport police officer asking for the employees to serve as eyes and ears for law enforcement. The employee interrupted the conversation to tell the officer that occasionally the neighboring Islamic center's children marched in formation on weekends through the vacant parking lot adjacent to the closed businesses. The supervisor said the students' marching itself wasn't particularly a concern; the problem, he said was that the 12-year-old participants would chant, "We are al Qaeda. Who are we? Al Qaeda."

"Good one," the officer smiled sourly. "You're a comedian without a gig."

"I'm not kidding," he insisted with a serious expression. "It's happened in the past, on many occasions." After realizing the employee was serious, the officer told him he would contact their investigation unit, and they would call him for an interview.

Where did this go once the investigators interviewed him? Were there surveillance, covert operations to see who was inspiring these young children to chant the name of America's enemy? The airport watch commander couldn't say, nor would it be right for him to speculate in a situation like this. Would any man or woman when presented with these facts have concern for this airport's security?

To me, as an airport watch commander, looking at all of these fragmented stories is like putting a puzzle together without the puzzle box lid: We don't have the overall picture of what happens when investigators take over a case, just the strange shapes, and color that each incident provides. But while we might not know exactly how the pieces fit together, we know the situation could be a forecast of threats to our homeland security.

A Third Terrorist Watch List Subject

Let me give you another piece of this worrisome puzzle that slowly assembles and serves as a call for the interminable heighten defense of our airports. At a regional airport on the East Coast, a law enforcement investigator walked in one evening and told the airport watch commander to brief the airport gate guards to be on the lookout for a man who had recently returned unexpectedly to the U.S. from a former province of Russia. This person was a general aviation pilot, and the investigation led them to believe that he may be planning to rent an aircraft at an airport in the region tonight.

The investigator said the suspect is the focus of a homeland security investigation, and if he arrives at the airport perimeter gates, the officer at the gate should stall his entry. He said to notify him immediately, and he would provide additional directions at that time. The investigator said he was unsure if the subject would come to the airport, but as a precaution, he wanted the airport police alerted. The airfield patrol officers received instruction to keep their vehicles on the south and north ends of the airfield as a precaution, and the gate guards were instructed to notify the police dispatch covertly if he arrived to enter the airfield.

A few hours later, the gate officer called dispatch and notified them that the subject was at the gate. The watch commander immediately called the investigator. The investigator answered and said he would call his superiors right away and promised to call right back. The investigator called back moments later, and the watch commander reminded him that he could not think of any legal standing to prevent the subject from entering the airport and using the rented aircraft. Without a direct order from investigative officials, the subject would be allowed to enter the airport, prep his aircraft and take off. The investigator told the watch commander the matter had been taken out of the regional officer's jurisdiction and had "gotten larger." He said this operation was in the greater metropolitan jurisdiction with oversight by the national incident command center. With a heightened concern, the watch commander asked him if the security of his airport was in jeopardy. All the investigator could say was to go ahead and let him in like any other pilot but to stand by for further orders.

The watch commander called the gate officer and told him to allow the subject access to the airfield. The subject drove in, parked his car next to a fix wing general aviation aircraft, and started preparation for the aircraft flight. The watch commander called the investigator and said, "Our guy is preparing his aircraft for takeoff." The control center's camera had zoomed in on the subject and was recording his every move. "He's pulling the plane out of the parking space as we speak. What are your instructions?"

"Central is in control now," the investigator answered. "This has gone to the *highest* level." The investigator said he was waiting to hear from them to see if they wanted to stop the aircraft from taking off, and he would call back as soon as he heard from Central. He ended by stating the surveillance unit had just arrived at the airfield gate and was standing by outside of the airport fence.

On the camera monitor in the control center, the subject was seen taking the aircraft window coverings down and removing the anchor ties off the aircraft. The airfield officers were radioed instructions to prepare to stop the aircraft with their police vehicles if necessary, using them as a barricade to prevent it from taking off. By the time they were alerted, the subject had pulled the aircraft out of the parking space and the taxiway and was completing his final pre-flight checks of the wings and flaps.

The officer's move within proximity of the aircraft as the watch commander called the investigator. When the investigator picked up the phone, he was hurriedly told, "The aircraft's engine has started, and the pilot is completing his pre-flight check. When he completes the flight preparation in a minute, he'll be on the runway taxiing for takeoff. What are your orders?" The watch commander could hear some voices talking frantically in the background, shouting over one another; it seemed the investigator was talking to many individuals around him, all of whom appeared to have an opinion on the situation. The airport police waited anxiously for his reply. Then, after a moment, the investigator yelled into the phone, "Stop the plane from taking off! Stop the plane from taking off!"

The phone slammed down, and the officers were called to make a traffic stop of the aircraft and directed not to let the aircraft take off. Police units raced in from the north and south ends of the taxiway. With their red and blue lights flashing like fireworks, they made a very unusual police traffic stop of an aircraft on the airfield. The watch commander had many tense moments in law enforcement; but for almost 40 minutes from the time this subject entered the airport until officers pulled in front of the aircraft, this one adrenaline rush was one of the top ten in his career.

Arriving at the location where the officers had stopped the aircraft, the watch commander entered the gate just as the investigators pulled up and took over. The police waited near the aircraft while the investigators talked with the subject and searched his aircraft. They loaded the subject into one of their sedans and drove off; as the police watched the taillights wink out of sight. Once again, the subject and situation raced off into the black hole where no information returns.

As one of three shift watch commanders, I have met or interacted with subjects on the Terrorist Watchlist during my tenure at the airport. How many unknown terrorist watch list suspects have tacitly passed through American airports without airport police knowledge? Have other terrorists monitored my airport while I drove or walked by them unknowingly? These questions were troubling as I conducted my daily airport security duties.

A TERRORIST WATCHLIST SUBJECT PROTESTS SECURITY MEASURES

Incidents that shape an airport law enforcement perspective do not always have an intensity that takes a few days off of their life expectancy. At an American airport, the watch commander received a call that a man in screening lanes was on the terrorist watch list's "selectee" screening list, and was arguing with TSA. The subject said he is not required to go through secondary screening because he was supposed to be taken off the terrorist watch list. The watch commander went to the screening lanes and motioned to one of their TSA administrators who happened to be in the terminal. This TSA administrator was a very experienced and insightful person; invaluable in the situation at hand.

They contacted the subject in question as he was boarding the aircraft. The man presented a photocopied form letter from TSA that merely said they would look into his request for removal from the selectee list; there was no mention made of his removal from the list as he had claimed in the screening lanes. After a few minutes of questions and answers, the subject continued to the passenger aircraft after he completed a secondary screening. Following the encounter, the TSA administrator said based on the subject status as a former roommate of one of the 9/11 hijackers before the 9/11 attack; al-Qaeda links are possible. The subject travels to the Middle East multiple times per year and is a possible terrorist intelligence operative. According to sources, the feds did not have enough evidence to arrest him as a supporter of terrorism; but even so, he will remain on the selectee list and subjected to extensive scrutiny at screening lanes each time he flies.

My airport and many of our country's other airports are visited and watched by groups that mean to do harm, once again, to our commercial aviation industry. The evidence is irrefutable and demands that our airports' security standards be second to none. David Shtulman is the Director of Agency Endowments for the United Jewish Federation Foundation. Shtulman offered this viewpoint of the possible type of airport attack that may occur in the United States:

"If you want to destroy the airline industry in the U.S., you do not have to blow up airplanes in the sky. All our defenses begin with security at the check-in process. However, low-tech suicide bombers in five airport lobbies around the country on the same day would accomplish the same thing. People will be afraid to go to the airport and security will have to screen people as they enter the terminal, making air travel a nightmare. After a few months when things begin to return to normal, use car bombs in airport parking lots and disrupt the system again?"[60]

It's clear these think tank terrorism scenarios are played out by good and bad people, and even the news media host experts who tell their versions of any number of terrorist attack probabilities and their methods.

ASYMMETRIC THREATS AND AMERICAN AIRPORTS

"The stakes are enormous. Nowhere is the asymmetric threat
of terrorism more evident than in the area of aviation security."

OFFICE OF THE INSPECTOR GENERAL, MAY 12, 2016

Kenneth F. McKenzie, Jr., is a Lieutenant General in the Marine Corps and senior military fellow at the Institute for National Strategic Studies at the National Defense University. McKenzie authored McNair Paper 62; *The Revenge of the Melians: Asymmetric Threats and the Next QDR*, where he remarks that there is an asymmetrical threat from hostile nations and groups who are seeking ways to undermine U.S. strength by attacking its vulnerabilities. The core principle of this concept is that a weaker power will find ways to diminish the power of the strong. In this concept, the asymmetric threat moves into asymmetric operational warfare where the inferior attacker's strength leverages the vulnerabilities of a stronger opponent weaknesses. This method of attacks strives to undermine the stronger force's will to strike back at the weaker forces,' thus achieving, the weaker forces strategic objective.[61] The next decade will be pivotal in America's foreign policy and its ability to garner the much-needed allies to combat the future terrorist threats.

The asymmetric threat to our Homeland comes from diverse groups whose goals are to weaken our country and diminish our dominance in the world. Threats come from nations' governments, such as North Korea and Iran, or terrorist groups such as Pakistan's 'LeT' Sunni militant groups, al-Qaeda, Somali's Al-Shabaab, and the Islamic State of Iraq and the Levant, to name a few. An example of an asymmetric threat facing an airport in the United States could be a lone wolf who bypasses strong terminal security and uses an explosive-laden fuel truck to ram through the perimeter fence of the airfield. On the airfield, the terrorist has multiple targets, such as airliners full of passengers on the runway and at the terminal and the ramp side of the airport terminal. One or the other would create catastrophic death, destruction and a prolonged cessation of aviation flights for days. A single person in this scenario could use conventional weapons at a point of his opponent's weakness rather than his strength. This simple assault would provide any terrorist objectives of physical destruction, death, news media attention, propaganda, and losses to the nation's economy.

The Islamic extremist converts are living in virtually every airport region in America as evidenced by FBI Director Comey November 2015 release that declared his agency is investigating over 900 'homegrown' ISIL cases in all 50 states. An example in my airport region occurred when the FBI arrested four Southern California men in Riverside County who converted to Islam and radicalized by extremist literature and online videos. These radicalized converts, whose ethnic origins were Filipino, Mexican, and Vietnamese, conducted training in firearms at paintball war game locations. The FBI arrested them just before they attempted to leave the U.S. to join the Taliban in Afghanistan where they planned to kill American soldiers.[62]

These homegrown terrorists chose to kill Americans elsewhere, but what of the many other homegrown terrorists that we are unaware of, who are plotting to kill Americans in our communities? As mentioned earlier, U.S. citizens are returning after learning combat and bomb-making skills in the Iraqi, Afghanistan and Syrian wars. What are their plans, to assimilate in their 9-to-5 jobs and return to a peaceful family life? Alternatively, will they and others plot to attack U.S. targets as a sleeper cell or as a single long wolf attacker for whatever misguided cause they claim to follow? Sometimes fiction merges with reality and provides a reasonable possibility outcome of the terrorist mindset as to why they want to kill Americans. This quote from the movie 'Traitor;' may apply in the real world and would describe a terrorist possible conviction and goals:

> "In chess and in war the key to winning is to anticipate what your opponent will do in advance. Think two moves ahead. The art of asymmetrical warfare is less about inflicting damage than provoking a response. Terrorism is theater. And theater is always performed for an audience. Ours is the American people. But they are dispersed across a large country. The question is how to convince them that nowhere is safe."

The San Bernardino California husband and wife, terrorist team, slaughtered their civilian co-workers who called them friends, in December 2015. Does this terrorist mayhem create fear and distrust in work groups with employees of different faiths across America? Six months later in June 2016, a son of Afghan immigrants, raised as a Muslim, declared his allegiance to ISIL on the cell phone call to the 9-1-1 operator as he killed 50 people and wounded an additional 53 people in the Orlando Night

Club attack. America continues to slide into an abyss of fear caused by 48 radicalized Islamic murder incidents since 9/11 that has taken 139 lives on American soil and seems to be increasing unabated.[63]

Do Neighboring Countries Harbor Threats for America's Airports?

My county and its neighboring Los Angeles County meet many of the risk conditions identified in the START report and as such are considered possible targets or staging grounds for emerging attacks.[64] But it's not just my region. It applies to virtually any airport in our nation as the porous borders, and the speed of movement by various transportation modes allows people to be anywhere in our country from any of our borders within 24 hours. New York and Seattle are to the Canadian border, as my city is to the Mexico border. Only an hour-and-a-half drive from Mexico, international or domestic terrorist organizations easily and clandestinely navigate across our unprotected southern border. The Senate Homeland Security Committee in 2011 made it clear that illegally entering America has been easy by the terrorists, extremists, and criminals not only from Mexico but from Canada, as well. In July 2014, the United States Southern Commander Marine Corps General John Kelly said our Mexican border is a "crime-terror convergence" of everything imaginable to include weapons of mass destruction.[65]

Judicial Watch provided an alarming example of terrorist groups accessing the United States unseen via our porous southern border in a December 8, 2014, news story. The FBI placed Adnan G. EL Shukrijumah on their most wanted list of terrorist operatives for his participation in the plans to attack Oprah Winfrey's television studio, New York, and Britain's subways, and the Chicago Sears Tower.

For many years, Shukrijumah came into and out of the U.S. across the Mexican border to meet his fellow terrorists so they could plan how to destroy U.S. targets and kill Americans. Judicial Watch confirmed through government sources that Shukrijumah piloted a private aircraft

MOST WANTED TERRORISTS

ADNAN G. EL SHUKRIJUMAH

Conspiracy to Use Weapons of Mass Destruction; Providing Material Support to a Foreign Terrorist Organization; Conspiracy to Provide Material Support to a Foreign Terrorist Organization; Receiving Military-Type Training From a Foreign Terrorist Organization; Conspiracy to Commit an Act of Terrorism Transcending National Boundaries; Attempt to Commit an Act of Terrorism Transcending National Boundaries; Use of Destructive Device

Digitally Enhanced Photograph

DESCRIPTION

Aliases: Adnan G. El Shukri Jumah, Abu Arif, Ja'far Al-Tayar, Jaffar Al-Tayyar, Jafar Tayar, Jaafar Al-Tayyar, Hamad

Date(s) of Birth Used: August 4, 1975   **Place of Birth:** Saudi Arabia

Hair: Black   **Eyes:** Black

Height: 5'3" to 5'6"   **Weight:** 132 pounds

Build: Average   **Complexion:** Dark

Sex: Male   **Citizenship:** Guyanese

Languages: Arabic, English   **Scars and Marks:** None known

REMARKS

Shukrijumah may wear a beard and has a pronounced nose.

CAUTION

Adnan G. El Shukrijumah was indicted in the Eastern District of New York in July of 2010 for his alleged role in a terrorist plot to attack targets in the United States and the United Kingdom. The charges reveal that the plot against New York City's subway system, uncovered in September of 2009, was directed by senior Al-Qaeda leadership in Pakistan and was also directly related to a scheme by Al-Qaeda plotters in Pakistan to use Western operatives to attack a target in the United States. Shukrijumah is thought to have served as one of the leaders of Al-Qaeda's external operations program.

SHOULD BE CONSIDERED ARMED AND DANGEROUS

from Mexico to the Cielo Dorado Estates private airport in Anthony, New Mexico. Cielo Dorado is one of the hundreds of private airports in New Mexico, and one of over 15,000 private airstrips throughout the United States. The story of this terrorist ended when a Pakistani Army raid in the South Waziristan province killed Shukrijumah.[66]

On August 4, 2016, the FBI arrested Erick Jamal Hendricks in Ohio on a federal complaint of conspiring to support the Islamic State of Iraq and Levant (ISIL). Hendricks declared his ISIL brothers covert cells were just across the United States southern border in Mexico. Hendricks was recruiting others in Ohio to launch terrorist attacks throughout the United States.[67]

Another example of what dangers are just across the Mexican border became evident when the Mexican Government arrested three Hezbollah terrorist suspects in Merida, Mexico. One suspect was Rafic Mohammad Labboun Allabounm, who is an American citizen. Allabounm quick extradition to the U.S. occurred when the Mexican authorities leaked his role in 9/11.[68] Current and retired Immigration and Customs Enforcement officers are declaring the government is hiding the facts from the public that large numbers of smuggled Somalis, Iranians, Syrians, Afghans, and men from Yemen continue across the border into the United States. Many are suspected to have ties to Al-Qaeda, Al-Shabaab, Hezbollah, Hamas and other terrorist factions. Sheriff Paul Babeu of Pinal County Arizona said the border is a U.S. security problem, "There is intelligence that we have that is very troubling, and we can't tell the public."[69]

These events and testimonies provide security managers awareness of the threats in our communities from areas we assumed were safe and protected. Texas Republican Congressman Ted Poe told CBS's local Dallas-Fort Worth News he believed that ISIL would use Texas's southern border to enter the United States. "Of course, the way they would come to the United States would be through the porous border with Mexico. The drug cartels will bring people into the country no matter who they are–for money."[70]

The northern border is hardly better, and an example of what dangers are just across the Canadian border is Ahmed Ressam. Ressam had trained in Afghanistan terrorist camps before he came to Canada. Ressam was driving to Los Angeles when he crossed the Canadian border, and a Canadian border officer gave him a second look. The officer said Ressam was acting "hinky." After a search of his car, they discovered hidden in the wheel well of his car's trunk were explosives and detonators that would have successfully detonated a bomb with the force of 44 times that of a typical car bomb. The Los Angeles International Airport Terminal was his target, with his attack planned on New Year's Eve.

The founder of the Islamic Supreme Council of Canada Imam Syed Soharwardy said jihadist groups are 'recruiting under our noses in universities and mosques.' The Canadian imam promotes pacifism in his teachings and warns extremist militant groups are recruiting in Canada. Because of his pacifist position, he has received a death threat from one of the members.[71] In June 2017, the Flynt Michigan Airport police lieutenant was patrolling the airport terminal when a lone wolf terrorist stabbed him in the neck. Soharwardy assessment is correct as Canadian citizen Ftouhi legally entered the U.S. from Canada and stabbed the airport police officer in the neck while shouting "Allahu Akbar." Etouhi was radicalized in Canada and played out his beliefs hoping to be martyred in the attack.

These are snippets, placed into a concise glimpse of what our nation faces in threats to the aviation industry infrastructure. These threats and thousands of other examples encapsulate one of the greatest threats to our nation's airport security: the Homegrown Violent Extremists (HVE's). The Los Angeles Airport HVE Paul Ciancia attacked the LAX terminal to "instill fear in traitorous minds."[72] The FBI arrested HVE Sami Osmakac for his plan to attack an Air Force base in Tampa, Florida. HVE Hesham Hadayet carried out an armed attack with two handguns at the El Al Airline ticket counter at LAX by shooting at the 90 passengers standing in line. He killed a customer service agent and, as passengers huddled nearby, he started shooting at them, killing one and injuring four until an El Al security guard shot and killed him.[73]

There are many examples of threats our nation's airports face and how law enforcement interacts with potential threats in and around their airports. The cat-and-mouse "game" between airport police and terrorist elements isn't a one-day, one-month, one-year term. It is decades of intelligence gathering, prevention, and deterrence on a 24-hour, seven-days-a-week continuum. Only such an effort will keep our airports safe from the threats facing them. Anything less is only a façade to provide you, the passenger, a false sense of security when you step into an airport terminal.

ISIL gave America a warning in 2016; ""Paris isn't far from you—we will by Allah's permission do to your country what we did to Paris. We will kill, slaughter and burn your people."[74] The American aviation industry remains a high-value target for terrorist organizations. From our nation's borders to the communities next to our airports, the threats are real and present. Terrorists will strike our airports and airlines again. They will conduct surveillance, operate from within, and initiate future attacks with callous disregard for innocent lives to accomplish their goals and inspire religious extremist recruiting. What we do now will prevent, deter or mitigate the next event. Brussels and Istanbul Airports are a warning; failure is not an option.

"U.S. has 55 daily encounters with suspected terrorists.
U.S. officials said the encounters, which involve airport and border security personnel as well as federal and local law enforcement officers, are reported to the Terrorist Screening Center (TSC), an interagency unit led by an FBI official based in a tightly guarded building in northern Virginia."[75]

MARK HOSENBALL, REUTERS, MAY 12, 2011

CHAPTER 4

The Open Front Door: 50 years of Airport Attacks

———

"I hope they will design an airport with
the idea that security is forever."

Arnold Barnett, Aviation Safety Specialist,
Professor of Operations Research at
Massachusetts Institute of Technology[76]

As a watch commander at the John Wayne Airport in Orange County California, I walked the terminal entrance sidewalks and admired the architectural beauty of the infrastructure around me. On many occasions, I walked the terminal and parking structures at great length to know every nook and cranny of the mile long corridor of airport buildings. Knowing my airport's infrastructure gave me the knowledge to make immediate and correct decisions when security events occurred in these areas.

One day I asked my bomb squad personnel to walk with me, and I asked them what would happen in a series of scenarios that I posed to them. We walked the upper-level of the terminal entrances and its lower level baggage claim exits, and I focused my questions on vehicle-borne improvised explosive device detonations and suicide bomber detonations at various locations. I asked the bomb squad to conduct a blast radius analysis in various areas of the airport to determine what assets would be intact after an attack with an explosive-laden vehicle. The answers were unsettling as to the extent of damage that would occur at my airport.

The design of my airport terminal and construction occurred over twenty-two years before my assignment there, with the goal of providing the best home for airlines and other businesses to serve the citizens of Orange County. The terminal cost $150 million in 1986 and provided the state of the art accessibility and conveniences to the traveling public. The John Wayne Airport did not plan for the al Qaeda or ISIL threat to our nation's homeland 22-years ago. Now, years after 9/11, I had many concerns and a strong desire to prevent or mitigate any threats that may come to the John Wayne Airport.

I used my training and experiences from fifteen years as a Sheriff's Special Weapons and Tactics team member to train deputies and special officers in airport active shooter or mass shooting team exercises. Using airsoft weapons, we formed assault teams to search for active shooters and engage them in role-playing hostage scenarios in the closed airside terminal. Somewhat realistic training like this revealed to me the vulnerabilities of my airport terminal and many other airports throughout the nation. Historical data shows the following airports possessed the same inherent vulnerabilities in their airport infrastructure where terrorist using firearms, grenades, suitcase bombs, and suicide vests in multi-assailant attacks wreaked havoc on the infrastructure and the innocents inside the terminals.

ISTANBUL, BRUSSELS, MOSCOW, LOS ANGELES, NEW YORK, PARIS, ROME, FT. LAUDERDALE

On March 22, 2016, the Belgium Brussels Airport terrorist attack shocked the world. Within minutes, the social and news websites were filled with images of the infrastructure destruction and the wounded and dead lying in the airport terminal. Governments of every nation and officials in virtually every field of security and law enforcement made public statements that this attack should not have happened. Three months after Brussels on June 28, 2016, terrorists, using precision military tactics breached one of the most secure airports in Istanbul, Turkey. Suicide bombers using AK-47 type military assault weapons killed 41 and wounded 239 passengers and airport workers.

Over fifty years of history documented airport attacks in the terminal or on the airport runways were not an anomaly, but rather evidence of our airport's security vulnerabilities from which we failed to learn from year after year. From the 1965 Aden Airport attack, the 1981 New York Airport terminal bombing, the 1983 Orly Airport attack, to the Rome Airport terrorist assault in 1985, these incidents were effectively billboards declaring airports were desirable and easy terrorist targets. Were the worldwide demands for greater airport security as pronounce when terrorist attacked Athens Greece Airport in 1968 or the Tel Aviv International Airport in 1971? What international tribunal formed to assemble a master plan to prevent future airport attacks after Russia's busiest international airport suffered a terrorist suicide bombing in the Moscow Airport terminal arrival baggage area in 2011. What procedures changed, and improvements to airports terminal infrastructures were made to stop future attacks in the open airport terminals of every airport in the world? Was the international call for changes in airports security throughout the past five decades as great as the Brussels and Istanbul Airport bombings security failures revealed?

Terminal planning and construction over the last 50 years were never designed to stop a terrorist from reaching unguarded passengers or the interior of terminals. Airport and airline administrations pushed to make larger accessible and beautiful terminals so they could attract customers and reach their airport's goals of maximum passenger capacity. Many airport construction designs modeled large pane glass windows and defenseless architectural façades whose sole purpose was to provide customers beautiful surroundings instead of preventing or mitigating certain types of terrorist threats.

"Many other airports today will incorporate a large glass façade at least in the front of the terminal to allow light in but will not use reinforced glass or create the proper stand-off distance."[77] Raffi Ron, former director of security, Tel-Aviv Ben Gurion International Airport

The general public uproar is short lived after each airport terrorist attack. Our fellow man reacts to airport security attacks, and within a relatively short span of time, their attention returns to their lives and the business at hand. The politicians react to these outcries from the public and initiate legislation. These types of reactive incident legislations often run into roadblocks from airlines, airport groups or related political advocate groups during the ensuing months and sometimes years of investigations, reviews, debates and the final Congressional vote. These groups common goal is to mitigate portions of proposed legislative airport security improvements for a variety of reasons. They often cite cost factors and the desire to maintain the passenger's convenience and ease of access to airports. There are, however, some dedicated politicians and citizen activist that continue to fight to improve our nation's airports security and attempt to overcome these obstacles for the greater good.

The facts reveal little significant changes to airports exterior infrastructure occurred over the last 50 years that decreased the vulnerability to various types of terminal or runway terrorist attacks. September 11th brought concrete bollards or rails to prevent vehicles from driving into the terminal from the roadway. Many other recommendations by airport governing bodies after 9/11, suggested placing concrete barricades in a zig zag pattern to slow cars approaching airport field gates or strengthening airfield fences to name a few. Many airports improved screening security, with few measures implemented for their airport terminal infrastructure.

Through each airport attack, decade after decade, airport governors did not, for only reasons they could testify to, renovate or design from the ground up, airports that would provide deterrence to terrorists whose plans are to kill passengers inside the terminal or on the runway. They did not consider the previous types of terrorist attacks in airport terminals and on the runways. For decades, the airport administrators did not seize the opportunity to add to their building design the attributes that would prevent or mitigate the suicide bomber, the vehicle bomb, or assault with firearms.

These government and airport administrators did not heed history warnings of what happened at airports in over 70 previous airport terminal attacks that occurred throughout the world. Nor did virtually any other airport in America pay attention to these lessons. Issac Yeffet, the former director of security for El Al, the Israeli National Airlines, toured American airports with Life Magazine writer Edward Barnes in 1989. They reviewed security operations at O'Hare, La Guardia, Stapleton, Miami, San Francisco and Los Angeles airport. Yeffet made a compelling statement in his assessment concerning airport administrators:

"Airline [airport] executives have made security a low priority. There is no reason to believe this will change until there is a major disaster at an American airport."[78]

INDIANAPOLIS INTERNATIONAL AIRPORT

The Indianapolis Airport was one of the first airports to design and build a passenger terminal after the September 11, 2001, terrorist attacks. Dan Goldblatt of the Indiana Public Media News posted in 2011 how Indianapolis International Airport was designed and built for greater security measures when completed in 2008. Right after 9/11, the TSA and Indianapolis collaborated to make the terminal more "open" for the security and passengers. Goldblatt stressed the improvement made to the screening lanes were the focus of the post 9/11 terminal security concerns. The Indianapolis Airport is a beautiful structure and resembles a giant glass house. But what is not apparent to most, is the glass installed is designed to be blast resistant and if a bomb exploded nearby, it will fold like a drape when broken instead of becoming shrapnel that would kill and maim passengers. The RAND Corporation promoted the blast resistant glass idea in a 2003 study that emphasized a reduction in the number of victims from an airport bomb attack would occur if airports glass windows received a shatterproof glazing, reduced window panes size, and the use of stronger window frames.[79]

Indianapolis terminal façade design incorporated concrete infrastructure components that will stop many types of terrorist attacks throughout the new terminal. As I learned from my bomb squad and through explosive training, distance from explosives is a friend and protects infrastructure, but more importantly people. In Indianapolis, they created large distances from the terminal and strengthened terminal walls with added steel and concrete to prevent these threats from posing as serious a problem as they may have been. This type of infrastructure is an improvement over the majority of other American airports and reduces susceptibility to any number of devastating terrorist attacks from the landside or the airside.[80] There are, however, steps Indianapolis can take to continue to lead other airports, and become one of the safest airports in the nation.

KANSAS CITY INTERNATIONAL AIRPORT

The Kansas City International Airport (KCI) designer, Ron Hicks, helped with the design plans for the Kansas airport in the 1960's. The wave of hijackings in the seventies resulted in improving the KCI terminal to thwart the possibility of hijackings at KCI. KCI is a long series of terminals laid out in three circle shaped terminals. The layout of these terminals allows passengers into their airline's screening lanes quickly with a short walk to their airplane. The city debated over the last few years to tear down the current airport and build a single passenger terminal airport. When interviewed by the reporter, Hicks objected to the proposed new design and said "Our facility, and the way it's designed, is not terrorist friendly. This current design is the ideal design for safety."

Hicks said the Brussels Airport attack gave him concern that the proposed new KCI airport terminal would mirror the Brussels "centralized security zone." Hicks reasoning was the centralized security zone would make KCI more attractive to terrorists as the larger number of passengers would consolidate into one location. The current KCI terminal layouts are "pod design" placing passengers at three different terminal locations. KCI elongated multiple terminal entrances reduces the 'dwell time' affording quick access into the secure airside of the terminal. The term 'dwell time' is used in many types of security planning and this context conveys the period of time a large number of passengers will bottleneck at ticket counters and screening lanes in airport terminals.

What dangers did Hicks see in the new terminal design? Hicks told Kansas City News Chanel 41 KSHB "the new terminal could have dangerous possibilities…. plans for a new terminal could make the facility more of a target for terrorists."[81] Only a month after Hicks interview, airline and aviation leaders attended the Kansas City Council meeting and made a pitch for the new terminal. Kansas City Aviation Department Deputy Director of Aviation, Justin Meyer, emphasized to the council the new terminal would provide passengers more conveniences with additional restaurants, play areas and restrooms to name a few.[82] In May 2016, the city opted to delay consideration of building a new KCI single terminal with a centralized security zone. Could Hicks passionate plea have resonated with the city council?

The KCI saga continued when in July 2016, the TSA wrote a letter to KCI and asked for security adjustments. The TSA wanted to consolidate the screening lanes in Terminal C into one checkpoint so the 'Precheck Program' passengers can quickly get through the security lines past the other passengers waiting for screening. Airport Committee member and Northland Councilmember Teresa Loan said: "I'm not sure it would be safer, safety should be the higher priority."[83] A Year later in August 2017, KCI accepted four bids for a one billion dollar new terminal. Pending a public vote in November 2017, it looks like KCI will have a single access terminal.

Is Kansas City Airport an example of airport directors, the TSA and airlines placing a higher emphasis on the business model over better infrastructure security as Yeffet assessed? Attracting passengers is the goal of any good airport business model and is important to the success of airports and airlines, but most important is the security of an airport. Security and safety after 9/11 is and will remain the foundation of a successful airport for many decades to come. The most secure airport will be one built from the ground up or renovated with designs that address the many threats facing an airport terminal and its runways.

I have heard many critics of airport safety state that our current level of security is a façade. The next time you walk through any American airport terminal, your assessment will conclude the airport's infrastructure will not stop the type of terrorist attacks that occurred in Brussels, Rome, Moscow and the over 70 other airport terminal attacks.

DWELL TIME AND THE FAA EXTENSION, SAFETY, AND SECURITY ACT OF 2016

The House of Representatives released Bill H.R. 636 with amendments in July 2016 and addressed the TSA mandates to eliminate dwell time with new recommendations and directives. The TSA mandate included assessing their Headquarters staffing and to pull out non-essential employees for duties in the screening lanes. TSA also received directions to return TSA officers who have screening certifications back to screening duties and have non-certificated employees conduct the duties of "restocking bins and providing instructions and support to passengers in security lines." Although this personnel usage is common sense in nature, Congress placed those directives in the H.R. 636 to help TSA reduce passenger wait times in screening lanes. Congress also directed the TSA to use their Behavior Detection Officers at 'PreCheck Program' screening lanes to expedite passengers who enrolled in the program. Less time in a screening lane means reduced exposure as a target should a terrorist walk in the front door of an airport terminal.

The Daily Telegraph reported on August 26, 2017, the Australian Airport "Bosses" and government officials were extremely concerned about the dwell time passengers spend in line at the country airports. The police earlier arrested a terrorist cell that attempted to check a bomb as luggage onto a passenger aircraft. If not for the device being too heavy, it would have destroyed a passenger plane in mid-air and created a disaster for Australian airlines and airports. During the investigation, the police discovered a second attack planned inside the passenger terminal where large crowds gathered to enter the screening lanes. The terrorist planned to release a gas chemical attack and kill as many people as possible. [84]

A Study by the Rand Corporation

"And the threat is real: terrorists are obsessed with attacking airplanes."[85]

Brian Jenkins, Rand Corporation

The Rand Corporation released an "Occasional Paper" report by Brian Michael Jenkins in 2012 titled "Aviation Security: After Four Decades, It's Time for a Fundamental Review." Jenkins is a highly regarded expert on terrorism and aviation security. He emphasized in his paper the great need for a comprehensive review of our current aviation industry security posture. An emphasized course of action suggested by Jenkins was for a "clean start" to achieve the optimal level of aviation security in our nation's 450 airports.

Jenkins listed some obstacles that would impede a clean start. These impediments to name a few, ranged from Congressional partisanship, differing ideologies and the lack of courage by the many national security stakeholders to ask questions and seek new answers. Jenkins said:

"Two or three non-government research institutions could be selected to independently design an optimal aviation security system, beginning not with the four decades of accumulated security measures currently in place but with a clean slate."[86]

A Variety of Perspectives on Improving Airport Security

In 1977, the University of Pennsylvania Law School released an in-depth review of two terrorist attacks on international airports. This examination of alternative approaches to securing airports from terrorist attacks focused on suggested reforms by waiving sovereign immunity laws and applicable tort laws. This law review made an interesting statement:

"It is to be hoped, however, that the governments' interest in promoting tourism and stimulating commerce and foreign investment, as well as an ordinary sense of responsibility, would combine to create an interest in rigorous security measures at international airports."

We know the U.S. Government enacted laws to enhance aviation security, from the 1961 Aviation Act to prevent aviation piracy up to George W. Bush Homeland Security Act. These and other security measures were added in response to each new threat, and these new measures were built on the existing airport's infrastructure. Did these decades of increased security measures make our airports any safer?

The Penn State Law School review using the Athens Greece Airport Terminal attack in their synopsis focused on victim restitution and who was responsible financially. In 1973 two terrorists opened fire inside the crowded Athens Airport passenger terminal. They threw grenades into an estimated crowd of 1500 people who were waiting to board or were boarding passenger aircraft. The BBC news story revealed:

"One American passenger described how the man standing next to him had his whole chest ripped by bullets and died on the spot. Another older man was also hit."

"A German radio correspondent said he saw a young child hit in the upper body and a woman screaming for her child as blood spurted from her own shoulder."

The law review noted the Greek Police provided security for Athens Airport, and it suggested governments should be held liable for terrorist attacks to improve international airports security. The law review surmised that placing liability on airlines and the government would force them to respond with improvements in airport security and a safer airport from which commerce, tourism and the economies of countries would greatly benefit. Making the airlines responsible for the safety of the passengers or making the government responsible for airport safety were arguments and a voice for that day by the University of Pennsylvania Law School.[87]

David A. Baker, Ph.D. Program Coordinator of Hospitality Management Professor at the Tennessee State University stated a very straightforward message on the various views on how to address our nation's airport security issues. Baker provided this thought on airport security in his 2015 paper 'Tourism and Terrorism: Terrorist Threats to Commercial Aviation Safety & Security.'

"If airplanes and passengers, as well as property and people on the ground, are to be protected, potential perpetrators of aviation terrorism must be prevented from breaching security checkpoints and gaining access to "secure" airport areas and to aircraft."

Baker emphasized that a considerable amount of vigilance is required to protect our aviation industry and stressed any single lapse in airport security would cause untold deaths, destruction, and harm to our economy. He made a valid point when he said: "Despite general agreement on what aviation security entails and the goals of an aviation security system, public controversy abounds on how to regulate and provide this important activity."

The RAND Corporation discussed similar ideas in another analysis twelve years earlier. In 2003 RAND released an "Issue Paper" called Designing Airports for Security, An Analysis of Proposed Changes at LAX." Terry Schell, Brian Chow, and Clifford Grammich reviewed the Los Angeles International Airport (LAX) expansion plan section titled 'Alternative D.' Alternative D emphasis was for the security of airport workers and passengers by:

* Maintaining the current annual passenger numbers (less number of passengers, lesser attractive target)
* Removing all parking structures
* Restricting passenger drop off to only large buses and other mass transportation vehicles
* Building a ground transportation Center away from the terminal where passengers would be dropped off and picked up
* Constructing a mass transit system to move people from the ground transportation center to the terminal[88]

In 2017, Los Angeles International Airport has taken proactive steps to safeguard their airport and the people who work and fly out of their airport. They elected to build a new system regulating the flow of passengers and vehicular traffic to their main airport terminals. LAX is the busiest origin and destination airport in the world and deals with heavy vehicular and pedestrian traffic. With congestion anticipated to grow in time, LAX is building a six-station people mover that will connect rental car, airport parking, and Metro train facilities to the airline terminals. Three stations will provide convenient pedestrian walkway systems in the Central Terminal Area. The planned rent-a-car center will merge over 22 rental car locations into one and will eliminate all rental car shuttles in the terminal areas.

LAX has signed off on two Intermodal Transportation Facilities (IMF) that will collectively handle airport parking for private vehicles and passenger drop-off/pick-up. Connections to hotels, shuttles/commercial vehicles and transit are part of the plans. Detailed pictures and the planned renovations can be found at http://www.connectinglax.com/.

Terminal access reconfiguration may have a positive effect in preventing known types of terrorist attacks such as bombs or firearms (the full extent is unknown). A small vehicle bomb would likely, not reach the terminal under these current renovations and the terminal would continue to function if a terrorist attacked the IMF instead of where passengers currently stage for arrival and departure inside the airport terminal. The greater distance people are required to travel to the terminal will provide security personnel extra time to spot a potential suicide bomber or active shooter suspect. Yes, the passengers dwell time increases at the IMF locations, and that will necessitate an increase in the airport span of control by security personnel, necessitating an increase in security personnel.

THREE SCOTLAND AIRPORTS

In 2007, researchers conducted a case study of three Scotland airports security operations and found each airport handles different types of classes of passengers and types of air transportation travels. The study concluded these classes dictate each airport planning for safety and security should be airport specific. The study said airport security is largely about 'risk management' based on likelihood and hazard and suggested a variety of teams should analyze threat scenarios from different perspectives. These teams should convene and formulate the airport security, based on the teams "views on various risk scenarios, and based on experience or perceived opinion either learned or acquired."[89]

Raffi Ron gave a similar viewpoint, with emphasis on experience team members formulating airport security. Raffi Ron is the former director of security at Israel's Tel-Aviv Ben Gurion International Airport. Ron provided an insightful measure that would improve airport's security during an interview with reporter Penny Jones of Airport Technology. Ron said each airport design or operation process must include a security subject matter expert who would be intimately involved in the concept, development phase, design phase, and the airport implementation process. Ron said the majority of U.S. airports do not use any personnel with security skills in their designing phase or in the construction companies. Ron summed it up with; "Security omissions at the point of design are leaving most of the airports open to attack."[90]

AIRPORT POLICE STAFFING AIRPORT AND TERMINALS

Airport Police Officers stationed at key portals of every airport is an essential component of a successful airport security matrix. The failure to have police stationed at the Los Angeles International Airport (LAX) screening lane and the Ft. Lauderdale International Airport (FFL) baggage arrival terminals locations enhanced the outcome of each HVE attack. An armed officer would have engaged the LAX and the FFL shooters immediately, potentially preventing or reducing the number of deaths and injured.

FT. LAUDERDALE INTERNATIONAL AIRPORT

Investigative reporters Michael Sallah and Kristyn Wellesley, USA Today Network, did an outstanding job on their recent news story titled 'Staffing cuts left the area of Fort Lauderdale airport, FLL), shooting unguarded.' This news story revealed Lauderdale civilian airport administrators reduced the number of law enforcement officers assigned to the airport despite the massive increase in passengers and flights added over the last few years. Would additional airport police positions and strategic placement of personnel have prevented or decreased the number of victims?

I feel FFL is not alone, as I learned from my experience and from the many airports I studied, that airports eliminated police officers positions to reduce airports cost. The San Jose Airport story in Chapter 11 is a detailed example.

Having managed and supervised airport police officers at a commercial airport, I learned the weak points of an airport infrastructure. I also learned where police officers positions should be for the best security posture. I gleaned this knowledge from handling police response to terminal security breaches, airfield fence breaches, terminal evacuations, aircraft on airfield emergencies, criminal airport incidents and a host of Homeland Security incidents that consisted of terrorist watchlist subjects and suspicious incidents.

Through my experiences, I learned police officers in the right positions immediately ended a threat and also learned police officers not in the right places, greatly enabled the risk by time and outcome. The following airport infrastructure graphic represents my opinion on what the baseline police officer staffing positions numbers and deployment posts should be in every airport terminal:

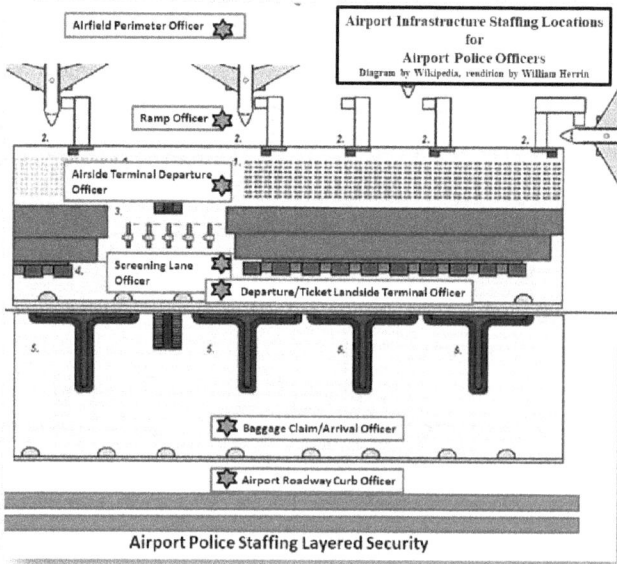

Airport Infrastructure Staffing Locations for Airport Police Officers
Diagram by Wikipedia, rendition by William Herrin

Airfield Perimeter Officer

Ramp Officer

Airside Terminal Departure Officer

Screening Lane Officer

Departure/Ticket Landside Terminal Officer

Baggage Claim/Arrival Officer

Airport Roadway Curb Officer

Airport Police Staffing Layered Security

Obviously, a larger terminal and airport acreage size will require additional officers at the number of depicted locations above.

Every airport should have a foundation of basic security components at their airport. This includes a minimum number of armed police positions that is a standard in every airport in America. This should not even be a debate, or, part of probability/risk/threat assessment issue. Police in the right positions in our airports will not only stop the active shooters but also will deter and/or arrest the criminals that prey on our open and soft airport infrastructure through a variety of airport crimes.

I have received some arguments that armed officers are not necessary everywhere as the "fix all" to our airport's security. Of course, they are not the 'fix all, ' and I never believed they were. Some arguments stress application of risk analyses and a look through the lenses of the potential threat at airports by their size, location, and enplanements. I get their points, ones most often based on how far the airport dollar can go, but I completely disagree with this argument, and I would be safe to say the people who died in the LAX and FLL airport attacks would disagree with this as well.

The headline on January 24, 2017, said: "Terrorism soars with a number of attacks rising 25% every year - and ISIS is responsible for a third. In 2015 there were 18,987 terror attacks in the world, with terrorism being defined as violence committed by "armed non-state groups and individuals." I feel there is no method of predicting the increasing violence in the world and where the carnage will strike next. But, in the interim, staff your airport security adequately, train your security forces well and deploy and protect your airport portals as you stand tall against the odds.

Conclusion:

"Being able to kill opponents on a large scale would allow terrorist groups such as ISIS to make a powerful showing.

We believe such an act of terrorism would ideally be carried
out in areas where people are concentrated and vulnerable,
such as the Nation's commercial aviation system."

GENERAL JOHN ROTH, DHS INSPECTOR, MAY 12, 2016

Protecting our airport terminals is problematical regarding each airport's location, current infrastructure, the financial cost of security renovations and inconveniences that change will create. Protecting our airports is a challenge, and we must take the additional steps to strengthen the airport terminals of the 450 primary U.S. Airports. The threats against our aviation industry will not wane with time; rather the threats will only grow with new, unimagined threats that will surprise the most experienced and educated security minds. The case study of three Scottish Airports made a bold statement alluding that the terrorist threats to the world aviation system will continue for decades. The case study predicted; "Future aircraft will be resistant to terror attack [as they will be} built like military planes [and] are able to resist some amount of battle damage."

CHECKPOINTS OF THE FUTURE

Congress directed the Aviation Security Advisory Committee (ASAC) to provide recommendations for improving the passenger screening processes. Congress titled Subtitle E, "Checkpoints of the Future." The lofty goal of Congress in this inclusion in the July 2016 House of Representatives Bill H.R. 636, is to start a pilot program with selected airports. This program will have the participating airports consider reconfiguring and installing security systems that will "increase efficiency and reduce vulnerabilities in airport terminals."

The end game for designing the checkpoint or airport terminals of the future is to create new security concepts for the curb to curb process, designs that will prevent security breaches, address all vulnerabilities, use technology innovations, and the configuration of an airport checkpoint. Congress gave ASAC until June 2017 to report on the results and any recommendations for improving passenger screening processes. Let us hope that ISIL and Al-Qaeda will wait until we obtain our goals for a safe front door.

RECOMMENDATIONS:

1. Base airport designs and renovations early comprehensive planning on the security threats of a post 9/11 world with the inclusion of security subject matter experts in the concept, design and construction phases of all airport infrastructures.[91]
2. Define airport dwell time and mass gathering of passengers in airport terminal locations for regulatory agencies for safety standards implementation and protocols. These protocols will be designed to prevent extended waits and large gatherings of passengers in one specific area anytime during the standard operations hours of an airport.[92]
3. Each airport security stakeholders should convene and discuss their viewpoints on their airport infrastructure, class of passenger's needs, types of travel needs, detailed review of airport threats and define each stakeholder responsibilities.[93]
4. Conduct a vulnerability assessment of the airport and convene all airport stakeholders to discuss solutions to the potential threats and create solutions to the airport infrastructure weaknesses.[94]
5. Mitigate threats to airport infrastructure by blast proofing walls and installation of shatterproof glass, and proper installation of roadway/entrance bollards to prevent a vehicle-borne improvised device from entering the terminal landside areas.[95]
6. Create various airport screening entrances and screening lanes for quick access to the secured side of the airport terminal.

7. Create greater standoff distances from roadways and airport terminals.[96]
8. Eliminate vehicle drop off and pick up at all airport terminals[97]
9. Raise the level of required training and standardize the training for all airport security personnel.
10. Ensure proper management and oversight of airport security and screening personnel to mitigate overworking employees, reduce fatigue and poor working conditions.[98]
11. Cap large airports enplanement passenger numbers.
12. Promote ownership, building, and management of private commercial airports to distribute passenger enplanements near all major travel hubs. (Increase in the number of smaller passenger airports will provide less incentive for a terrorist to attack large to medium hub airports. The increase in the number of airports will ensure greater resiliency for maintaining passenger and cargo transportation in the event of terrorist attacks on the aviation industry.)
13. Take immediate action now, based on current threats and the methods and techniques used by terrorists in the airport terminal attacks in Brussels, Moscow, and Istanbul. Airports should not wait for the TSA and ASAC to complete their pilot programs. Each airport configuration is vastly different from the next, and each airport must modify their geographical layout and current infrastructure design that will allow for an increase in protection of passengers and the terminal.

CHAPTER 5

The Insider Threat

———◆———

"The insider threat presents a significant threat to
commercial aviation security. A person on the inside
is a subject matter expert in his area of operations
as well as having an above average knowledge of
the workings of the airport and its security."

ALAN BLACK, VICE PRESIDENT & DIRECTOR OF PUBLIC
SAFETY, DALLAS-FORT WORTH INTERNATIONAL AIRPORT[99]

ONE DAY BEFORE THE START of my patrol shift in the early 1980s, I was
in the Orange County Sheriff's Department North Patrol Operations
locker room changing into my uniform. A fellow deputy sheriff came
into the locker room and started changing out as well. I said, 'Hi Tom,
what's new?" Tom mumbled a sluggish reply that I didn't quite understand. I responded by rambling about my family and department related
topics as we donned our uniforms and started walking to the patrol
briefing room.

At the time, I did not know my co-worker was a heroin addict. Tom
was estimated to have been using heroin and working as a patrol deputy
for a few months before his arrest. As young deputies, my peers and
I daily supervised incarcerated drug addicts and dealers doing time as
inmates in our County Jail. When a deputy graduates from the police

academy, the jail is the first training grounds in our law enforcement career. We learned, working inside the jail, from the experienced street inmates of their drug addiction, how addicts behaved, drug selling methods, and motives. After promotion to Deputy Sheriff II, we transferred to the Operations Division to patrol duties. Daily we went hunting for criminals that included the sellers and users of illicit drugs in the streets of Orange County, and most of us could spot a drug user a block away. We did not see, or we subconsciously overlooked, what was evident about Tom: his behavior, wearing long sleeve shirts on warm days, his loss of body weight and other obvious clues. In our minds, there was no way one of us could be one of them.

Tom compromised the internal security of the Sheriff's Department. Speculation was, his relationship with the criminals he previously arrested may have provided the criminals the means to avoid our patrol and narcotic units. Tom's addiction to heroin turned a law enforcement officer into a criminal in sheep clothing. Other than embarrassment, no actual damage occurred to my law enforcement agency by Tom's drug addiction episode, but the potential was there.

Flash forward 35 years later in 2016 and Orange County Sheriff employee Nooshafarin Ravaghi was teaching jail inmates English language skills in the high-security county prison. Ravaghi used her insider position to help three prisoners escape, resulting in a massive manhunt that lasted a week. If an insider threat can pierce the security of a law enforcement agency, then our public airports are certainly at risk.

During my years as a watch commander at John Wayne Airport, I walked through my airport terminal and waved at employees, stopped and talked to them about business and family or the current sports team season. Trusting my fellow airport employees was essential to the airport daily operations safety and security according to the Department of Homeland Security. However, in the back of my mind, I found it difficult to put my complete trust in my fellow airport partners. The Homeland Security manual even stated that airport employees were "trusted employees" who were our partners in Homeland Security, and I was supposed to rely on them while performing my law enforcement and Homeland Security duties. In reality, many law enforcement personnel often use the adage of President Reagan, "Trust but verify."

An airport employee who is a <u>criminal</u> or <u>terrorist</u>, who has obtained "trusted" worker status with unfettered access to the most secure part of America's airports is one of the greatest threats to any airport. Historically, adjudicated criminal cases reveal how the trusted airport employee had placed passengers and co-workers in harm's way through the criminal acts they committed in airports throughout the world. Insider threats in airports have been evident as far back as 1955 when a Hong Kong to Jakarta flight blew up in midair. In this incident, a custodian airport employee placed a bomb on the passenger aircraft to kill the premier of China who he thought would be on the airplane.[100] An airline mechanic is a likely suspect in the Egyptian airport where the Russian Metrojet Flight 9268 departed and blew up in midair over the Sinai Desert in October 2015. The suspect airline mechanic has family ties to ISIL and may have planted the bomb in a handbag on the aircraft before takeoff. Police officers and a baggage handler were also arrested who may have assisted the mechanic. The crash killed 224 passengers.[101]

Barely three months later, in February 2016, a Mogadishu Airport Employee handed a terrorist a laptop computer containing a bomb. The terrorist boarded his flight, and if not for the delayed departure, the subsequent detonation of the bomb by the suicide terrorist would have crashed the passenger aircraft. The aircraft had not gained enough altitude to pressurize the cabin, and the heroic efforts of the aircraft pilot saved the passengers with the exception of the terrorist who disappeared out of the gaping hole that the bomb created.[102]

The majority of airport employees are honest and trustworthy folks. However, a percentage of our nation's airport employees have committed crimes before and during their employment in our airports. On virtually a weekly basis, police arrest airport workers at airports across our country for a variety of crimes. These arrests reveal the continuous crimes of theft, employee drug use, employee smuggling of illegal drugs and contraband has not diminished. The criminal and terrorist groups seek out current airport employees who have committed crimes or have the malevolent forethought to commit crimes. These same criminal and terrorist groups also have or will try to place their terrorist or criminal operatives into airport jobs. Once inside, these now "trusted" airport employees will work within the secured area of our nation's aviation infrastructure to accomplish the terrorist or criminal organizations' goals. These airport employees are law enforcements' greatest concerns—the insider threat.

The World's Airports Insider Threats

The airport insider threat is worldwide. Employees in other nation's airports have and will continue to be a concern for U.S. Homeland Security. When security breaches occur in other countries' passenger or aircraft cargo, and these planes then fly over our soil, they become a direct threat to the safety of our people and national resources.

The French government, for example, cannot protect their citizens from the terrorist threat inside or outside their aviation industry. In 2006, the French investigated employees at French airports and took away the security badges of 72 airport workers at Charles de Gaulle airport in Paris, when an extensive investigation revealed these "trusted" airport employees had visited terrorist training camps in Pakistan and Afghanistan. One of the dismissed airport workers had close ties to al Qaeda through Algerian terrorist groups. Even more shocking, one of the workers was a close friend of Richard Reid the British shoe bomber who, in December 2001, attempted to blow up a plane that flew from Paris to the United States.[103] The French efforts in 2006 seemed to have been futile as in December 2015; the French Government again discovered 70 radicalized airport workers at the Charles de Gaulle Airport with terrorist ties. The airport took away their high security 'Red Zone' badges. The recheck by the police was the result of the largest terrorist attack in France since World War II, and the discovery terrorists were plotting to target a French airport.[104]

Many aviation terrorist events and arrests reveal terrorist organizations recruit airport employees based on their positions, skills, levels of access to critical areas, or because of their physical/cultural characteristics. White Anglo-European or American Islamic converts are of particular interest for terrorist recruiters. European countries are aware of this problem, and they are making airport security improvements in this area. On March 3, 2010, the arrest of a Heathrow Airport employee for a terrorism-fundraising plot occurred. According to an article written by *The Sun's* crime editor Mike Sullivan, it seems this airport employee was raising money for an attack on a passenger aircraft.[105]

Naval Reserve aviator and commercial airline pilot Steven Goff gave his opinion in an article he wrote for *The National Interest*. Goff aviation security expertise led him to suspect that an airport employee aided the Antwerp Belgium Airport large diamond robbery that occurred on the runway. Goff notes the liberties and the knowledge that airport employees have of their airport terminal are what the terrorist or criminal covets. He emphasizes that there is always the potential for terrorists to bribe or apply coercion or other ways to pressure airport employees to do tasks for them.[106]

Goff's suspicion was correct that an airport insider threat might one day kill innocents as evidenced by the 2015 Russian Jetliner bombing in Egypt. Another insider threat example is the German news agency story on January 29, 2015, that an employee of the Frankfurt Airport in Germany close friend is a member of the ISIL terrorist group. The employee was dismissed from his position at the airport.[107] Still yet, another example is the British Airways employee, Rajib Karim, who was convicted of preparing acts of terrorism. Karim was acting under orders from al-Qaeda Al-Awlaki and in one message told Awlaki, "I personally know two brothers, one who works in baggage handling at Heathrow and another who works in airport security... but I am not sure if they are at the stage to sacrifice their lives."[108] These news stories span the globe and are revealed in many news venues as shown by the Garuda Indonesia Airlines mechanic, Muhammad Syahrir's, arrest for being part of a terrorist network that conducted terrorist bombings.[109]

The Royal Canadian Mounted Police's conducted a two-year drug smuggling and human trafficking investigation highlighted by CBS News Canada, and it revealed the ominous news. Numerous crime organizations infiltrated eight of Canada's largest airports according to the Royal Canadian Police. Our nation's security management must understand a few of the troubling findings of the investigation. Criminal organizations work throughout our nation and internationally and these organizations need to have access to points of entry to other countries. Canadian Senator Collin Kenny stated, "Smugglers don't much care about what product they are carrying, and they don't ask about what's in the bag they are moving. Crime groups work at corrupting existing employees or by placing criminal associates into the airport workforce."[110]

The United States and Our Airports' Insider Threats

America opened its arms and welcomed Somali refugee Abdirahmaan Muhumed to safety and refuge so he could live a life away from the threat of hunger and death in his homeland. Muhumed found a job at the Minneapolis St. Paul International Airport and was granted a security clearance and issued a Secured Identification Display Area badge (SIDA). This badge allowed him access to the security side of the airport, where for ten years he refueled passenger jets with Jet-A fuel from fuel trucks. Muhumed then took another job for three years, where his duties were primarily cleaning passenger jets.

At one point in Muhumed's life, he decided to join the terrorist group ISIL and was confirmed as a death casualty in Syria during the ongoing conflict between ISIL and the Syrian government. Muhumed's incident is alarming, but an investigation revealed the problem was even greater.

Two other airport employees at the Minneapolis St. Paul International Airport also left their jobs at the airport and joined a terrorist group in Somalia. In Somalia, each one blew themselves up in suicide missions. One of these suicide bombers worked at the Minneapolis St. Paul International Airport's coffee house across the aisle from the customs office and the other was a bus driver who shuttled passengers from one air ramp gate to another to make connecting flights.[111]

In February 2017, The U.S. House of Representatives Homeland Security Committee released a report entitled, "America's Airports: The Threat From Within." The chairman of the committee stated: "America's aviation sector remains a crown jewel of ISIS and other terrorist groups targeting our homeland." The report emphasized how the over 900,000 airport employees who work in our nation's airports are able to bypass traditional screening requirements and enter the most vulnerable areas of our airports. I explore the dilemma of airport employee screening in chapter eight, but the report summarizes an overview of the problem in this statement:

Moreover, the vulnerabilities shown by recent incidents at both domestic and foreign airports demonstrate the troubling reality that current security standards would likely fail to prevent a determined adversary with insider access from causing harm to an airport or aircraft. Industry infighting, jurisdictional battles, inconvenience, and cost concerns are not justifiable reasons to cause delays to enhancing the security of the American homeland and our aviation system.[112] America's airport insider threat continues to evolve and pose greater dangers each day. Terry Loewen is an American, born and bred. Loewen was a 58-year-old avionics technician employed at Wichita International Airport, the busiest airport in Kansas. On Friday, December 13, 2013, Loewen drove to work with his car loaded with explosives. Loewen arrived at the airfield gate that he entered every day to go to work. But that day was different. That day, he intended to drive his car onto the airfield, park his car near the busy terminal filled with passengers, and detonate the explosives in a suicide attack. Loewen was arrested by the FBI when his airfield gate access card failed to open the gate. He discovered his car was full of dummy explosives that he obtained from an undercover FBI informant posing as a terrorist. U.S. Congressman Mike Pompeo posted on his government website Loewen's stated purpose, which is every airport police agency's greatest nightmare:

"By the time you read this I will - if everything went as planned - have been martyred in the path of Allah. There will have been an event at the airport which I am responsible for. The operation was timed to cause maximum carnage death. My only explanation is that I believe in jihad for that sake of Allah for the sake of my Muslim brothers sisters. Fact is, most Muslims in this country will condemn what I have done. I expect to be called a terrorist (which I am), a psychopath, and a homicidal maniac."[113]

I have to ask the question, what if Loewen had decided to conduct his martyrdom terrorist planning alone. It would be safe to answer: If Loewen learned to build a car bomb on his own, he would have successfully detonated the car bomb in the airport terminal ramp adjacent to the passenger airplanes and populated terminal. Loewen's igniting the bomb would have been the FBI and local law enforcement first awareness of the plot, and burying the dead and rebuilding the airport would have been the outcome.

WHY AIRPORT EMPLOYEES BECOME INSIDER THREATS

Throughout the history of aviation security, the strategy has always focused on the external threats, with little attention or resources devoted to the insider threat. Any airport employee may be an insider threat for reasons that may not seem to be a serious problem for most people. Gambling habits have a tremendous ability to corrupt people from all occupations. In September 2013, dozens of local TSA agents working at the Pittsburgh International Airport were terminated or suspended for participating in an illegal gambling ring. Gambling addiction leads to debt, and debt often leads to poor decisions to resolve one's debt.[114] The Department of Homeland Security released a report titled, "Combating the Insider Threat" advisory on May 2, 2014. In the report, one of the signs of vulnerability that may lead to an employee becoming an insider threat was gambling.[115]

An illustration of the seriousness of a trusted airport TSA officer employee-gambling problem is the notorious Lufthansa Airlines JFK Airport theft case. A JFK airport employee, who owed $20,000 in gambling debt to the Mafia's Lucchese Crime Family in 1978, compromised the security of the airport as an insider threat to eliminate the debt he owed to the mafia. The airport employee assisted the crime family in stealing more than six million dollars and jewels from a temporary holding vault on the airport's property in one of the nation's most infamous airport thefts. The airport employee gave vital information to the thieves. He showed them where to park their vans and provided a one-of-a-kind key to access a maze of terminal passageways. He provided details of the number of employees on duty and locations where they worked.[116] Thirty years later in 2014, the FBI arrested five of the Mafia members for the robbery that was one of the largest cash thefts in American history.[117]

From gambling to bribery, the insider threat employee can have many reasons to betray the trust placed in them. The TSA Investigators discovered this when they conducted a security test in North Carolina at the Charlotte-Douglass International Airport on November 19, 2010. An undercover agent walked to a ticket counter agent of a major airline and told him that he needed to get the package he was holding to Boston that day. The undercover TSA agent handed the ticket agent a hundred dollar bill, and the employee placed another passenger's name on the package and sent it on the flight.[118] Simple human greed is the lynchpin in an airport employee crossing over and becoming an insider threat.

Many of the airport security topics of concern written in these passages may cross over into each other. The insider threat is certainly one that merges into the many security issues depicted in the following passages. Employees who smuggle drugs into airports are one of the greatest insider threats. On July 15, 2015, a Los Angeles International Airport American Airlines clerk was arrested at the airport. She used her airport insider position to place suitcases full of methamphetamines unscreened, onto passenger jets for flights to St. Louis, Missouri.[119] Seven months later, a Jet Blue Flight Attendant, used her insider status and attempted to smuggle 70 pounds of cocaine through the passenger screening lane.[120]

The same thing holds true for the Delta Airlines employee who smuggled a backpack into the airport containing $282,400 in March 2016. Employee Jean Yves Selius had been paid $1000 each time he carried a large amount of money into the airport and then hand it to an unidentified passenger in a bathroom on the security side of the terminal.[121] Your imagination will immediately go to the dark side of what the possible contents of the unscreened bags could contain. Criminal airport employees do not search the bag they receive from the drug courier before they enter the secured side of the airport through the employee door. They have no idea of what is inside the bag as they hand it to a courier who then boards a passenger jet with the unscreened carry-on bag.

I draw from my experiences as an airport watch commander to describe the acts of criminals employed at America's airports in the subsequent passages of this book. During the years at my airport, I interacted in arrests and investigations of airport employees who committed crimes. I tried to understand how these criminals gain employment and how they could work for years before the discovery of their crimes. I attempted to find what measures implemented by airport administrations would prevent an insider threat from working in our nation's airports. I asked myself and sought answers to this critical concern of airport law enforcement during my tenure in the airport division. Many answers to my questions left me with little hope for an immediate solution to this greatest threat facing our aviation industry.

RECOMMENDATIONS:

In the coming chapters, I submit to the reader some recommendations that will provide a variety of solutions to prevent airport crime and as a byproduct help prevent the airport insider threat. Additionally, the recommendations for improving employee screening and background checks in upcoming chapters will collectively and significantly decrease the airport insider threat described in these previous passages.

CHAPTER 6

Drugs at Airports

—————◆—————

"You personally exacerbated one of this
nation's greatest blights."

JUDGE NICHOLAS G. GARAUFIS TO AN AMERICAN AIRLINES
BAGGAGE HANDLER CONVICTED OF TRAFFICKING MILLIONS OF
DOLLARS OF DRUGS ON COMMERCIAL JETS, OCTOBER 2012. [122]

AMERICA'S AIRPORTS FACE CERTAIN DANGERS when drug traffickers use our passenger aircraft to transport illegal drugs. We find the extent of the drug trafficking problem in our airports in the arrests and the news media publishing of these incidents. With every arrest, it is unknown how many undiscovered illegal drug shipments pass through our airports hidden among cargo, passenger luggage or even secreted within compartments of the aircraft themselves. The law of averages declares a much larger amount of drug shipments get through our airports than are stopped by law enforcement.

Drug smuggling organizations, like any business, have a profit margin. If the drug cartels use of the airlines to smuggle drugs, makes them a profit, then that method will continue to be used by the cartels. The publicized news accounts that the public sees of airport drug arrests, the gangs and cartels loss of employees and loss of drugs and money are simply part of the operating cost of the drug cartels and gangs business operations.

I believe many of the cartels and gang's drug shipments via the commercial passenger aircraft flights are successful, and they continue to smuggle their drugs through this mode of transportation despite the loss of shipments due to law enforcement. Why else would they continue to use passenger aircraft to smuggle drugs year in and year out? Los Angeles International Airport is an example of drug cartels and gangs continuous use of the aviation industry. The 2016 news headline, "LAX Is Going Cocaine Crazy" reveals some high profile drug smuggling arrests at Los Angeles Airport.[123]

In 2014, a TSA agent was arrested at the Los Angeles International Airport for helping drug traffickers smuggle drugs onto passenger aircraft. Organized criminal drug traffickers gave the TSA agent $1,000 each time he allowed a drug courier to bring a bag full of drugs through his screening lane.[124] Your calculations can quickly add up the monthly profit the TSA agent was making if he allowed only one drug courier through a day, much less two or three times a day. As decades of airport drug trafficking arrests decline, there is no doubt, our nation's airports are a continuous conduit for this illegal activity.

Smuggling drugs through airports is a far-reaching problem, but our airports also face a potentially greater danger when airport employees use illicit drugs. The drug using employees span all types of airport jobs, from administrators, the passenger aircraft cleaners, ground crews, flight crews, and the sundry of other airport workers in the airport transportation industry. As I mentioned before, even a police officer is not immune to the use of and addiction to illicit drugs that continues to be a national problem in every occupation. A more recent example of this is the London Luton Airport counter-terrorism police officer who tested positive for using cocaine in March 2016. [125]

Drug Trafficking at America's Airports

The public's memory of airport crimes fades over time until a new crime emerges that, unfortunately, rarely rekindles a faint recollection of similar past airport crimes. The 2003 example of a report by The New York Times details a massive drug ring of twenty or more baggage handlers. This story typifies decades of our nation's systemic airport drug problems. The Times stated, "they were moving so much cocaine that the police named the law enforcement investigation; "Operation Snowstorm." A police spokesman told the NY Times, "We take this very seriously, especially after 9/11. Today its narcotics; tomorrow it could be explosives."[126] The Times also quoted the acting assistant secretary of the Federal Bureau of Immigration and Customs Enforcement as saying, "A network of corrupt airport employees, motivated by greed, might just as well have been collaborating with terrorists as with drug smugglers." In this JFK drug ring arrest, the baggage handlers worked for four contract baggage handling companies, as well as American, Delta, and United Airlines. Law enforcement estimated the ring operated from 1992 to 2002.

The ongoing investigations into drug smuggling at JFK revealed yet another massive drug smuggling operation that overlapped with the previous "Operation Snowstorm." From 2002 to 2009, operating with impunity under the nose of airport police and TSA, this multi-million dollar operation came to light after the arrest of American Airline employee Victor Bourne and six other airport employees. In October 2012, Bourne received three life sentences for his drug smuggling crimes.[127]

Bourne trafficked large volumes of drugs into American cities that eventually harmed and probably killed some of the users of his smuggled illegal drugs. His dangerous methodology of smuggling the drugs in the wing compartments of commercial aircraft was so precarious that it could have caused an airliner to be disabled in flight and possibly crash. One witness testified that Bourne came into the cargo hold of a commercial aircraft one day with two empty duffle bags and went to the plane that carried his latest shipment of cocaine. Bourne removed the interior airliner wing's metallic panel covering the location of sensitive aircraft avionics and other vital flight equipment and removed what they said was 60 bricks of cocaine that weighed 132 pounds. It was sheer luck Bourne's criminal efforts did not cause the death of passengers on the thousands of aircraft flights he used to smuggle drugs. The investigation resulted in the arrest of nineteen other airport employees for working in Bourne's airport drug operation.

United States Attorney Loretta E. Lynch said, "Using his insider status, Bourne turned American Airlines into his personal narcotics shuttle service, running a criminal organization that ignored passenger safety and security in the pursuit of their greater goal–enriching Victor Bourne."[128] An insider airport employee like Bourne could just have easily placed explosives in a multitude of aircraft. What would happen if 12 passenger airplanes fell from the sky within minutes of each other, in flights over various U.S. cities? Could this be our nation's next 9/11?

The common technique used by drug smuggling airport employees' use is the transportation of drugs into the airport through unmonitored employee portals. An example of this common tactic occurred at the San Diego Airport on March 18, 2014, when the police arrested four baggage handlers of the Delta Global Services for passing drugs to couriers on the secure side of the airport. As trusted airport employees, they easily avoided the police and homeland security and passed the drugs to couriers who earlier walked through the TSA screening lane. The airport employee and drug courier pre-planned meetings at a designated restroom stall located on the secured side of the airport. There, they passed the drugs under the stall wall divider to the courier, who would then board the passenger jet and fly to their destination.[129] Any prudent person immediate thought, is instead of drugs, could the bag the trusted airport employee brings in contain a gun, hand grenade, homemade bomb, or other serious weapon or device to commandeer a passenger airplane? The answer is yes, as Delta Airlines employee Eugene Harvey used this very same smuggling procedure to smuggle assault rifles and handguns from the Atlanta Airport to New York. Law enforcement documented twenty flights from Atlanta to New York where he carried unscreened bags of firearms. Criminals purchased these guns for use on the streets of New York.[130]

Airport criminal employees are motivated by greed, and greed, as case after case reveals, is the primary reason they choose to violate their trusted employee status. Greed was the motive for the fifty-nine Miami International Airport employees arrested in two undercover operations titled "Operation Ramp Rats" and "Operation Sky Chef." The latter named operation was the name of a company that provided food services for airlines in airports across the nation. After a two-year undercover investigation for smuggling heroin, explosives, and weapons, the arrest of the airline food service employees occurred. The agent in charge said, "It's an issue here not only of narcotics but an issue of the airport and the security of the flying public."[131]

The previously cited TSA officers arrested for allowing drug dealers to smuggled drugs through their screening lanes at Los Angeles International Airport were not alone. In March 2015, the FBI and Drug Enforcement Agency arrested two private airport screeners contracted by the TSA for the same crime at the San Francisco International Airport. These two airport employees allowed pounds of methamphetamine through their screening lanes in carry-on luggage and onto passenger flights. Airport workers throughout our nation airports are participating in these types of crimes after succumbing to the temptations of large cash bribes.[132]

If you were to ask the average passenger or airport police officer about employee smuggling cases that occurred five, ten, or twenty years ago, many could not remember, or they never knew of the thousands of past cases that occurred at our airports. Airport employee contraband smuggling onto passenger aircraft will continue to occur due to ignorance of historical airport crimes and continuous dumbing down of the public. The only true way for successful prevention of 99% of these crimes is the implementation of 100% screening of airport employees into and out of the airport.

DRUGS SMUGGLED INTO THE U.S. FROM OTHER COUNTRIES

A criminal drug smuggling operation in August 2013, presented a greater danger to the Homeland Security of the United States. Two Philadelphia U.S. Airway employees smuggled baggage full of cocaine from the Dominican Republic into the Philadelphia airport. The criminal airport workers' took the luggage loaded with cocaine from the aircraft that arrived from a foreign territory, bypassing the U.S. Customs arrival luggage inspection area, to another domestic arrival baggage area where the luggage was removed from the airport premises without the drugs being discovered. This method allowed baggage into the U.S. unscreened where anything from bio to nuclear threats could have made it unseen into our country.[133] Only your imagination can limit the potential threat this smuggling operation posed.

CRIMINAL STREET GANGS AND AIRPORT DRUG SMUGGLING

As the sophistication of criminal gangs increases, our nation's airports are primary target venues for their unlawful activities. One of the major way gangs makes money is by moving and selling illicit drugs. Retired Los Angeles County Sheriff Sergeant, Richard Valdemar, a member of the California Prison Gang Task Force, investigated and helped prosecute members of notorious street gangs. Valdemar wrote a news story for PoliceMag.com in 2008 that describes how he examined the interior cargo holds of commercial aircraft at the Seattle International Airport. Valdemar conducted an analysis of investigative reporters' pictures that depicted graffiti of both the Bloods and the Crips who are California-based criminal gangs. This graffiti prominently marked the walls of the luggage compartments inside the belly of the aircraft. I selected two airport employees' comments who work at the Seattle International Airport from the Airliner.net forum site. They reveal an airport ramp worker's inside view of what goes on during their work shifts while loading baggage and moving aircraft around the airport.

In the Airliners.net forum, airport employees blog and comment on the topic of the day. During the gang graffiti news story, employees posted their views on gang members, drugs, and alcohol on the airport ramp:

Hey, it's the ramp. The general public is not supposed to be down there anyway. Yeah, it looks bad but how many of those doing the graffiti are gang member wannabee's? Probably the vast majority."[134]

Felons working on the flight line, bypassing the background check by getting visitors badges from the port. Gang members walking the tarmacs. And yes, there are taggings that relate to the Seattle area. Ask the Seattle Police Gang Unit if REDACTED has visited them recently, and learn that REDACTED was warned that there are tagging's related to the Seattle area that should be looked at seriously. Don't forget to add in all the REDACTED transfers from Los Angeles. Employees under the influence of alcohol and narcotics."[135]

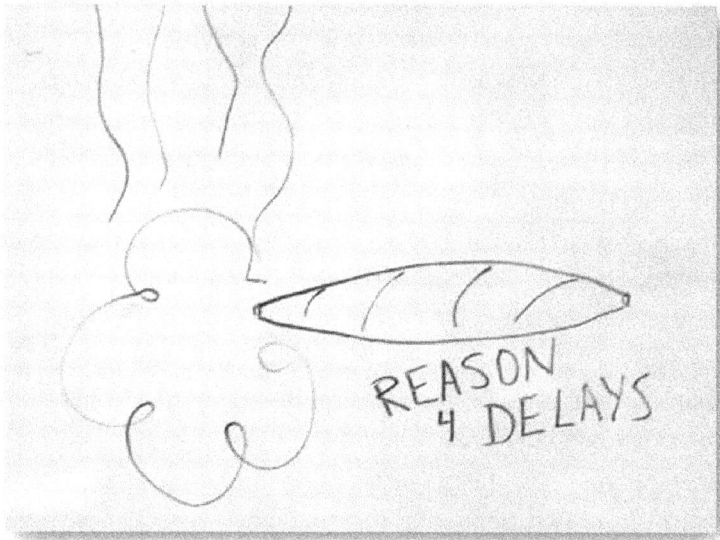

Graffiti inside Passenger Airliner Luggage Hold,
Rendition Illustration Source: W. Herrin

The Los Angeles International Airport takes the gang problem at their airport seriously. This proactive airport police agency created a Gang Intelligence Unit. The gang unit identifies and goes after people conducting gang activity at the Los Angeles International Airport. They work through aviation employee's information to find gang member relationships that may be active in the airport's airfield area and their possible link to terrorism or crime.[136]

The Royal Canadian Mounted Police (RCMP) conducted a two-year investigation and revealed 58 organized criminal gangs were smuggling drugs into Canada's airports. They cited many of the gang members were airport employees, and many of these airport employee criminals were still working at the airport upon conclusion of the RCMP report.[137]

AIRPORT EMPLOYEES AND DRUG USE AT THE AIRPORT

The ramp at any airport is in the hands of airport employees who are intimately familiar with every nook and cranny of the airport's infrastructure. They spend eight-to-ten hour shifts moving into and out of the secured and unsecured sides of the airport. They know its passenger boarding areas, baggage carousels, maintenance repair rooms, administrative offices, and employee locker and lounge rooms to name just a few of the airport ramp and terminal areas.

A variety of airport workers operate inside and around the ramp of the airport, where they tow aircraft, pump jet fuel into aircraft from fuel trucks, restock meals for the next flight, clean aircraft, load and unload luggage. Additionally, aircraft maintenance workers conduct preflight checks of hundreds of aircraft that land and take off.

The nature of the work on a 24/7 schedule is grueling. Airport ramp workers face an arduous workday, but they also have to meet rigorous airline flight schedules and ever-changing timelines. An air carrier's on-time record is crucial to its success and is a powerful marketing attribute for airlines to promote in the very competitive air transportation industry. One unfortunate example of how airport employees are under constant pressure from the airlines was the accidental death of a Menzies Aviation employee who died when he was "hustling to pick up airline baggage" and crashed his ramp cart. The co-worker of the deceased employee told *USA Today,* "They were told if the plane were late, it would cost them a lot of money. They would always be rushed."[138]

These demanding and labor-intensive jobs create an opportunity for the introduction to the use of illegal drugs. These drugs, when first used by the ill-informed airport employee, seem to be initially helpful, but these drugs lead the employee down the road to addiction and self-destruction. The hustle on the ramp is ongoing throughout the day and night as ramp supervisors push their employees to meet airline schedules for daily inbound and outbound flights. As a result of the pressure, they work at high levels of vigorous physical activity, sometimes for long stretches of time. At these moments, illicit stimulant drugs like amphetamines, become a temptation to solve their fatigue.

One day while driving on the airfield roadway, I turned on my overhead red and blue police vehicle lights and pulled over a ramp baggage supervisor who was speeding on the ramp. The supervisor was driving a tug pulling a chain of luggage trailers. I told him I stopped him for unsafe driving and cautioned him about the dangers of racing around the aircraft and fuel trucks on the busy ramp. The supervisor looked at me with disbelief and said he has a schedule to keep and that I would be at fault for delaying his airline flights. I looked back at him with the same disbelief, finished the administrative citation, and released him to his duties. This airline supervisor is one example of an airport job that brings above-average stress levels resulting in employees not following safety protocols at the airport.

There are varieties of drugs used by airport employees. Alcohol is a drug, classified as a depressant, and is the most widely used drug in the world. When used by an airport employee on the job, alcohol is just as dangerous as any narcotic or stimulant drug in pill, powder or smoking form. Take for example the San Diego Airport fuel truck driver arrested in April 2015 for driving a fuel truck intoxicated three times over the legal limit. The employee was attempting to fuel passenger airliners on the ramp when his fellow employees reported him to the airport police.[139] At the Detroit Airport, the police arrested an American Airlines pilot for being intoxicated while in the process of inspecting his aircraft for takeoff in March 2016 and is an example of how far the alcohol abuse problem reaches to all levels in the airline industry.[140]

Drugs and Airport Employees - a Case Example

At an airport in the mid-west, the airport police arrested a ramp employee on an outstanding warrant issued for his failure to appear on a charge of using an illegal drug called methamphetamine. The ramp employee was a cargo luggage handler and had unfettered access to the entirety of every aircraft operational area of this busy airport. His duties permitted him to drive an airport luggage cart or cargo truck around jet aircraft.

Because of his criminal warrant, the airport police arrested him and booked him into the county jail. A week after his arrest, he showed up at the airport, trying to use his deactivated security badge and the police questioned him on his eligibility to work in the airport. The employee protested and said he works for the airport luggage contract company that provided service to the airport. The employee said his original felony charge is now a misdemeanor, and according to his employment agreement, this allowed him to return to work on the airfield. He was correct, the FAA and Homeland Security policies at this time allowed airport employees with only misdemeanor criminal records to work in the most secure part of our nation's airports. The police told the employee his online state records showed his conviction was a felony, and if the charges changed from a felony to a misdemeanor, he had to provide documentation from the court of those changes.

The ramp employee went to the courthouse and obtained a copy of the court order showing that his felony is now a misdemeanor. He then went to the airport administration, who told him that since it was "only" a misdemeanor, he could have his security access badge and return to work for the airline. Several months later, an outside police agency arrested the airport employee for possession of methamphetamine drug paraphernalia. When he tried to return to his shift at the airport, the watch commander met him at the gate and asked him about his recent arrest. The ramp employee said, "I fell off the wagon again [Used Meth], but I've gone through rehab, and I'm okay." With pressure from the airport police, the airport administration had no choice but to withdraw the airport employee's security clearance. With no Secured Identification Display Area (SIDA) badge, his employment was terminated by his airport contract company. This personal airport employee story is an example of a drug-addicted and criminally convicted, employed airport worker, who gained employment in one of the most secure areas of our airports.

The airport police arrested one of the baggage loaders at JFK Airport, Erroldo Weatherly, in 2002 for drug smuggling. Before his arrest, his past criminal cases included a felony for assault and yet he still maintained trusted worker status on the secured side of the airport. His trusted worker status gave him the opportunity to commit crimes in the airport that resulted in his arrest for smuggling the drugs in 2003.[141] This news story reveals how systemic the problem is at many airports. Employees like these find their way into airport jobs because of poorly legislated ordinances, federal statutes, company work policies, and lax hiring practices. These workers jeopardize the safety of millions of people at our airports.

Police and Homeland Security face an enormous task in protecting an airport, in particular, the high-security side of the airport ramp. The ramp is at the center or hub of the entire airport where the majority of aircraft, ground vehicles, and pedestrians are in continuous movement around each other. The inherent nature of airports' 24/7 operations places the airport ramp, in particular, at great risk from airport employees under the influence of illicit drugs.

A Second Airport Employee Drug User Example

An airport watch commander received a call from an airport employee who said a co-worker was going to kill himself. According to the witness, the airport employee was sitting in his car and was slowly tightening a tie in a noose around his neck. The employee worked at a restaurant on the secure side of the terminal and was still in the airport parking lot when the watch commander and his officers located him.

"Are you trying to kill yourself?" an officer asked the employee through his partially rolled-down car window. At the employee's affirmative nod, the officer asked, "Are you serious about this?"

"I am," the employee answered.

"Do you have anything in your pockets I should know about?" the officer asked as he took the employee out of the car, handcuffed him and removed the noose. "Anything you might hurt yourself with?"

"I have a pipe," the employee answered.

"A pipe? What kind of pipe?"

"A meth pipe." The employee handed the officer two glass pipes, both with crystal meth residue on them. The subject was subsequently arrested and taken to jail.

Employee drug use is a threat to any company's successful operation. But airport employee drug use threatens themselves, the lives of other employees, and the very people they serve, the airline passenger. When an employee uses drugs, he puts himself and others in danger. His addiction becomes his obsession and his primary concern while everything else becomes secondary—including his job and the safety of passengers. The threats posed by drug-addicted and drug smuggling employees is an unacceptable part of airport life, one that's hard to eradicate from an airport's employee work culture that's hidden from outsiders. In support of my opinion is the unfortunate example of a Newark Airport employee who died at the airport from an overdose of heroin in 2016. The employee brought an unscreened and unauthorized woman into the airport at two a.m. to accompany him while he used heroin inside the airport. When he lost consciousness and died, she wandered the airport looking for help and then called 911.[142]

An extreme example of how some airport employees' groupthink can spiral out of control is the previously cited arrest of JFK employee Bourne and his ten-year drug smuggling operation. A juror in the trial told the *New York Times* that witness after witness in the trial testified that "everybody did it," [airport employees]. As reported in the *New York Times*, the testimony of an arrested airline employee revealed how much corruption among the employees had spread;

> "What percent of the airline's employees would you say engaged in this conduct (theft, drugs)?" a federal prosecutor, Patricia E. Notopoulos, asked Matthew James, a defendant in the case who pleaded guilty and testified for the prosecution. "About 80 percent," the employee answered."[143]

A THIRD AIRPORT EMPLOYEE DRUG USER EXAMPLE

Across from the airport ramp at an American airport in the Western United States is the 'fuel tank farm' containing four Jet-A fuel tanks that hold over a million gallons of kerosene grade jet fuel that power today's passenger aircraft jet engines. The kerosene fuel has a flash point above 38°C (100°F) and as with any combustible fuel; it demands all precautions and handling in the safest method.[144] The airport fuel tank farm has supervisors who oversee the daily loading and unloading of Jet-A fuel into four large fuel tanks that are a mere 35 feet away from the perimeter fence line. The fuel is loaded onto fuel trucks and driven by the contract company workers who service the Airlines passenger jets, privately operated jets, and general aviation aircraft throughout the airport.

Fueling a passenger aircraft, photo by W. Herrin

Fuel truck operations occur hundreds of times a day on the airport ramp. A fuel truck operator drives his 3,000-gallon capacity Jet-A Fuel truck up to a parked passenger jet that is typically loading passengers from the airport terminal into the aircraft. He gets out and using wire cables with clamps, bonds the fuel truck to the aircraft that includes the hose nozzle ground attachment creating a conductive path to equalize the electrical potential between the truck and aircraft. The fuel truck employee then hooks up pressure fuel hoses and pumps jet fuel into the wings of airliners. Fuel truck drivers train extensively under the FAA safety protocols.

At this airport, an airfield fuel farm supervisor was in his office one day when he looked out his office window and saw a fuel truck driver behaving oddly. This employee behavior concerned the manager because he was operating a fuel pump siphoning fuel from one of the airport's million gallon tanks into his fuel truck. Disturbed, the supervisor left his office and approached the employee, asking, "What are you, high?" The supervisor stood there silenced by the employee smile as the employee nodded affirmatively and continued to operate the fuel pump filling his truck with jet fuel. The employee continued to ramble; "But it's no big deal," he assured the supervisor. "There's an airline supervisor on the ramp who takes care of us. It just helps us get through our shifts, man." "Who's the supervisor who gives you the stuff?" The fuel truck driver just smiled and finished filling the fuel truck tank.

The fuel farm supervisor deliberated for a few days whether to report his conversation with the fuel truck driver to the police. He knew he would be at odds with the tightly knit airport employee community and feared snitching on another airport employee would make him the focus of fellow employee's ire and retribution. The fuel manager struggled with the choices and elected not to report the employee.

Months later, the supervisor heard rumors that other employees were using illicit drugs while fueling passenger aircraft at the airport. Weeks later, an airport police officer stopped into the office and asked how the supervisor was doing. The supervisor summoned some courage and told the police officer his story. He expressed his concerns and worries about the safety of ramp workers and passengers alike and told the officer he did not know the name of the suspect driver.

The police officer reported to the watch commander, and they reviewed the fuel supervisor statement. The watch commander called the airport police department's narcotics investigator and gave him the details of the allegations. When the investigator attempted to contact the fuel service supervisor, he found that the supervisor had resigned from his job just days before. The investigator tracked the former supervisor to the other side of the state to interview him. The investigator found the former supervisor's information credible and substantial enough to start an investigation at the airport.

A meeting between the watch commander, the investigation unit, and the Airport Police Command staff convened. A discussion summarized that there are no named suspects or probable cause to conduct a criminal search in the private leased spaces of the airport. Using an undercover police officer as a baggage handler was one suggestion tabled that everyone agreed is the best way to catch drug using and drug selling airport employees on the ramp. The airport administration estimated it would take months to place an officer in an airline employee position and to gain the trust of other employees and wanted to find another way.

The narcotic investigator suggested using the Law Enforcement Agency's 12 narcotics detection dogs to conduct training searches of the airport ramp offices, lockers, and all secured areas. This type of operation would be a two-edged sword; first, it would provide training for the K-9 teams and second; there will be a strong chance of discovering airport employees who harbored drugs on the secured side of the ramp area. This massive airport search operation would consist of over half a mile of airside terminal infrastructure. The airport infrastructure included the locker rooms, offices, and maintenance rooms leased by ten major airlines. The search would also include common areas, baggage conveyor belts, and a variety of other rooms such as storage closets, stockrooms, and bathrooms.

The watch commander contacted other municipal, state, and federal agencies for best practices for the proposed operation. The watch commander was hoping not to have to recreate the 'wheel' by learning from past drug interdictions at other commercial airports. He found the only agency who conducted a search of a commercial airport with drug dogs was the Drug Enforcement Agency (DEA). He contacted the DEA, and their investigators told him their operation had targeted only one airline office in a terminal at a time during searches for illegal drugs, but never an entire airport terminal in one operation.

After clearing any legal concerns with the city legal counsel, Homeland Security Lawyers, DEA, and the District Attorney's Office, the watch commander took the operation plan to the civilian airport management. The response was less than enthusiastic as the possibility of news media highlighting employee drug arrests at their airport was not desirable. The operation plan scheduled start time of 4:30 a.m., coinciding with ramp workers arriving for work to service aircraft and load luggage. This start time would provide the best window of opportunity to discover employees carrying drugs into the airport. The organized training mission would give law enforcement personnel legal access to the entire airport contingent on approval from the airlines and contract companies to search their leased work areas.

The training mission required a large number of law enforcement officers to support the operation. The watch commander recruited a 55 member task force from his agencies, various divisions. The TSA assisted and monitored the operation for any Homeland Security concerns related to arrests made at the airport.

The watch commander called each airline's national corporate security manager and justified the law enforcement operation, asking them for approval to search through their private leased offices and workspaces. The watch commander requested the training mission remain confidential from the airport workers and the onsite airline management. Some security managers approved the concept immediately but with one caveat; they had to talk to their corporate airline administration and attorneys first. A few days later the watch commander started to receive replies from the national corporate airline administrators—some would not grant permission for their airlines to participate and would not allow police dogs into their offices or leased work areas. These airline companies said they would make an exception if the watch commander confided with their airline station managers and included them in the operation planning. Other airline administrators gave approval without restrictions.

The watch commander held a meeting with the airline station managers and briefed them on the details and purpose of the operation. The watch commander asked them to keep the operation confidential from all airline employees. The watch commander explained the narcotics K-9 teams would discover illicit drugs their airport work area. He mentioned if an employee carried drugs on their person and strayed near the dogs during the searches, the K-9 team could detect the employee drugs.

The day before the operation, the watch commander contacted several station managers to discuss last-minute details, answer any pending questions, and stressed the need for the mission confidentiality. The watch commander made his first phone call to one airline manager's office, and the secretary answered. After he identified himself, she cheerily asked, "Is this about the drug search tomorrow?" The watch commander was alarmed that the office clerical staff knew 24 hours in advance of the imminent drug dog search and more than likely the rest of the airline employees were aware of the operation as well.

The watch commander believed at this time, the employees who used drugs at the airport were now alerted, and they would remove the drugs from their hiding places. If the workers planned to bring drugs into the airport, it was obvious they would leave them at home that day, rather than have a police K-9 shove his nose in their backpack and risk arrest.

On the morning of the search at four a.m., 55 law enforcement officers assembled and received details on the operation plan. The briefing included an advisement that no narcotic training aids are in the search areas, and if the dogs alerted, they would have a crime scene. The sweep started at 4:30 a.m. with twelve K-9 teams fanning out to predetermined start points at intervals on the terminal ramp side. Each K-9 team had a spotter team that would secure and mark a dog's alert location and implement crime scene containment if the dog alerted. If a dog detected drugs in an area, they would immediately bring in a second dog to verify the accuracy of the first dog's alert. The suspected drug hiding areas would be cordoned off, and a posted officer would protect the scene until a police search of the location was conducted.

Police narcotic dogs alerted for drugs five minutes into the search. The following areas were deemed a crime scene when the first K-9 team and then a second dog verified the scent of drugs at these locations:

1.   A personal tool storage bag in a maintenance room.
2.   An airline employee lockers #34 and #14.
3.   A second airline employee locker. Discovered was a cellophane baggie containing marijuana residue.
4.   A third airline employee locker.
5.   A fourth airline stockroom locker.
6.   An airline contract baggage company file cabinet.
7.   A fifth airline office area.

The K-9 alerts confirmed that illicit drugs were in these locations within the last 24 hours. Well into the first half hour of the search, they had seven narcotic K-9 alerts. Confirmed employees drug stash locations were found on the airport ramp as the dogs continued to alert on additional marijuana residue in empty employee lockers. The Narcotics Unit Lieutenant called the watch commander over, and they agreed the employees were aware the pending search yesterday. They called the search off after 90 minutes due to a large number of alerts and only residual traces of drugs found.

The police had designated two areas, one; a file cabinet in an office and two; a locked employee locker where drugs dogs alerted. The police officers secured the areas until the investigators obtained search warrants. The investigators returned to the locations on the terminal ramp, relieved the officers, and searched the locked cabinet and locker. Again, like the other locations, drug odor or residue located, indicated these places harbored illicit drugs at one time.

Out of the 11 airlines that fly into and out of this airport, four of them had illegal drug residue detected by the narcotic K-9 teams in their operational areas, and two contract services companies had confirmed drug alerts. No employee detentions or arrests occurred, and the watch commander concluded the problem remained in the airport.

The drug search of the ramp had a short-term impact, in that it created a deterrence that potentially reduced airport employees bringing in or using drugs at the airport—for a while. As in most venues, the tide flows in, the tide flows out, and there were no gauges at this airport to assess the airport employees who continued to use drugs.

Charles Slepian of the Foreseeable Risk Analysis Center conducted a series of remarkable criminal investigations at the JFK and Los Angeles airports and wrote about them in 2004. The airport drug investigations occurred in 1986 when the airline's employees went on strike. Slepian was hired to protect the in-flight airline employees and the airlines' property. Slepian tells the details of several months of his investigations of airport employee crimes and violence in the two airports he investigated. Undercover agents used in the investigation revealed a great amount of narcotics trafficking, in addition to theft rings, employee fraud, and gambling. They identified airport employee drug users, sellers, and thieves who worked for the airlines, the airport, parking lot companies and a sundry of other aviation related employers. But what was most disheartening, was Slepian's findings that airline managers and supervisors were not part of the solution, rather they were in some cases part of the problem. The following quote from his article brings a touch of reality to the past and current state of affairs in our airports today:

> "Management personnel were not immune from temptations either.....some managers, in the face of the ready availability of illegal drugs or free alcohol, would partake long before the end of their work day. Other management personnel quit their jobs, went back to line positions, or risked their safety and quite possibly their lives because they would not accept what was going on around them."[145]

During my career in law enforcement, I've seen many examples, in diverse areas of police operations, where employees used illegal stimulant drugs in their long hours of shift work. Taxi cab to truck drivers, teachers to executives in corporations are users of illegal drugs, and yes, even law enforcement officers have been documented as succumbing to using illicit drugs as the previously mentioned London Luton Airport police officer use of cocaine attests. Professor Katherine Deck of the University of Arkansas in Fayetteville conducted research that shows illicit drug use by employees is in every workplace. She conducted a study in a county with 100,000 workers. Her study revealed:

> It takes four methamphetamine users to do the work of three nonusers. In addition, a meth user is five times more likely to be absent from work than a non-using co-worker. What's more, the study found meth users in all industries and walks of life, from the government to doctors' offices to poultry processing facilities. There is no industry or occupation that is exempt, Deck says.[146]

If Deck's study is correct, then every airport has employees who use and are at risk of using illicit drugs. In Hawaii's Honolulu International Airport, the FBI arrested an American Airlines fuel truck driver in April 2013. The airline fuel truck driver sold cocaine and crystal methamphetamine for several years while working at the airport. He used his security credentials to move his drug selling enterprise around the airport and to transport the methamphetamine and drug money back and forth between Honolulu Airport and the Los Angeles Airport.[147]

SOME LAST THOUGHTS ON AIRPORT EMPLOYEES AND DRUGS

Airport ramp workers own statements declare the presence of illicit drugs at airports, as does the high-profile airport drug arrests and news accounts.

It is evident that people with criminal backgrounds or malevolent mind-set find employment at our nations' airports. At an American airport on the West Coast, the local police narcotic investigators were working on a suspected drug dealer who worked as an airport employee at the county airport who had prior convictions for felony drug sales. The investigation also revealed the employee lied on his employment application so he could obtain an airport security badge. His lies on his employment application gave him access to the airfield, and he roamed freely around the airport among the aircraft. The suspect even brought his cousin onto the airport ramp to help him wash the many aircraft—a cousin who wasn't an employee and unscreened by the employer or Homeland Security.

The U.S. Department of Transportation (DOT) and the Federal Aviation Administration implemented the Airport Improvement Program (AIP) Sponsor Certification for the airport's Drug-Free Workplace requirement. In the FAA AIP, it, unfortunately, specified that airport employees who use drugs are supposed to "self-report" in writing, any convictions for "a violation of a criminal drug statute occurring in the workplace no later than five calendar days after such conviction." To secure a grant for FAA funds, the FAA states:

"When airport owners…accept funds from a FAA administered airport financial assistance program; they must agree to accept certain obligations. Obligations imposed by the grant assurances will extend beyond the completion of the project."

The FAA AIP Section 740 – Drug-Free Workplace Requirements states:

* Airports 'will' provide a drug-free workplace for their employees.
* Airports must make a 'good faith' effort on a continuing basis to maintain a drug-free workplace.
* State to employees that the unlawful manufacture, distribution, dispensing, possession or use of controlled substances is prohibited in the workplace.

* Notify employees action will take place against those who violate the prohibition.
* Notify employees as a condition of employment, they will notify the airport if they are convicted of a violation of a criminal drug statute.

I have to be cynical here, but really? What self-respecting drug using airport employee is going to tell his employer of his conviction for using methamphetamine?

Nine TSA employees tested positive for drugs and alcohol at the John Wayne Airport between 2010 and 2016. Are the John Wayne Airport baggage handlers, maintenance workers, janitors, airline employees, airport employees and the many private business airport employees drug-free? Alternatively, is random testing for drugs on these employees even conducted? If so, how many drug-using employees were terminated at John Wayne Airport from 2010 to 2016 for positive drug/alcohol tests? TSA disclosed their employee's positive drug tests due to a freedom of information order. I advocate the TSA and airports disclose, on their own accord, their annual efforts to rid the aviation industry of employees who use illicit drugs and alcohol while conducting their assigned tasks in and around passenger airliners. Is asking this of our aviation industry too much to ask? I do not think so.[148]

All work locations, including aviation, have a percentage of employees who abuse drugs. As revealed in the 2010 U.S. Department of Justice Drug Assessment; "32 percent of workers stated a coworker's drug/alcohol use affected their job performance."[149] The 2013 U.S. Department of Health and Human Services Substance Abuse and Mental Health Services Administration reported that 9.5 percent of full-time workers and 9.3 percent of part-time workers were current drug abusers. The 9.5 percent equated to more than 11.3 million full-time employees who were drug-dependent adults.

Tug pushing back passenger aircraft after loading
for takeoff, photo by W. Herrin

The National Survey on Drug Use and Health estimates 20 million Americans used illegal drugs in the past 30 days. An estimated 48 million Americans abuse prescription drugs, which equates to 20 percent of the population.[150] An airport watch commander told an airport administrator that the airport should mandate drug testing for all employees. The administrator replied; "We would lose a third of the airport employees if we drug tested them."[151]

RECOMMENDATIONS:
The Department of Transportation requires random drug testing of the flight crew, attendants, instructors, dispatchers, maintenance, and ground security coordinators. These same standards must be consistent

throughout the U.S. aviation industry. Drug testing should include all baggage handlers, food services drivers, fuel truck drivers, and a host of employees and subcontractors who are not currently drug tested. All airports' current employees must be part of a drug testing process before and continuously through their employment at an airport.

* All airport employees must be non-drug users or show an abstinence from any drug use over a five-year span before consideration for employment in American airports.
* All airport employees must be physically screened before every entry and screened upon exiting the airport to deter employees from carrying illicit drugs, and for that matter, passengers' stolen luggage items into and out of an airport.
* Inspect all cargo handlers and their vehicles before every entry and exiting of airport property.

Enhance Federal and state laws with harsher sentencing guidelines for 'aviation' employee drug use, sales, and smuggling. Coupled with consistent testing for substance abuse, greater penalties, and drug testing provides the increase protection for the safety and security of our vital aviation industry.

The National Institute on Drug Abuse (NIDA), states:

"Employers who have implemented drug-free workplace programs have important experiences to share:

Employers with successful drug-free workplace programs report improvements in morale and productivity and decrease in absenteeism, accidents, downtime, turnover, and theft.

Employers with longstanding programs reported better health status among employees and family members and decreased use of medical benefits by these same groups.

Some organizations with drug-free workplace programs qualify for incentives, such as decreased costs for workers' compensation and other kinds of insurance."[152]

The Orange County Sheriff's Department for years has conducted random drug testing of all sworn deputies and staff. This necessary security procedure, if implemented by a business, ensures the integrity and safety of the business, their employees, and the people these businesses serve.

CHAPTER 7

Airport Luggage and Other Thefts

—⬥—

"Over the years when I was there, the pilferage of baggage
was always a problem. It was always tempting for people
who worked at the airport to pilfer bags for valuables."

Michael DiGirolamo, Former Deputy Executive Director
of Operations Los Angeles International Airport[153]

Today, an average of one and a half million people per day will arrive
at an airport in the United States with a suitcase, carry-on bag, or laptop computer bag and will take a seat on a passenger aircraft for their
flight. When a passenger arrives at the airport terminal on the curbside,
with check-in and carry-on baggage, they have two choices: give their
luggage to the airport sky-cab employee located on the outside of the
terminal, or check in at the ticket counter and hand the ticket counter
employee their luggage.

The airline employee will take the passenger check-in luggage and
send it to a large cavernous TSA scanning room where TSA officers
X-ray it and often open and check the luggage. From here it goes onto
a maze of conveyor belts to a baggage receiving area named "baggage
makeup" area. This area is where baggage handlers sort out the different
airlines' luggage and place bags on a motorized tug. The luggage arrives
at the aircraft via airport tugs where another crew of baggage handlers

places the luggage, carefully balanced for an even weight distribution, into the belly of the passenger aircraft. At the arriving airport, crews of baggage handlers move the baggage off the aircraft onto tugs and drive it to the airport baggage makeup area where the baggage conveyor belt takes it to your arrival carousel.

Passengers expect quality service from an airline and trust their luggage to the airport baggage handlers. Of all the worries associated with flight and travel since 9/11, the safety of your belongings shouldn't be one of them. But the disturbing fact is this: Every airport has luggage ramp workers who rummage through passengers' suitcases for anything of value. Some airports have large groups of baggage thieves who work together; others have small groups of criminals, and this evolves and changes as employee attrition, and new hires occur. The theft of items out of passengers' bags, referred to as pilfering, is included in the numbers derived by airlines that account for the approximately 1.8 million bags annually that were lost, stolen or damaged.[154] In the U.S. alone, airlines have lost as many as 10,000 bags a day that equates to roughly $4 billion worth of luggage annually. Worldwide, airlines in one year have 'lost' 25 million pieces of passenger luggage. That comes out to just under 3,000 bags every hour of every day, all year long.

As you sit in your seat on the airplane, you may wonder what exactly goes on just a few feet below you in the belly of the aircraft where your stored luggage lies after you check your bag and watch it disappear on a conveyor belt. While you're waiting for takeoff or getting a sandwich before boarding your plane, airline employees or the airlines' contracted employees may be stealing from your luggage or even taking your entire designer suitcase for themselves. There's a good chance that a baggage handler could remove your luggage from the conveyor belt so it would miss the flight you are on, allowing an airline employee to rummage through it at leisure after you're already in the air.

An airline security manager shared with me an interesting baggage theft case he investigated and pointed to my airport as the location of the theft. He told me that a passenger who flew on his airline filed a police report concerning stolen valuables taken from her luggage on a flight that originated at my airport. The passenger found a half-eaten slice of pizza that the thief apparently left in the luggage. The security manager's subsequent investigation revealed that the airline company next to his airline's loading area threw a pizza party for their ramp workers the day of the theft. The pizza party took place during the time that the victim's luggage was on the ramp waiting for loading onto the aircraft. The security manager believed that a baggage handler of the other airline had placed the half-eaten slice of pizza in the open luggage while he was pilfering the passenger's belongings. The crook was probably disturbed while rummaging through the luggage and closed the suitcase in haste, accidentally leaving the pizza behind. As a result, the incriminating pizza took a flight to Hawaii instead of the passenger's valuables, and the thief got away with the crime.

Airport Baggage Handlers

Airport workers jobs range from baggage handlers, cabin cleaners, equipment handlers, laborers, and other classifications. In the U.S., there are close to 2 million of these employees at our airports.

Baggage handlers are a vital part of a cohesive airport-ramp ground crew team. They receive on-the-job training on how to follow the many procedures and guidelines that govern moving and loading luggage in a busy airport. They must be alert in their work areas at all times, and there is little room for mistakes. Inside the belly of a passenger aircraft, the baggage handlers must properly secure luggage to prevent movement during flight. The safety of the airliner is in jeopardy if the weight of the interior cargo of the aircraft suddenly shifts mid-flight. Unbalanced luggage holds can cause severe consequences, in the worst case; it may lead to an emergency landing or crash. The National Aerospace Laboratory issued an executive summary titled, "Analysis of Aircraft Weight and Balance Safety Occurrences," and stated:

"What happens if the certified limits as defined in the centre of gravity envelope are exceeded? From design, the aircraft flight characteristics will be adversely affected whenever the certified limits are exceeded. For instance as centre gravity limit moves aft, the aircraft will become less stable as the centre of gravity approached the neutral point. If the centre of gravity lies aft of the neutral point the coordination and control motions required to maintain a stable flight condition will exceed the capability of the pilot and the aircraft will become uncontrollable."[155]

Loading passenger baggage, photo by W. Herrin

Loading luggage and cargo is, therefore, a crucial responsibility of every ground crew member. They cannot daydream or afford distractions by committing crimes; rather they must focus on the critical accuracy of their work. Baggage handlers also must move fast and efficiently to make sure their airline flights stay on schedule. Maintaining flight schedules requires baggage handlers operating motorized tugs, mobile conveyor belts, trucks, and a variety of motorized lifts to unload luggage, travel from one side of an airport to the other and reload the luggage onto the respective connecting flight aircraft very quickly and promptly.

Baggage Handler positions require no prior training and are entry-level jobs with minimum education requirements of a high school diploma or GED certificate. Some baggage handlers I interviewed at my airport did not have a GED or high school diploma, as some were from South America and some could not even speak English. Baggage handlers receive low wages for hard work. At the Logan Airport in Boston, the workers planned a strike and other protests because of low pay and the SEIU Union Local 615 proposed to help. The union claimed most contracted workers who provide such services as gate security, airplane janitorial and baggage handlers at Logan make $8 to $9 an hour while others make less than minimum wage.[156] Tim Cigelske worked for a major airline in Milwaukee as a baggage handler from 2005 to 2007. He wrote a short story called "Confessions of a Baggage Handler" and said, "At $7.50 an hour baggage handling is boring and strenuous. The pay is terrible and the hours are worse (shifts begin at 4 A.M.)." [157]

Airline companies assign a ramp manager to oversee airport baggage employees' specific ramp duties and ensure adherence to the procedures that govern the baggage employees. The airlines' ramp offices are adjacent to each other, and their supply rooms, lockers, and other nearby company leased areas. Most airports ramp infrastructure obscures baggage handler's movements in their work areas, as the employees move around quickly from task to tasks. Monitoring their movements is a difficult job for the ramp supervisors and the few law enforcement officers on the airside. These ramp workers play a vital role at the airport, but with low pay and minimum supervision, the leap from baggage handling to luggage thief is not a difficult one.

Nerea Marteache Solans wrote a 2012 dissertation titled, "Employee Theft from Passengers at U.S. Airports: An Environmental Criminology Perspective," at Rutgers University. Solans' study reveals some of the problems in understanding airport baggage theft. Solans cited Baumer &

Rosenbaum's study on employee theft that highlighted employee attributes that will likely lead to stealing from work locations. Solans study indicated these workplace elements are consistent at airport ramps throughout the U.S. and increase the likelihood of employee thefts:

* Low pay and entry job positions
* Employees unhappy with their working conditions, amount of work, and management
* Work locations that provided easy access to valuables
* Employees who believe there is only a small chance of getting caught
* Businesses without thorough background check and theft prevention policies[158]

Moreover, airport employees know intimately the daily activities of their neighboring airline companies' employees, police patrol frequencies, airport officials inspection schedules, and virtually all other pedestrian and vehicle movement in their work areas. The daily routines revolve around a very structured flight timetable. When someone or something appears in their work area, chances are it is on the employee's schedule and is a normal occurrence; if it isn't, the person in question is immediately apparent to the employee. Ramp workers and baggage handlers are familiar with each of the restrictive, high-security portals to and from their work area, and as a result, they can monitor the comings and goings of their peers, supervisors, and law enforcement personnel. If an airport employee is committing crimes on the secured side of the airport, and the airport police officer walks through the door and onto the secured side of the ramp, cell phones are buzzing reporting the presence of law enforcement.

CRIMES OF OPPORTUNITY

The biggest headache to airport law enforcement and any law enforcement agency in the nation for that matter is the crime of opportunity. People in every city, workplace, school or public area will leave valuables momentarily unattended, and front doors of homes and offices are left unlocked and unoccupied. Many people start the day with no malevolent intent to steal while many others specifically look for an opportunity for personal gain at the expense of another. A person passing by an unattended purse or briefcase may see the opportunity and seize the item for its potential value. Or if they knock on a door of an office or home and find it unlocked and unoccupied, this moment presents an opportunistic time to commit a criminal theft. As with the public and private domains, the airport is a perfect setting for crimes of opportunity. How does the opportunity arise at an open airport with hundreds, sometimes thousands, of employees and passengers continuously moving throughout the facility?

In "Theft by Employees," a general criminal behavior study by Hollinger and Clark, they found that employees with unfettered access to merchandise, items of value, and money, coupled with diverse types of products had greater levels of employee thefts.[159] In Felson and Boba's study and book, 'Crime & Everyday Life,' it cites employees with specialized access to areas containing valuables are a common nexus of theft crimes. Felson goes on to say that this type of crime is "a criminal act committed by abusing one's job or profession to gain specific access to a crime target."[160] Hollinger and Clark surmised in their study that one-half to a quarter of a company's employees had stolen valuables or money during the tenure of their employment. In my experience at commercial airports, I learned the opportunity for baggage theft crimes in an airport are: airport baggage employees have special access to the airport high-security areas, marginal-to-no supervision, hard work with low wages, and work in areas that their activity is not observable by supervisors or law enforcement.

Charles Slepian's findings in his airport crime investigation at JFK and Los Angeles International Airports revealed the same culture of crime and opportunity exist, to one degree or another, in virtually every airport in the nation. Slepian said, "As in the case in most workplace settings where illicit activity is present, we found 10 percent of the [airport] workers were always alert for opportunities to break a rule or a law for personal gain; 10 percent refused to participate in any phase of those activities even when threatened, and the rest went along to get along."[161]

Jack L. Hayes 25th Annual Retail Theft 2013 Survey supports the reasons for theft by employees that other studies cited. In it, he reveals one out of every 40 employees was arrested for stealing at work. Out of 23 major retailers, employee theft apprehensions increased 5.5 percent in 2012.[162] I found employee luggage theft causation, enabled by the merging of an employee's motivation to steal, his ability to steal created by his workplace, and the opportunity to steal. The following 'Crimes of Opportunity' graphic illustration best describes my viewpoint.

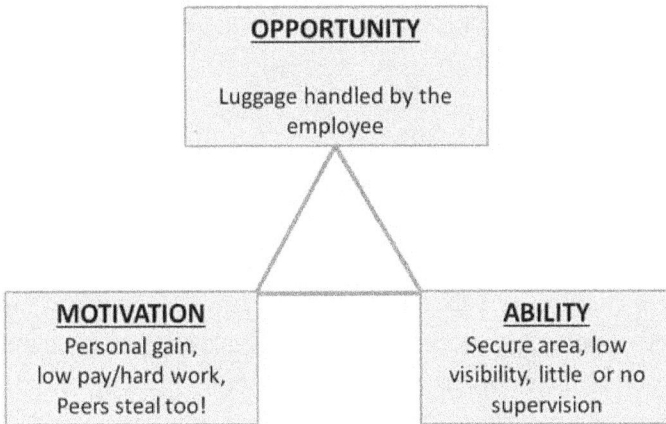

OPPORTUNITY

Luggage handled by the employee

MOTIVATION
Personal gain,
low pay/hard work,
Peers steal too!

ABILITY
Secure area, low
visibility, little or no
supervision

Airport Employee Crime of Opportunity Triangle
Source: W. Herrin

The airlines and airport police must strive to eliminate the employee baggage theft and pilfering crimes of opportunity. Management and supervision with strong character and ethics can eliminate a crime of opportunity triangle 'ability' component with proper supervision and oversight. Airports and their law enforcement personnel can increase electronic surveillances, active random patrols of employee work areas and exit screening of all employees and weaken the 'opportunity' component of the triangle. Airlines and contract companies can provide a fair wage, benefit packages, and develop positive employee relations that will help lessen the 'motivation' component of the triangle. Any success by just one of the airport stakeholders will symbolically collapse the triangle and reduce thefts at airports.

> "Virtually every significant case of employee misconduct had warning signs that leaders either ignored or failed to recognize as important. Furthermore, leaders themselves lie at the core of both the cause and solution to corruption. Past research has repeatedly confirmed that most scandals start with one employee doing relatively small unethical acts and grows to whatever level the leadership allows."[163]

Jamarcus Domonique Harper was one of three baggage handlers arrested at Las Vegas McCarran International Airport for stealing from passenger's luggage over several months in February 2017. Harper said: "Stealing from luggage was a common practice among his coworkers."[164] Where was the proper supervision of the three McCarran employees? Was effective police and security patrols ad surveillance in place to prevent and deter? The contract baggage company must answer for these airport employees' failure, and violation of the Homeland Security 'trusted employee' failure and violation of passenger rights and property.

> A former Austin airport baggage handler who bought marijuana with guns he took from passengers' luggage was sentenced to 18 months in prison on Friday in U.S. Western District Court. August 25, 2017, American-Statesmen Staff

Reporting Airport Luggage Thefts

What do airports do when customers report stolen items from their luggage or a missing/stolen bag? JetBlue, Southwest, and Frontier Airlines contract of carriage at the time of this writing only provided domestic airline passengers four hours to make a claim for lost, stolen or pilfered luggage. Other air carriers like United and Delta gave 24 hours to report the mishandled luggage.

Have you ever called an airline and tried to reach a live person? Passengers tell me that it's nearly impossible to find a live person on an airline phone system. Many of the victims of baggage theft return to the airport and attempt to talk to the ticket counter agent, who is typically busy processing a long line of passengers waiting to enter the airport screening lanes. When the passenger tries to resolve the whereabouts of the missing bag, frustration quickly sets in for both the airline employee and the passenger. In these instances, it's not uncommon for the airport police to quell the unruly airline customer and act as intermediaries until the airline and passenger resolve the problem. Officers at my airport have been to countless ticket counter incidents, which we title a "keep the peace" call. On rare occasions, we've had to use the threat of arrest to calm the irate passenger—all because the passenger is frustrated, feels violated, and just wants his or her missing luggage or items.

During my investigations of luggage thefts, I spoke to various airline ticket counter employees who expressed to me, through words and body language, annoyance at customers who reported lost baggage or thefts from baggage. Based on my conversations with these employees, I believe this annoyance is due to their working conditions; overworked and sometimes understaffed, these employees seem numb to the daily complaints from passengers.

You have probably experienced similar situations at your job—daily interruptions that annoy you but are an inevitable part of the job. You probably pass such annoying situations to coworkers whose job it is to handle them. When a passenger suffers the invasion of privacy by a theft of their personal possessions, or the loss of valuable business data that disappeared with their stolen laptop, they are often enraged and feel violated. A ticket counter employee can view an airport luggage theft report as an everyday event. It's a crisis and the first time for the passenger; but for an airline ticket counter employee, this is the fifth reported incident today, and through time it becomes a normal part of the business for airline employees.

A passenger on a national airline in 2012 boarded the aircraft and found there wasn't room for her carry-on bag containing her laptop computer. The flight attendant told the passenger they would stow the bag in the cargo hold. Upon arriving at her destination, her bag was gone. The next day the airline delivered the bag, minus the laptop. The passenger filed a complaint and received a letter explaining that since each piece of luggage must go through a complicated process of government checkpoints, multiple carriers on connecting flights and sub-contracted employees, it was not always possible to determine where any particular loss occurred. Making the results of the investigation complex occurs when the airlines deem the process is confidential and point to the muddied waters of federal law. The letter stated:

> "Because baggage is channeled through government security checkpoints, other airlines and sub-contracted employees, it's impossible to determine exactly where the loss occurred."

This letter is available online at http://fstoppers.com/us-airways-stole-my-laptop-and-wont-replace-it

Even if you do report your damaged, missing, delayed, or stolen luggage within the airline's specific timeframe, the odds are you won't receive your property or if it was stolen, see the responsible party punished.

My Research of Luggage Thefts

During my career in law enforcement, I encountered many property crime cases throughout my assignments with the Sheriff's Department. In the latter part of my career and as a current airport watch commander, I had developed an intense desire to curtail criminal activity in my area or responsibility as much as I could. As in any law enforcement officer career, they encounter thieves in all walks of life. In my career, arresting burglars in a warehouse in Aliso Viejo to arresting a mom for shoplifting from the Sears store in the Laguna Hills Mall gave me insight as to the reasons and the methods people steal and the simple to complex property crime variances.

The airport division commander walked into my office one day and asked what the extent of thefts at our airport was. I told him, as the new kid on the block at the airport, I wasn't aware of any property crime tracking by the division, but would look into answering his question. He went one step further and assigned me to research the depth and breadth of the airport's baggage pilfering and theft from passengers' luggage. In my initial review, I discovered the division had no tracking in place, logs or any measuring system.

I searched for any studies made on airport crime trends and found there were sparse studies written on the subject from a research perspective. I initiated a division tracking log that detailed any luggage or pilfering thefts reported to the airport police at my airport. For over a year our police baggage theft reports from passengers or airlines were very low in numbers. My logs showed some months we would have one or two reports of pilfered items or stolen bags submitted to our officers. I knew our officers were doing a good job on prevention patrols, but even with that assumption, the numbers didn't ring true in light of other airports' reports of theft rings and news coverage of their luggage theft and pilfering.

I determined it would be best practice to rely on combined statistics generated by airlines and my law enforcement agency. I also networked with other airport police agencies from across the nation to grasp the size of the problem at their airports. Another method I used in my quest for information on baggage thefts was to query Airlines' ticket counter representatives and obtain their policies on passengers' theft complaints and what actions they took when passengers reported a theft to them. Some airline employees said in past situations, they refused to take the passengers' theft reports and instead told the passengers to read the airline's contract of carriage on their tickets, which said in small print, "Do not pack valuables in your suitcases." They then lectured the passengers that they shouldn't have placed any valuables in their suitcase.

The airline's reply led me to a surprising finding, one that I did not expect. I discovered that airlines will first try to remedy the problem without submitting the complaint to corporate for reporting to the Department of Transportation (DOT). The airline often convinces passengers not to report thefts either by convincing them it's their fault for not following the contract of carriage warning on their ticket. Some airline managers will try cajoling passengers into taking a gift voucher for free drinks on their next flight in addition to the settlement refund limits provided by the airlines. This form of public relations effort occurs at other airports as well, as aptly said by another airport's employee concerning their methods of placating upset passengers in the Airlines.net forum:

> "Topic: RE: REDACTED Airlines Gang Bin Graffiti
> You are right about the AS employees. They have every reason to, as they are getting nothing from the uppers to support them when 140 angry customers are at their counters. Then when the big wigs tell the employees to give them a $5.00 food voucher, it certainly does not make being a CSA any easier."[165]

My months of airport theft report's data were insufficient to reach a conclusion as to the extent of a luggage theft or pilfering problem. The best way for law enforcement to stay on top of a crime trend is to apply police manpower and assets in the higher crime rate areas; if we knew which airline had the highest number of thefts, we would know where to start fixing the problem. To help me determine the extent of the theft problem, I contacted ten airline security managers and requested their last six months of reports on stolen or pilfered luggage or items. Some were very responsive and helpful; others, however, were reluctant. The result of my attempt to obtain accurate statistics failed. Each airline had its particular methodology and software database for compiling their individual airline mishandled bag statistics. A few airlines gave their data with no explanation of the statistical columns, and others took months to turn over the data that was vague and ambiguous regarding lost, mishandled, or pilfered. I viewed eleven airlines statistical spreadsheets. None of the airline's data files were even remotely similar regarding their various methods of accounting and organization of the data. The numerous 'mishandled bags' categories had a column on thefts and pilfered luggage or depending on the airline; they merged everything together under mishandled bags. The lack of accurate and credible data stymied my research to accurately determined the extent of pilfering and baggage theft at my airport.

Based on my research into airport luggage theft, I found it was very probable that airlines rarely reported thefts from baggage or stolen luggage to my law enforcement agency. The airline ticket counters and administrative offices were within a two-to-five minute walk from my agency offices. Our officers stood merely a few yards from the ticket counters during operational hours, and no valid reasons were evident as to why an airline employee could not direct victims of theft to law enforcement at my airport. Explanations that I encountered from airline employees varied from being too busy; it's up to the customer to decide to report it to the police, or they sent a report to corporate who would add another mishandled luggage statistic to their list but would not notify the airport law enforcement.

Supporting my findings is a wide-ranging study on airport crimes called "Crime Investigation in a Commercial Environment: Airports" written by Detective Inspector Lawrence Nunn of the Metropolitan Police, Great Britain Home Office. Nunn found that theft from passengers' luggage was rarely reported and obtaining statistics on which police could track patterns of theft was impossible.[166]

Legally, if the passenger decides not to report the theft, the airline is not in violation of the Code of Federal Regulation governing the enforcement of airline reporting requirements. When this happens, the theft is not reported to the DOT as there is no victim, and then technically there is no crime. Is this the best way to handle this issue? Is the DOT statistics giving us the accurate picture, or is the image skewed by the airlines' methods in handling passengers reporting lost or stolen luggage? Are airlines able to marginalize or stifle theft complaints to keep the thefts from becoming part of the theft statistics? Based on my experience, I feel the numbers reported to the DOT are significantly understated. One ticket counter employee made me smile when I asked her what her airline's policy was concerning reporting theft of luggage or pilfering. She looked perplexed, raised her eyebrows, looked up at the ceiling, and said, "I don't know, but I'll print it off of our website and give you a copy."

A part of a passenger's airfare ticket goes toward paying airline employees' wages. In return for these salaries paid by the airline passengers, employees should maintain the passenger's luggage with safety and care. In the case of airport luggage thefts, the thieving employees receive wages and a dishonorable bonus when they pilfered from victim passengers. "It's the cost of doing business," airlines and airports callously have said to others and me. However, in truth, it is this very attitude that has led to the consistent rampant baggage theft problems we have today.

The following true stories occurred at my airport or other airports that I researched or worked with during investigations or training. I did not name the airport, as these crimes are systemic throughout America's Aviation Industry. Additionally, I provide corroborating news stories of these crimes in conjunction with my criminal investigation experiences.

Airport Police Luggage and Pilfering Theft Investigations

A passenger at an airport in America was distraught when an airport employee stole her $1,400 Louis Vuitton luggage with her personal jewelry and over $6,000 worth of clothing that she had just purchased at the local shopping mall. She checked her bag at the airport, trusting the integrity of the airlines and our aviation security. But when she arrived in Michigan, her bag never showed up in the baggage claim. She filed her claim with the airline and told the airline employee her many articles of clothing still had price tags on them from the mall stores near the airport where she'd purchased them. An airport police investigation at the departure airport included contacting the mall clothing stores, and the store clerk. The clerk informed the officer, they thought the person who returned the sweater was the customer that purchased the item, and they credited a return to the victim's credit card after refusing the theft suspect request for cash. It was easy to determine this airport employed the airport baggage thief. The investigation hit a dead end with no witnesses or video surveillance to identify the thief.

The 'Crime against retail and manufacturing premises: findings from the 2002 Commercial Victimization Survey,' by the United Kingdom Home Office revealed the problems with employees who steal and the companies that employ them. Many businesses in the survey felt that it would be "inappropriate" to call the police on an employee theft incident. The study revealed that many businesses choose to deal with employee theft internally, as the survey found employers reported only 42% of employee thefts to the police.[167] During my tenure as an airport watch commander, I found many of the airlines at my airport fell into the examples of the above Commercial Victimization Survey findings.

The Martin Gill book; 'The Handbook of Security, Chapter 9 'Employee Theft & Dishonesty' by Richard Hollinger and Jason Davis found some businesses would put up with employee crimes because; "It is significantly less expensive than paying employees a more equitable wage." A finding that should be poignant to the Aviation Industry was in the research; "employee theft is the most costly form of larceny experienced by the business world."[168]

The Great Britain Metropolitan Police Inspector Nunn study; "Crime investigation in a commercial environment: airports," included an analysis of crime at five of America's international airports: JFK, Anchorage, Los Angeles, Newark, and Seattle. The study said police at these airports reported employee theft from luggage was a widespread problem, but airlines and passengers weren't reporting the thefts, which resulted in marginal if any, statistics to support their intelligence.[169]

An Airline Method of Handling Theft Problems

An example of an airport theft problem reported to the airport police occurred when the airline implemented a new baggage scanning system for loading and unloading the luggage from the aircraft. The new scanning system for passenger bags showed that passenger luggage was arriving at the airport on the ramp side but was not making it to the baggage claim. In other words, baggage ramp employees were stealing bags. The station manager reported the situation to the airport watch commander. The watch commander told him he'd like to start a law enforcement investigation to confront the problem head-on, but the manager declined to participate. Instead, he asked the watch commander to talk to his workers during an employee meeting of his airline ramp workers. The watch commander was opposed to this because if he had to resort to a covert investigation at a later time, such an investigation would have less chance of success once the police watch commander gave the ramp baggage handlers a "We know you're stealing, and you shouldn't do that" speech.

The station manager refused to cooperate, and his replies to the watch commander inferred he wanted to mitigate the problem without police action. The watch commander conferred with the airport police command and determined that they could not force the airline manager to report a crime. The watch commander decided to offer his services as a public relations gesture, called the station manager, and told him he would address his luggage theft problem and the criminals working for his airlines at their employee's meeting.

The day of the employee meeting, the watch commander stood in front of the morning shift of airport baggage employees. "There's a baggage theft problem going on at this airline," he told the group. Most of the employees sat there blank-faced while others looked at him with obvious contempt; many were not willing to look him in the eye. He looked around at each of them, forcing eye contact where he could. "Some of you sitting here are suspects in the thefts, or you may know who is stealing the luggage. The stealing needs to stop."

The watch commander couldn't believe he was doing this but went on to highlight the public's negative opinion of their airlines with the ongoing baggage thefts. He told them their airlines would lose passengers, and this will directly affect their airline financially; subsequently, their salaries and benefits would suffer. He gave the legal consequences of stealing, such as jail time and financial penalties. As he spoke, more and more employees began to avert their gaze or fidget uncomfortably. Having been through the Homeland Security Behavior Detection Officer Training, and with over 30 years of arresting and interviewing criminal suspects, his visual assessment told him many of the employees sitting there exhibited guilt of some type in their body language.

The watch commander thanked the station manager and the workers and left the meeting. The next day, he met with the station manager and told him the admonishment and pep talk wouldn't work, and he would never do something like this again. The loss statistics the station manager provided, revealed the unreported thefts had been mounting for quite some time. A simple lecture from a police officer was not going to stem the tide of employee thefts; rather the lecture would make future police investigations more difficult. The watch commander asked him why no one notified the airport police when the first theft occurred and why he had allowed the crimes to continue without asking the airport police for assistance. The manager just looked away and mumbled something about corporate procedures.

Two weeks later, the airport station manager called and said the situation had taken a turn for the worse. The number of bags stolen or pilfered was increasing dramatically, despite the 'officer friendly' talk the watch commander had given. The airline manager said he called in his corporate security manager from the Midwest instead of calling the airport police for assistance. He said his airlines still wanted to handle the thefts internally through their corporate procedures, as their new scanning system was pinpointing when and where the luggage thefts occur. The watch commander was furious with the airport employees who must have felt immune from being caught as they arbitrarily continued the pilfering and stealing of luggage. The watch commander told the manager he added resources and personnel on the ramp since their last meeting for increased high-visibility patrols. The watch commander told the station manager he was disappointed with his lack of cooperation and would brief his administration on the details of his airline's failure to cooperate with his law enforcement security partner.

AN AIRPORT POLICE LUGGAGE THEFT INVESTIGATION CASE STUDY

Two weeks later the police dispatch placed a call on the radio for a possible theft from the luggage carousel. The call informed the area officers that a passenger was reporting only one of her bags were on the arrival baggage carousel, and the other one was missing. The watch commander immediately thought an airport employee on the ramp side had the missing bag. As the watch commander arrived at the airline terminal location, he found this side of the airport was on the opposite end of the terminal from his baggage thieves. The watch commander officer told him the missing bag had a zebra-skin pattern, had been hand scanned electronically coming off of the arriving aircraft, and never arrived in the designated baggage carousel. The watch commander knew if the airport employees have not hidden the bag where they could not find it, they would be able to spot this type of bag quickly on the security side of the terminal.

He assigned his officers to search systematically every area of the airline's ramp around the arrival passenger jet. They were directed to question each ramp worker, as if they were the suspect and ask where the zebra bag was, using their best accusatory tone of voice in hopes of someone snitching on the thief. They were out of luck that day. The zebra bag, like so many others before and after it, disappeared into the airport ramp's black hole.

The next day, the watch commander was in his office when he received a phone call from his police dispatch. Someone at the front counter wanted to see him. When he went to the counter, an elderly Hispanic man was waiting for him. He could not speak English, so the watch commander called one of his Spanish-speaking officers to interpret. The Hispanic man was in his early 60s and was one of the ramp workers whose area they searched the day of the stolen zebra bag. Stressing that he wanted to keep his job, the elderly Hispanic man said he had not stolen the zebra bag but knew others at his airline were responsible. The airport ramp employee was a permanent resident alien since he moved from Peru in 2006, and said he worked two jobs and could not afford to lose his airport employment.

With the help of the officer interpreting, the informant told the watch commander he was frightened the previous day when an airport police officer searched the area the employee was sitting at while another officer on a cell phone looked directly at him. He believed the officers thought he had stolen the bag and was worried the police thought he was a suspect. The informant worked on the opposite end of the airport from the airline who asked the watch commander to speak to their thieving ramp workers. The watch commander suspected baggage thefts at his airport were occurring in many of the airline companies varied terminal locations, and the informant was about to give him the facts to support his assumption. He told the informant the airport police will not tolerate any thefts at the airport and said he needed to know who the thieves are. The watch commander emphasized that his identity and cooperation would be confidential.

With a trusting nod, the elderly informant said the luggage thefts were numerous where he worked. When he first started working for the airline contract company, he slowly began to see his coworkers taking things from passengers' luggage. He first thought it was just a couple of employees who were stealing. These workers would operate as a two-man team: One would stand lookout while the other would unzip or access by other means, luggage on the baggage makeup area, where tugs with carts load onto or off of luggage carts from a large continuously moving carousel. This baggage makeup carousel is the repository of passenger luggage transported from the various airlines' ticket counters via an extensive system of conveyor belts. These employees would take anything of value quickly from the bags on the conveyor belts and bags inside the belly of the aircraft luggage hold.

The ramp employees offered the informant chances to participate in the luggage thefts, but he refused. Knowing his co-workers were stealing made him feel guilty, and he reported the co-worker's thefts to the ramp supervisor. With a somewhat clearer conscience, he waited to see if the airlines would act on his information, but days passed, and he noticed the supervisor ignoring the thefts. Eventually, he discovered the supervisor received stolen items as gifts from the employees he supervised. Nervous by the extent of the corruption, the informant withdrew socially from his fellow airport workers. He looked away when his fellow employees were stealing and quit speaking to anyone he didn't have to and concentrated on his duties.

The informant said it was common for the airline ramp workers to steal anything edible as well; thefts of food were a joke to the employees. They would take boxes of chocolates or other snacks from passengers' luggage and put them on the employee break table so that everyone could have some of the candy or food—courtesy of their unsuspecting airline passengers.

Ramp theft, according to the informant, was highly systemized. He said the ramp workers developed a complete operational system for their criminal enterprise. They devised hiding locations where they could store small items like watches or jewelry by placing them on a ledge under the conveyor belt. At the end of their shifts, they would pocket the items as they left for home. They knew no one monitored them entering or exiting the secured side of the airport, and they would simply walk out with the stolen items. The watch commander told the informant he needed to see the locations where the employees hid the stolen items, and he agreed.

The watch commander was thrilled that he now had a man on the inside. Covertly, without other employees knowing, the informant directed the watch commander to two separate stolen-items stash locations. With this preliminary information, the watch commander contacted his investigators.

A Second Informant on the Same Day

A few hours into preparing the initial case informant information, the watch commander received a phone call from his airport control center officer. The officer told him he had a caller on hold who wanted to report luggage thefts on the airport ramp.

The watch commander grinned to himself, leaned back in his desk chair, and told the officer to transfer the call to his office phone, as he believed the caller was the elderly informant he interviewed hours earlier. After a momentary pause from the dispatch officer, the officer said this caller is someone else, and he's a little anxious.

Perplexed, the watch commander answered the line. The caller introduced himself as a ramp worker, one who worked for the airline the watch commander addressed at a meeting a month earlier; this person was present when he had given the luggage theft speech to him and his coworkers. The employee told him that he walked off the job just a few hours ago, abandoning his luggage handler assignment on the airport ramp and now wanted to report his coworkers who were stealing from passengers' luggage.

The watch commander leaned back in mild disbelief; within the last few hours, two informants came to him accusing their fellow employees of stealing. The two informants were from different airlines whose work areas were half a mile from each other on the secured side of the airport terminal. This second informant said he was a new employee with the airport baggage contract company and had worked at the airport for only a few months. Until recently, his job was on the evening shift, and he enjoyed working with his co-workers.

His transfer a week prior, to the early morning shift, happened against his wishes. On his first day of his new day shift, he observed his new coworkers pilfering from luggage and even stealing the bags. Daily, his coworkers, and field baggage supervisor offered him some of the stolen items, but he refused to take any. Throughout his shifts, his fellow employees insisted everyone shares in the spoils, even the administrative clerks in the ramp office accepted gifts of stolen items. They said the crew had a good thing going and told him he had to participate—or else. The pressure from his coworkers and supervisor was tremendous, and the new informant faced a difficult decision.

Days passed as the second informant pondered what to do. He wanted to keep his job and stay out of trouble, but under the mounting pressure, he felt he had to do something. He decided to tell the ramp airline manager, about the thefts from passenger's luggage. Before he called the watch commander, the second informant met with the airline ramp manager and told him that he wanted to leave the morning shift and go back onto the evening shift. The second informant told the ramp manager the details of the thefts the manager's employees were committing. After listening to him, the contract company ramp manager looked indifferently at him and without hesitation told him that he would be staying where he was. The manager then told him to get back to work.

Shocked, the second informant told the manager he was working overtime and was going home early. He walked out of the office and exited the secured side of the airport. While he was on the shuttle to the employee parking lot and even after he arrived home, all he could think about was that he had probably lost his job. He was young, just a few years out of high school, and his parents were poor and could not support him, and he needed his job. He called the airport police so he wouldn't be incriminated with his fellow employees in the event the police were investigating and caught his co-workers stealing.

The watch commander felt somewhat overwhelmed at the totality of the situation with the elderly informant coming forward this morning and the second informant this afternoon, both divulging a mountain of information. The watch commander continued his interview with the second informant who told him the ramp workers operated in small crews of six to ten employees, depending on the flight schedules. One of the ramp workers was picked by the ramp manager to be the baggage-loading supervisor. The second informant said the baggage handler supervisor acquired his job using a fake work-visa. The ramp supervisor bragged he arrived in the U.S. under a Guatemalan work-visa and gained his airport job under an El Salvadorian work visa.

The baggage handler line supervisor designated himself as the "shot caller," who scheduled the day shift luggage workers hours and duties. "Shot Caller" is a jail and prison term used by inmates for the designated leader in the jail cell. In a prison or jail setting, the shot caller controls the other prisoners in his cell by fear and sometimes force. This line supervisor was empowered by the ramp manager not only to conduct the line supervisor's duties but many of the baggage manager's duties as well. Essentially, his primary job was to keep everyone in line, and not to bother the baggage manager who spent most of his time in his office. The line supervisor scheduled and coordinated the baggage handlers loading and offloading of the passengers' luggage, and coordinated distribution of the stolen property. The line supervisor kept the employees happy by ensuring their assignments allowed them equal access to locations where they could steal in parity with their peers. To create equal opportunity for his co-workers, if one employee had scored too many expensive items during the shift, he distributed the stolen items equally among all employees. His socialist style distribution system seemed to work for his crew.

The second informant believed the entire theft problem grew to this point because the ramp station manager rarely left his office to check on his employees. He initially wondered if the station manager knew about the thefts and turned his head while the El Salvadorian baggage ramp supervisor ran the crew. After reporting the thefts to the manager and told to go back to work without any comment, the second informant was convinced that the station ramp manager was aware of the thefts.

The second informant set out the details of the theft ring: The morning theft crew would load the luggage into the airline passenger jet for the early morning flights. The employees took turns loading the bags into the belly of the airplane. The employee's unzipped bags or broke locks to pilfer from the passenger's luggage inside the cargo hold and would take valuables before the airplane's scheduled departure time. To be as stealthy as possible, employees turn off the interior lights before sunrise and work with flashlights while they rummage through bags for valuables. In the dark of the early morning hours, the thieves operated without detection by remaining out of sight from the police ramp patrols. The theft crew used a lookout that was on the ground or peering out from the aircraft's' baggage hold. While you're at an airport, look at the baggage being loaded on the luggage belt, if the employee isn't loading while others are loading, he's a possible lookout.

The second informant told the watch commander there were a large variety of stolen items as passengers placed anything and everything in their luggage. Virtually every type of electronic device is stolen—laptops,

Possible lookout? Photo by W. Herrin

tablets, cell phones, cameras, and many other types. He told the watch commander that passengers put jewelry, souvenirs, and designer clothing in their luggage and it was all fair game. If a bag looked valuable, especially if it were a name brand like Gucci, the thieves would either target it for pilfering or steal the entire suitcase.

To get the stolen items (including entire bags) out of the airport without being caught, the thieves got creative. They designated a specific luggage tug to transport the stolen goods and wrote the name "Sam's Cargo" on the side of it to identify the tug with stolen luggage from the hundreds of other airport tugs. This particular tug had zip-up side panels to keep luggage from falling out when it was moving on the airport road and, in this case, it served as concealment for stolen goods. When the airline flight schedule permitted, they would drive the tug with the stolen suitcases to the other side of the airport and off airport property through the airport's freight gate. This freight gate is the exit from the airport to the cargo building located outside of the airport fence perimeter. The cargo building is the distribution point for all air cargo transporting onto the airport runway and eventual loading into aircraft. This warehouse is a two-way conduit of outgoing and incoming cargo and U.S. Mail that arrives and leaves on flights.

At the freight gate, the airport police stationed an officer whose job was to inspect all incoming vehicles, both inside and out. As with most airports, no one checks outgoing tugs and vehicles, just the incoming. The second informant wasn't sure, but he assumed that the stolen goods were stashed either in the warehouse or a designated employee vehicle parked near the warehouse. At this airport, it was common to see tugs and airport vehicles on the public roadway adjacent to the airport driving to off-airport warehouses.

The second informant said the airline employees would keep the stolen property for personal use or sell the property through a number or ways. One method used by thieves was to sell the stolen passenger items by driving down local city streets and brazenly yell out to people and offer the laptops or iPods at a fraction of their usual cost. Other favorite ways were to dispose of stolen property by selling items on the internet via some web-based companies or taking items to a pawn shop or an electronic device resale shop.

After the watch commander had completed his interview of the second informant, he met with investigators to discuss the thefts and the Homeland Security insider threat potential. They included the airline station manager, who oversaw the accused ramp station manager, and his airline corporate security manager flew in for the meeting as well. During the meeting, one of the investigators recognized the baggage supervisor from photos of the employees as a person he'd investigated at a large nearby international airport. Another employee theft suspect had a criminal record and was a member of a local city tagging crew. Tagging crews travel around their home city and paint graffiti pictures and their moniker names on virtually every flat surface that is exposed to the public. You can imagine how the airport watch commander felt to discover such quality trusted security partners were handling his airport's luggage and valuables at the airport.

The investigators went to work with a number of surveillance techniques. In Italy, the Italian Airport Police placed covert cameras in the aircraft cargo holds of the aircraft and caught baggage handlers stealing from passenger's luggage. The covert camera technique used in Italy wasn't possible according to the airline corporate security manager. The manager said installing cameras in his airline's type of passenger aircraft would cause problems with the electrical or electronics of the aircraft. In May 2013, the Italian Police, however, did not find it difficult to install luggage compartment surveillance cameras in their passenger airlines when a rash of luggage pilfering reached epidemic proportion. The temperature and pressure resistant cameras caught airport employees stealing from passenger's luggage at Rome's airport and various other Italian airports.[170]

The investigation continued, and the ramp baggage manager resigned under the mounting scrutiny by the airline management and police participation. The investigation subsequently stalled due to the failure of surveillance methods, and priority criminal/Homeland Security cases that took two investigators off the case. The only investigator left on the case neared retirement and was juggling his other non-airport jurisdictions' caseloads, and the airport property crimes took a backseat. The airport theft case remained open for the new investigator and the pending caseload. At this airport, the case eventually closed pending new leads despite the informant's assistance.

This case highlights airport investigation difficulties and the mistakes made by "trusted airline partners. The airport's airline and police administration who collaborated in the waning months of the case are the only ones who know the reasons for the failure of this investigation.

"Exclusive: The Stunning JFK Airport Baggage Scandal; 200 Thefts per Day JFK airport law enforcement sources told Kramer that thefts at the airport have Increased at a staggering 200 a day and that's every day. Baggage handlers, Jetway workers and even security people are all in on the ongoing scam to steal you blind. The belly of the airplane has become like a flea market for airport employees. They go in there and go through the luggage unencumbered, unchecked."[171]

At an airport in America, a police investigator told the watch commander that during a recent investigation, his team discovered a memo from a large regional airline at the airport. The memo contained theft allegations from their airline supervisor against a ramp employee. The corporate airline management sat on this charge for a year before taking any action. When they did act, what did the airline do? Did they notify the airport police? Did they fire the employee or pursue any disciplinary course of action? The answer to all these questions is, unfortunately, no. Their solution was to transfer the employee to another state's airport, where he probably continued pilfering from passengers' luggage.

How the Airline Industry Track "Mishandled" Bags & Statistics

"Do not put your faith in what statistics say until you
have carefully considered what they do not say."

William W. Watt

By law, U.S. airlines are required to report to the Department of Transportation (DOT) all passenger reports of mishandled baggage for all domestic flights each month; "Carriers are required to report all domestic reports of mishandled checked baggage, including lost baggage, pilfered baggage, damaged baggage, and delayed baggage. Carriers must count a mishandled baggage report (MBR) even when the MBR does not result in a claim for compensation."[172]

There are many concerns with the aviation industry in transit baggage accountability. During baggage theft investigations, airline employees told me they didn't know if the missing bag was stolen or lost because a certain amount of time had to elapse to determine if the bag was lost, delayed or stolen. When I went directly to the airlines, I did not receive the full cooperation of every airline in baggage theft investigations. Many varied reasons given by the airlines pointed back to corporate policy and procedures. These corporate procedures were designed to exhaust every possible reason the bag was not in the passenger's hands, and theft was one of the last reasons airlines would arguably want to declare as the reason for the missing bag.

When an airline employee receives a written or in-person complaint from a passenger that his bag didn't show up, a check by the airline employee is made to see if it was diverted or missed the flight. Information has to be updated in the airline database to change a bag from "lost" to "stolen," and it's questionable if the missing bag classification is updated.

I perceive there are unintentional design flaws in the gathering, categorization, and communicating of the Airlines and the Societe Internationale de Telecomunications Aeronautiques (SITA) lost baggage statistics to their airport security partners. SITA is an aviation communication technology business that strives to solve the many problems the aviation industry encounters in its day-to-day business operations and is owned by 350 partner airlines.

Airlines and airports self-report statistics of theft to the DOT, and to SITA. In my search for enlightenment on the complex problem of tracking mishandled, lost or stolen airline bags at my airport, I read the 2012 through 2016 SITA Baggage Reports. The SITA 2016 report stated in 2015, 23.1 million bags were mishandled.

In the 2016 baggage report, SITA used an outline of a suitcase as a graph called; 'Reasons for Delayed Bags in 2015.' The graph depicted the categories and percentages for delayed bags. The categories were mishandling, loading, ticketing and tagging errors. In the 2016 report, these categories equated to 92 percent of delayed bags and are the result of human handling errors, and 8 percent of the errors resulted from weather and various regulations. The 2016 SITA report cited 15 percent of mishandled bags were classified as pilfered and damaged bags while 6 percent were classified as stolen or lost. The two categories of pilfered and stolen totaled 21 percent of the mishandled bags category.[173]

The 2016 SITA Baggage Report defines a mishandled bag as; "delayed, damaged or pilfered bag which is recorded by either an airline or its handling company on behalf of the passenger and handled as a claim."[174] In North American statistics, what SITA fails to tell you is there has been an enormous drop in checked bags due to the higher cost to check luggage for a flight. The airlines made over 3.8 billion dollars just on checked bag fees causing more and more passengers to take a light load in carry-on bags versus paying the high cost of checking a bag.[175]

Scott Mueller is an expert in the aviation industry's commercial passenger baggage operations. Mueller managed 52 cities for airline baggage services and baggage systems and based on his experiences, he wrote the book *The Empty Carousel*. Mueller said the airlines provide the DOT an average of the four baggage claim categories of lost, damaged, delayed and pilfered luggage. So one combined number is sent to the DOT and airlines do not have to provide a breakdown of the four categories, which makes it impossible to track airlines' passenger property thefts.[176] Mueller gives clarity from an airport insider viewpoint as to the how the airlines' statistics are inadequate and do not provide accuracy:

> "Baggage statistics are broken out by the airline in four categories. These four categories are lost luggage, damaged luggage, delayed luggage, and pilfered luggage which are claims of property stolen from luggage. Airlines are not required to reveal how many thefts they have in a month or how many bags are lost, stolen or delayed per category. Airlines also determine their percentage of mishandled luggage based on 1000 passengers boarded. For example; the end results are based on the assumption that all 1000 passengers that board an airplane checked a bag. Now if only 500 passengers out of 1000 who board an

aircraft actually checked a bag. Then the airlines statistic of 4.5 bags mishandled per 1000 passengers boarded would actually be double. So statistics are not a good measurement of an airlines' baggage handling performance."[177]

SITA also recognizes Mueller's accurate assessment, and in their 2016 Report, they admitted the metric used could be skewed, and their figures may "mask poor performance" due to the increased cabin baggage carriage as an example of cause and effects. SITA plans to reassess their methods used to count bags. No matter how many times you may fly in a year, read Mueller's book for insight and methods on how to protect your luggage when traveling. It is a guide through the maze of airline baggage claim procedures.

The mishandled bags' category common denominator is the human handling of baggage at the arrival, transfer, and departure airports. The greater cause of luggage delayed, misrouted, pilfered from, or stolen entirely are predominate because some baggage handlers are either careless, lazy, or thieves. Scott Mueller had this to say, "The airline employees are the number one cause of mishandled luggage. Carelessness in handling the luggage and employee error during the check-in process is the number one reasons bags do not make it to the same destination as you do."[178]

Without accurate vital statistics, law enforcement agencies at airports are hamstrung without knowing the extent of employee thefts in their jurisdiction. Airport police chiefs who are members of an organization called "Airport Law Enforcement Agencies Network" (ALEAN) are attempting to track baggage theft trends using these statistics via SITA's WorldTracer software.

Can any current airline tracking method accurately analyze whether bags are missing due to theft or if the airline lost the bag? How can we know just how serious the baggage theft problem truly is without accurate data? Even our national database of crime index is inaccurate, and supporting statistics are not complete. Marcus Felson and Rachel Boba in their study, "Crime and Everyday Life" asked the question "how much crime is there?" In the real world, they said that as a student of crime "you must know the limitations in truly measuring crime." The Uniform Crime Reporting Program and the National Crime Victimization Survey are the two noted measurements of crime in the U.S., yet they contain only a percentage of the crimes committed. Felson states, "Even with a clear definition of crime; we still have problems counting it up in the real world. In some cases, only the offender knows what he or she did. With other crimes, a victim knows but won't tell anybody. In still other cases, there seems to be no victim at all…statistics are thrown at you that don't paint the entire picture."[179]

When a private researcher tried to assess the extent of employee theft at airports, she ran into roadblock after roadblock in the search for the truth. Nerea Marteache Solans revealed the great difficulty in assessing the airport theft problem she encountered during her research on the subject:

> "The search for data to conduct this research has encountered several obstacles. First airports are critical infrastructure. As such, most of the data related to their baggage handling and managing practices, as well security measures is considered Sensitive Security Information, and is therefore not made public. Second, some relevant information that is not "classified" is gathered by agencies and companies that only grant access to the data to members of the industry. Third, the fact that one of the theft types studied in this research (theft from checked luggage) is committed "in transit," makes it difficult to establish where exactly a theft was committed or what type of employee committed the crime without access to TSA or airport police records."[180]

Laura Ingraham is the host of a national talk radio show, a former litigator, bestselling author, and Fox News contributor. Ingraham highlighted the problems encountered with luggage theft by sharing her experience of the theft of her jewelry at Newark Airport. Ingraham told 'TheDC' news, "She has been getting a total runaround while trying to track down answers about the theft and information about how to proceed. The only people who, it turns out, were helpful, were the nice people at the Port Authority Police Department at Newark Airport." Ingraham said it took many hours for a Continental Airlines employee to respond to her dilemma and when they did respond, Continental Airlines told her it was her fault for placing her jewelry in her luggage. Ingraham said; "Blaming the victim is also a really lovely way to deal with the flying public." Ingraham was assisted by the Port Authority police, who helped her file a criminal theft police report. She said; "the process of reporting these kinds of crimes is so cumbersome that many people don't have the time or willpower to get to the bottom of them."[181] A SITA survey found approximately one-quarter of all passengers [206 million] said there should be vast improvements in airline baggage handling.

SITA CEO, Francesco Vilante, prefaced SITA "Baggage Report 2012," where he gave the following advice in his opening remarks: "We need to come together as an industry to make additional breakthroughs [in reducing baggage mishandling]. For one thing, this means adhering to standards. But it also means adopting a culture of openness—bringing about more proactive data sharing among all industries stakeholders. Only then can we gain clear visibility of the bag's journey, combining our insights to find new ways to prevent mishandling."[182] In a spirit of openness, Vilante's words promote sharing the information among all aviation stakeholders in a unified effort to solve the problem. Vilante's suggestion is the beginning to solving our nation's problem with airport employee baggage thefts.

WHAT TO DO IF YOUR LUGGAGE IS STOLEN OR PILFERED

If something is stolen from your luggage and it's identifiable using the bags unique characteristics or serial numbers, victims should immediately file a report with the airline and airport police. Within minutes of filing the reports, immediately, victim passengers should start checking eBay, Craigslist, 'Offerup' or 'Letgo' selling websites to name a few and local airport pawnshops for the next 72 hours. Your stolen item could be on one of these websites or in a pawn shop within hours. If you do find your item listed for sale on a website or in a pawn shop, call your local law enforcement agency so they can track and locate the seller and arrest them for possession of stolen property. The Government Accountability Office (GAO) compiled an "Organized Retail Crime" Report for the House of Representatives. Depicted below is the average life cycle of stolen items and methods of disposal:

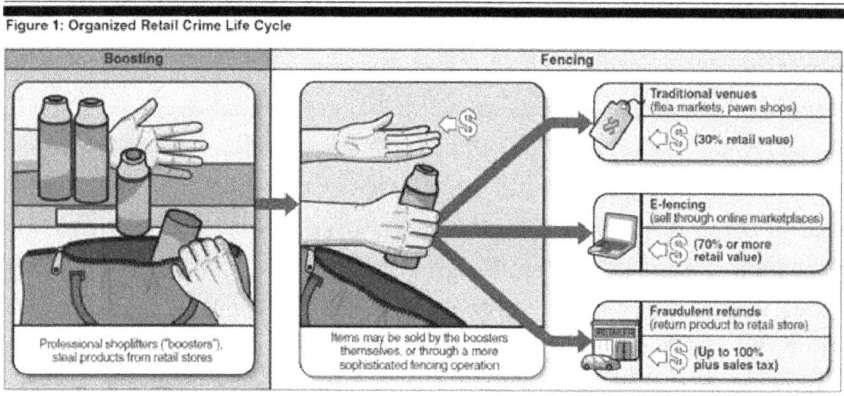

Figure 1: Organized Retail Crime Life Cycle

Boosting

Professional shoplifters ("boosters"), steal products from retail stores

Items may be sold by the boosters themselves, or through a more sophisticated fencing operation

Fencing

Traditional venues (flea markets, pawn shops) (30% retail value)

E-fencing (sell through online marketplaces) (70% or more retail value)

Fraudulent refunds (return product to retail store) (Up to 100% plus sales tax)

GAO/NRF Crime Life Cycle Diagram, Source:
Congressional Accountability Office

An example of airport employees using pawnshops to dispose of stolen goods is in the FBI press release of June 2013. It announced the arrest of Miami International Airport Fleet Service Clerk Marco Cruz, who took a box of six gold bars from arriving American Airlines flight 902. Cruz took the gold to a pawnshop and sold them for $250,000 in cash. The police arrested Cruz and the pawnshop owner.[183] Here's an example from another airport that caught their ramp workers stealing from the passengers' luggage and selling the stolen goods on eBay:

"In Portland, Ore., Northwest Airlines baggage handlers were caught stealing items and posting them for sale on eBay right from a supervisor's airline-owned computer. Baggage theft reports are up nearly 50% this year, according to airport spokesman Steve Johnson."[184]

Every airport in the nation suffers baggage theft crime sprees. At Hartford, Connecticut's airport, Lieutenant J. Paul Vance of the Connecticut State Police Agency investigated his airport baggage handlers and arrested many of them for pilfering luggage in the aircraft while loading luggage. Vance said they stole laptops, electronic devices such as iPods, cameras, and jewelry.[185]

SITA and the airlines have financial inspiration to solve this critical aviation industry problem as Congress passed the 2016 Aviation Innovation, Reform, and Reauthorization Bill (AIRR). AIRR allows passengers reimbursement for their baggage fees by airlines when the passenger's bags are still missing after 24 hours. This congressional act will certainly decrease the 3.8 billion airlines profit from baggage fees and be a major motivation for baggage accountability reform.

AIRPORT ARRIVAL LUGGAGE CAROUSEL THEFTS AND SECURITY NEEDS

Airports view baggage claim areas as a low-security risk when considering adding additional security to the arrival carousel areas. Brussels and Istanbul Airports attacks have not changed America's airport's security views on these areas. Many airports' arriving baggage claim locations are easy targets for active shooters, but also by baggage thieves. Baggage claim carousels are typically just a few feet from secured terminal egress portals that lead directly to the high-security departure side of an airport terminal. High security in these areas is essential to a safe airport.

Door to a passenger airport airfield next to a public
arrival baggage claim, Photo by W. Herrin

There are valid reasons for restricting any person who has not passed through an airport screening process from entering the arrival baggage carousel areas of our nation's airports. A primary reason is the security of the airfield ramp from an open baggage carousel where anyone off the street can stand next to a door and watch airport employees swipe a badge and walk into the airfield. A secondary reason for restricting non-passengers into a baggage claim area is it will deter and prevent outside luggage thieves from walking into the terminal and stealing a suitcase off the carousel. Baggage carousel thieves conceal themselves easily when walking through the hundreds of other people in the baggage claim area.

Open public baggage claim makes it difficult to spot
the luggage thief, Photo by W. Herrin

In 2013, at the Portland International Airport, airport police arrested four adults and two children for luggage theft. The police said several luggage thefts they were investigating are related to these criminals. The baggage claim employees said, "it's a known problem with people on the MAX (light rail passenger system). People come in on the MAX, steal bags, and go back out on the MAX."[186] In 2014, a 37-year-old Newark man was arrested at Newark Airport the 40th time for stealing luggage from the carousel.[187] Newark has a similar light rail system adjoining the airport.

In Phoenix Sky Harbor International Airport, a husband and wife team stole over a thousand pieces of luggage, simply by driving up to the curb, walking in, and taking passenger luggage off the arrival carousel.[188] Denver International Airport police arrested a man for stealing numerous suitcases. The man was the lead suspect in the stealing of the famous rock star Peter Frampton's luggage from the arrival carousel. Three years earlier the police investigated the suspect when he posted on eBay items taken from passenger's stolen luggage, but due to lack of evidence, the police did not file charges at that time.[189]

During a news channel filming at the Denver Airport concerning the arrest of the baggage theft suspect, airport spokespersons were providing details of the arrest to the news media. As the media crew was taping the news segment on the airport thefts, coincidentally, another thief was stealing a bag off the carousel. During the interview, the security camera caught the thief's actions, unbeknownst to the news and airport media persons standing adjacent to the thief. The Denver airport police did confirm to the news agency that the thief stole the luggage from a baggage carousel next to the one where the interview took place.

The Denver Airport representative told the CBS Denver News the number of stolen bags was minimal, and there was not a major problem. The Denver airport police in a follow-up interview told the news media; that luggage and baggage theft numbers, "may be higher," since passengers may report the theft of their luggage only to the airline they flew on in hopes of financial compensation. Another passenger who was a victim of luggage theft told the CBS Denver News they were at the airport during the Peter Frampton bag theft episode. The passenger went to the Denver airport police who told him they had a "bit of an issue" in regards to expensive luggage thefts from the baggage claim carousels. We can take from the CBS News investigation that the statements by the airport information administrator and the police were at odds as to the extent of the seriousness of baggage thefts at their airport.

The Denver airport police were also in the dark as to the magnitude of the stolen bag numbers at their airport because their airport passengers were indeed reporting their thefts only to the airlines who did not report the thefts to the airport police.[190]

At Hartsfield-Jackson Atlanta International Airport, a passenger whose bag was missing on the carousel went to the airport police to report the crime. The police told him they were suffering an epidemic of carousel baggage claim thefts. The police investigator told the passenger that he reviewed the surveillance video and saw the theft suspect had positioned himself at the carousel before the passenger's arrival. The theft suspect timed the bag movement on the carousel—as it was nearest to the exit—grabbed it, and darted out the door. The investigator told the passenger that once outside the door there's no video of that area, and the thief becomes lost in the crowd, and there's nothing they can do.[191]

At my airport, we occasionally received reports of missing luggage from the arrival carousels. Our airline's baggage claim offices were near the carousels, and the airline often placed non-claimed baggage outside their offices located conveniently next to the terminal exit doors. Due to the 'open-door' to the public policy of airports' arrival carousel areas, observing and catching a baggage thief on surveillance video or from a police officer positioned nearby is a low percentage of success endeavor. A thief standing in the area stealing luggage and a passenger picking up his luggage are virtually indistinguishable from each other. A police officer stationed near the baggage carousel span of control is beyond one officer's ability to deter successfully or prevent luggage thefts off of the carousels. The Denver Airport thief stealing a bag while police, airport personnel, and news media are standing two carousels away makes this point perfectly—not a theory but a simple fact.

On a more positive note, Delta Airlines initiated an active identification baggage check program at their arrival carousels in December 2013. Delta paid their employees to staff the operation during the trial period while the airport provided stanchions to cordon off Delta's baggage claim area from the other airlines.[192] I applaud Delta Airlines for taking the right step in this direction for safety and security of their passenger's possessions. It is a small first step, but nevertheless a step in the right direction. Orlando Airport in Florida took a giant proactive measure when it added $5 million to its budget to upgrade the security for their arriving luggage carousel locations. Orlando had suffered a significant increase in baggage thefts from their carousels.[193]

An ominous warning concerning the openness of America's Airports arrival baggage claim is the Moscow Airport suicide bombing that occurred at their arrival baggage claim location. On January 24, 2011, a terrorist detonated a bomb among arriving passengers that killed 37 and seriously wounded 87 people. The airport spokesperson said the arrival area was open to the public "to which people who are not passengers have free access."[194]

RECOMMENDATIONS:
Management of Airport Employees Recommendations:

1. Airline corporations must empower their airport station managers with unbridled authority to prevent employee misconduct as it occurs. When the airline station manager suspects a baggage pilfering/theft trend is developing, the airline station manager must place all disciplinary and investigatory options on the table. The station manager must not be hamstrung by corporate management image concerns and must act in partnership with local airport police and prosecute the problem immediately within the Federal and State criminal laws.

2. Airline station managers' hiring by the airline corporations must include prerequisites that the prospective manager applicants have strong leadership, character, and ethics. In turn, airline station managers must hire and support line supervisors who will hold employees accountable for their bad behavior, lack of good character, and dishonesty. These supervisors must

have zero tolerance for misconduct of any kind. These types of supervisors and managers, when hired, will uphold the integrity of their respective airlines, walk the ramp, and engage their employees with sound supervisory fundamentals and consistent monitoring. The first line supervisor will make or break an airline's ground operation. A supervisor who has knowledge of misconduct and whose response is deliberately ignoring employee misconduct must be removed from airport employment in the most legally-expeditious way possible.

> "We respectfully submit that positive leadership, and the examples set by management and supervisors can make the difference between a workforce that "looks the other way" and one that does not give opportunity to criminals or terrorists."[195] National Association of Airline Passengers

3. Implement a Lost/Stolen Luggage Unit (LSLU) in the Nation's Airports

    This proposed LSLU unit based at each airport would be a jointly-funded operation by airlines. The unit's primary purpose would be to investigate and follow up immediately on passengers' reports of stolen, missing, and lost property. The Unit would provide a single location at every airport terminal in the nation where passengers from all airlines would be directed to address their claims of lost or pilfered luggage and other thefts. This will free the airlines' ticket counter agents and other airline personnel so they can accommodate their busy daily flight schedules. All airlines will be required to provide open access to the LSLU of all flight manifest, daily employee rosters, and luggage data.

    With SITA and ALEAN (Airport Law Enforcement Association Network) already in place, the LSLU would bring together all aviation stakeholders' investigations through a fusion center that would provide accurate theft, pilfered, and lost luggage statistics previously entered into a central database. The LSLU units receiving of missing/stolen bag information would institute simultaneous investigations of on-duty airport baggage handlers, TSA, and other airport employees who handled the bag during the hours the flight was at their airport. All airlines will be required to send all passengers to the LSLU to report their pilfered, lost or stolen luggage complaints. Further changes to the present system would include:

* The LSLU office will be adjacent to each airport's police agency office.

* The LSLU agents would take immediate reports, initiate timely investigations, and work in unison with airlines, airports, and a dedicated law enforcement officer liaison.

* The LSLU and involved police agencies of both departure and arrival airports would use the current crime trend technology and target the thieves with available information from the airline's database (flight number, passenger info, destination, arrival time based on SITA's current and planned technology, etc.). Roster's and timelines of luggage handlers' duty hours that are available immediately would allow real-time investigations.

* The LSLU in partnership with airport police will have the unbridled authority that would span throughout the airport and airlines. They are authorized to conduct immediate investigative searches; if necessary, on the scene in any area of a leased airline office space or work locations, including employee lockers, office spaces, and any area that is accessible by baggage handlers. LSLU searches are based on preapproved, contractual consent by all airport stakeholders under each airport's security plan and will be part of the employee employment contract. Luggage thief's methods have shown that there is a window of opportunity

of as much as four-to-eight hours to find stolen items or bags before the criminals leave at the end of their work shift.

* The LSLU consistent investigative actions would create a prevention and deterrence posture with the promotion of the program to airport employee groups.

4. Airport Police Security Experience Attrition and Methods of Recompense:

Airport law enforcement personnel will enter and leave an airport police agency through new hires, retirements or transfers. When transitions of airport police members occur, there must be a fluid and organized transference of learned skills, knowledge and best practices from the departing personnel to the new personnel. Transference of knowledge does not occur as a standard operating procedure in most airports. This highlighted concern from a study out of seven European airports is one of the root causes of the failures in many airport security operations. The study said, "Inadequate organizational learning mechanisms where lessons learned [at airports] are lost with a high turnover of employees."[196]

In this and countless other examples that I've seen at many airports, law enforcement employees leave the airport division, and there is a subsequent loss of their years of acquired airport security knowledge. This knowledge is not appropriately transferred to new staff nor documented in a detailed database of policy and procedures best practices. Criminal investigation knowledge loss specific to commercial and cargo airports directly affects the proposed LSLU and its baggage theft investigations. Airport police agencies should review the study entitled, "Airport Security: An Ethnographic Study." The study suggested the use of a gathered historical information is a source of reference as part of the annual training of airport police in airport crime case histories and best practices.

5. Effective Exit Checks and Security of Arrival Baggage Claim Locations:

Airlines are responsible for ensuring the passenger receives their baggage upon arrival at the passenger's destination airport. The airport provides the security of their work areas for reuniting the baggage with the passenger on the arrival carousel. Both the airlines and airports work together in accomplishing this task. Up until the late 1990s, airline personnel would check the passenger's luggage ticket with the luggage to verify ownership when the passenger would leave the arrival carousel. Due to airlines' budget cuts, the majority of airlines no longer provide that security procedure. The majority of arriving-luggage carrousel thefts are committed by people who come to the airport with the intent to steal the luggage from the unsecured baggage claim areas. The Las Vegas McCarran Airport case serves as an excellent example where thieves found it extremely easy to drive up to the curb, walk in, and take suitcases and bags.

Airports and airlines should supply security at every airport baggage claim area and restrict the baggage arrival area only to inbound arriving passengers. This will eliminate the majority of baggage claim luggage thefts. Security at baggage claim locations will provide an additional homeland security component in addition to luggage theft prevention. Airport police should staff entrances, or the use of armed, trained security guards whose duties are to monitor egress and ingress of these portals is an essential component of the baggage area security. The airlines will pay for the cost of the security personnel.

6. Enact legislation For Stronger Airport Crime Related Laws.

Increased consequences for crimes committed by airport employees are a deterrent to recidivism airport thefts. Aviation crime statues with increased penalties for crimes committed on airport property by the state and federal legislative process to increase the safe airport zone is necessary.

7. Precautions and Tips to Avoid Thefts While Traveling:

    While the airport and Homeland Security ponder their next steps to tighten airport security and eliminate criminal employees, the following are tips to assist you in securing your belongings while traveling. The products listed in these recommendations can be found with a web search using the keywords included in the following recommendations:

    *   Avoid Using Soft Body Zipper Bags. Baggage thieves can access a locked zippered suitcase with merely a ballpoint pen. The pen opens the zipper quickly, allowing access to the contents of the luggage. Just moving the zipper tabs that are locked together with a small padlock will reunite the zipper teeth; it will appear the suitcase was never breached.
    *   Use hard-shell luggage. Current designs offer high strength but low weight polycarbonate material with TSA-accessible, embedded lock mechanisms in their designs.
    *   Use brightly-colored luggage-locking straps as another alternative.
    *   Use luggage sleeve covers that slip over the luggage and present a harder target for pilfering thieves and also provide a waterproof cover for traveling in inclement weather.
    *   Use adjustable, high-tensile stainless steel flexible wire mesh: These products are designed to cover your belongings in a net-like fashion, thereby protecting a variety of bags and packs from tampering, pilfering, and theft. They need to be locked using TSA-approved locks.
    *   Buy a unique bag. Do not buy an upright black bag with wheels because these types are most common.
    *   Avoid expensive name-brand luggage or baggage that appears expensive.
    *   Put a colorful, unique, and distinctive marking on your bag.
    *   Book direct or nonstop flights.

- Video record the items that you're placing inside the luggage.
- Take photographs of your luggage with your cell phone or digital camera. Having pictures to show the claim representative will make it easier to describe your luggage.
- Label your luggage inside and out with your name, address, email address, and cell phone number.
- Record your bag's size and any unique features. The more details, the better.
- Don't pack items that are banned.
- Use locks approved by the TSA, if not, don't lock your bags. Your bag may signal TSA that it needs extra screening and if secured with an unapproved lock; it may not make your flight.
- Do not place valuable items in checked luggage. Ship items separately to avoid handling at the airport.
- Use plastic zip ties to prevent baggage handlers from opening your luggage. TSA can cut them if they need to inspect your luggage. Most baggage handlers will then look for an easier target.
- Check in early. Remove old tags.
- Confirm that new tags are attached and that the labels list the correct destination.
- Avoid switching flights at the last minute. If you make this mistake, your bags may fly with your original flight and sit around for hours and possibly days at the wrong destination, where they will be susceptible to crimes of opportunity.
- Do not pack anything electronic that will vibrate—or if you do, take the batteries out. Suspicious sounds or vibration coming from a suitcase while a baggage loader is handling your bag will initiate a police investigation, and you and, your luggage will miss your flight.
- If your bag isn't at the baggage claim, file a police report before leaving the airport and ask for directions on how and

when you can receive a copy of the report. Then file a report with the airlines via ticket counter or phone, and be sure to get a reference number and mark the time you filed the report. Create accountability. If you get the name, direct phone number, and email address of the airline's representative agent with whom you filed the report, you make them part of the solution to your problem.

* Secure all credit cards, cell phones, and laptops. You might think your jewelry and expensive clothes are the most important belongings you take on your flight, but of equal importance is the data stored on your credit cards and your laptop, tablet, and cell phone. Identity thieves use high-tech scanning equipment that copies your credit information from these items simply by walking by you. But there are products available that will shield your identity information.

* To provide additional safety for your valuables - if you choose to pack them in your luggage - you can purchase "diversion safes." These are simply everyday items with false bottoms, such as a plastic mug, book, or even a can of potatoes chips or soda. Diversion safes are disguised as such unremarkable items and can hide your jewelry or other valuables from the attention of luggage pilferers.

CHAPTER 8

Screening Airport Employees?

———◆———

"A better solution would adopt a 100 percent screening
program for all aviation employees. The infrastructure
already exists for this increased level of security. The
safe operation of commercial aircraft in the skies over
the United States is critically important to our economy,
national security and the psyche of the American people."

CAPTAIN STEVEN GOFF [197]

AIRPORT EMPLOYEES THROUGHOUT OUR NATION's airports have unfettered
access to the secured side of the airports with merely a swipe of a card
on an electronic card reader. The employee can stow any item he wishes
in his backpack, lunch pail, or tool box and walks alone into the most
secured side of the airport through a private door. The airline employee
will leave through the same entrance and walk to his car parked nearby
without anyone seeing or knowing what he placed in his container during his work shift. What type of Homeland Security and potential crime
risks is possible with these employee access procedures?

A courageous airline pilot, Chris Liu, took cell phone videos of San
Francisco Airport employees bypassing security screening by entering
into employee-only doors and accessing the security side of the terminal. These employees would take carts of tools, boxes of supplies and a

host of other items needed to perform their job in and around aircraft. Liu was not only an airline pilot, but he was also a volunteer Homeland Security Armed Flight Deck Officer on his passenger aircraft. As a flight deck officer, Liu trained with a government issued handgun to protect his aircraft from criminals and terrorists. As a professional passenger jetliner pilot, Liu understands the vital need for homeland security at our nation's airports.

Liu felt it was his duty to let America know what TSA and every custodian, baggage handler, airport police officer, and maintenance worker in America's airports already know about this type of unscreened employee access. Liu posted his video of the door and other areas of the airport on YouTube. Three days later, four Federal Air Marshals and two Sacramento deputy sheriffs showed up at Liu's home and confiscated his federally issued handgun. The Air Marshal said Liu allegedly revealed the weak security of the airport and impaired the efficiency of TSA and caused the loss of public confidence in TSA.[198] I had never seen a force of local police officers with armed Air Marshals go to a person's home in force to confiscate a person's federally-issued firearm when that person did not commit a crime. Homeland Security specifically conducted this show of force and tyranny to scare the airline pilot and any others who may emulate the pilot's freedom of speech in airing his concerns about airport security. If Homeland Security summoned Liu by phone to come to their office and turn in the issued handgun, Liu would have complied without any hesitation.

People called Liu the Patriot Pilot for wanting to change what he perceived are serious security flaws in our airports. San Francisco Airport management disagreed and pointed out in a rebuttal that the only door highlighted in Liu's video led to a private lunchroom for airport ramp employees and not to the ramp below. However, the San Francisco Airport Administrative statement that refutes Liu is a distraction. Like many big airports, San Francisco has many other doors that lead directly to their ramp without screening and just a swipe of an employee's badge, just as Liu attested. Liu resigned as a Federal Flight Deck Officer rather than go through the TSA inquisition and continued as a pilot for his airlines. This vindictive overreach by TSA resulted in one less capable and armed pilot who would defend his aircraft in our nation's airports.

INSTITUTE MANDATORY AIRPORT EMPLOYEE SCREENING AT ALL AIRPORTS

America's airports and Homeland Security can strengthen our airport security by instituting mandatory screening of all airport employees before they enter the secure areas of the airport grounds. At present, baggage handlers, mechanics, fuel specialists, and other employees do not receive the same daily physical screening as airline flight personnel and passengers. Airport management estimates screening all employees as they go in and out of the airport infrastructure is cost prohibitive. They also claim screening employees would make security lines longer for passengers.

The former security chief at Northwest Airlines, an aviation consultant, and advocate for the screening of all airport employees, Douglas Laird, said in an interview with *USA Today* about two airline employees in Orlando who smuggled 14 guns onto a Comair flight, "Not screening airport workers is a terrible vulnerability. The system is totally wide open. It's long overdue."[199]

But what is very disheartening to me is the spokesman for TSA, Nico Melendez, and his statement in the Brian Sumers story in the *Daily Breeze*. Melendez said, "It is not possible to check every employee when they arrive each day, especially when many of those workers have access to potentially dangerous or disruptive items once they are on the job." Melendez's arguments emphasize the airport employees are our "trusted" security partners, and reporter Brian Sumers wrote; "At its core, airfield security is built on trust."[200]

In October 2013, two trusted Los Angeles Airport employees devised dry ice bombs and detonated them on the security ramp side of the airport. While the dry ice and containers are readily available on the secure side of airports, it is common knowledge among the employees and to anyone with common sense; a bomb is just a swipe of an airport employee's card from entering any airport in America. It is no secret and in hundreds of documented open source investigations, news reports and airport security papers detailing airport security breaches.

The British newspaper *The Telegraph* reported that the United Kingdom government-commissioned report said hundreds of airport workers in England had been allowed to work in high-security areas of airports without proper background checks. The study emphasized that terrorists are attempting to place "sleepers" in airport jobs on the inside of the airport security areas. A review of British airport security occurred after an Islamic employee, Samina Malik, was arrested under the UK 2000 Terrorism Act. Malik worked as a store clerk on the security side of Heathrow Airport and was found to possess a library of books on techniques of terrorism, firearms, poisons, and hand-to-hand combat written by Islamic extremist groups. Malik wrote poetry describing how she wanted to be a martyr and admired the Mujahideen.[201] One ominous phrase Malik wrote, read: "The desire within me increases every day to go for martyrdom."[202]

DALLAS FT. WORTH AIRPORT

Three years after Pilot Chris Liu made his statement, employees in Dallas-Fort Worth Airport (DFW), raised alarms about what they called a national security issue. Two employees speaking anonymously to local Fox Channel 4 News said they were concerned about who was being hired to work on the secured side of the airport and how they accessed the security side. They cited employees would swipe their card and enter the security side unscreened while other employees would follow quickly behind them before the door closed to avoid having to swipe their cards.[203] In airport security, we call this "piggybacking," it is expressly forbidden and is a violation of all Airports Security Plans (ASP).

Fox News investigated and filmed DFW airport employees entering the secured side of the airport revealing many examples of piggybacking in their investigation. The investigation highlighted the nation's airports' inadequate security procedures where unscreened contract workers enter the secured side of the airport to clean airplanes and perform other ancillary duties.

NBC News investigated Dallas Ft. Worth Airport a second time for employee security door breaches. NBC News-5 Reporter Michael Dorstewitz discovered a number of incidents where the airport employees violated Homeland Security protocols:

- An off-duty Continental employee drove his family in a van from the cargo side of the airport to the airport terminal via the airfield roads on the secured side of the ramp to avoid the Homeland Security passenger screening.
- The Chief Executive Officer of American Eagle Airlines used his badge to escort his wife to avoid screening to meet their daughter who was on an inbound flight.
- An American airline pilot on a personal trip used the employee entrance to avoid the long lines at the screening lanes.
- A flight attendant used her badge to sneak a carry-on backpack through the employee door without it being screened and gave it to her husband who was a passenger on a flight to Germany.
- A TSA supervisor let an employee in without a badge into the secured side of the airport without being screened.
- A Federal Aviation Administration manager was caught using the employee door to board a personal, non-business flight.

The NBC News-5 report even discovered a Dallas Ft. Worth Airport analyst employee using her trusted status to bring her unscreened husband through an employee door to board a flight. Reporter Dorstewitz interviewed the TSA consultant Chaim Koppel and asked, "If you're catching that many employees, how many are you not catching?" Koppel said for every employee caught entering illegally through the "trusted" employee door; three to four are not caught.[204] Koppel's statement was reflective of how the U.S. Attorney's Office successfully investigated and arrested airline employees in the Houston Airport System where these trusted airport employees turned to crime;

> "Oct. 19, 2012. Escober and Molina were employees of Express Jet and DAL [Delta Airlines] Global Services, respectively. Court records indicate they conspired together to use their positions as employees at the airport and their knowledge of security to circumvent airport security and smuggle items in exchange for pre-negotiated sums of cash from an undercover Homeland Security Investigations (HSI) special agent who they each believed to be a narcotics trafficker."[205]

An undercover federal agent hired Escober and Molina to smuggle fake identifications, passports, and heroin through the "trusted" employee door in unscreened bags into the sterile area of the airport. The agent would go through TSA screening and once on the sterile security side of the terminal; he would go to a designated bathroom stall and wait for Escober. Once Escober entered through the employee door into the secure side of the airport, he would take the drugs and identifications into the designated restroom and pass the satchel under a bathroom stall divider back to the federal agent. The agent would then pay Escober for the delivery and board a flight to Miami.[206]

EVERY AIRPORT IN THE NATION HAS A PROBLEM
The ease of employees entering an airport in America unscreened and unmonitored opens doors to threats that could bring death and destruction to our airports. *The Boston Globe* reported in March 2014 that five airline employees were arrested for smuggling $417,000 worth of

drugs in a suitcase through employee security doors and onto flights to Miami. Nine indictments were handed down by the courts for drug money smuggling operations.[207]

Across the nation on the West Coast in the same month, a massive drug operation was busted in March 2014 that involved airports in Hawaii, Baltimore, New York, Nashville, and Detroit. Assistant U.S. Attorney Michael Wheat said in an affidavit to the Southern District Court of San Diego, California, that the operation revealed a severe problem regarding airport baggage handlers circumventing security by entering and exiting the airport ramp, and moving drugs onto and out of airplanes and into nearby cities. Many of the airport employee drug couriers would take the unchecked and unscreened handbags of drugs through airport employee only security doors by swiping their employee identification card. Once on the secured side of the terminal, they would place the drugs in the passenger aircraft overhead bins for flights from city to city. San Diego was the base of this drug smuggling operation for the Mexican Drug Cartel. Six arrested baggage handlers were on the cartel's payroll to deliver drug shipments on passenger planes to these different airports. The U.S. news release said;

> "The indictment alleges that Felix Samuel Garcia, Paulo Mendez Perez and Saul Bojorquez, all current or former employees of Delta Global Services, which provides ground services for several airlines, flashed badges numerous times and walked through checkpoints with drugs in their backpacks. Brian Alberto Gonzalez, also a DGS employee, allegedly worked as a courier."[208]

This trend continues as revealed by a Delta Airline's employee arrest for smuggling $282,000 in a backpack on April 28, 2016. The employee planned to pass the money under a bathroom stall to a passenger who previously went through screening.[209]

I found during my law enforcement career that every retail business has an acceptable loss percentage of the products they sell. Drug cartels and organized crime syndicates also have an acceptable loss ratio. I believe that the larger percentage of drug smuggling efforts are successfully completed, and those who get caught are written off as just a cost of doing business.

From the East Coast to the West Coast, incident after incident, decade after decade, criminal airport employees violate the trust placed in them. For days and weeks after criminal airport workers are arrested for using the employee airport security portals in criminal acts, the news media venues are filled with politicians, security experts, law enforcement officials and the airport administrators, bellowing about the Homeland Security dangers that could result in such incidents. Months afterward, the news moves to another headline-grabbing event and memories fade until the next employee is arrested for carrying guns or drugs through the unmonitored employee entrance.

On December 24, 2014, the news once again erupted with the story of a Delta Air Lines baggage handler arrest and resulting charges of helping criminals smuggle over 100 guns through the airport and onto passenger aircraft. From Atlanta International Airport to New York, these guns traveled in the carry-on compartment, some loaded with ammunition, while passengers sat below the compartments. We have to ask; what was done to prevent each past incident that occurred during the last 30 years of our nations' airport crime history, after each arrest of drug or gun smugglers occurred? What new procedure was implemented to safeguard our vital aviation industry? We can answer these questions with the litany of airport employee's smuggling incidents previously cited. It is safe to say; nothing of any worth was done to eliminate the problem of the "trusted" airport employee criminal activities. The one exception is the Miami International Airport, which saw the light in 2015 and started screening their employees because of the following criminal incident:

FBI arrested Atlanta baggage handler for his role in airport gun running.

"The complaint alleges that Harvey repeatedly evaded airport security with bags of firearms, some of which were loaded," said United States Attorney Sally Quillian Yates. "He then passed the guns off to an accomplice who transported them as carry-on luggage to New York, where they were illegally sold."[210]

House Bill H.R. 3102

Congress released Bill H.R. 3102 in July 2015 and required the TSA to conduct an 'Employee Screening Study' of the cost of screening 100 percent of airport employees who enter the SIDA locations of airports. Mandates required the TSA to create a risk-based model for screening airport employees. The TSA conferred with the Aviation Security Advisory Committee (ASAC), comprised of a group of aviation industry experts to examine the gun and drug smuggling airport employee problem. These experts used a "risk-based approach" and gave 28 recommendations. ASAC expected their suggestions would "mitigate" or diminish airport employee criminal activity on the secured side of every airport ramp and terminal in America.

After reviewing the 28 ASAC recommendations, it seemed some were a rehash of existing airport security protocols to one extent or another. ASAC final course of action was to implement random employee screening. They chose this direction as the "cost-effective solution." ASAC said; "100 percent screening of airport employees does not appreciably increase the overall system-wide protection."

Congress reviewed the TSA findings and considered the factors that may enhance airport employee screening and security by:

* Ensure those airport employees with access to SIDA areas are authorized.

* Ensure airport employees whose credentials are withdrawn and are immediately denied access to SIDA area.
* Differentiate who has access to SIDA areas and people who have access to a 'particular' area of an airport.
* How often employees are 'require' to use SIDA access points at airports.
* Can airports reduce the number of employee SIDA access points?
* Can the TSA in conjunction with airports create an employee randomization screening plan that will fit all airports?

The National Association of Airline Passengers

ASAC held their annual public meeting in late November 2015 and attached the National Association of Airline Passengers (NAAP) rebuttal to their ASAC recommendations on airport employees screening. NAAP is a non-profit association formed in 2010 to protect the rights of airline passengers, crew, and airport personnel. The NAAP started their rebuttal of the ASAC with this admonishment.

> "We have reviewed the FINAL REPORT OF THE AVIATION SECURITY ADVISORY COMMITTEE'S WORKING GROUP ON AIRPORT ACCESS CONTROL. We believe it is our duty to take issue with this report, to call to your attention its deficiencies,...."[211]

The NAAP opposed and chastised the ASAC recommendation for random airport employee screening with a thesis fact filled argument supporting their recommendations. The NAAP gave the following in their subsection titled "Problems and Shortcomings of the Working Group's Report."

* The report did not recognize TSA's specific statutory duty to require "screening or inspection of all individuals."

- The current proposals would not have stopped past incidents of airport employee smuggling.
- Airport employees and their bags will be allowed to continue into the SIDA areas of airports unscreened.
- TSA's workforce criminal activity is ignored.
- Lack of airport supervision and management was not addressed.

The NAAP concluded, "less than 100% screening of airport and security employees invites and encourages abuse by those who would not ordinarily be tempted." The NAAP went on to declare any security vulnerability can be exploited, improved background checks and random screening will not guarantee trustworthiness and integrity of employees, a secure environment will only be maintained by uniform standards that govern employee entrances into the SIDA of every airport.

If mandatory screening for every airport employee is not implemented, I stand firm in my belief that the TSA and the ASAC will fail to protect us from one of the most serious threats to our nations' airports, the insider threat.

> "What good is all the screening at the front door if we are not paying attention enough at the backdoor? The answer is common sense."

> Representative John Katko, Chairman of a
> House Homeland Security subcommittee[212]

Airport employees cannot be surprised or caught off guard by a wandering group of blue shirt badged TSA officers who randomly sat at a table near an employee entry portal to screen airport employees as they walk in. Airport employees are adept at texting and cell phoning each other in real time when they see anything out of the norm in their work area. Any illegal gun smuggling airport employee with a minimum level of intelligence will pre-plan using operatives on both sides of the employee door giving an 'all clear' or a 'do not enter' message when it's time to load the next stash of guns or drugs on the designated flight. It will not matter to the employee if he or she has to wait for the same flight to depart on the next day at the same time to the same destination. Charles Slepian, the founder of the Foreseeable Risk Analysis Center, sums up the problem succinctly:

> "It is simply reckless security practice to allow some 900,000 workers at America's commercial airports to come into the workplace without going through the same physical screening process those passengers and flight crews go through each time they seek access to the security part of the airport. I have heard all of the arguments about "trusted worker" programs, background checks, inconvenience, and slowing down the process, and I remain unconvinced that we cannot procedurally secure aircraft, baggage, and cargo from exposure to the risk of ramp-side terrorism. I know what every airport worker in America knows: Our airliners are more vulnerable to explosives from the air side than the passenger side, and until we correct that, aviation security remains a `crap shoot."[213]

FAA Extension, Safety, and Security Act of 2016

The Congress passed the FAA Extension, Safety, and Security Act in July 2016 and ordered an increase in "red-team" covert testing of employee entrances and other secure areas of our airports. Further, Congress directed the TSA to review airports that have implemented enhanced airport employee access points screening to include vehicles in the Secured Identification Display Area (SIDA) of airports.

The Act takes the ASAC recommendation to conduct random enhanced and "unpredictable" physical inspections of airport workers who work in the SIDA by verifying credentials, checking them for prohibited items and verifying they are following procedures at the employee SIDA portals. Congress directed a development of performance metrics. These metrics consist of percentages of employees adhering to protocols of airport access points, use of credentials, employees who work outside and inside the secured areas, their access requirements, and the differences in the secured access points types and requirements. Congress requires the TSA to submit the findings by July 2017.

HOUSE HOMELAND SECURITY COMMITTEE MAJORITY STAFF 'AMERICA'S AIRPORTS: THE THREAT FROM WITHIN' 2017

The February 2017 House Homeland Security Committee report found the "much more needs to be done to improve the state of access controls and mitigate the insider threat facing America's aviation sector." 900,000 airport employees and contractors bypass physical screening requirements and are an increasing concern for possible insider threats.

The report stated a vast majority of the nation's airports do not have employee screening at the security access doors leading to the airport ramp side and most vulnerable areas of the airport. As of November 2016, only three airports in the nation required 100% physical screening of all airport employees who worked at their airports. The insider threats were listed in great detail and recommendations were offered.

H.R. BILL 876

The 115th Congress in April 2017 referred 'AN ACT' to the Committee on Commerce, Science and Transportation titled the "Aviation Employee Screening and Security Enhancement Act of 2017." This bill authorized a cost study if all employee access points from non-secured areas to secured areas of airports were to have the following:

- A secured door utilizing card and pin entry or biometric technology
- Surveillance video recording, capable of storing video data for at least 30 days
- Advance screening technologies, including at least one of the following
  - Magnetometer (walkthrough or hand held)

o   Explosive detection canines
o   Advance imaging technology
o   X-ray bag screening technology

The ACT required proactive effort by requiring that each airport employee must submit a social security number to Homeland Security for proper vetting. They also required a continuous vetting of all credentialed aviation workers through the FBI "Rap Back' program that requires a fingerprint-based criminal record history checks.

One critical requirement that the ACT placed into motion was the establishment of a national database of individuals who have had either their airport or airport operator-issued badge revoked for failure to comply with aviation security requirements.

The weakness of the ACT is the delay in mandatory 100% employee screening. During the lengthy study that may go as long as 2022, the ACT implemented covert testing and inspections and 'recommended' assistance for air carriers, foreign air carriers, and airport operators to conduct their own employee inspections as needed.

In August 2017, the TSA placed a 'Request For Information' (RFI) to the public sector and asked for input on developing an airport employee screening system. The RFI stated; "develop an employee access security model using intelligence, scientific algorithms, and risk-based factors. The goal of the model is to give aviation employees working in the secured areas of airports the expectation that they may be subject to security screening/inspection at any time while working at an airport." The TSA continues to go in the wrong direction, as only 100% screening will be adequate to safeguard our airports from the employee insider threat.

RECOMMENDATIONS:

Assistant Director of Public Safety and Security of Miami-Dade International Airport Lauren Stover oversees the 100 percent screening of all airport employees with her team of security and police personnel. At Miami-Dade International Airport, 35,000 employees access the high-security side of the airport through four screening portals. Additionally, there are seven access gates to the airfield where vehicles are inspected before entry. In 2014, through their efforts, the airport confiscated 209 employee ID badges for violations of security protocols and restricted them from the secure side the airport until they received retraining on the security procedures. Stover cited a large drug smuggling operation in the 1990's at the Miami-Dade airport as the chief reason for implementing 100 percent employee screening. But more importantly, Stover said the insider threat is a grave concern for her, and she is working on new programs to eliminate this potential problem at her airport.[214] In July 2017, Stover completed a six-month pilot test using advanced X-ray equipment and trace explosives detection at one of its employees screening checkpoints. Stover and Miami-Dade International Airport have set a standard of security far above other U.S. Airports.

> "We have intercepted guns, drugs, large sums of money…..It's really not that costly when you compare the costs versus the consequences of not having a program [100 percent employee screening] like this.
>
> LAUREN STOVER, DIRECTOR OF PUBLIC SAFETY AND SECURITY MIAMI-DADE INTERNATIONAL AIRPORT[215]

An airport's security infrastructure can be hardened to prevent and deter potential criminal and terrorist threats from its employees who work daily in the secured and non-secured sides of its infrastructure.

I recommend mandatory airport employee egress and ingress screening; airside pedestrian portals and vehicles:

1. Implement 100 percent screening of all airport personnel. All employees who come into and depart through the secure side of the airport are screened each way. This airport employee entry

and exit screening process enhance airport's homeland security. Weapons, drugs and many forms of contraband will be eliminated from entering the secure side of the airport, smuggled aboard airliners or into the airports' surrounding communities from arriving airline flights. Employees who carry with them a personal use amount of drugs to consume on the secured side of the airport will be more apprehensive of being detected. Additionally, transporting contraband for street gangs or cartels will be curtailed from this point of entry and exit. Airport employee thieves who steal or pilfer airport, airline and passenger luggage will have second thoughts when they walk out with their backpacks containing stolen items, drugs or cartel cash and are required to open them up to the TSA, law enforcement officer or security exit lane guard screener. This screening is possible through the creation of employee-only screening portals, with the number of these portals commensurate with the size of the airport's terminal and security areas. Miami-Dade International Airport logs all electronics that their airport employees bring in and out of the secured areas. This procedure significantly reduces the transportation of stolen goods out of the airport by criminal airport employees and should be replicated at all U.S. Airports.

2. Airports' screening of all inbound vehicles should be a protocol (including airport vehicles and ramp carts) when they come into the area of operations (AOA) gates. Reverse screening of outgoing tugs and vehicles should be mandatory.

3. Fence line over/under preventative measures: Every airport must prevent airport employee who smuggles unscreened luggage over, through or under the airfield fence to a waiting accomplice. Although a severe security weakness, it can be overcome by an increase in effective airport police officer operation planning and procedures that encompass video surveillance, fence alarms, clearing vegetation from perimeter fence lines, and dedicated airfield police officers patrols.

"All a terrorist needs to do to penetrate security is to get an ID. The absurdities and flaws in airport security *must* be exposed in order to improve them, and, as is painfully obvious to anyone who covers aviation security, the current system isn't working. It's harming tourism and air travel, leaving passengers with a false sense of security, and paving the way for an inevitable re-run of 9/11."

Ron Wilson, former San Francisco Airport employee.[216]

CHAPTER 9

The Perimeter: Our Airports' Greatest Weakness

———

"What I've learned since taking on this fight in Congress
is even more alarming. In the last decade, there have been
over 1300 known breaches to our airports' perimeter
security throughout the country. In September 2011, the
Homeland Security Committee heard testimony from Mr.
Lee Hamilton, the former vice chair of the 9/11 Commission
and current member of the President's Homeland Security
Advisory Council, as well as former Secretary of Homeland
Security, Governor Thomas Ridge. They both cited
perimeter security as an overlooked yet incredibly important
security issue that continues to exist—long after the 9/11
attacks—at airports throughout the United States."[217]

US Representative William R. Keating

On April 9, 2015, the Associated Press (AP) reporters Martha Mendoza
and Justin Pritchard detailed a story on perimeter breaches at U.S.
Airports.[218] All I could think about was why did the press wait so long
before they reported the obvious problems that our airports' perimeter
security have suffered over the past four decades. The AP stated they
found 268 perimeter breaches since 2004 at a large number of airports in

America. The AP and the rest of the news media do not know the exact extent of this problem on a national scale. If we were to use the known number of airfield perimeter breaches that occurred at my small commercial airport since 2004 and multiply them by the 450 airports that the TSA protects, you would have an astounding 3,150 airport breaches since 2004. This equates to 286 airport perimeter breaches a year in the United States during the last eleven years. Theoretical you say? Based on my knowledge of airport fence line breaches, research during and after serving as a watch commander at a commercial airport, and the wide-ranging media news stories that repeat themselves almost weekly, I firmly believe the right numbers are higher than my hypothetical number.

I finished this particular subject matter chapter a few years before the completion of the final manuscript. As I completed the various other chapters, I found myself revisiting this subject monthly to update it with airport perimeter breaches reported in the news. I derived the following from my experiences, studies, and networking with other airports in a quest to understand the extent of the problem of airport perimeter incursions and use this knowledge in an attempt to safeguard my airport from the perimeter breaches plaguing our nation's airports.

My First Efforts to Understand the Extent of the Problem

I interviewed the Sky Harbor International Airport Phoenix police about an incident at their airport. I found they had serious concerns about their airport security and were working diligently with their airport administration to correct the problems they faced. The police told me the airport administration had tentatively approved measures to strengthen their perimeter fences. Concern increased when a vehicle drove through the fence of the Phoenix Sky Harbor Airport in an attempt to get away from their SWAT team. The SWAT team was seconds away from stopping him as he sat with his vehicle's engine running in the fire department's parking lot next to the airport runway fence. The suspect had been the object of a long city street pursuit by city police units that culminated at the perimeter of the Sky Harbor International Airport. The suspect paused and then drove his truck through the fence at approximately 20 miles per hour. Even at this relatively slow speed, the fence put up no more resistance than a row of toothpicks. The suspect then proceeded onto the runway, passing under the wings of a moving passenger aircraft to evade the pursuing police. The vehicle was trapped by a third chain link fence while attempting to exit the airport.[219]

Truck fleeing police approaches SkyHarbor fence,
Permission by; ABC 15 News, June 30, 2005

Another example of an airport perimeter failure occurred at Southwest Florida International Airport when 34-year-old Jack Brems fled from his home after a Lee County Sheriff's deputy arrived in response to a disturbance call at the home. Brems arrived at the airport

Truck breaches SkyHarbor fence, fleeing police,
Permission by; ABC 15 News, June 30, 2005

Truck drives under passenger jets wings, Permission
by; Phoenix ABC 15 News, June 30, 2005

and drove his car crashing into and through a security access gate to the airfield and down the runway. Brems forced a Southwest Airlines pilot to take off suddenly to avoid hitting Brems' car. Brems said he realized he was playing chicken with a 737-passenger jet when the plane on the runway was heading toward him, and he moved out of the way with 20 yards to spare.[220]

Brems drove at estimated speeds up to 130 mph under the wing of a taxiing USA 3000 flight that was preparing to depart.[221] Airport spokesperson Susan Sanders said that at 7:40 p.m., airport communications cameras spotted someone driving down a runway. Transportation Security Spokesman Christopher White said the airport's electronic access control alarm alerted authorities when Brems was on the runway. According to Sanders, the dispatchers alerted the airport police who chased Brems for 15 minutes on the airfield and arrested him when he crashed into a pond.[222] The spokesperson for Southwest Florida International Airport felt its security perimeter was adequate, and enough safeguards were in place to protect the airport.

These perimeter breach reports, along with the results of my extensive investigation of America's airports' perimeter security failures, gave me concern. The Phoenix Police Department told me Dallas/Ft. Worth Airport was strengthening their perimeter, and it serves as a role model of methods to improve airports' perimeter security. I arranged a tour through the Dallas/Ft. Worth Airport Police and flew to Dallas and visited the large international airport. I was impressed with their efforts to provide great perimeter security for their airfield that hosts 27 million passengers each year. Dallas/Ft. Worth is a perimeter security model to emulate.

I applaud Phoenix Sky Harbor International for their proactive efforts to initiate improvements and safeguard the 19 million people who annually fly from their airport.[223] Unfortunately, their perimeter security improvement efforts were under construction when ABC 15 News reported on April 2010 that a man jumped over the perimeter fence and stole a U.S. Airlines vehicle and drove across several active runways before the police captured him. And yet the airport security fence was tested a third time during Sky Harbor International Airport perimeter improvement. According to Phoenix Police Sgt. Trent Crump, a woman, breached a secure area at 10:00 p.m. by ramming her 1997 Saturn into the north/east gates and gained access to the active runway.[224]

Incidents demonstrating the weakness of our airport perimeter security are routine news stories. Reported by CNN, on Christmas day 2013, "A man climbed an eight-foot and then a ten-foot fence at Newark Airport. The suspect ran across two runways to Newark's Terminal C without anyone seeing him. An airport employee captured the suspect and held him until the airport police arrived. Two thousand miles away on the same Christmas day, a man climbed the airport perimeter fence at Sky Harbor International Airport and ran onto the runway and taxi-way. The suspect ran up to a Southwest Airlines jet and pounded on the jet engine with his hands until the airport police drove up and arrested him."[225]

As history has proven time and time again, terrorist planning and attack methods evolve. The many extremist organizations that conduct terrorist operations are intelligent and are good at intelligence gathering. Terrorist groups see these news accounts of U.S. airport perimeter fence breaches. Their intelligence operatives compile this type of information into their data files, which they may use to analyze, plot and implement the next 9/11 in the United States.

Will your perimeter fence protect you from a terrorist or drunk driver while sitting on a passenger jet on a congested airfield? Photo by W. Herrin

AN AIRPORT'S FIRST LINE OF DEFENSE

"The House of Representatives Committee on Homeland Security believes that state of access controls at domestic airports is in need of direct and thorough scrutiny in order to mitigate perimeter breaches and insider threats to aviation security." July 1, 2016[226]

The first line of defense at any airport is the perimeter boundary. When you are sitting in your departing aircraft with your family, and you look out to see the airport runway fence perimeter, you probably feel a sense of security. You are on a runway guarded by patrolling law enforcement officers, and security camera monitored restricted-access airport property. You probably get a similar feeling when you lock your front gate to your property, or lock the deadbolt on your front door, or arm your security system.

At airports in America, that sense of security is utterly false. Today's designed perimeter protections at most airports do not protect the airport from a criminal trespasser or terrorist with destructive intent. In most cases, the poorly maintained fencing is the greatest security weakness in American airports today. An unprotected perimeter means vulnerable people, aircraft, fuel tanks, and other critical airport assets to include the terminal itself. Proactive measures must occur to harden the airport's first line of defense, and not just the terminal entrance and screening lanes. Without comprehensive full-perimeter security in place, our airports are in harm's way.

July 1, 2016, House Bill H.R. 5720, directed the TSA to conduct a system-wide assessment of airport access control points and airport perimeter security. The goal of this bill is to collect system-wide data for access controls and perimeter trends that will assist aviation security to make "better-informed risk management decisions." This information will be used by the TSA to update the existing 2012 National Strategy for Airport Perimeter and Access Control Security. This effort is long overdue, but unfortunately, will still take years to implement in ways that will improve our nation's airports perimeter security now rather than later.

The Government Accountability Office (GAO) studies and conducts analysis on aviation security and compiles reports to the government. In these reports, the GAO defines airport perimeters as the fence surrounding an airport, including access gates and access controls that prevent unauthorized access to restricted areas.[227] I think the operative word in this description is "prevent."

Many of American airports fence perimeters are inadequate
and in a state of disrepair or poor maintenance
Photo by Nathan Worden

Airport administrators have to look at the facts and place their airport perimeter security priorities above the other expansion improvements to their airports. A leading global consulting, engineering and construction firm, CDM Smith, produced their 2013 Economic Report that detailed and encouraged new airport expansions that will accommodate the forecast growth in passengers and cargo transportation. But we cannot continue to put the cart in front of the horse in regards to our airports' perimeter security needs and place it secondary to other airport improvements. It will be difficult to convince the nation's airport administrators to slow down on capital improvement and put the perimeter security first. These executives know the forecast of passenger travel will grow from 713 million to more than one billion passengers in 15 years. They also know they need over $71.3 billion to improve or build new terminals, runways and other infrastructures by 2017 alone.[228]

PALM SPRINGS INTERNATIONAL AIRPORT BREACH

The Palm Springs International Airport perimeter breach serves as yet another example of airports not addressing their perimeter security until an incident happens. The Palm Springs Airport was on the news when I saw the video of a drug-crazed, mentally-ill ex-convict who drove his truck through the chain link gate early one morning and stopped on the runway in front of a taxiing passenger jet.[229] I went to Palm Springs and spent the day with the airport police re-enacting the sequence of events. The police gave me an account of the suspect's actions as we drove around the Airport. The officer told me the suspect drove his truck through a locked airfield chain link gate, knocking it down and then drove onto the airfield. He turned in front of a taxiing smaller regional passenger jet and stopped his truck blocking the path of the airliner. A maintenance crew was piloting the jet and conducting a test of the aircraft's jet engines by taxiing the plane down the runway. The suspect exited his truck, ran to the jet's door, and pulled on the door lever, yelling, "Take me to Mexico!" The mechanics inside held the door shut as the suspect pulled so hard he broke the handle off the door. Luckily, there were no passengers on board.

When his crude hijacking attempt failed, the suspect returned to his truck and drove across several runways to a private jet center, where police confronted him. During a standoff, the suspect said he was going to shoot the police officer. Without warning, the suspect drove off as police officers opened fire on him. The Palm Springs police showed me an airline company sign with the bullet holes.

The police told me the suspect raced across the runway to the airport's perimeter chain-link fence and for the second time, drove through it with alarming ease and exited the airport. After a lengthy street pursuit, the police cornered and shot the suspect in downtown Palm Springs in a densely populated area. The felon survived and received 15 years in a state prison. His actions placed many officers and civilians in jeopardy but imagine how much mayhem this man could have caused if his actions had taken place during a busy time of takeoffs and landings. You can view the entire news video showing the actual shootout on the airport at http://www.spike.com/video-clips/mjwvs9/palm-springs-psycho-palm-springs-psycho-standoff.[230]

The Palm Springs Airport spokesman in response to the news media inquiries said, "You can't address everything and anything that might happen."[231] Seven years later, Palm Springs Airport started strengthening its perimeter fence. In the City Council Staff Report issued on July 6, 2011, the city manager, David H. Ready stated:

"The airport security project is specifically designed to improve the condition of the airport's perimeter fence, a primary component of the airport's overall security program, by replacing several thousand feet of old and worn fence line with new product... Some lengths of the existing fence do not meet adequate height requirements as outlined in the *TSA Publication Recommended Security Guidelines for Airport Planning, Design, and Construction*.... Federal Regulation CFR 1542 requires the airport operator to maintain a security program that will prevent criminal acts against civil aviation.... Moreover, keeping the airfield, taxiways and runways clear of unauthorized people and wildlife is one of the highest safety concerns at any airport given the potential catastrophic effect on life and property of an aircraft strike."[232]

I conducted an analysis to determine if weak perimeter fencing is common among with all airports. In addition to inspecting Dallas Ft. Worth and Palm Springs Airport tours, I toured with the airport police agencies for the San Jose, San Diego, Burbank, and Long Beach airports. I examined their perimeter infrastructure and studied the law enforcement agencies that patrol their airport's perimeter to obtain the most accurate data on airport perimeter security. I reviewed the individual airport's policies and procedures, as well as their airfield perimeter. I additionally studied many photographs of airport perimeter security throughout our nation's airports. Aiding my research was the Google Earth aerial maps and half a dozen internet social or photo-sharing websites where photography hobbyists post intimate behind-the-scenes photos of airports fence lines, gates, and other security features.

An accurate examination of our airport's perimeter fencing and its security required me to review the Federal Aviation Agency and the TSA guidelines and protocols. The current set of "guidelines" released for the nation's airports is the 2011 "Recommended Security Guidelines for Airport Planning, Design, and Construction." This Federal publication begins with a disclaimer by TSA who states:

"The U.S. Government assumes no liability for the contents or use. This document does not create regulatory requirements or mandates of any kind. There are recommendations and guidelines that might be considered highly beneficial in one airport environment while being virtually impossible to implement at another airport. The purpose of the document is to provide as extensive a list of options, alternatives, ideas, and suggestions as possible for the airport architect, designer, planner and engineer to choose from when first considering security requirements in the early planning and design of new or renovated airport facilities."[233]

The FAA and TSA Rules

An extensive review of the FAA written guidelines for airport perimeter fencing reveals their minimum standards are not adequate to ensure our nation's airport perimeter security needs in a post 9/11 world. The FAA failures to mandate strong airport perimeter security is evidenced by hundreds of reported airport perimeter breaches that have occurred since 9/11.

The following excerpt from the FAA website shows how dangerously behind the times the FAA is when it comes to securing the safety of our airports. The FAA following directive seems to prioritize wildlife as the top concern and Homeland Security secondary. While it is essential for the safety of aircraft operations to keep wildlife off airport property, the fact is in our post 9/11 world, a terrorist poses a significantly greater threat than a deer or stray dog. But the disturbing fact of the matter is this: many of our nation's airports' perimeter fences are not built to these wildlife prevention standards. If it were capable of preventing wildlife from accessing the airfield, significantly better security would be the result, rather than the current eight-foot chain link fence with three strands of barbed wire airport requirement. The wildlife hazard assessment type/height of the fence and structure is written in the FAA recommendations;

> "Generally, it recommends a 10-foot chain link fence topped with 3 strands of barbed wire, and a 4-foot skirt attached to the bottom of the fence. The fence skirt should be buried at a 45-degree angle on the outside of the fence at least two feet into the ground to prevent animals from digging under the fence and to reduce the chance of washout. This fencing configuration is the most effective for keeping deer and other wildlife off an airport; it also greatly increases airport security."[234]

The FAA and TSA declare that the wildlife fence significantly increases airport security. Why doesn't the government meet both types of security objectives with one set of regulations for airport perimeter fencing?

Shouldn't all fence assessments be based on the "manmade" threats? If TSA provides best practices for wildlife threats, why not provide best practices for the human threats as well?

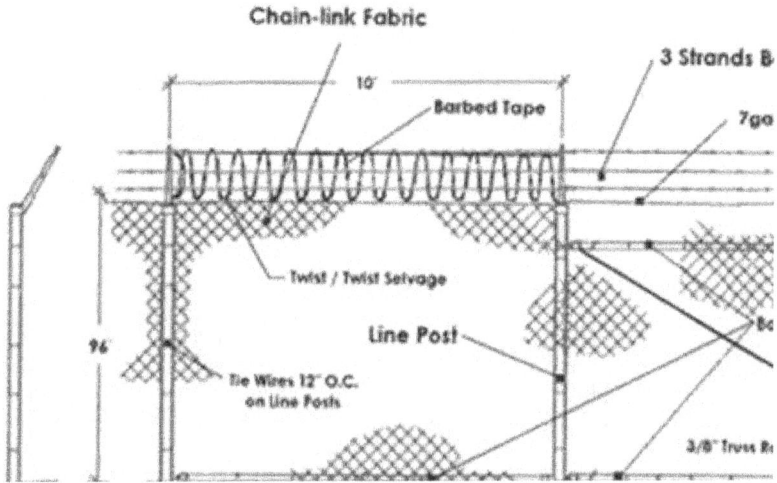

TSA Recommended Airport Chain Link Fence
(Source: www.tsa.gov/airport_security)

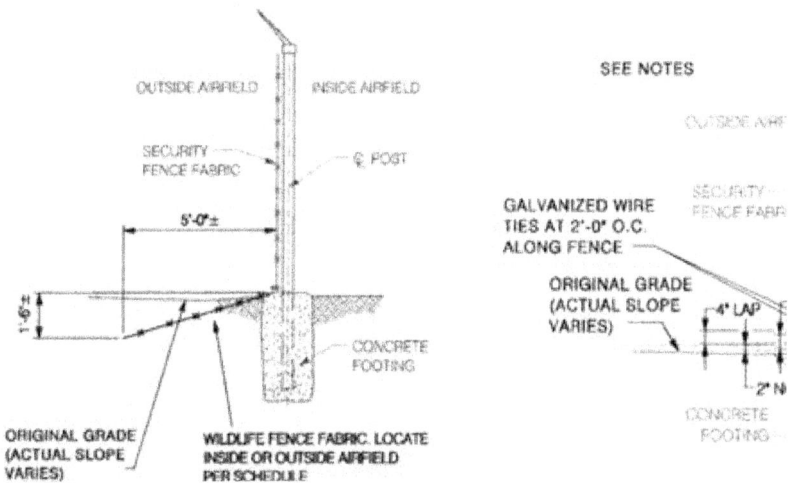

TSA Recommended Airport Wildlife Fence
(Source: www.tsa.gov/airport_security)

On page 24 of the above-referenced document, TSA recommends that chain link fencing is used to construct a perimeter fence because it is the most cost-effective method to deter unauthorized entry. Keep in mind; this suggestion does not make forced entry the primary objective in using chain link, it emphasizes that chain link is only a basic deterrence.[235]

A Poorly maintained commercial airport fence,
photo by permission of Audio Bob

TSA's aviation security standards are established through regulations and security directives. To create these regulations and directives, TSA often borrows from other regulatory federal agencies that govern an airport's operations. This legal foundation provides a comprehensive, national aviation security program that facilitates the creation of an individualized Airport Security Program (ASP) for every airport in the country. Each ASP is based on the unique characteristics of a particular airport, such as its location and size. Each airport integrates specific security elements within secured areas and the Airport Operations Area

(AOA). These factors include, but are not limited to, detection and pre-vention of illegal entries of subjects and vehicles and their movements.

Naturally, each airport must approach these concerns differently due to their particular physical location, as they comply with federal regula-tions. Some airports have recognized this problem and have addressed it by installing crash resistance gates, high strength wire mesh perimeter fences, and other barriers that go over and above the TSA requirements.

An American airport successfully strengthened its
perimeter fence, photo by W. Herrin

But most airports have not remedied the weak fence perimeters. These airports cite budgetary restraints to capital improvements and ongoing airport maintenance or improvements elsewhere as priorities over airport perimeter fence security strengthening. Former O'Hare Airport Security Chief and 30-year Chicago Police Veteran James Maurer called Chicago's O'Hare Airport the least secured in the nation. He summed up the airport administrators placing $15 billion in mod-ernization and expansion plan as a priority over the basic perimeter and other airport security components. According to Maurer statement, this airports prioritization could potentially allow terrorist opportunities that would have catastrophic consequences.[236]

Federal and state laws govern airport civilian administrators' actions and reactions. When a security breach takes place at an airport, civilian officials at other airports may have to respond to that event by making changes to or updating their security measures and procedures. Generally, civilian airport administrators, in my years of observation, do as much as is required of them by state and federal regulations regarding providing security—and no more. One must keep in mind how important it is to protect the people and aircraft on the airport runway during the busy ramp activity.

A busy U.S. international airport ramp, Photo and Permission by Mark Kwiatkowski

THE IMPORTANCE OF SECURITY ON THE AIR OPERATIONS SIDE OF AN AIRPORT

First and foremost, ramp security has to be one of the top priorities at any airport. The "ramp" is the hub of the airport, the place where virtually every single person passes through who has business at an airport. The ramp is a large concrete parking lot for passenger aircraft, where the aircraft is fueled, cleaned, and mechanically maintained. Luggage and cargo, flight crews, passengers, and security personnel move in and out of this location throughout the day. The principal protection of this vital area is the airport perimeter fencing. The following diagram contains the basic essential components of an airport security perimeter.

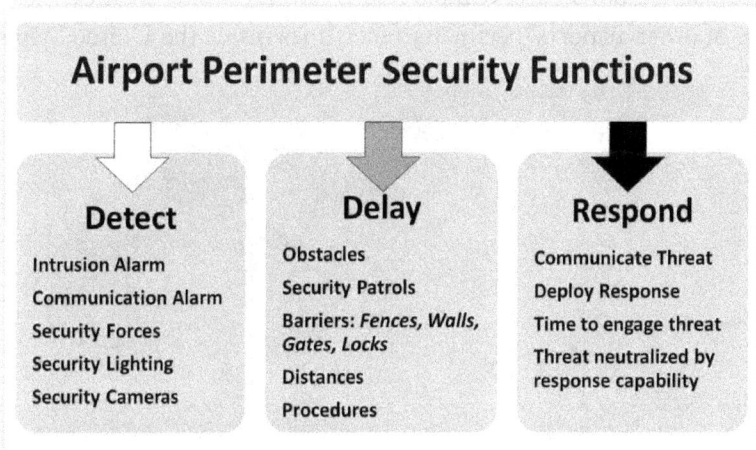

Airport Perimeter Security Functions

Detect
Intrusion Alarm
Communication Alarm
Security Forces
Security Lighting
Security Cameras

Delay
Obstacles
Security Patrols
Barriers: *Fences, Walls, Gates, Locks*
Distances
Procedures

Respond
Communicate Threat
Deploy Response
Time to engage threat
Threat neutralized by response capability

The components of an Airport Perimeter Security
System and its functions, source: W. Herrin

Law enforcement at every airport in the nation must contend with providing the proper level of security that will protect their airport. When airport security fails, and a fence line breach occurs, the airport police will evaluate the failure, assess a solution and ask the civilian airport administration to fund and implement perimeter fence strengthening to meet recent and future perimeter threats. The airport administration will weigh the cost of this security improvement request and consider the needs of the requested improvements over other priorities. Airport administrators at times, for reasons they deem necessary, will often make a risk-based decision to implement, forgo, or delay requested airport perimeter security improvements for other airport business priorities.

How and Why Airport Perimeter Fences Are Breached

If you assess your airport perimeter security, you will partly base your assessment on a comparison of other American airport perimeters with your airport perimeter. More than likely, you would also review the security incidents that breached the other airport perimeters. Then you would compare them with any incident that your airport perimeter has suffered. I will go out on a limb and surmise your airport perimeter fence assessment reveals your fence is comparable in strength and weakness to an average of other airports' perimeter fence lines inside the United States.

Dense vegetation on an airport's perimeter can
pose a security risk, Photo by W. Herrin

There are many components, which create a good airport perimeter security matrix. One important element is the ability of the perimeter security cameras and airport police to view their areas of patrol. A lack of visibility of an airport fence line due to trees and shrubbery is an important security problem, preventing both the police officer and the airport security cameras from doing an effective job of monitoring the airport perimeter. Even with the strongest fence in place, the fence security is degraded with a lack of visibility. The easiest way to prevent bad guys from committing a terrorist or criminal act is to have the opportunity to see and stop them before they can reach the fence or as they attempt to breach the fence line. TSA guidelines suggest removing vegetation and trees from the fence line, yet many airports do not heed that recommendation. In my law enforcement duties, I've given neighborhood watch presentations to homeowners. I told many citizens to trim the shrubbery around their home to prevent a hiding place for criminals who may want to break into their home undetected by neighbors or passersby. This simple crime prevention doctrine is even more applicable to our nation's airports in our post 9/11 world.

Objects next to an airport fence will aid a breach
of an airport, Photo by Nathan Worden

It is easy to drive a car through, climb the fence or cut a fence it with a pair of wire-cutters at most American airports. No grappling hooks, welding equipment, or armored tanks would be needed to breach the perimeter—just a little bit of upper body strength, a tool you probably have in your garage at home or an automobile powered by a four-cylinder engine.

On August 27, 2016, a man climbed over the Eppley International Airport fence in Omaha Nebraska and stole an airport truck. While passengers were boarding a Southwest jet, the man crashed the truck into the front wheels of the aircraft at a high rate of speed. The aircraft pilot and flight attendant were injured.[237]

Eppley Airport Perimeter Breach, Photograph & Permission by David Postier

In July 2014, at approximately 3:00 a.m., a person climbed the eight-foot tall fence of Houston Airport. From the fence, the person made it to a fuel tank truck fully loaded with jet fuel and drove it across the runway with the trucks lights out. The airport police found the truck but not the suspect. At the time of this news story, the police didn't even know if it was a man or woman. When asked, the airport's general manager said he said he didn't know anything about the airfield breach incident. The reporter offered the police reports to the general manager, and without saying anything, he drove away. The airport released a statement saying they are always evaluating their airport security and would be "moving forward, both inside the terminal and along the perimeter fence line." The news story speculated what a person could have done with the fuel truck, such as driving it into the path of a landing passenger jet or running it into the terminal and setting it on fire.[238] How much and what type of security improvements are needed for the air side of our nation's airports?

AIRPORTS MILITARY STYLE FORCE PROTECTION

One vital component of any airport security analysis is a review of force protection and how effective it is in supporting the airport infrastructure. Force protection is a military phrase that when applied to a commercial airport security, can be defined as measures to maintain freedom of airport activities, provide protection of the airport terminal, people, and supporting infrastructure it is designed to protect. Force protection essentially guards the airport people, infrastructure, and vital resources from asymmetrical attacks.[239]

In 2002, The Orange County, California Grand Jury reviewed the John Wayne Airport security operations where it specifically addressed its airport fence security after 9/11. Included in these recommendations, were military style force protection components. The Grand Jury made the following recommendations for immediate implementation:

1. Inspect the fence and have trees that are too close removed and ensure that there are no gaps between the fence and the ground.
2. Place K-rail (cement rail vehicle barriers similar to the ones that separate freeway lanes dividing opposing traffic) at locations conducive to penetration by ramming vehicles.
3. Close all private Fixed Based Operators (FBO) gates that may allow penetration of the airfield by ramming vehicles.
4. At gates that remain in use, place K-rail in a configuration that will ensure vehicles must proceed slowly (to the entrance gate of the airfield to prohibit gaining enough speed to ram through the entrance gate).

The following recommendations for long-term implementation were:

1. Study the feasibility of installing an alarm wire along the full length of the fence and a motion detection system at specific locations inside the perimeter fence.

2. Install a second perimeter fence (or replace as needed) to form a "clear zone" around the airfield.

3. Re-install existing perimeter fence (or replace as needed) on a low concrete base to prevent penetration by vehicle and erosion.

4. Install articulating, hydraulic type barriers at ACS (Access Control Systems) enabled gates.

The Grand Jury recommendations are sound judgments and if implemented would strengthen this airports' perimeter security force protection from terrorist threats. What did the airport do to with these recommendations?

QUESTIONING AND DEBATING SECURITY PARTNERS ON AIRPORT FENCE PERIMETERS

As an airport law enforcement official, you must ask the tough questions and seek the realistic solutions to security problems our airports face. Sometimes law enforcement will not agree with the answer from the airport administrators. Our nation's airport law enforcement agencies must push to obtain the security needs regardless of the opposing view and obtain their security goal or at a minimum, a satisfactory compromise with the civilian administrators.

At an airport in America, an airport police watch commander asked an airport administrator a hard-hitting question: "What if an airport perimeter fence breach incident occurred, like the Palm Springs and Sky Harbor International airports, and someone was hurt because we failed to strengthen the perimeter?" The airport administrator said insurance would cover the cost of the damage, injured or dead passengers. The watch commander was startled by the answer as he expected something on the line of a discussion of how an airport can mitigate the potential danger of a weak perimeter airfield fence as the given reply. This administrator's mindset may be more commonplace among out nation's airport managers than we think, where a risk versus cost mindset is predominant. For years, we have reacted to security incidents at airports. We are better than that. We must strive to break decades of reacting to airport security breaches and incorporate an anticipatory preventative mindset for our airport perimeter security needs.

In 1945, Professor George Vold of Northwestern University authored a prophetic paper describing post-war aviation and crime. Vold said new developments in aviation would make some crimes more profitable or convenient to carry on, such as illegal drug movement, human trafficking, organized crime, and subversive efforts to overthrow the existing form of government. But most breathtaking of all, Vold said the future of aviation could result in aircraft used as weapons of mass destruction with the deliberate spreading of infections or contagious diseases or "other acts that would jeopardize the safety and well-being of an entire people."[240] Our post 9/11 aviation industry world need visionaries like Vold and each airport law enforcement chief, and airport director must look inwardly and address the obvious potential security failures of their airport's infrastructure with vision and foresight. These aviation officials must eliminate the decades of aviation industry groupthink and envision what can occur on the perimeter of their airports and take measures to prevent them.

An American Airport proactive measure to strengthen its airport gates security, Source: Futurenet Security Solutions, a Future NetGroup Company: 'Grab' Retractable Airport Gate Barrier

An Airport Who Failed To Heed Warnings

In an American airport, the airport police presented a perimeter analysis report to the airport administration with recommendations to strengthen the airport perimeter. After the study had been submitted detailing different ways the airport fence could be breached by criminals, accidents or by a terrorist assault, the airport did not act upon the recommendations. Over the ensuing years, a series of security breaches occurred at that airport. Each one of these breaches in the report contained the details of the many ways this airport perimeter fence could suffer an incursion. The following chronological sequence of airport fence breaches took place at this airport after the submitted study was received by the airport administration:

1. A man climbed over the fence near the airport's four fuel tanks and ran across the runway, stopping a taxiing 737 passenger aircraft. The FAA tower received a radio call from an American Airlines pilot on a taxiway reporting a man was running from the fence line toward his passenger aircraft. The man ran in front of the airliner, then headed north on the taxiway and ran behind a Southwest airliner waiting for takeoff on the airport's main runway. A Continental Airlines pilot waiting on the taxiway observed the man being blown backward by the Southwest airliner's engine thrust. The man then ran south on the runway, where he stopped approximately 50 yards away from the Southwest airliner. An airport operations civilian employee coordinated with the tower to put out an "all stop" order and close the airport for air traffic. The airport police arrived, arrested the suspect in the middle of the runway, and transported him off the airfield.

2. A closed airfield perimeter gate was breached by a car that crashed into the fence, easily driving through the chain link barrier and onto the airfield. The gate was near a highway, and drivers leaving the nearby local nightclub, in a drunken stupor, would somehow mistake the shut gate as a highway entrance.

For a number of years, drunk drivers would ram their vehicles directly into the gate or through the chain-link fence next to the gate with alarming frequency. The airport tried water-filled barricades that also failed. Concrete jersey barriers seemed to solve the problem until a female drunk driver in a 2007 Toyota four-door sedan crashed through the gate by driving on the grass next to the concrete barriers, through the fence, and onto the roadway. The vehicle continued driving onto the airfield passing rows of parked general aviation airplanes. Approximately 15 minutes earlier, a private passenger jet took off from the runway where the drunk driver was crossing. The suspect drove across both runways and turned north toward the terminal ramp where over half a billion dollars' worth of passenger jet aircraft were parked and loaded with fuel for morning flights. The drunk driver drove past the ramp police officer, proceeding at a slow speed due to her damaged vehicle rear flat tires. The airport police officer ran from his guard station, alongside the driver and yelled for her to stop. The breach suspect continued driving at approximately 10 mph, approaching the commercial aircraft at the South aircraft parking ramp. The officer unholstered his gun and pointed it at the driver and yelled for her to stop again as he ran alongside the vehicle. The police arrested the driver after she stopped 50 yards from the parked passenger jetliners, in the middle of the taxiway.

3. On New Year's Eve, the third incident occurred at an American airport where a heavy coastal fog limited visibility to 100 feet. At approximately 2:00 a.m., a custodian cleaning the sterile side of the terminal saw a man walk out of the jetway from the ramp and into the secured side of the terminal where the custodian was preparing for the arrival of passengers. This closed sterile area of the terminal is off limits to non-screened people. The man was drunk and was found by the police and arrested for trespassing. The suspect told police he was walking home from

a bar and climbed the airport fence, not knowing that it was an airport with the fog shroud obscuring his view of where he was going. He walked across the airfield until he reached the terminal and started jiggling doors; eventually, he found one of the jetway ramp doors unlocked and entered the terminal. The police officer asked the suspect how much he had to drink, and he replied that he had been drinking all day and didn't know. The police officer administered a Breathalyzer test that showed a .138 blood alcohol content (BAC). To put this in context, that's between five and six highball drinks within one hour for a person weighing 150 pounds.

Airfield Jetway stairs, similar to one breached
by a trespasser, Photo W. Herrin

4. This same American airport suffered yet another breach of its perimeter security when an airport police officer saw a man walking on the airport property among the parked general aviation aircraft. When he walked closer, the officer became suspicious

and detained him. An investigation revealed that the man dug a hole under the fence with his hands and crawled under the fence onto the airfield. The man confessed he was taking a shortcut to the other side of the airport.

5. The 5th infringement of this airport perimeter fence occurred when an airport police officer discovered a breach of the chain-link perimeter fence occurred on the side of the airport near the fuel farm. It appeared an unknown suspect or suspects, concealed by the heavy brush on the fence line, used a cutting tool to create a hole large enough to climb through and enter the airfield. No suspect was seen or found.

6. A 56-year-old man driving under the influence of alcohol crashed through the airport perimeter chain-link fence and hit a parked aircraft so hard that it pushed it into another parked aircraft.

7. Airport Federal Aviation Administration Ground Control notified the airport police of a suspicious male climbing over the perimeter fence near the airport's general aviation area. Law enforcement personnel subsequently arrested the individual outside of the airport perimeter. The 22-year-old male claimed he did not know where he was or how he had arrived at the airport.

Seven perimeter fence line breaches occurred at this airport as media stories broadcast the weaknesses of other American airports' perimeters year after year. The problems are real and continuing as evidenced by the Florida International Airport gate fence breach by three men who easily jumped the airport fence and entered the secure runway area while being pursued by law enforcement.[241] Without stronger perimeter fence regulations, our airports will not provide consistent and effective security for our nation's airports.

An incident occurred at JFK Airport where a stranded man on a jet ski, scaled the eight-foot perimeter fence onto the airfield, walked across two other airfields and into the terminal. The summer before, a nude man swam onto the beach next to the JFK Airport fuel tanks.

The airport officials said he was very near the fuel farm containing millions of gallons of jet fuel. Another official said if he were a terrorist, he could have caused catastrophic damage and death to the airport.[242]

Last Thoughts on Airport Perimeter Security

A final illustration of the urgent need to secure our nation's airport perimeters occurred at the Philadelphia International Airport. Chief Inspector Joe Sullivan of the Philadelphia Police Department's Homeland Security and Counterterrorism Division said an intoxicated man drove his old Jeep Cherokee through the airport's fence. An FBI special agent's statement in a court affidavit stated: "As an airplane approached the airport in a final descent for landing, the driver suddenly crashed the airfield gate, heading toward the plane after accelerating to more than a 100 miles per hour."[243] As police were preparing to capture the suspect, the pilots of a US Airways flight were beginning their touchdown. They averted a collision with the drunk driver when they pulled up and circled.[244]

USA Today Travel Reporter, Jelisa Castrodale, was very blunt about the state of San Jose International Airport perimeter fencing when she said: "Did she pole vault over the worthless collection of chain links?" Castrodale sarcasm was due to the TSA refusing to provide video of 20-year old Deanna Predoehl scaling the airport fence and trespassing onto the airfield in April 2015. Castrodale said in her news reporting that San Jose International Airport, after five major perimeter fence breaches, has received a grant from the Federal Aviation Administration to heighten the airport fences to ten feet, add motion sensors and improve their surveillance camera systems. Will each airport in America have to suffer numerous perimeter breaches before they improve their fence line? Or will the airport managers across the country keep regurgitating the same defensive statement as San Jose Airport spokesperson Rosemary Barnes stated to KGO

Channel 7 News in reply to the airport fence breaches "Our fence line in all areas of airfield meets federal standards."[245] I feel Barnes statement should have said; 'Our airport's fence meets federal regulations that are inadequate for the safety of airports across the nation." -

We have to learn from history, and history has taught us hard lessons in airport passenger security. Protecting an airport's perimeter is essential to the wellbeing of the aviation industry. A flimsy chain-link fence is often all that stands between your security and a criminal or terrorist threat when you are on an airfield. Our nation's airports have interwoven wires on fences and gates that are so easily cut, climbed, dug under, or run through. At most airports in the United States only unarmed security guards, desk attendants and one or two mobile police patrols are all that keep your airport perimeter "safe." Hold that thought next time you're inside a passenger aircraft on the airport runway.

RECOMMENDATIONS:

1. Strengthen All Airports Perimeter Fencing:
   * Strengthen existing chain link fence to withstand a vehicle strike.
   * Install secondary vehicle intrusion prevention barrier.
   * Install razor wire instead of the standard three strands of barbed wire. Razor wire will dissuade or slow a suspect from climbing over.
   * Install intrusion alarm sensors on the perimeter fence to alert police to respond immediately to the incursion location.
   * Upgrade All Perimeter Gates: Install hydraulic or pop-up grab barriers for all perimeter vehicle gates (see Dallas/Ft. Worth Airport continuous efforts).
   * Place breach deterrent barriers at all closed perimeter gates such as removable bollards inserted into metal sleeves padlocked in the ground.

2. Remove all obstructions along perimeter to ensure visibility for law enforcement:
   * Remove vegetation, hedges, and trees that afford hiding places next to the airport perimeter fence line.
   * Partner with the community around the airport to remove existing items on the fence line that afford makeshift ladders that assist people climbing over airport fences.
3. Utilization of Current Security Technology:
   * Thermal sight outdoor sensors.
   * Video analytic camera systems that detect unauthorized movement.
   * Fiber optic intrusion detectors.
   * Ground radar supplemented by a visible light closed-circuit television camera and an infrared CCTV camera allowing visibility through multiple types of visibility conditions including smoke, rain, dust, fog, and low light conditions.
4. Observation tower placement, portable or permanent, along heavily-traveled industrial airport fence perimeter.
5. Staff Armed Mobile Airfield Guards whose numbers are consummate with airfield size.
   * Mobile airfield police should be trained in stopping a vehicle that breaches the airfield fence line with techniques such as "pitting/ramming" maneuvers.
   * Mobile airfield police should be equipped with high power military style rifles capable of penetrating a vehicle engine block.

CHAPTER 10

The Security Challenges of Fixed Base Operators and General Aviation

———————

"Drug smuggling aircraft and pilots walk
through, fixed-based operators every day. The
community should pay more attention." [246]

"This Joint Intelligence Bulletin is intended to provide federal,
state, local, tribal, and private sector partners with new insight
into the enduring interest of al-Qaida and violent extremists
in targeting general aviation, particularly small aircraft."

HOMELAND SECURITY/FBI JOINT INTELLIGENCE
BULLETIN, SEPTEMBER 2011

AS A NEW WATCH COMMANDER at my airport, I drove up to the private jet
center, located at the end of my airport's runway. I parked my police unit
on the ramp airside and walked into the terminal through sliding glass
doors. I looked around and noticed there were no security guards in the
lobby of the two-story private aviation business. I walked through the
lobby and out the front door to the landside public parking lot adjacent
to the main public road. I turned around, looked at the openness of the
private jet center, and felt our nation's private jet centers have been left
behind by the federal post 9/11 security plans.

At virtually every commercial airport in the country, there are private passenger jet centers called Fixed Base Operators (FBO). FBO aircraft operate on the same taxiways and runways as regular commercial passenger airlines. FBO employees, general aviation pilots, passengers, maintenance, and a host of service contract employees regularly access the FBO terminals that lead directly onto the commercial airport runways. Transient pilots from other states and even other countries fly into FBOs taxiways and terminal ramps. Flight schools and student pilots are regular customers at FBOs, where they fuel their general aviation aircraft, use rented parking, or store their aircraft in hangers.

There are more than 3,000 FBOs in the United States and 400,000 flight student and pilots whom frequent FBOs. These pilots use a broad range of aircraft such as the Bombardier, Gulfstream G450s, to the midsize and light passenger Lear and Citations model jets, as well as fix-wing propeller engine airplanes and helicopters.

Private aircraft operators, for the most part, are patriots who would do anything to safeguard the aviation industry, but not all are good guys. Jason Barbour of Manhattan Beach, California, received a sentence of 136 months in prison for transporting marijuana from Canada to cities throughout the United States by way of private general aviation aircraft. Barbour would buy cocaine in Los Angeles with the marijuana cash sales and then fly the drugs to drug dealers in Canada. How easy is it to transport drugs by private aircraft from airport to airport in America? Quite easy as there are no checks, no inspections or systems to track the hundreds of thousands of annual flights by private aircraft pilots.[247]

Gates Scott is Vice President of Aviation Aerospace and wrote an article on crime and general aviation. Scott estimated that the drug cartels use private aircraft to transport 65% of their cocaine traffic from South America to the United States. Scott went on to say the general and business aviation has a major hand in smuggling drugs into the U.S., by acquiring the aircraft and logistics to make the Cartel smuggling operations successful. Drugs can be smuggled into any airport in America by way of general aviation aircraft. If drugs can be smuggled into the U.S.

on this massive scale, can components to make suicide vest bombs, hand grenades and automatic weapons be smuggled just as easily?[248]

General aviation is a significant component of the aviation industry as approximately 200,000 general aviation aircraft amount to 77 percent of all air traffic in the United States. FBOs and general aviation account for over a million jobs that produce over $219 billion in economic outlay in America.[249]

The TSA provides the FBOs and general aviation, recommended security guidelines that offer suggestions to the owners of the FBO on how to implement security, but it holds the FBO and the commercial airport responsible for the security procedures under the airport security plan.

A busy airport Fix Base Operator adjacent to an airport's primary runway, Photo and permission by Brian Bartlet

AIRFIELD FBOs SECURITY BREACH INCIDENTS

Are our FBOs secured as best they can be? Are they a direct danger to the security of the commercial airport where they reside? I was driving with a San Jose Police officer as he gave me a tour of the San Jose International Airport. We stopped on the ramp near an FBO and watched a privately owned car drive up to an electronic gate that led onto the airfield. The driver entered using his airfield access card, and as the gate arm opened, the car drove onto the airport ramp. As the gate started to close, a motorcycle whizzed through the gate without swiping a card. I turned to the officer and said, "We call that piggybacking at my airport." He looked embarrassed and said he's calling an officer to cite the motorcycle rider. Our conversation immediately went to the obvious; what if the motorcycle was laden with explosives, like the motorcycle suicide bomber that killed two U.S. soldiers and ten Afghan students in Afghanistan. What would be the catastrophic effects if an explosive-rigged motorcycle drove through a gate by "piggybacking" and targeted a fueled and passenger-laden jet parked at the terminal?[250] We both knew the answer. No one could stop it in time if the motorcycle were the instrument of a terrorist plan. We also discussed the vulnerability of the FBO gate and inability of an FBO employee to visually check the identity of the driver of cars entering the airfield.

Years later, on November 23, 2014, at another FBO at Mineta San Jose International Airport, 39-year-old Miguel Zaragoza trespassed onto the FBO airfield taxiway and was spotted by an FBO employee. At first, Zaragoza cooperated with the employee but then ran away and commandeered a City of San Jose truck and drove it to the curb of the airport's terminal 'B' where the airport police arrested him.[251]

The vulnerability of an FBO at a commercial or general aviation airport in the United States is a unique security problem. TSA's "Security Guidelines for General Aviation Airport Operators and Users" publication A-002, September 11, 2013, state airports FBO's are self-regulated. FBOs can utilize security guards but are not required to and have the option to use the attendant behind an openly accessible counter to verify whom the person is and why they want to access the airfield. Anyone can walk into an FBO from the public landside without saying a word, sit down, and simply watch the business interaction between the attendants, pilots, and passenger. In time, an attendant offers a polite, "How can I help you?" if they're not too busy. There is little funding in Homeland Security budgets for general aviation. The funding that is allocated goes to Washington D.C. airports for the protection of the national capital.

One example of the problem encountered with the security at FBOs occurred at an airport in America. A watch commander went to his airport FBO terminal on several occasions concerning homeless or mentally ill people during his time at the airport. One frequent visitor was a homeless female transient who demanded to fly to Washington D.C. to see President Obama. In one incident, the homeless person had walked a few feet from the glass doors entrance onto the airfield where many parked and taxiing private passenger jets were on the ramp. On two occasions, a mentally-ill person walked out onto the airfield by "piggybacking" with other passengers and pilots. Airport police arrived to arrest the trespassing suspect as he was attempting to enter a private jet without authorization.

There are many different types of security concerns at our nation's FBO's. Jeffrey Goldberg wrote an article for *The Atlantic* titled, "Private Plane, Public Menace." Goldberg hitched a ride on a private eight-seat plane from New Jersey Teterboro Airport to Dulles Airport. Goldberg describes entering the FBO with his friend. Upon entering the FBO terminal, the friend merely gave a few numbers of an aircraft identification tail number to gain access to the airfield where they met the pilot of the plane whom they'd never met before and climbed aboard. Goldberg has been a critic of TSA for years, and the wheels were turning in his mind, as he was thinking of how a terrorist would hijack the aircraft he was flying in as a passenger. Goldberg asked his friend, "So let's say that I'm a terrorist pilot, and I have a bag filled with handguns, and I shoot these two pilots, and then I take control of the plane and steer it into the headquarters of the CIA. What's to stop me?" His friend replied, "There's nothing stopping you, all you need is money to charter or buy a plane."[252]

The FAA makes it very easy to find the full name and address of an airplane owner simply by typing the tail number in the FAA search engine. This is open source information and may aid an unauthorized entry onto an FBO airport ramp. FBO counter personnel become complacent over time or in a busy period in the terminal. This leads to a failure to check a person's identification and simply open the door for a person to walk onto a ramp as he sounds off with a tail number and name. An FBO employee must provide excellent customer service and often will bend the rules for customers who are the lifeblood of their business. This is a Homeland Security concern that all airport security stakeholders should question.

In Marvin Cetron's report, '55 Trends Now Shaping the Future of Terrorism,' Cetron describes a terrifying scenario of a four-seat general aviation Cessna 172 that flies out of an airfield in Massachusetts heading for the Boston Distrigas liquefied natural gas depot. His frightening description of the terrorist who packs the Cessna with explosives and crashes it into the gas tank depot has disturbing but realistic possible outcomes. Cetron estimated the terrorist flying the Cessna would kill 197,525 nearby citizens from the explosion of the tank field that calculations measure would have the force of 50 Hiroshima bombs.

In an incident reported by the *Dallas News*, a man named Rueben Martinez drove up to the FBO business jet center gate. Rueben as reported in the news story; "he pulled up to the gate in his 2007 Chevy Tahoe and started punching buttons on the gate-access pad. One employee opened the gate to talk to him." Rueben, seeing the gate was open, and he could drive onto the airfield, took off toward the airport at an estimated 100 miles per hour. Dallas police officers located him in an aircraft hangar and arrested him.[253]

I conducted a general aviation airfield access study at a sister commercial airport in my state. While driving on the airside with the airport police, I became acutely aware of the lack of security for the airfield area of operation and their FBO terminals. At one FBO, a pilot or person who wishes to access the airfield drives up to a gate swipes an electronic card and enters the airfield unmonitored. If the individual doesn't have a card, he communicates with the attendant by an intercom, provides a name that is on the authorization list, and the gate is opened remotely from the FBO terminal for him to enter. Are these types of procedures 'Best Practices' for an airport FBO after 9/11?

The Congressional Research Service study titled, "Securing General Aviation" by Bart Elias states the U.S. general aviation industry poses serious concerns. The report said a terrorist could exploit general aviation by using the general aviation aircraft to attack critical infrastructure or high-profile targets such as corporate business executives and CEOs. This study reminded the reader and Congress that the 9/11 terrorists learned how to fly general aviation airplanes at flight schools in the United States before carrying out their attacks.

JEREMY ROGALSKI INVESTIGATION

Jeremy Rogalski is an Investigative Reporter for KHOU-TV in Texas. His exhaustive investigation of the accessibility of general aviation aircraft at airports in the Harris County City of Houston Texas resulted in his testifying in front of Congress. At The House Hearing titled: General Aviation Security: Assessing Risks and the Road Ahead, Rogalski revealed some problems he found with our general aviation airports.

Rogalski testified he was able to walk through unlocked doors and entered unlocked executive jets parked near commercial airlines. Rogalski cited access controls at locked gates as failures when he simply drove up and told an unseen attendant that he needed to get to his airplane on the gates remote intercom. With no questions asked of who he was, the out of sight attendant electronically opened the gate. At the Long Star Executive Airport, Rogalski drove onto the fenceless airport and parked next to a passenger jet with opened doors with no one around. No one on the airfield questioned them or seemed concern.

Rogalski made a point in 2007 when Daniel Wolcott, with four friends, snuck into a GA airport and took a ten passenger Cessna Citation on a 350-mile joy ride. Wolcott piloted the aircraft from St. Augustine/

St. Johns County Airport in Florida and landed at Gwinnett County Airport in Georgia. No one noticed the aircraft was missing from St. Johns for a few days. The plane was on Gwinnett County airfield for 24 hours before it was determined suspicious by airport employees.[254]

Rogalski cited many other GA aircraft and airport security failures with an emphasis on the GA aircraft being used as a weapon for terrorists in the Houston area "target rich environment." He cited the Port of Houston container ships carrying everything from fuel, Chlorine Tankers, and other toxic chemicals. Rogalski said a government study revealed 17,000 people would die in a GA aircraft strike on a chemical ship or nearby chemical plant. Pulling out the trump card, Rogalski gave Congress reports by the leading national expert concerning chemical tankards destruction scenarios, Dr. Jay P. Boris of the Naval Research Laboratory. Boris assessment of the outcome of one such attack would be "far worse than 9/11."[255]

ROGALSKI, U.S. GOVERNMENT ACCOUNTABILITY OFFICE, AND THE JAPANESE ZERO

On July 15, 2009, Assistant Inspector General for Inspections U.S. Department of Homeland Security, Carlton Mann, rebutted Rogalski investigative findings at the U.S. House of Representatives Subcommittee meeting. Mann said the GAO and the Congressional Research Service were consistent with his views of GA aircraft being used as a terrorist weapon. Mann said the lack of fuel capacity, small size and minimal destructive power of "most" GA aircraft make them unattractive to terrorists. Mann said "aircraft in flight are highly visible by large audiences, and most airspace, particularly airspace near major metropolitan areas is well monitored by civil and military authorities. Mann said the terrorist would probably use large truck bombs to accomplish any terror acts instead of GA aircraft.

Mann beliefs are in great error. The airplane used in prolific massive suicide attacks, the World War II-era Mitsubishi A6M Zero fighter plane, is comparable to many of our current GA aircraft in the United States. Many other GA aircraft that could be used by terrorists are larger and faster than the Zero. The Zero had a maximum takeoff weight of 5000 pounds and was armed with four 130-pound bombs or a single 530-pound bomb, plus extra fuel tanks to increase the damage.[256]

A small fiberglass boat loaded with an estimated 400 to 700 pounds of explosives motored up to the U.S.S. Cole anchored in Yemen. The two boat occupants stood up, saluted, and then detonated the bomb that killed 17 sailors and caused this massive hole in the side of an armored warship.

Today, the single-engine Mooney Acclaim SM20TN can fly at 272 MPH and carry a payload of 100 gallons of gas and 700 pounds of cargo. Strip the Mooney down a little more, and you're almost at half a ton of payload. Granted the Zero could fly at 330 MPH, but the speed and inertia difference would be negligible with a Mooney loaded with 900 pounds of explosives flying into a Chlorine Tanker Ship as Rogalski stated in the congressional hearing. Go ahead and let your imagination pick any number of critical infrastructure targets or any venue with 100,000 people sitting in the stadium as potential targets of a terrorist attack a Mooney or comparable GA aircraft.

What would American's think the next day after terrorist's use of GA aircraft in an attack in the United States as they look up at one of the hundreds of thousands of GA pilots flying their aircraft on a leisure trip or vacation? After a terrorist attack, terror would fill our hearts every time a GA aircraft drifted overhead in any town in America. Even worse, the problem is greatly amplified if multiple GA aircraft were timed in different states or from the Mexico and the Canadian borders to launch a terrorist attack on the same day at a variety of U.S. targets. Step up the terrorist tool to an 11-passenger, 15000-pound, King Air 350 twin-engine GA aircraft with a 2500-pound payload and the situation is much worse.

An unfortunate example of what damage a GA aircraft can cause is revealed in an accidental airplane crash in Wichita Kansas. A King Air

GA aircraft crashed into the roof of a commercial building at Wichita Mid-Continent Airport and injured five people, killed the pilot and three people inside and destroyed the building. The FAA investigators had to use a crane to retrieve the aircraft data recorder due to the extensive damage to the commercial building.

GENERAL AVIATION CRIMES AND TERRORIST ACTS

Some high-profile incidents have occurred with student pilots and other experienced general aviation pilots. For example, in Boyd/ Greenup County in Kentucky, police arrested an organized drug smuggling crime ring of five members at Ashland Airport. One of the members, Edward Edwards, is a local general aviation pilot who is also a flight instructor and has a commercial pilot's license. Edwards piloted many trips to Mexico and brought back hundreds of pounds of illegal marijuana and prescription drugs. In September 2016, he was caught with a load of 800 pounds of marijuana hidden in his small GA aircraft at the small Kentucky aviation airport. John Stines is one of the Ashland Airport local GA pilots and said this about the suspect Edwards, and the drug arrest: "Who would have expect…we're a quiet small airport, everybody knows everybody, pilots that fly into here are regulars, we never expected anything like this."[257] Instead of marijuana, it easily could have been eight hundred pounds of C-4 Explosives, or Anthrax, or radioactive dirty bomb materials, or a biological disease cargo. We know there are unlimited possibilities of what other GA aircraft that flew undetected into the United States have already deposited on our soil.

Charles J. Bishop was a Florida student pilot who committed suicide in a single-engine airplane by flying the aircraft into the Bank of America skyscraper. Bishop was a 15-year-old high school honors student and was in flight training. He was seated in a Cessna 172 when the instructor left the plane to perform a pre-flight check of the aircraft. Bishop took off alone while the instructor was still outside the aircraft.

Bishop left the following note in his pocket stating his reasons for committing suicide by flying the Cessna into the Bank of America building;

> "I have prepared this statement in regards to the acts I am about to commit. First of all, Osama bin Laden is absolutely justified in the terror he has caused on 9-11. He has brought a mighty nation to its knees! God blesses him and the others who helped make September 11th happen. The U.S. will have to face the consequences for the horrific actions against the Palestinian people and Iraqis by its allegiance with the monstrous Israelis—who want nothing short of world domination! You will pay—God help you—and I will make you pay! There will be more coming! Al Qaeda and other organizations have met with me several times to discuss the option of me joining. I didn't. This is an operation done by me only. I had no other help, although, I am acting on their behalf."[258]

Even more disturbing was Frank Eugene Corder, who stole a four-seat Cessna 150 from Aldino Airport in Churchville, Maryland. Corder flew the plane at treetop levels and crashed the small-engine airplane at full throttle with flaps up into the south lawn of the White House. Corder was killed on impact and was found later to have been under the influence of cocaine and alcohol.[259]

Last but not least, Joe Stack, angry at the IRS, flew his Piper Dakota into the IRS building in Austin, Texas, killing two and wounding 17 people. Investigators speculated that Stack took out the back seats and loaded two 458-pound drums of fuel into the airplane before the collision. Stack left his statement as to why he became a homegrown terrorist on the internet:

> "It has always been a myth that people have stopped
> dying for their freedom in this country...I know there
> have been countless before me and there are sure to be

as many after. But I do know that by not adding my body
to the count, I ensure nothing will change…but violence
not only is the answer, it is the only answer."[260]

ANDREW JOSEPH "JOE" STACK ONLINE STATEMENT
BEFORE HIS SUICIDE CRASH OF HIS PRIVATE AIRCRAFT
INTO THE AUSTIN, TEXAS OFFICE OF THE IRS

At the Georgetown Airport, where Stack flew his plane out of on his
deadly suicide mission, the security was questionable. As of April 2016,
you could go to the airport web page where a question and answer is
listed for airport visitors. One question was how to get into the airport.
The following was taken directly from the website:

"How do I enter or leave the airport when the gates close at night?
Slowly approach the gate in your vehicle and the gate will open
automatically. If you are walking or riding a bike, the gate will
not open. However, to enter or leave the airport, press the button on the south side of the gate on Terminal Drive."[261]

The Georgetown Airport also has self-serve fuel service where you could
swipe your card and place as much fuel in your aircraft tank, or for that
matter, as Stack was have purported to have done, into 50-gallon barrels
inside your aircraft as well. The following was also on the website:

"Can I purchase fuel after the terminal is closed?
The Self Service Avgas Pumps are available 24 hours per day, 7
days a week."

Georgetown did have a security advisory on their web page as
of June 2015 that spoke of 9/11. Unfortunately, like most general
aviation airports, as in the case of Joe Stack, it did not do much
good. The following is posted on the airport website:

"Security Awareness: General Aviation
You should be aware of the two principle general aviation security objectives following September 11, 2001: Protecting passengers and aircraft from attack, and preventing aircraft from being used as weapons directed at sensitive targets on the ground."

Aftermath of Stack's suicide mission, Photo & Permission by Jeff Lake

FLIGHT SCHOOLS AND FOREIGN STUDENTS

A national security breach occurred at the La Verne Airport flight school in California when the police arrested a flight school owner for visa fraud. The flight school owner wasn't authorized to receive foreign students. News story accounts alleged she used fraud to allow people from Egypt, Sri Lanka, and Taiwan to enter the U.S. and enroll in her flight school by creating fake visa documents for foreign students. This flight school owner wasn't alone. Flight school owners in El Cajon, California, and in Massachusetts at the Stow flight school and TJ Aviation Flight Academy at Minute Man Air Field, 30 miles northwest of Boston, were also arrested for creating fake visa documents for foreign students.[262]

A flight school curriculum starts with a myriad of aircraft operations such as flight systems, air traffic control communication and during the second phase of flight instruction, a minimum of three solo flights are completed by the student pilot. An introduction to instrument and night flying leads to the third step of flight instruction that requires learning about our National Airspace System, Navigation, GPS systems, non-directional beacon navigation, take off and landings, and includes a minimum of three cross-country solo flights. During these flights, the student lands, refuels at an FBO in and out of a variety of airports in different cities across the nation. Student pilots learn the infrastructure of our local and national airports through flight school training.

Flight schools have in the past, and may still be used by covert terrorists posing as students to obtain the knowledge and skills to attack our aviation system again as the student pilots did on 9/11. At my airport, just after midnight, a general aviation propeller powered airplane landed and taxied to a closed FBO. We drove to the aircraft and two Pakistani national student pilots stepped out of the plane and in broken English said they wanted to use the closed FBO. We told them the airport FBOs are closed for a few hours each day, and they would have to fly to an airport that had 24/7 FBO service. Their identification and pilot licenses were valid, and they flew off into the night. The ease that student pilots can enter any airfield in America makes it paramount that every student pilot is vetted, authorized and is a known person whose identity is instantaneously accessible in every airport's security database.

U.S. Representative Mike Rodgers, in his Majority Staff Report in late 2012 stated, "…not only was TSA unable to account for all foreign nationals taking flight training in the U.S. as reported by the GAO, but U.S. citizens on the 'NO FLY LIST' could receive flight training, including flying unaccompanied."[263]

Flight Students Are Not Properly Vetted

"The 9/11 hijackers exposed a gaping hole in the security of U.S. flight Schools, the federal government establishing the Alien Flight Student Program [with] TSA has been responsible for vetting foreign flight students. In July 2012, the Government Accountability Office reported those significant weaknesses in flight school security persist."[264]

A TSA analysis found that more than 25,000 foreign nationals in a Federal Aviation Administration (FAA) database were not in the TSA's database, "meaning that they had received a FAA airman certificate but had not been successfully vetted or received permission from the TSA to begin flight training." At a Boston-area flight school in 2010, the Department of Homeland Security's ICE division discovered 25 illegal immigrants who were enrolled and taking flight lessons. "That's not the worst of it," Representative Rogers notes. "The owner of the flight school was also here illegally." The aspiring student pilots had nonetheless been approved by the Transportation Security Administration (TSA) to take the lessons, despite their illegal immigration status.[265]

Within the last couple of years, the U.S. Government has taken significant strides to prevent foreign flight school students who may be a threat to America. According to the Aviation Security Advisory Committee (ASAC), in 2012, 47,000 foreign nationals were vetted by the TSA to attend flight schools in the U.S. ASAC also posted the University of North Dakota findings that 45% of all commercial pilots written tests in the U.S. were taken by foreign citizens.[266]

Current TSA procedures collect and retain biographic and biometric data for covered foreign individuals seeking flight school status. A passport is required, but if the person cannot obtain one because they are refugees, asylees, or classified as a temporary protected status, they must produce a refugee travel document or a permanent/conditional resident card, or a 'document' issued by the U.S. Citizenship & Immigration

Services. Accurate vetting of these types of flight school students is essentially impossible.[267]

Other critical security issues are still on the table concerning Alien Flight School regulations at the ASAC Meeting on July 28, 2016. Concerns were aired against the current five-year frequency for vetting foreign students by the TSA, emphasizing the vetting was not frequent enough to "manage risk." One member of ASAC, Mr. Witkowski, asked for additional details on a requirement for security awareness training for employees of flight schools. Mr. Witkowski asked that flight schools be required to notify the appropriate Federal agency when persons attempt to pursue initial flight training in large aircraft. "Currently it is expected that flight schools would provide such notification based on their security awareness training, " but apparently flight schools are not "mandated" to report this.

The Government and ASAC should expedite its efforts to adequately provide the comprehensive measures to prevent the wrong people from receiving pilot training inside the United States. According to the preliminary investigation of a plane crash in East Hartford, Connecticut, our flight school pilot vetting system failed. On October 12, 2016, Jordanian flight school student Feras M. Freitekh, altered the cockpit controls before the flight and intentionally crash the aircraft with his instructor on board. The instructor survived the crash and told the FBI that Freitekh directed the aircraft toward the ground and due to the alteration of the controls; he could not regain control of the aircraft from Freitekh. The headquarters of military jet-engine maker Pratt & Whitney was near the crash site.[268]

Other Examples of Unsecured GA Airports and Aircraft:

* 18-year old Geoffrey Biteman, a self-taught pilot, took a Cessna from Moseau Municipal Airport in North Dakota frequently for joy riding flights. Keys to the Cessna were in the aircraft whose owners were away on military duty.
* Four Cessna aircraft were stolen from the Fullerton Airport in California. It was speculated the suspected crime method was an

aircraft would fly into Fullerton Airport, drop off a pilot who then steals an aircraft parked at the airport and flies out.

* GA pilot, Mario Mercier, was sentenced to jail for stealing avionics from GA aircraft at more than 20 private airports in eight states from 2004 to 2006. It was his ninth conviction.

* 19-year old Colton Harris Moore was suspected of stealing a high-performance plane from a Monroe County Airport locked hanger in Indiana. The plane was recovered ditched off an island in the Bahamas. The manager of the airport said: "how could an airplane fly from Bloomington, Indiana, and fly across states and airspace's and international waters and never be detected?"

* A Piper PA-32R-301T was stolen from the Chapel Hill Horace Williams Airport. The plane was determined to be stolen when its emergency beacon activated after it crashed and the suspect fled.

I have a great fear that someday, terrorists will weaponize small general aviation aircraft or large private jets and use them against American homeland targets. 40-year U.S. Marine General John Kelly told Congress in 2015 that he was very concerned about the nexus of drug cartels and terrorists at our Southern Borders. The evidence is in the hands of the Federal Government, and the evidence reveals GA aircraft are readily available for any number of possible terrorist purposes along Mexico's border with the United States.

I am not worried about 99% of America's GA pilots, but there are some I fear. I am also very concerned for a larger percentage of foreign pilots that frequent our skies. I'm also greatly worried about the lack of security for GA aircraft. These few stories and incidents send an urgent message to airport stakeholders of the security weaknesses in our aviation industry.

Is our current general aviation security that predominantly relies on our trusted security partners in the GA field adequate? Did it work at the Ashland or Roseau Airport? Alternatively, do we need greater security measures for general aviation aircraft? I strongly feel each airport owner must be required to mandate general aviation aircraft owners employ every reasonable security measure to safeguard their aircraft. The Risk Management Matrix needs to be tossed out the window, and mandatory aircraft security procedures and security training of general aviation personnel must be a requirement to safeguard our skies.

Last but certainly not least, our northern neighbor incident of a stolen GA aircraft that crashed killing the 20-year old suspect in 2016, resulted in these non-unified comments on security at private Canadian airports;[269]

- Patrick Gillian, vice president of operations with the Canadian owners and pilots association, said the theft of planes is so rare most private airports and aerodromes (small general aviation airfields) don't need additional private security.
- Transport Canada states on its website there is no standard for "the security of private air operations." "Although there is currently no International Civil Aviation Organization (ICAO) standard for the security of private air operations, Canada, along with a number of its major international partners are in the process of developing plans to enhance general aviation security," the agency says.
- Mathieu Larocque, a spokesperson for CATSA, said the agency is not responsible for perimeter security at airports. "The airports where we are present we are not responsible for the security of the airport," said Larocque. "The security of the airport itself, like the airport perimeter, access to the tarmac, security guards at the airport, that is local responsibility handled individual airport authorities."
- "These more regional, perhaps almost part-time airports where there is not a lot of activity, it's not fully under CATSA's mandate for standards of protection. The security gets quite a lot lower and certainly in some cases can lead to concerning incidents like this one."

✦ Aviation expert Jock Williams expressed concerns about the airport's security. "We leave our planes unlocked because a person breaking into a plane could do tens of thousands of dollars' worth of damage and cause the plane to be grounded until it was fixed," he said. "Whereas if you leave the door open, the person opens the door, looks in, finds that there is nothing to steal and goes away."

In March 2016, Curt Epstein wrote an article on AINonline titled "Security More important Than Ever at FBO's." Epstein noted the FBO's famous and wealthy clientele might be vulnerable to the threats of international and domestic terrorists and airport criminal activity at airports. Epstein stressed FBO employees must have "situational awareness" as a central component of an FBO security plan. He also placed emphasis on the need for proper physical elements such as well placed lighting, cameras, and so on.[270] I commend Epstein insightful and accurate assessment. In 2006, I developed a terrorist and criminal airport watch curriculum. I gave the two-hour course to my airports FBO's employees. As in any good law enforcement neighborhood/business watch program, situational awareness is a critical teaching point and one that all FBO employees must integrate into their daily activities on the airfield.

Recommendations:

1. Increase stricter security access controls at all FBOs.
2. A legal form of picture identification will be verified by employees before admittance into an FBO or General Aviation area and be required for entering through general aviation terminals and FBOs.
3. Armed security guards will be placed at all FBO Terminals.
4. Required Risk Assessments with a review every two years for all FBOs and their security procedures.
5. 100 percent contraband screening of FBO passengers and employees for admittance onto an active commercial airfield.

6. Required 24-hour video surveillance monitoring of commercial airports FBO terminal, hangar, ramps, and points of entry.
7. Mandatory TSA "Airport Watch" or airport business watch participation.
8. Mandatory background checks on all FBO and general aviation employees.
9. Mandatory vetting of all general aviation pilots through TSA.
10. Mandatory physical security anti-theft measures for general aviation aircraft.
11. Mandatory background checks requirement for flight school instructors and students through DHS and local airport police.
12. The TSA twelve-five security program requirements are mandatory for all general aviation aircraft over 12,500 pounds in weight and compliance with general aviation aircraft that transports 60 or more passengers with additional TSA security measures.
13. Fingerprint-based criminal history records check for all flight crew members who operate large private or corporate aircraft.
14. Terrorist watch list checks of all passengers of large private or corporate aircraft.
15. Mandatory security inspections of all large private or corporate aircraft.
16. Mandatory completion of security compliance audits every two years.
17. All general aviation flights will be tracked at U.S. Borders with sufficient radar technology to detect low flying aircraft.

CHAPTER 11

Airport Administrators, Chiefs of Police, and Airport Security

———◆———

"No matter what specific duties an airport director has
each day, the number one responsibility of an airport
director is a safe and efficient airport. The overall quality
of the national airspace system depends on it."[271]

STATE OF MAINE AIRPORT MANAGERS STUDY GUIDE

ONE MAY SAY TO OBTAIN the safety of an airport; the Federal Aviation
Administration guidelines must be implemented by an airport governing authority. Another could argue that emphasis on improved, post-9/11
security measures in the context of added security and law enforcement
resources, would define the degree of safety at our nation's airports.
Through my experiences with Airport Directors and Law Enforcement
Administrators in many commercial airports, I found the level of security at our country's airports varied considerably.

At my airport, I learned firsthand, the nature of airport manager's
security decision-making while working as a law enforcement watch
commander. I observed their logic and self-rationalization for their security decisions that defined the level of security and safety of my airport
and other airports. Based on my experience and assessments, I believe
our country's current airports management models cannot provide the

optimal level of security that is warranted based on a continuous threat to our aviation industry, a threat that will last for decades.

In our nation's current airport security matrix, the airport itself holds the primary responsibility for maintaining airport security and its safety. The airport is accountable for maintaining compliance with the Federal Aviation and Transportation Security Administration requirements. The airport police department in some airports is a division of a local law enforcement agency that contracts with the airport to provide police services. In other cases, it is an organization of the airport municipal corporation owned by a city, county or state. These law enforcement agencies are a sub-division of an airport's operations and fall under the airport civilian administration's governance. The airport management of aircraft operations under FAA protocols is a complex undertaking by the airport operators. An airport airfield and terminal operations alone are a daunting task that encompasses oversight of the huge number of protocols and procedures that apply to aircraft, flight crews, security, and a variety of airport support and maintenance employee groups. Since 9/11, the airports have greatly increased layers of security requirements and protocols and the overall workload for airport administrators has increased proportionally.

Our nation's airports' security incidents require unique, informed and expedient decisions. During my time at the airport, I wrestled with the correct representation and components that best define a safe airport. I was enlightened on best security practices for airports when my administration asked me to conduct a study of 21 airport police agencies located throughout the country and their individual airports' security plans. The results of nine months of research helped me to define and formulate a view of how a safe and efficient airport model should operate and what it should look like in our post 9/11 world. Through this study, I conducted interviews with various airport directors or assistant directors (or their appointed representatives), the TSA deputy federal directors, chiefs of police, budget officers, and the airports' operation supervisors and police officers. As a result, of this analysis, I believe the current nationwide system of airport security governance needs a significant change.

For decades, our nation's airports have operated under the same business management template and structural hierarchy. The facts presented in the previous chapters spotlight the failure of our nation's airports' ability to solve the fundamental security problems with emphasis placed on a "safe and efficient airport." Is there a better business model from which airports may thrive as a successful enterprise that will provide the best post-9/11 security for our nation's safe and efficient airports? What training and background must a person possess to effectively run both the business and security of a commercial airport? What skill sets, education, training, and expertise do our airports require of directors and managers to safeguard our aviation industry from post-9/11 threats?

To answer these questions, we must first understand how our nation's airport directors and airport commissions make security decisions; who they are and how they are selected to govern an airport in our post-9/11 world. I examined a series of airport case study examples that details airport manager's decisions in these recounted airport incidents. The examples come from my fellow airport police agencies or ones I have been involved in or shared by others within our nation's airports. These events provide insight into how airport security decisions are made in a variety of airports in the United States. These examples only serve to generate a discussion on managing security decisions among the airport security stakeholders inside our nation's airports.

Airport Security Management Case Example 1: Airport Vehicle License Plate Reader Cameras

An airport in the United States was offered an electronic camera system termed 'License Plate Readers' (LPR). The electronic camera system would identify vehicle license plates when they drove into this airport's roadways and parking structures. The system is provided by a federal grant, free of cost, and could identify as an example, a stolen car or an

Amber Alert (kidnapping) vehicle. The LPR system would also alert authorities of vehicles owned or associated with people on the terrorist watch list if it came onto or near the airport. The license plate numbers are stored in a database for tracking and referencing criminals and suspected terrorists who travel through the airport.

The airport police gave a demonstration to the Airport Director of the LPR system capability and used a mobile unit that was currently in use in cities nearby. After the demonstration, the Airport Director did not give a decision for months and eventually turned down the system for two cited reasons. The first reason the airport refused the LPR federal grant was the airport was planning to install a future license plate reader camera system in the parking structures. The airport planned the LPR installation years in the future from the current law enforcement proposal date. The Airport Director said the airport wanted to install a complete system at one time that would also include the use of the system in the airport parking garage. The parking garage LPR system would identify absconding parking patrons who left the airport parking lots without paying. At the time, the airport police were told the airport declined the grant; the full truth was not revealed. The second reason was told in more confidential circles as it pertained to the airport director's feelings that he didn't want a "big brother" at his airport.

I offer this airport director's decision, as I will other examples, to discuss the how and why of airport managers' decisions from a perspective that should be open to public discourse but rarely are. Was this airport director's decision correct when he declined the free LPR system that went against the airport police chief's and homeland security insistence to improve the airport security? The proposed law enforcement LPR system was capable of meeting any future expansion into the parking structure, thus negating any credible reason not to install the LPR system. Many believed the airport director's personal doctrine and views resulted in the loss of this additional layer of security for the airport.

The current hierarchy of airport management has not changed since the 1950's. There are hosts of managers inside an airport, each with particular responsibilities on a cascading level of decision making. The airport director provides the strategic plan for the airport while mid-level managers with operational managers run daily airport operations.

AN AIRPORT GOVERNANCE OVERVIEW

All airports work under a single airport director who manages virtually every aspect of airport operations. The appointment of an airport director is by the airport's governing state, county or city-elect body of politicians where the airport's jurisdiction resides. States, counties, and cities own the various commercial airports throughout the nation. An airport governing body is also advised on airport matters by a separate organization called the Airport Commission. While airport management organizations will differ depending on the size of the airport, its location, and the management philosophy, each has developed its business model from more than six decades of aviation industry growth, specific to each airport's region and state.

The airport director manages and creates policies for a commercial airport. He or she partitions the areas of a commercial airport into major airport divisions depending on the size and needs of their respective airport. These airport divisions have a variety of titles such as Airport Operations, Business Development, Facilities, Finance & Administration, and Public Affairs. The second in command is the assistant airport director who aides the airport director in the management of all airport activities by administering the operational policies of an airport. The airport director and assistant directors control the five or more airport divisions, the airport budget, human resources, and the regulatory and compliance statutes required of commercial airports.

Under the director and assistant director are a determined number of deputy airport directors. Some airports designate these positions as deputy executive directors or other titles, but for this conversation, we'll use the "deputy airport director" title, and I'll use the acronym DAD for brevity. The following concise descriptions of the various DAD's duties used in this context is not a complete list but rather title headings of responsibilities that have great more details within those duties.

Airport Director

Assistant Airport
Director

| Deputy Director of Operations | Deputy Director of Business Development | Deputy Airport Director of Facilities | Deputy Airport Director of Finance & Administration | Deputy Airport Director of Public Affairs |

Chief of Police

Fire Department

A General Example of an Airport Organization Chart, source: W. Herrin

The DAD of business development creates, implements, and monitors all contracts of the airport for its property usage, rentals, and leases, as well as provides all the equipment and vehicles.

The DAD of Facilities is responsible for all areas of facilities management and engineering for the entire airport.

The DAD of Administration and Finance is responsible for airport finances, the planning and writing of the airport budget, overseeing its expenditures, bookkeeping, budget reports and also provides all administrative support to the other airport divisions.

The DAD of Public Affairs is the airport representative for communications inside the airport and liaisons with the media, community, and government.

The DAD of Operations coordinates the airport law enforcement, the fire department, and the access controls of the airport. The DAD of operation is the security coordinator as required by Homeland Security and the TSA primary contact. The DAD of operations has a myriad of responsibilities that include the administration of general aviation, parking facilities, and ground transportation. The airport under the DAD of operations manages both the airside and the land side of the airport.

These general summaries of the deputy airport directors' duties reveal how running an airport is a massive and complex operation. Over the decades, our airports have attempted to make adjustments to meet the complex needs of an ever-demanding traveling society and the accelerating development of technology implemented in its domains. The needs of airport tenants place tremendous demands on the Operations DAD in managing their regulatory compliance of the daily commercial and general aviation activity. Since 9/11, the enormous responsibility of security and safety for the airport and its adherence to the federal regulatory laws and protocols has impinged on the airports by requiring an unprecedented increase in Homeland Security at each airport.

AIRPORT COMMISSIONS

Each airport typically has a commission consisting of members who are appointed by the state, county, or city-elected officials from the airport location of jurisdiction. The number of members of the commission varies with the size and complexity of the airport itself. The appointment of airport commissioners can range for 4 to 5-year terms, and the majority of appointed members do not have aviation industry experience. The airport commission provides advice to the local government politicians on matters of the airport operations, planning, and other issues. The airport commission also conducts investigations of issues facing the airport, as it deems necessary in the exercise of their mandated powers.

I reviewed many airport commissions across America, as well as the commission members' professional backgrounds and discovered there was a vast diversity among the members regarding skills and employment experiences. The following are two examples of airport commission members' backgrounds and job experiences. Observing the range in types of backgrounds of these airport commission members provides insight into the governing member's capabilities, their life experiences and what fields of expertise they possess in assisting a commercial airport.

This first example is from a medium-sized airport in America. These commission members' vocations were: a restaurant owner, a city council member, an owner of a website developing company, a realtor land manager, industrial engineer and a CEO of a wireless engineering and service company.

In another example, an airport's commission from a large international airport was chosen. In this commission, members' backgrounds and job experiences consisted of seven distinct areas of expertise. These commission members professions were a real estate fund sponsor operator that invests in residential properties, an estate planning attorney, a corporate member of a real estate investment and development management firm, a former state assembly member who specialized in K-12 education bonds, a corporate member of a real estate company, a Corporate member of an entertainment law firm, and a University Director of a Psychiatric Clinic.

As you can see from these two examples of airports commission's backgrounds, they are quite diverse in their life experiences. In these examples, the experiences ranged from a myriad of business, industry and political environments. An airport commission can provide oversight and sometimes can be an arbiter for their airport and advises on the development and formulating of airport policy. The commissioners provide inroads with local, county, state and federal political entities that have the authority to approve airport ways and means to ensure the success of an airport operations business plan.

But what is most glaringly noticeable with our current airport commissions' membership in the post 9/11 world, are many airport commissions lack of Homeland Security or law enforcement professionals. Homeland Security and law enforcement members on airport commissions are as necessary, if not more so than the politicians, lawyers and businesspeople who predominately make up most airport commissions.

Airport commissions must have the ability and skills to provide our airports the knowledgeable support and insight to promote necessary security improvements.

An airport commission is essential to the governance of an airport. Sometimes, though, an airport commission influences in an airport can turn negative and depending on the circumstances, the safety and security of the airport may not be best served. An example of this is an international airport in a large American city. The airport hired a nephew of one of the airport commission's members as a senior management assistant where his duties were to improve security and safety by properly certifying and training airport employees. The nephew finished 70th out of 76 people on the eligibility list. The airport previously employed the nephew who resigned from his job due to illicit adult materials on his work computer. He was rehired and later was given disciplinary rebukes and a suspension for sexual harassment in one incident and another when he assaulted his ex-girlfriend's beau in the airport terminal and made harassing phone calls to her from his work phone.[272]

How and Why Airport Directors Are Selected

In the United States, in my opinion, there is a lack of continuity in the selection criteria and requirements for airport directors or their assistant managers. In a nationwide review, selections it seems, are left to the airport governing authority to use their rules when choosing airport directors who govern airports and make the critical airport security decisions.

Curiosity led me to examine the DAD's backgrounds in airport security operations, as well as the reasons for the security decisions they made. In an assessment of airport administrators and managers from various airports, I found that some civilian airport management members do not come from aviation, law enforcement or security job backgrounds when hired for their first job at an airport. I also discovered they are not required to have an aviation or law enforcement security education to manage an airport or its security. In some cases, a person can be hired by an airport and receive 'on the job' training as the entry method of learning their new aviation industry job. The airport directors and DAD of operations examples are best depicted from an actual random sampling of selected airport directors and managers from major international to small city airports.

This first example came from an airport in the Midwest, where the DAD of Operations transferred into the county-owned airport from a county probation department. A second example is a city employee who transferred from a large urban city department of planning and development job to the director of an airport. A third example is an airport director who was a city staff attorney when appointed to an important airport director position.

The airport directors chosen by these various governmental agencies create the complex airport security plan based on the myriad of FAA and TSA guidelines and recommendations. The results are varying degrees and levels of expertise in airport security network operations throughout the United States. America's airport directors have been competent in providing for the security of their airports under federal mandates. Sometimes airport directors fail in providing the best security for their airport, and wrong security decisions are made for their airport's security infrastructure protocols and procedures. During my time in airport law enforcement, I found the security management methods of airport directors often conflict and differed with those of the chief law enforcement commander hired to maintain the safety of the airport.

Airport Security Management Case Example 2: Airport Perimeter Fence Security

The security issues related to the perimeter fencing at airports, as discussed in Chapter 9, reveal how airport security stakeholders can move from collaborators to adversaries regarding perimeter fence breaches. In this situation, the airport director was provided the airport police perimeter analysis that revealed their fence could suffer many types of failures. The airport director dismissed the security analysis and placated the airport police with the caveat that the airport will improve the airport fence sometime in the next ten years as other airport improvements are made. Over the next five years, airport perimeter breaches occurred at this director's airport seven different times. Accurate facts and high probabilities were provided to this director showing the weakness of his airport fence based on the perimeter fence current condition and using other airports fence incursions examples.

Five years earlier the county grand jury made similar recommendations for the airport's perimeter fence based on the 9/11 threat level and assessment data. The director chose to ignore the studies recommendations.

In one of the seven incidents at the airport director's airfield fence, a vehicle breached the fence and made it onto a runway. A sequence of the airport security partner's management reviews and decisions were made in reaction to this particular security breach. The airport police conducted an immediate assessment with a detailed summary of improvements that would stop repetitive airfield incursions. The airport TSA Federal regulatory agency reviewed the incident, inspected the fence, and cited the FAA minimum standards stating the fence complies with federal codes. The Airport Director reviewed the incident and stated the breached fence was built to federal regulatory specifications for airport perimeter fences and no improvements were needed. After each of the seven other airfield incursions by suspects climbing over, under or crashing through the airport's fence, the director placated the recommendations of the airport police and did not strengthen the perimeter fence line.

This is where the collaboration breaks down between the airport security stakeholders. Based on the incursion, the airport police asked the airport administration to improve the airport fence to stop future perimeter fence breaches. The TSA states the fence in its current configuration is in compliance, and the airport director states the airport is in compliance and improvement isn't necessary at this time. The result was the fence is left as is, despite the strong possibility for future incursions by vehicles and persons.

Many airport directors are slow to change their management methods and philosophies that may conflict with their fellow airport security stakeholders' recommendations. For one to put off an airport security improvement of an area that continually failed its intended specific purpose is wrong by any definition. The perimeter fence provides the safety for the airlines to maintain timely flights by preventing interruption of those flights from an incursion on the runway. It also creates a safe environment so that passengers will choose to travel to and from that particular airport. The strong security matrix of any airport is easily a public relations selling point to the public who use the commercial airport. A strong, safe, breach-resistant airport perimeter fence with good airport police manpower staffing, along with the post 9/11 heightened terminal security that when marketed appropriately, not only reassures passengers but tells criminals and terrorists that this is a hardened target. Terrorists prefer soft targets, not hardened ones.

AMERICA'S AIRPORT SECURITY AND RISK MANAGEMENT

Since 9/11, America's aviation security is managed by organizations whose agents are interconnected. The meshing of these interrelated groups has created an elaborate committee of security stakeholders who have varying degrees of experience and authority that they use to provide security of our airports. Since 9/11, these security networks have failed to perform as a team with seamless, unified airport security approaches to meet our airports Homeland Security goals. Rather, the security network process has steadily become dysfunctional and seems to intensify each passing year.

At my airport, each security stakeholder (TSA, airport police, airport directors, and airlines) is responsible for their area of risk. The term 'risk' has many meanings. In this context, it will cover several areas defined in the 2010 Department of Homeland Security (DHS) Risk Lexicon. The DHS uses this dictionary to clarify the elements of risk-informed decisions using the risk classifications. The airport security network stakeholders use terms in the Lexicon such as Absolute Risk, Acceptable Risk, Adaptive Risk, and Adversary Risk and so on.[273] Assessing risk has many critical components. One significant part of the risk assessment process is having or acquiring knowledge of who your adversaries are. Different enemies will proffer different threats. At our nation's airports it is critical to get risk assessment right, but in reality, the whole risk assessment process comes down to a roll of the dice with the hope your number comes up.

The National Association of Airlines Passengers submitted a rebuke of the TSA and ASAC use of the risk matrix. The NAAP said, "The assumptions used by the Working Group in the context of applying a Risk Based Security Approach Model to criminal activity were flawed, and the conclusions reached on this subject cannot and should not be relied upon."[274] This NAAP is an interesting counter argument to the DHS risk matrix used in our airports and one that I support.

Douglas and Wildavsky in their book 'Risk and Culture;' purport dangers are infinite regarding the types of threats facing a person or entity. In an airport, clearly, the number of threats can be insurmountable, and one may imagine the many types and methods of possible threats. Douglas and Wildavsky proposition that a prioritization of the dangers in a risk analysis is essential as it is impossible to address every threat. What strikes near and dear to me is Douglas and Wildavsky reasoning "only social consent keeps an issue out of contention," implying risk is a societal process and interpreted differently in many countries and for that matter in the many organizations that provide for aviation security as well.[275]

Will the Airport Director, TSA Federal Security Director, and the Airport Police Chief all perceive risk identically? Lennart Sjoberg argued people sense only threats and dangers, and risk cannot be detected. If this is the case, the risk is a possible outcome that has yet to occur, and is not in the present analysis of the situation at hand, but is imagined or interpreted as a possibility. So assuredly, these different security stakeholder organizations interpret risk differently from each other to one degree or another.

"Misapplication of Risk Based Security Principles
Risk Based Security involves analyzing risks and taking steps to avoid, control, and mitigate that risk. We respectfully submit that the working group made a serious misjudgment when it concluded that...there were significant differences between the threats posed by criminal activity and terrorism..." National Association of Airline Passengers[276]

The security choices managers make at our nation's airports must be intelligence based on potential threats that are in and around each of our nation's airports and less on broad brush strokes of assumptive probability outcomes that are typically used in many airports risk assessments.

The Brussels Airport police threaten to go on strike after the terrorist suicide bombings in their departure terminal. In an open letter to the airport management, they stated "Every police officer in any police force at Zaventem knew this day would come," and the letter continued with accusing the airport management of not preventing the "Huge flaws in security."[277] Brussels airport management may very well have used the 'acceptable risk' approach and rolled the dice. They lost.

I believe every airport police department has personnel who disagree with some of their airport management security decisions that the airport implemented over the objection of the airport police. These internal battles between airport security stakeholders rarely make it outside the conference room and into the public ear, yet they occur more frequently than outsiders think.

Can we hedge our bets on making the wrong choices? Yes, we can. The anticipation of all threats, applied prevention and mitigation efforts in an airport, on a broad scale can be successful with the collaboration of all airport security stakeholders. The following case example reveals an airport police agency's conflict with the airport director in an attempt to implement a crime and terrorist watch prevention program that would aid the police in finding actionable intelligence from the community of potential unknown threats.

AIRPORT SECURITY MANAGEMENT CASE EXAMPLE 3: AIRPORT BUSINESS/TERRORIST WATCH PROGRAM

At an airport in America, a police manager created an airport criminal/terrorist business watch program for airport employees and the companies around the outside perimeter of the airport. The police based the business watch program on best practices of the National Neighborhood Watch Program and a variety of terrorist watch programs and groups. The central purpose of the airport business watch program was to enlist the airport employees and nearby businesses' employees who work in the buildings surrounding the airport. Recruited workers are trained to be sentinels, and to report suspicious incidents and behavior of people to the airport police.

The pilot program was given to a select number of employee groups to evaluate and critique the merits of the program. These employees after receiving the course were given a survey and asked to provide answers anonymously. One hundred percent of the test group members stated the airport business watch program was a valuable tool for airports to use for homeland security. These surveys results were documented after each presentation and were given to this airport administrator for his approval and implementation in both the airport and surrounding community. The airport director and DADs reviewed the curriculum and concluded that the program would "scare people" and would cast a negative public relations shadow on the airport, so they chose not to approve the program. The airport chief of police, instead of creating a rift with the director of the airport, tacitly allowed the program to be given by his staff to the surrounding businesses.

The Forecasting International Incorporated, a private think tank, produced a U.S. Government publication written by Dr. Marvin Cetron and Owen Davies, called, "55 Trends Now Shaping the Future of Terrorism." Cetron and Davis said:

> "Having the experts watching potential targets isn't enough. We need to get as many eyeballs on them as possible. Ordinary citizens need to know where the dangers lie. Every indication is that the terrorists' determination to hurt America is undiminished."[278]

The airport police used the risk mitigation option to reduce potential criminal and terrorist activity by educating members of the surrounding airport communities on the Homeland terrorist and criminal threats. The police were prompted to create the program based on risk indicators of activity around the airport where suspicious vehicles, persons, and actions were occurring.

This example of decision-making by two airport security stakeholders in an airport concerning a proposed security improvement program, reveals the civilian management's opinions, beliefs, and views are distinctly different than the airport law enforcement's or federal homeland security member's views. Different views, in this case, resulted in a significant number of probable citizens <u>not</u> being trained and used by the airport police as eyes and ears for airport Homeland Security and crime prevention. This failure was the result of the airport administration exercising its authority not to grant broad latitude of employee involvement in the prevention program. Chad Whelan and Darren Palmer's report, 'Responding to Terrorism through Networks at Sites of Critical Infrastructure: A Case Study of Australian Airport Security Networks,' states:

> "The complex dynamics of such networks are intensified when membership (airport security network) necessarily extends to the private sector, [airport administrators]. The protection of

critical infrastructure is thus a task of engendering enhanced responsibilisation in the private sector, something that requires considerable effort."[279]

Airport Security Management Case Example 4: Airport Surveillance Cameras

At an airport in America, a passenger airport obtained security cameras and monitors from a large nearby international airport who had recently updated their camera system with new equipment and technology. As the old technology aged, the airport police surveillance of critical portions of the airport was hampered due to maintenance issues and quality of the optics from the cameras and monitors. The airport's strategic 10-year plan included new cameras and monitors for the airport security surveillance.

The airport delayed purchasing the new security camera system but did purchase new cameras and monitors in their facility's baggage makeup control room. Civilian airport employees staffed the baggage makeup room and observed the intricate and multi-level baggage conveyor belts in operation. The airport's goal was to increase the number of areas that could monitor baggage conveyor belts and carousel areas and quickly locate jams and breakdowns.

Staff viewing the new large TV 40-inch screen monitors and cameras would detect the location of luggage jams and expedite the repair, saving airline passenger's time. Quick and efficient transference of airline passenger baggage from the ticket counters to the airplane helped maintain airline companies' lease retention, profits and passenger satisfaction for their flight's timely departure and arrivals. The airport director chose to increase business infrastructure improvements over the airport's security infrastructure much-needed improvements. A decade passed, and as of January 2017, the old surveillance systems at this airport still await the final phase of upgrades to their surveillance systems.

I toured dozens of airports and examined their security camera monitoring systems and the personnel who operate them. My findings lead me to highly recommend every airport self-examine the actual capabilities of their airports' camera monitoring systems and the personnel who staff these vital components of our airport's security functions. The surveillance systems of every airport must be the best available for airport security.

AIRPORT DIRECTORS, AIRPORT SECURITY STAKEHOLDERS, AND ADVERSITY

The airport director has the final word on every decision made at the airport to include the security improvements that meet or exceed hundreds of federal regulatory requirements. Proposed law enforcement or federal security stakeholder's solutions to solve an existing airport security problem can differ from an airport director thoughts. These differences can create an adversarial working relationship during the negotiations for a solution. In the July 2011 House Oversight Committee Hearing of the Subcommittee on National Security Homeland Defense and Foreign Operations, a number of airport security stakeholders made statements that reflect their continuing adversarial relationship in our nation's airports. Florida Congressman John Mica offered a politician's viewpoint in response to an airport security problem he observed.

> "Now, there's a new airport administrator. He wasn't familiar with all of the details but we're going to do a thorough investigation of this. This is just one instance, again, of a non-thinking Agency."[280]

Charlotte Airport operator Director Jerry Orr attended and spoke at the same hearing. Orr gave his opinion of TSA in the hearing;

> "I have been critical of the performance of the TSA since its inception. I am not critical of its mission. I am critical of its measures.

In my judgment, the effectiveness of the TSA is compromised by a rigid attitude of arrogance and bureaucracy. I am confident that I am not the only airport operator with significant concerns about the effectiveness of TSA. An adversarial relationship between airports and the very Agency entrusted to help safeguard them is clearly detrimental to the goal of safety and security."[281]

Rafi Ron is the former director of security at Tel-Aviv Ben-Gurion International Airport and the Israeli Airport Authority. Ron is a consultant to airports and an aviation security subject matter expert often called on by the U.S. Government for advice in these matters. In a Congressional hearing concerning aviation matters, Rafi Ron stated:

"There is a vague division of responsibilities between the airport authority, local law enforcement agencies, and the TSA. Depending on the nature of the security concern at any given time, one or more of the agencies may be called on to respond. Although they have some degree of coordination, no one person at the airport is in charge of security and proactive programs may be undertaken or skipped by any of the three without consulting the others."[282]

Over the years as an airport watch commander, I've observed a series of conflicts between airport administrators and their security partners that resulted in difficult working relationships. Rather than one of collaboration between the airport management, airlines, airport police, and federal agencies, these security partners were at odds with each other to such an extent that it affected the level of security at these respective airports.

Robert Poole and Viggo Butler of the Cascade Policy Institute made a bold statement on how to improve airport security soon after 9-11. They argued that the primary problem with airport security was that everyone involved in the airport was responsible for security. Poole and

Butler's reasoning meant no one person was really in charge of this type of airport security matrix. In their two-page commentary, they argued that using the European model of holding the airport owner/operator strictly accountable for all security at their airport would significantly enhance security. Telling an owner/operator that their security failures will result in the FAA yanking their license to operate would inspire airports to prioritize security over other business line items. I agree somewhat with Poole and Butler's suggestions, but I would offer a different airport management process.[283] I recommend placing all airport security operations on the shoulders of a qualified and skilled law enforcement director whose duties are the Aviation Homeland Security and Aviation Crime specific areas. The chief of airport police position should be empowered with equal authority as an airport director for the specific task of managing an airport's security and its law enforcement in an airport administrative duo management. I argue no airport director should have the authority that would subvert a decision by an airport head of security in our post 9/11 world.

Are Two Heads Better Than One?

Can our current model of airport management give way to a new airport management organization that will improve its security management? For decades, the airport management ideology dictated the airport director has sole proprietorship of the airport functionality. This airport management model, more than any other business industry model, has historically suffered worldwide-prolonged terrorist attacks. Through these decades of airport terrorist attacks and crimes, airport director's security decisions have been based on their personal values, goals, acquired education, and world experience. Airport police chiefs operate with knowledge of critical infrastructure protection, law enforcement, and homeland security. In our current airport business philosophy, this single Chief Executive Officer (CEO) top-down management style has dominated our airports organizational business models in the United

States since the early days of the aviation industry. A CEO is a lone ranger at the top making the final critical security decisions for his airport.

I propose consideration of duo management of commercial airports where the business model and security model of each airport are separated systems that work together with equal voice to provide the airport's master business and security plan. Some businesses have broken the single top-down CEO model. The Dell Corporation is an example; the founder and CEO Michael Dell and President Kevin B. Rollins share decision-making power. Both Dell and Rollins have an agreement that they will not make major decisions unless they both approve. The Dell Company continues this management style throughout their corporate ladder and places two corporate executives, as they term it, "in the box," on any important project. The executives "check" each other's weakness, but also share the success or the blame.[284]

In their book, 'Shared Leadership, Reframing the How's and Why's of Leadership,' Craig Pearce, and Jay Conger delves into the concept of shared leadership. They state, "As organizations and their worlds grow more and more complex, it is increasingly difficult for a single individual holding the position of chief executive officer to lead."[285] Pearce and Conger note the current top-down concept in businesses has been the prevailing model for many decades. The need for shared leadership in today's airport security plans has never been more evident. Before 9/11 the complex nature of running an airport business under federal/state/local laws was a quagmire itself for airport directors. Since 9/11, the burden of airport security has increased substantially with continuous threats posed by international and national terrorists. As Pearce and Conger suggests, senior leaders in today's world do not have the complete information to make critical, practical decisions in our complex and ever-evolving world. We would be wise in considering Pearce and Conger's concerns with our post 9/11 national airport management system.

Can a shared leadership concept provide the best management of our country's airports? In light of 9/11 and the continuing threat of terrorism, would it be more efficient to handle the business and security models under two executive officers to obtain the best of both worlds? Solomon, Loeffer, & Frank wrote of two individuals who simultaneously shared one leadership, and introduced a co-leadership theory as early as the 1950s. These types of shared leadership theories were heresy in the early to mid-1900s, as the leadership model was command and control, with influence remaining vertical and only in one direction; downward, with the leader and subordinates in the industrial age often having different and separate goals.[286]

One significant change in today's business management and the fastest growing organizational unit is the team unit concept. What distinguishes these groups from traditional organizational forms is the absence of hierarchical authority. This concept makes the appointed leader a peer in the organization. The purpose of the team is to bring a very diverse set of functional backgrounds together. Here the leader is highly dependent on the diverse team's backgrounds to solve problems that the leader has no knowledge or experience with the topic.

As far back as 1924, Mary Parker Follett, who created the concept of "The Law of the Situation," tabled a radical shared leadership concept. This concept suggested that the company should follow the lead of the person with the most knowledge regarding the situation at hand, rather than the lead of the person with the formal authority in the company. Again this concept was considered interesting but often dismissed by business leaders in the age of command and control and downward-only influence of leaders to subordinates. Follett stressed that leaders must be aware of the complexity of the exceptional situations that arise in business and to defer to the co-leader who had the most knowledge of the subject to handle the situation.[287] Another interpretation of Follett's theory is that conflict between two parties should be resolved by reference to the facts of the situation and not through a power struggle.[288]

The Amana Corporation has not had a single CEO since 1995. The corporation has four co-leaders who divide the company by industry lines of farming and forestry, utilities and construction, manufacturing, retail, and tourist services. Before 1995, Amana had not made money except for its famous refrigerator line of products. The company is now quite profitable under the shared, equally yoked CEOs, despite its varied number of goods and services.

O'Toole and Galbraith in their paper titled, 'Two Heads Are Better Than One,' emphasize that two joint leaders must understand what the other is good at, and where their direct leadership is needed for the organization to succeed. O'Toole and Galbraith emphasized how duo leaders can effectively coordinate and communicate with each other. The single largest factor in the success of the co-leadership operation of the company is the absence of the "ego" and "what's-in-it-for-me" type of thinking. Sometimes, not controlling one's ego is the hardest part of the co-leader management, and management of egos is essential to the safe and efficiently run business and security of an airport. If an airport director and the airport chief of police take the cooperative fluid approach for the responsibility of their leadership tasks, goals, and missions, they will have an efficient and increasingly successful business and security outcome.[289]

AIRPORT SECURITY MANAGEMENT CASE EXAMPLE 5: "NO ONE DOES ANYTHING UNLESS I APPROVE"

A law enforcement agency networked and assisted all critical infrastructures within their jurisdiction by assessing their locations and creating an emergency first responders access database. These critical infrastructures ranged from public utilities, hospitals, schools, government facilities, commercial facilities, communication sectors and transportations systems.

The law enforcement agency assembled a team to conduct a detailed assessment of the airport and prepare a first responder access database. When ready, the agency told the airport director the assessment would begin on a certain date. The airport director told the law enforcement management that he was in charge at his airport and no assessment would be approved or allowed to be conducted on his airport. The law enforcement agency could not convince the airport director to allow the assessment.

This example of totalitarianism management of an airport is something that should never have occurred in our post 9/11 world. For reasons only known to this airport director, he decided to exert his authority in a manner perceived as egotistical by his fellow security stakeholders.

AIRPORT SECURITY MANAGEMENT CASE EXAMPLE 6: AIRPORT SECURITY GUARDS

An airport law enforcement police officers and armed special officers, both employed by the same police agency, provided security to an airport in the United States. The airport police officers went through a basic county sanctioned police academy while the special officers went through a modified 5-month police academy. Both officer classifications received annual law enforcement training and daily updates on airport security. Also, these two groups of law enforcement officers attended a 40-hour Peace Officers & Standards Training Aviation Security Course and were required to qualify with their firearms every month. The special officers served the airport for the past 30 years with distinction and were familiar with the entire airport's infrastructure, protocols, and procedures.

In budget planning, the airport director reviewed the law enforcement cost for his airport and decided to cut the number of special officer positions that included officer assignments to guard the perimeter vehicle gates. The director estimated the airport would save approximately $800,000 in annual salaries with cutbacks on special officer personnel. The director elected to replace the officers with armed private security guards. The security guard state license protocols required private citizen guards to receive 40 hours of training that included an 8-hour block on private person arrest procedures. The private security guards were only required to attend an 8-hour firearm classroom session and 6 hours on the firing range. Additionally, the firearm license was valid for two years and required the private guard to shoot his handgun to qualify only four times under state law within those two years to maintain the validity of his armed guard card license.

The airport police chief opposed the police officer position cuts and argued that the experienced officers' qualifications at these airport perimeter gates far exceeded the inexperienced and far less-trained security guards' skills. The airport police compared the special officer gun training and their firearms qualification with the security guards proficiency firearms training. Despite greater police training by the law enforcement special officers, coupled with their years of law enforcement experience at the airport, the County Board of Supervisors approved the Airport Director's security guard service contract request, and the armed security guards replaced the airport special officers.

The private security company selected was the lowest bid from three private security guard companies that submitted bids. The chosen security company and its guards never provided security for a commercial airport before this contract. In this instance, the airport director chose the least-expensive but nevertheless a TSA-approved level of security versus tested, experienced, law enforcement skills, and better-trained security personnel to save money.

Airport directors' primary job is to conduct business operations that will ensure profit instead of losses. Some airport directors will take the path of least resistance to ensure success in these endeavors. In this perimeter security example, the airport director did what his business sense told him, save cost, but unfortunately at a sacrifice of higher levels of security for its airport.

San Jose International Airport Law Enforcement Staffing Cuts

I toured the San Jose Airport with the San Jose Police Department, watch commander. The San Jose police agency provided airport law enforcement protection for the City of San Jose-owned San Jose International Airport in California. In a study of San Jose, I compared their airport policing to my airport, and we shared our airport security operational concepts with each other. San Jose Airport, at the time of my visit, was in the midst of a huge $1.7 billion terminal renovation.

A few years later the airport was in financial crisis, having overextended themselves with their investment bond payments becoming due. At the time of my visit, San Jose Airport staffed 47 armed police officers for airport security. Over the years since my visit, San Jose initially eliminated six airport police positions to save cost. The next year they reduced the number of officers to 41 to guard the airport on a 24/7 basis. A year later the airport director at San Jose Airport cut the number of police officers from 41 to 23, a total of a 51 percent decrease in police officers over two years. Part of the San Jose police duties was to respond to door alarms that indicated someone breached the passenger door and were now possibly on the ramp among the parked passenger airliners. After San Jose Airport cut the airport police positions by 50%, the airport assigned their civilian personnel to respond to these alarms.[290]

San Jose International Airport is an example that serves as a wake-up call to the nation regarding weakening an airport's security. I surmise the San Jose Airport Police Chief did not wholeheartedly agree to deplete the police force at his city airport by 50 percent. Only the San Jose Chief of Police, City Council, and the Airport Director can reveal the criteria and reasons for the police-staffing cut to the San Jose International Airport. Would the 16-year-old boy who climbed the fence and stole away on a flight to Hawaii in 2014, have been seen if there were more police officers on duty that day? On the other hand, would full police staffing stop some if not all of the five people who breached the security fence at San Jose?[291] As of July 2016, the San Jose Police Department was struggling with vacancies due to officers retiring or transferring to other agencies. San Jose Police Department, agency-wide, is stretched thin, and this directly affects the level of security at the San Jose Airport and should concern the citizens who use this airport.

But San Jose is not alone. I feel my airport and others throughout the nation are letting the memory of 9/11 fade as they downgrade, reduce or marginalize their security staffing levels.[292] On the upside, the San Jose Airport has improved several areas of their airport security infrastructure as reported to their Airport Commission in the May 8, 2017, Airport Security Briefing. Some of those improvements are:

* Updated fence standards
* Technology Upgrades
* Exit lane technology
* Perimeter camera improvements
* Inclusion of the Rap Back Program

Complacency is a deadly sin and cannot be tolerated in America's airports. Law enforcement classifies complacency as the number one killer of police officers in the line of duty. Complacency in our countries aviation industry can, and more than likely will result in weakened security. Weakened security foreshadows innocent people in our airports or on planes in our skies becoming victims again when the next 9/11 occurs in America. The Webster dictionary describes complacency as, "self-satisfaction especially when accompanied by unawareness of actual dangers or deficiencies." Burn and Harrell used a definition in their survey paper, "Threat Perceptions and Drivers of Change in Nuclear Security Around the World." Although directed at nuclear facilities, their definition applies perfectly if not more so to our nation's airports:

"Complacency – the belief that the threat is modest and the measures already in place are adequate – is the principal enemy of action. Hence, a better understanding of the reality is critical to getting countries around the world to put stronger protections in place."[293]

RECOMMENDATIONS:

The nation's passenger airports should be under the shared leadership of two Executive Officers, the Business Executive Officer and the Public Safety Executive Officer. Both Executive Officers will only have authority over their designated duties and responsibilities. The following is an outline of a proposed concept of shared leadership in America's Airports:

1. Airport Business Executive Director will:
   * Manage all airport landside and airside operations under the FAA and TSA regulations.
   * Manage the Airport Master Plan, Airport Operations, Airfield Facilities, Passenger Terminal Facilities Aviation Support Facilities, and Airport Operation Center.
2. Airport Law Enforcement/Public Safety Executive Director will be responsible for all aspects of Airport Security and Law Enforcement:
   * Responsible for updating and maintaining the Airport Security Plan and act as the primary security liaison between the airport and TSA.
   * Manage all airport law enforcement and security operations of the airport by FAA and TSA regulations. This will include a periodic review of all security-related functions to ensure compliance with the security program and applicable Security Directives from TSA. Initiate corrective action for instances of noncompliance, and conduct and review new airport job applicants' employment history and criminal background checks.
   * Acts as the designated Airport Security Coordinator.

CHAPTER 12

TSA: Transportation Security Administration

———————

"If you have 10,000 regulations, you
destroy all aspects of the law."

—WINSTON CHURCHILL

"No more essential duty of government exists than the
protection of its people. Fail this, and we fail everything."

----JUSTICE FRANCIS T. MURPHY

AS A NEW AIRPORT WATCH commander, I immediately realized my
working relationship with TSA must be an active and sustainable one
to meet my law enforcement goals of providing a safe and secure airport. Through my tenure as an airport watch commander, I networked
with other airport police agencies across the nation. I joined in many
discussions and participated with other airport police agencies in joint
training missions. I learned their difficulties and successes in working with TSA were similar to mine. During this time, we discovered
a clear understanding of TSA's operations was essential to a cohesive airport security partnership. Knowledge of the TSA at their airport provides watch commanders the ability to react to a situation or
emergency with foreknowledge of his TSA security partners response

procedures as the police rush to the scene of an airport incident. To obtain this edge, an airport watch commander must know everything about one of the most critical security partner, the Transportation Security Agency.

Before 9/11, the airlines and airports contracted with private screening companies who provided the passenger screening at airports. Since TSA took over the nation's airport screening, they have become the lynchpin in the machine that drives our airport passenger security. This is not by choice of the majority of airports' administrations and airport police agencies, but by a Federal law passed by Congress.

WHAT IS THE TSA?

In our nation's airports, the TSA is the regulatory power that sets the security parameters for the commercial aviation industry. The TSA does not have law enforcement powers and operates a variety of programs surrounding its core function of screening passengers for admittance into the secured side of our nation's 450 commercial airports. The TSA was created to provide screening of travelers, but along the way evolved and administered programs that allow them to move teams of screeners randomly to virtually anywhere in our nation's airports. The TSA operates in many formats, from the intelligence-gathering arena to checked baggage screening and TSA Behavior Detection Officers. There are TSA inspectors who test and investigate their employees and all company employees at the airport. TSA has program specialists, regulatory inspectors, security managers, and a variety of operation officers. TSA operates special programs such as the Visible Intermodal Prevention and Response (VIPR) teams who operate by:

> "Deploying at random locations and times in cooperation with local authorities to deter and defeat terrorist activity, or teams may be deployed to provide additional law enforcement or security presence at transportation venues during specific alert

periods or in support of special events. TSA routinely conducts thousands of VIPR operations each year in transportation systems nationwide."[294]

TSA manages special programs such U.S. Air Marshalls, Federal Deck Officer Program for flight crew's use of firearms, the "Secure Flight" program that identifies high-risk passengers and low-risk passengers, and a host of support personnel positions and trainers.[295] These positions are mostly filled by promotions within TSA entry-level employees.[296]

TSA Employee Hiring Qualifications and Employee Turnover

What has been the hiring success at TSA? When TSA started an online blog, it inadvertently revealed a startling statistic that revealed over 67,000 TSA employees left the agency within the last decade.[297] TSA employees incidents appear in negative print news stories and are common in television news for TSA employee crimes they committed, unethical conduct and lack of common sense in running a massive nationwide airport security organization. They have been the brunt of humiliation and sarcasm by every facet of American society.

Why is such a disproportional amount of adverse public opinion cast on TSA more so than on any other federal agency, even surpassing the Internal Revenue Service? One reason is the highly visible position the TSA screeners are in and the perceived power they inappropriately exercise when dealing with the public on a daily basis. Once the TSA walked down this road of adversity with the American public, it became a one-way trip.

To successfully apply and be hired by the TSA as a screener, you are required to have a GED or a high school diploma. The GED or diploma requirement isn't necessary if you have one year of experience as a security guard or as an X-ray technician. Many TSA employees apply for the screening job to obtain a path of entry into the federal job market that offers lucrative jobs within the federal government.[298] The newly-hired TSA screener receives an initial 40 hours of classroom screening training and 60 hours of on-the-job training. The new TSA recruit is then given a uniform and badge and is assigned the duties of keeping bombs, knives, and guns from passing through the screening lanes. Things don't get any smoother for TSA employees when hired. After their training, they receive an onslaught of new monthly (if not weekly) security directives and instructions on how to implement them. These security directives, without much customization, are applied at every large and small airport in the country.

Sometimes even the TSA management personnel make negative news stories. In the early formative stages of TSA, there seemed to be no rhyme or reason to the hiring criteria for Federal Security Directors (FSD) who managed each airport's new TSA program. In 2003, former FAA Inspector Margie Burns said new airport FSD had interesting backgrounds that lacked expertise in aviation security. Some were ex-military; several came from public affairs, political offices, or communication fields. The first wave of FSDs came from diverse positions such as a dean from the Naval Academy, an administrator at the El Paso FBI office, and the head of security for the Phillip Morris tobacco corporation.

Some controversy was linked to the initial hiring of FSDs, as in the case of the FSD hired after being removed from the DEA in the Southern USA area for interfering with a drug investigation. A California airport received an FBI official who had just retired from the FBI rather quickly, due to 75 FBI employees filing a joint grievance against him. Even lower level TSA managers such as Assistant Federal Security Directors displayed immediate problems, as exemplified by the one who stabbed his fellow TSA worker to death.[299] United States Congressional Representative John Mica summarized the TSA hiring practices years later when he gave his opinion on September 28, 2012: "TSA is probably the worst personnel manager that we have in the entire federal government. It is an outrage to the public and, actually, to our aviation system."[300]

TSA AND ITS AIRPORT SECURITY PARTNERS

The airport TSA Federal Security Director partners at airports are the civilian airport director and the sworn law enforcement airport police chief. Every airport has a security plan that the Federal Transportation Security Agency requires under section 1542 of their regulations. Airport directors create and implement the TSA approved Airport Security Plan (ASP). The civilian airport director manages the ASP and is responsible for implementation and adherence to the TSA regulations.

The law enforcement agency is a major security stakeholder at each airport and is TSA's enforcement partner. The airport police provide for the physical security and law enforcement of the entire airport. Most airports law enforcement officers operate police dispatch communications, surveillance cameras, emergency alarms response, and vehicle/foot patrols to name a few duties. The airport police enforce the airport ordinances, county/state laws, and the Homeland Security directives.

During my time at John Wayne Airport, I worked daily on the front line with the TSA screeners, supervisors, and management. As the airport police training supervisor, I instructed TSA personnel, as well as airport and airline personnel in emergency disaster planning and response. Through the implementation of security partners' cross training, common ground is created between the airport security stakeholders. Through years of training together, we became aware of each other's respective roles in the security of the airport, and each other's specific operational boundaries and where our duties overlapped.

In an airport comparison study, I conducted interviews with rank and file TSA officials, airport administrators, and police personnel at twenty American airports. In the analysis, I asked questions related to many facets of their airport's security operations. The study revealed accounts of security partners' incidents with the TSA that were both good and bad. But what stood out in the study were the many diverse airport security methods implemented throughout our nation's airports, while the TSA maintained a national standardized regulatory role throughout the 450 airports it served.

From the analysis, I concluded many of our security stakeholders' and TSA problems were very similar to my airport's conflicts. I found where airports' security partners' duties merged and overlapped, friction between them arose. The different security stakeholders methods of operations and territorial issues were at the core of many conflicts between the TSA airport security partners.

WHEN TSA AND THE AIRPORT POLICE CLASH:

A sister airport police department in California told me about a confrontation between their airport police agency and the TSA assigned to his airport. The event started when an off-duty police officer arrived at the airport for a flight and checked his luggage with the airlines. He declared to the airlines his duty handgun was inside a locked gun case, unloaded and secured inside his checked suitcase. The police officer left on his flight, and arrived at his destination and discovered his handgun missing from his luggage.

The airport police received a report of the crime at the departing airport, and they immediately started an investigation. The police went to the TSA screening room and reviewed the video during the time the bag traversed through the room and saw a TSA employee taking the gun case from the luggage. The airport police immediately asked to obtain a copy of the video and to speak with the TSA officer. Here's where things got dicey; the TSA supervisor refused both requests and the airport police went from partnership mode to a criminal investigator position and told the TSA supervisor to comply, or be arrested for interfering with a criminal investigation. The airport TSA Federal Security Director arrived, and a standoff occurred with both sides saying they would arrest each other.

The federal and state laws were on the airport police side, and after a contentious back and forth, the police were allowed to interview the TSA officer. The investigators received information before their interview that the TSA management told the suspect TSA screener he didn't have to say anything to the airport police. When the investigators interviewed the employee, his only statement was, "I was told I don't have to say a thing to you, and I'm not going to." The investigators continued their inquiry, and through interviews found a co-worker of the TSA employee who told the police the suspect TSA employee stole the gun from the luggage and sold it to a relative. Confronted with the new evidence, the TSA officer confessed to the theft and said his relative sold it to a local gang member. Once aware of the evidence and the range of jail time he could receive for his crimes, the suspect TSA officer coerced his cousin to buy back the gun and returned it to the police.

Charlotte Airport Director Jerry Orr commented in the Congress Oversight Committee report on TSA his concerns about the TSA relationship with his airport security stakeholders. Orr said in his working with the TSA at his airport the communication was poor at best and "TSA's lack of responsiveness and bureaucratic confusion undermines its airports' security efforts." This following sentiment that Orr expressed is more than likely shared by many airport administrators and security chiefs around the nation:

> "I am confident, as mentioned earlier, that I am not the only airport operator with significant concerns about the effectiveness of TSA. Where TSA has become an adversary rather than a partner for security, real needs are being lost."[301]

A TSA Protocol and Its Adversarial Effects with Their Security Partners

Another example of the TSA and airport police having a negative and confrontational relationship occurred at an airport in America. The TSA Inspectors' position at this airport has many duties, and one auxiliary function was to police the police. The TSA airport inspectors created a variety of "test situations," such as setting off alarms at terminal exit doors that lead to passenger aircraft locations. The TSA inspectors would time the airport police officers' responses to the alarms, often without prior notification to the police administration. This response testing took officers away from their real duties in an active airport and provided real potential threats a window of opportunity. Over a considerable period of time, the airport officers were incensed with the TSA, and the security partnership deteriorated.

The airport watch commander at this airport developed an amicable working relationship with one of the TSA assistant federal security directors. During the time of strife between the airport security stakeholders, the watch commander and the assistant federal security director discovered their similar goals allowed them to overcome many of the problems that caused conflict between their two agencies. On the other hand, other members of the TSA found it difficult to communicate with other airport security stakeholder members, except through other management level administrators. In the hallways of the police agency and the airport operation offices, there were constant disparaging of the TSA from the top down. The watch commander heard likewise, from his TSA security partner that the TSA employees disparaged the airport officials and his law enforcement officers in the hallways of the TSA work locations.

The TSA assistant director often said the TSA and airport employee's just don't get it when talking about their failure to understand the full context of the comprehensive homeland security effort. His TSA rank and file suffered from the fundamental lack of security awareness and took their daily jobs as a punch the time clock in and out shift work. He told the watch commander of his battles to prevent complacency and tried daily to keep the big picture in front of TSA employees.

The adversity between the airport security stakeholders became a norm in their work culture where conflicts between them were a daily part of airport security operations. The former commander of the U.S. strategic forces, General Eugene Habiger, said, "Good security is 20 percent equipment and 80 percent culture."[302] Conflicts between airport security stakeholders decrease the security of an airport. Airport security is more than the x-ray machines, alarm systems, and video surveillance; its success is in large part on the shoulders of the men and women who collectively work together in the various airport security positions.

HALF OF ALL TSA EMPLOYEES COMMIT MISCONDUCT

I wasn't shocked by when I read the House Homeland Security Committee Majority Staff Report released in July 2016, I was, however, found to be wrong in my previous belief that a lesser percentage of the TSA employees were culpable in some misconduct during the terms of their employment. The TSA's data itself revealed between 2013 and 2015, almost half of the TSA employees committed some form of misconduct that ranged from insubordination, ignoring policies/procedures, sexual misconduct, fighting, bribing, criminal conduct, and misuse of government property to name just a few listed in the report.[303]

What troubles me most is the House Homeland Security Committee title of their report: "Misconduct at TSA Threatens the Security of the Flying Public." The implications of this title along should be echoing down the halls of every airport terminal in America. With that being said, I will share an airport police insider view of interactions and incidents with TSA employees. The following information may provide stimulus for public discussion when considering sending their elected officials their concerns for the TSA. The following are personal accounts and stories from other airport law enforcement agencies of TSA employee's misconduct attested to the House Homeland Security Committee.

TSA AIRPORT SCREENING FAILURES

The enormous cost of TSA since its inception should naturally infer that the United States airport screening of passengers is the best in the world. Our airports' screening for explosive devices, weapons of all types, and contraband should be the most accurate system that ensures our aviation security. But the following examples possibly show the opposite is occurring. At an airport in America, the police received a call from the TSA supervisor asking for assistance at the south terminal screening lanes. The watch commander and police officer went to the screening lane to investigate and saw a subject accompanied by his ten-year-old daughter. TSA had earlier placed the man's backpack bag in the x-ray machine, and he passed through the magnetometer without any problem. The TSA randomly selected the subject for secondary screening, and they detained him and his daughter in the selectee area. During the hand-search of his backpack, two loaded 9-millimeter gun magazines were found by a TSA employee. TSA summoned the airport police.

Law enforcement completed a thorough search of the backpack, and they pulled a loaded 9-millimeter handgun with a round in the chamber out of the man's bag. The police officer interrogated the subject and determined he did not intentionally bring the weapon into the airport. The police cited the subject for carrying a concealed weapon, and after clearing a warrant/record check was allowed to continue his flight with his daughter without his gun. The initial x-ray of the backpack was not saved during the incident by TSA due to the failure to see the gun or ammunition magazines.

The watch commander took the handgun and asked TSA to run it through the scanner in the same place inside the luggage to understand why the TSA screener did not see the weapon. The police and TSA viewed it through the x-ray scanner and agreed the TSA employee should have seen the weapon. If the TSA had not selected this passenger for a secondary hand search, he would have been on an airborne passenger jet with a loaded handgun. This story, like many other incidents at our nation's airports, never made the news.

Another example of a TSA screening lane failures is the October 2012, ABC report of a gun undetected in the New Orleans Airport:

"Just one day earlier in Orlando, TSA officers missed another loaded gun. This time, a firefighter had mistakenly left the gun in her purse and carried it right through security screening and on to her plane. The firefighter realized on her own what had happened and alerted authorities."[304]

You have to wonder: How many guns make it through our nation's airport screening without being found?

The Department of Homeland Security Inspector General and the Government Accountability Office (GAO) test TSA screeners on the job at our country's airports. One series of tests revealed that Los Angeles International Airport screeners missed 75 percent of fake bombs while Chicago O'Hara missed 60 percent.[305] The failure rates for detecting prohibited items, weapons, and explosives during these tests are alarmingly high. A few years later, in mid-2015, the TSA tested their screeners again and suffered failures in almost every test given to them by undercover TSA inspectors. The screeners failed 67 out of 70 tests, resulting in the reassignment of the acting TSA Director.[306] In July 2017, Minneapolis-St. Paul International Airport TSA Agents failed 95% of the screening security tests conducted by the TSA Washington D.C. Red Team. TSA screeners missed items, such as weapons, explosive materials, and drugs.

TSA screening failures were not all due to ineptness, accident, or missed attempts. The TSA at Honolulu Airport fired 30 screeners for massive failures to screen baggage where they would falsify baggage as inspected without looking inside.[307] Even non-firearm weapons make it through screening as in this case at JFK Airport in March of 2013, when a rape suspect made it through screening and was waiting to board his flight when police arrested him and found an illegal stun gun in his possession.[308]

One of the most egregious security lane breaches happened in Dallas Ft. Worth Texas. A man boldly walked around a non-used metal detector and blended in with the screened passengers. As the man walks past a sitting TSA agent, the surveillance video showed the agent with his head lowered looking at his cell phone held between his legs. The man went straight to the passenger jet where he confronted his girlfriend, who was a legitimate passenger on the jet, in a domestic dispute. Fourteen minutes later, the police arrived and arrested the man.[309]

COMMON SENSE AND RATIONALITY

One of the TSA's biggest handicaps is their failure to incorporate common sense into this procedure. The TSA screener supervisor called my officers to our south screening lanes, one day, for an incident concerning a security breach that had just occurred. I arrived thinking some suspicious character had slipped by the TSA security and was now about to conduct some nefarious act on the secure side of the terminal.

"What's going on?" I asked the TSA supervisor as I approached him.

"A person went through without getting screened," he told me, pointing to a crowd of passengers near an airline check-in gate.

I scanned the crowd but didn't see anyone that stood out as particularly suspicious. Looking back to the officer, I asked, "Who's the suspect?"

He sheepishly looked down. "It, uh, was a baby, but I don't know where he is."

I asked more questions and found out a mother with her baby came into the screening lane to be cleared to board an airplane. The mother had an injury that required her to wear a steel leg brace and use a walking cane. Accompanying the mother were two other female relatives, and when it was the mother's turn to be screened, she handed the baby to a previously screened relative. The baby was taken to the airline gate by the relative while the mother went to the secondary screening.

In secondary screening, a person is given a pat-down and scrutinized closely for any security issues. Some people are randomly selected for secondary screening while others are chosen purposely for various reasons.[310] The mother was taken to secondary screening so the security officers could examine the leg brace and pat her down by hand. While this procedure was starting, one of the TSA screeners realized that the baby wasn't screened and notified the TSA supervisor, who in turn called me. TSA sounded an audible alarm and stopped screening passengers. My officers fanned out to look for the baby. I understand that a person could use an innocent baby to smuggle prohibited items into an airport, but the totality of the circumstances should be governed with common sense.

I found the two relatives with the baby and smiled as I asked them to bring the baby back to the screening lanes. They looked perplexed, but they willingly returned. The TSA screeners still had the mother sitting down, and she was taking the leg brace off as I walked into the screening lane. The relative returned the baby to the screening lanes, and a TSA screener started to feel the legs and arms of the nine-month-old and check under the car seat holder for suspicious items.

While the TSA officer frisked the baby, I turned around and was surprised to see the mother hobbling through the x-ray machine without her brace or crutch. Dumbfounded, I turned to the TSA supervisor and asked if he understood the liability if the mother further injured her leg because of this nonsensical procedure. The supervisor immediately took the cane to the mother and escorted her back to the chair and her leg brace. These type of procedures are not just a local problem, but it is systemic with TSA employees' not using common sense or should I say "moral sense." The TSA employees are completely overwhelmed by a massive, centralized regulatory agency's black and white policy and procedures. When TSA employees are off duty and at home, I have no doubt they exercise common sense in their everyday life and never conduct themselves at home as some TSA employees have at work that creates the embarrassing incidents that the news media has highlighted time and time again.

Aristotle was the first person known to discuss "common sense." His take was, as humans, we are capable of "real reason thinking, " and various philosophers have expounded on this common sense discussion throughout the centuries. I, being a simple man prefer to take the definition from the Merriam-Webster Dictionary and the Cambridge Dictionary with a recommendation to add this essential guide to the TSA policies. Merriam-Webster defines common sense as: "Sound and prudent judgment based on a simple perception of the situation or facts" and Cambridge states "The basic level of practical knowledge and judgment that we all need to help us live reasonably and safely."[311]

In February 2013, a Missouri family planned to fly out of the St. Louis International Airport to Disney World in Orlando, Florida. Their three-year-old daughter is confined to a wheelchair because she suffers from spina bifida. After passing through the TSA screening lane, the three-year-old was singled out for additional screening measures. The TSA told the parents they chose their daughter because she was in a wheelchair. The TSA agent said the child would be patted down and her wheelchair swabbed for explosives. For over 20 minutes the parents went through a horrific ordeal. The TSA took their daughter's comforting lamb doll away, patted her down, and her wheelchair searched. If Aristotle were present at the screening lanes, what conclusion would he have reached as to the reasoning for this search? The disturbing irrational acts are depicted in the video of the ordeal and are found at; http://radio.foxnews.com/toddstarnes/top-stories/tsa-detains-3-year-old-in-wheelchair.html.

TSA had tried to meet the ever-evolving challenge of an enemy who can camouflage his attack plans to meet the challenge of our nation's security efforts. To this end, TSA has mechanically placed procedures that are designed to fit all, yet distressfully fails without end. Let me provide you with a couple of concrete examples of TSA's lack of rational thinking regarding the real-world application. I received information that former Army General and Secretary of State Colin Powell and his wife would arrive at my airport for a departure flight. I had arranged a private pre-board screening for the couple, due to General Powell's status as the Commanding General in Desert Storm and his prior position as the Secretary of State in President Bush's cabinet. When he arrived, I met him and his wife and escorted them to a pre-determined area where I had staged two TSA screeners and their supervisor to accommodate their expedient entrance into our terminal for their security and safety.

The female TSA screener used a metal detecting handheld device to screen Mrs. Powell. Once finished, the TSA employee said to Mrs. Powell, "Now I'll need to pat you down, ma'am." I immediately looked from the employee to the TSA supervisor, who appeared equally in compliance with the plan. "That won't be necessary," I said. "There won't be a pat down of Mrs. Powell or General Powell, either one." The TSA supervisor immediately agreed and said; "Oh, of course not! No pat down necessary, of course not!" "Thanks for your assistance," I said with a smile as I escorted General and Mrs. Powell to the elevator.

My second example of TSA occurred when Nobel Peace Laureate, former Secretary of State, and National Security Advisor Henry Kissinger entered a TSA screening lane in a wheelchair in an airport on the East Coast. At the age of 89, the TSA asked Mr. Kissinger to stand up for weapons or explosives searching. Again, I recognize that a wheelchair or an elderly passenger can smuggle prohibited items into an airport, but common sense alone should tell you that Henry Kissinger is not a threat to our national security, airports or passenger jetliners.

The inappropriate screening procedures practiced on certain passengers so often reveals a lack of common sense that makes incidents like this a public relations plague on TSA. Another TSA screening standoff occurred in Nashville, Tennessee when TSA officers held Senator Rand Paul for a body pat-down after their screening x-ray machine suffered an anomaly. Senator Paul offered to go through the machine again, but the TSA employees refused and insisted on conducting a body pat down. Senator Paul refused to be patted down, resulting in a standoff. TSA is not preferential to Republicans only. They nailed Diane Feinstein, a Democrat and the chair of the Senate Intelligence Committee, for a pat-down as well.

None of those former government officials mentioned are above Homeland Security and the law, but they are not a threat to any aircraft that they are about to board! A quick, thorough cursory handheld electronic wand or metal detector walk through check is sufficient screening for such people. I think actor Bradley Cooper summed it up best, "I think if you live in a black and white world, you're gonna suffer a lot. I used to be like that. But I don't believe that anymore."[312]

A Snapshot Look at TSA in Newark Airport

The Newark New Jersey International Airport location is a testament to a TSA program that has imploded with a consistent decade of endemic instability. This is not exclusive just with Newark as many TSA groups at other airports have shared similar problems.

On a recent trip to Europe, I flew into and out of Newark. As an airport law enforcement member, I always observe the local police and TSA employees at the airports I travel through. During my three-hour layover in Newark, I saw a young male TSA screener working the x-ray carry on luggage duties. I stood nearby watching; the young man stares at attractive female passengers as bags proceeded through his x-ray screen monitor without him looking at the screen. I estimated three bags passed through without the screener so much as glancing at the monitor screen, his eyes glued instead to the women walking through the screening lanes. Having worked with TSA employees for years, I know this particular behavior was not an isolated incident, as it occurs at Newark, my airport, and many other airports. Newark has suffered failure after failure in its TSA airport security operations. On March 29, 2013, TSA announced:

> "After a year-long investigation of baggage screening at Newark Liberty Airport, the Transportation Security Administration moved to fire 25 screeners and supervisors and suspend 19 others. After nearly six months of due process hearings, the TSA announced that a total of four employees were dismissed, 32 were suspended, and six were exonerated."[313]

As I completed a research project on Newark Liberty International Airport TSA for this book, the number of adverse TSA incidents at the airport alarmed me. Since early 2003 when they officially took over the screening responsibilities, a decade of failures occurred. Examples of the TSA failures at Newark started when the *USA Today* News reported in 2004 of the removal of nine Newark TSA agents from their job for failing two proficiency tests. The screeners said the "do or die" test scared them and caused them great stress, and they felt they "weren't adequately trained."[314] That same year Newark TSA airport screeners told newspaper reporters that thousands of bags a day were not being screened for explosives and stated, "It's all smoke and mirrors" because TSA is understaffed, and they are pressured by airlines and the airport to keep the lines moving.

In 2005, TSA cracked down on 210 of its security screeners at Newark for abusing sick time. One-sixth of the TSA Newark workforce was told to bring in doctors' notes when calling in sick. The underlying reason for the chronic sick call-outs, as stated by TSA Newark screeners, was "poor morale." The *Newark Star Ledger* news article quoted Newark TSA employees that absenteeism is a major contributor to the continuing security troubles at Newark, causing forced long shifts where the TSA screeners could not do their job properly because of fatigue.[315]

A year later, in 2006, Newark TSA screeners failed 20 of 22 security tests that were conducted by undercover agents. During the tests, screeners did not follow operating procedures. Fake bombs were hidden in bottles taped to an agent's body and elsewhere were not discovered by the screeners. The Newark TSA official said, "We just totally missed everything."[316] Again, the problems were not just in the screening lanes. In 2007, a Newark TSA manager gave test questions illegally to a TSA candidate for a management position to ensure the prospective candidate finished at the top. Newark TSA problems revealed a top-down, bottom-up systemic failure as each year the news broke on yet another TSA problem in Newark.

I could go on with examples, year after year, of Newark TSA employee failures, but I'll culminate my list with a 2012, *ABC News* story on former Newark TSA screener Pythias Brown. Brown learned how to identify valuable items on the TSA provided x-ray scanner and used the same equipment to steal from the passengers. Brown also used his inside knowledge of the inoperable surveillance cameras locations as moments of opportunity to steal, and even his agency-owned TSA approved locks were easy to pick without anyone knowing. The core of the TSA employee problem as cited by *ABC News*, showed a "culture" of apathy that afforded TSA workers reasons to steal from passengers and placed the blame directly on managements' lack of oversight and collusion of fellow TSA employees.

THE TSA MANAGEMENT AT NEWARK INTERNATIONAL AIRPORT

The Federal Security Director at Newark Airport oversees all aspects of TSA's airport security plan. His job is to work with the airport administration and airport police in providing essential leadership in its implementation. Newark's first Federal Security Director (FSD) was a manager of various Federal Aviation Administration assignments that covered airport security issues. Three years after he started his job as the FSD, Newark Airport had suffered a plague of security screening lapses and low morale. No reason was given when the FSD left his post at the Newark Airport.

The replacement FSD hailed from public relations, lobbyist, and White House event planner position in two presidents' administrations. Even with experience as a senior director of the Port Authority of New York, he immediately came under fire for lack of a prior law enforcement or professional aviation background. According to news accounts, he raised TSA employees' morale, but Newark still suffered through many TSA employee failures during his brief 16-month tenure. The FSD decided to move on and take the FSD job at Miami International Airport for undisclosed reasons.

In stepped another Federal Security Director, whose background was legal counsel for a harbor commission, and the Bureau of Alcohol, Tobacco, and Firearms (ATF). This FSD resigned in 2011 and took another post at TSA. The fourth FSD at Newark Airport took the reins in 2011. In October 2012, the Newark FSD fired 25 TSA screeners for inadequate passenger screening, sleeping on the job, and failing to follow standard operating procedures.[317] Two years later in October of 2014, the Newark FSD received a promotion, and another FSD took the reins.

Through 12 years, five professional, highly educated, multi-skilled managers walked into the Newark TSA Federal Security Director Office, and they all suffered the same systemic failures. How does that happen? The revolving door of TSA leadership at Newark had a more adverse effect than positive ones, and this type of rapid leadership change would impede any company's progress and success. Reviewing the immense amount of data on Newark TSA, coupled with my experience working with TSA at an airport, led me to believe that the TSA span of control at 450 plus airports is too large. I feel the core reason for TSA problems are it's rigidly structured 'one shoe fits all' procedures and philosophy that stems from the centralized Washington D.C. Headquarters and its management philosophy. I believe this has been the genesis of many problems and various failures of TSA throughout the nation.

TSA Employee Criminal Conduct at America's Airports

Screening failures are a serious matter, but criminal acts by employees of a Federal regulatory agency, whose mission is to safeguard the citizen, are unconscionable. I've seen investigations and criminal convictions of TSA employees at my airport for thefts of passenger property perpetrated by TSA officers. In one case, a TSA officer found a gold bracelet left by a passenger in the property tray and took it. A week later, she wore it on duty while working the screening lane. When the police questioned the TSA screener, she confessed and was subsequently charged with theft and fired.

I mentioned TSA supervisor Pythias Brown earlier and his four-year rampage of stealing from passengers' luggage at Newark Airport. I have to start the subject of TSA employee criminal conduct by using Pythias Brown as the poster child for this subject.[318] TSA Officer Pythias Brown provided a stark testament to the core problems that are endemic to TSA at one level or another. Between 2003 and 2012, Brown was one of over 400 TSA employees who was involved in thefts from airport passengers. Brown admitted to stealing over three-quarters of a million dollars of items from passenger luggage and at the security checkpoints. Brown simply summed up one of the reasons as, "It became so easy, I got complacent."[319]

There are several contributing factors in the Brown case. First, as previously stated by Pythias Brown, the TSA employees developed a culture of indifference. This indifference diminished the TSA employee's moral conscious to protect the passenger's luggage and stealing from passengers' personal belongings became easy. As in most employee thefts no matter where they occur, failure to supervise the TSA officers is the chief contributing factor for TSA employee thefts. In Brown's case, it trickled down from the supervisors, where one told him management was talking about him, and that alerted Brown to take precautions while continuing his crimes. This tells you even when supervision suspected Brown of criminal conduct; they failed to stop him. Brown alluded to his criminal activities as being a drug type high, saying, "It was like being on drugs. I was like, what am I doing? But the next day I was right back at it." [320]

This reprehensible TSA crime story culminates with why Brown and his co-workers broke the trust the nation gave them. Brown said many of the TSA officers said they didn't care and cited one reason for their actions was not being paid adequately, and taking the passengers' personal property was justified compensation. Other TSA officers said the TSA management was mistreating them and the thefts, again, were compensation for the perceived injustice by the TSA management.[321]

But the most important reason that crosses over into all of humanity is pure greed. Referring to the extent of TSA officers' thefts, Brown said, "It became massive." Brown's four-year crime binge only came to an end when he did not remove all the News Corporation CNN stickers off of the CNN Network camera he had stolen and listed on eBay. After

Brown's arrest, investigators found Brown had current listings of video games, laptops, and 80 stolen cameras for sale on eBay.

Representative Mike Rogers, Chairman of the House Homeland Security Transportation Subcommittee, had this to say about TSA's image, "Stealing from checked luggage, accepting bribes from drug smugglers, sleeping or drinking on duty—this kind of criminal behavior and negligence has contributed significantly to TSA's shattered public image."[322]

TSA officers stealing are a grave concern for the safety and security of our nation's airports. But there is more egregious criminal conduct by TSA officers. An example occurred on April 26, 2012, when the police arrested four Los Angeles airport TSA officers for allowing luggage full of methamphetamines to pass through their screening lanes secretly. These officers didn't only miss the presence of the drugs; they were in fact paid thousands of dollars in cash bribes to turn a blind eye on this drug shipment. The officers would communicate through phone texting to coordinate the drug courier's entrance into their screening lanes.[323] The US Attorney said this represented a "significant" breakdown in the airport security system.

At another airport, one of the TSA officers failed to show up for work, and a subsequent investigation revealed she was absent because she was assisting her husband after he escaped from a minimum-security state prison. This particular TSA officer's moral indiscretion and wrong choices are similar to the many other TSA employee decisions throughout our nation's airports.

The criminal misconduct by TSA officers is not limited to theft and bribery, even crimes such as sexual assault misconduct occurs. This example will suggest there are no limits or reasons why TSA screeners fail. A male homosexual TSA officer devised a plan that allowed him to grope an attractive male passenger for the TSA officer's sexual gratification. The TSA officer recruited a female TSA officer to assist him by having her push the "female" button on the body scanning machine when a male would walk through. This would signal an abnormality as the male passengers walked through due to the female-male genitalia differences. The homosexual TSA officer would then conduct a secondary screening of the targeted male passenger by patting down the passenger's groin and buttock area. After months of complaints, the TSA supervision conducted surveillance on the two TSA officers and discovered the allegations were true. The TSA fired the two TSA officers.[324]

How the TSA Investigates and Disciplines Employees

The July 2016 House Homeland Security Committee report said the TSA was not prone to investigate a majority of employee misconduct cases. Misconduct cases rose between 2010 and 2012 by virtually 27 percent, yet from 2013 to 2015 the number of cases opened by the TSA to investigate decreased by 15 percent. In all the misconduct allegations in 2013, only 6 percent were investigated. The TSA did not investigate 94 percent of the reported misconduct cases in their active disciplinary system. In 2015, only 4 percent of all cases of alleged misconduct were investigated.

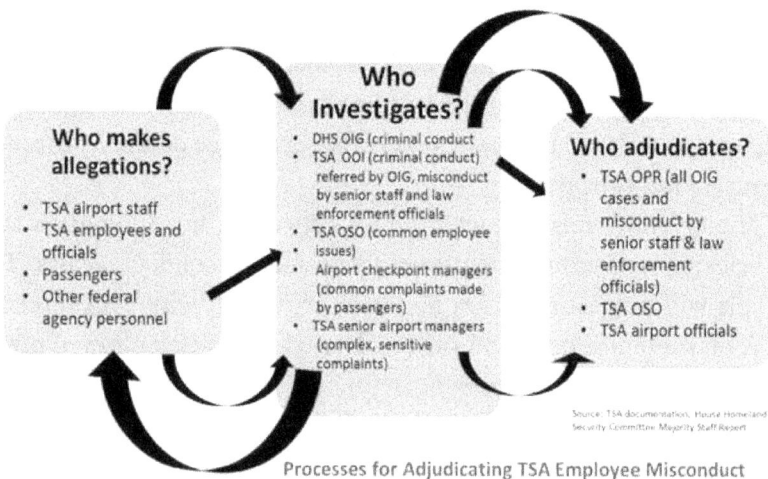

Processes for Adjudicating TSA Employee Misconduct

Rendition Graph by W. Herrin

So how did we get to this point? The House Report said the bureaucracy of the TSA system is responsible for the lack of oversight and responsibility in handling alleged employee misconduct complaints. The above illustration recreated from the House Report reveals the complex and disorganized TSA system now in place that reviews allegations of their employee's misconduct.

FEDERALIZATION VS. PRIVATIZATION OF SCREENERS

The nation's airports have witnessed the TSA successes and failures, and the pertinent question is asked: Are TSA screeners any better than private screeners? Before TSA took over the security screening at airports, screening was the responsibility of individual airlines and airport operators. Most airports selected through a bidding process, their contracted screening security companies. The Federal Aviation Administration (FAA) provided the oversight of airlines and airports' screening operations before 9/11. The airlines and airports were not receptive to the FAA regulations and often choose the least expensive private security screening companies and equipment so the overhead cost could be reduced, and profits increased. These security-screening companies' employees were inadequate in levels of performance. A good indicator that the airport screening was not doing well in 2000 was the red flag that the largest 19 U.S. airport security screening operations suffered an average of 126 percent in employee turnovers, from May 1998 to April 1999.[325]

Immediately after 9/11, the U.S. Senate opted with 100 percent of the senators voting in favor for a complete governmental takeover of all of America's airports' security. The House of Representatives was less enthusiastic and opted along Republican and Democrat party lines for airports to choose between private versus government airport security screeners. President Bush pushed for the "federalization" of all airport security screeners and tipped the balance for governmental control, thus putting in motion the creation of TSA.[326]

Since 9/11, the Government Accountability Office has analyzed the issue and came to the conclusion that the expensive TSA airport screening is not much better than, and in most cases equal to, the private company screening that was in place before 9/11. The five private screening companies that operate today at airports in the United States perform as well as, and, for the most part, better than, their federal counterpart. So why are we expanding an expensive government agency that performs equally and not better than the private sector?

Mr. Robert Poole is Director of Transportation Policy and Searle Freedom Trust Transportation Fellow at The Reason Foundation. Poole, an engineer who studied at MIT, has advised the Ronald Reagan, the George H.W. Bush, the Clinton, and the George W. Bush administrations. Poole first proposed the commercialization of the U.S. air-traffic control systems, and many have followed in his footsteps in echoing the need for change. Canada implemented a version of his corporation concept that is also heavily favored by several former top FAA administrators.[327] Poole best summarizes issues regarding the TSA screening responsibilities in his Policy Study 340 for the Reason Foundation:

"There are three basic flaws in the current model. First, the law presumes that all air travelers are equally likely to be a threat, and mandates equal attention (and spending) on each—which is very wasteful of scarce security resources. Second, the TSA operates in a highly centralized manner, which is poorly matched to the wide variation in sizes and types of passenger airports. And third, the law puts the TSA in the conflicting position of being both the airport security policymaker/regulator and the provider of some (but not all) airport security services."[328]

On April 5, 2013, Shon Agard researched and submitted a scientific thesis for Eastern Kentucky University titled, 'Civilian Aviation Screening: A Time-Series Analysis of Confiscated Firearms at Screening Checkpoints.' Agard used a series of quantitative data analysis's to compare the number of guns confiscated by airport screeners from 1990 to 2009. In the study, Agard reviewed the screening processes used by the private and federal methods and found the passenger screening models were identical. He also found the technology of X-ray machines and magnetometers remained consistent over the period of the analysis and disproved any argument that advances in screening technology had an effect on the number of firearms confiscated each year. Agard said as a result of his studies, "We can assume that, although two different groups of people and processes are being performed, the same results are likely to occur." "There is no significant difference in the level of firearm confiscations after the federalization of the civilian aviation screening process."[329]

In essence, he concludes that despite the enormous increase in cost by the U.S. Government, we would have accomplished the same number of firearms results if the TSA had never taken over the screening lanes.[330] Agard made a disclaimer that neither private nor public sector screening services are more effective than its counterpart, but they are equal in the number of confiscations.

The TSA contracted with an independent evaluator, Bearing Point, to assess the private screening operations in comparison to TSA screening operations. Bearing Point found that the private screenings were just as effective as TSA security screening processes, and, in fact, the airports that have private screeners experienced shorter wait times. The U.S. Travel Blue Ribbon Panel on Aviation Security summarized a core issue of the TSA's responsibilities for airport security:

"Some in Congress appear to have calculated that there are no political consequences to an inefficient and costly system, but great political consequences to a successful terrorist attack. This is a classic Hobson's choice that the American traveling public repudiates. The debate Congress must engage in is not strong security versus weak security, but rather how to create a world-class aviation security system that effectively manages risk, increases efficiency and embraces the freedom to travel."[331]

Representative John Mica, Chairman of the House Transportation Committee, expressed his concerns:

> "Having been involved with the TSA and actually picked the name for the Agency and helped craft its enabling legislation some 10 years ago, I've had a chance to monitor its activities closely. And unfortunately, I become more and more concerned with the billions of dollars that are being expended. Some of it just astounds me. We've created an Agency that's actually run pell-mell away from security and turned into a huge, unthinking, non-risk based bureaucracy. Everywhere I turn, I'm appalled at what's taking place."[332]

The Price of TSA Screening

In the previously cited airport security study I conducted of 20 airports, a segment of the study looked at airport police staffing duties and their cost. The airports I used were in South Carolina, Texas, Missouri, Indiana, Ohio, Pennsylvania, Washington, Oregon, and California. I targeted these specific airports due to their similar enplanement annual numbers of my airport. To accurately compare several airports' law enforcement personnel salaries cost in diverse economic areas, I used a medium-income and cost-of-living standard to create an accurate comparison. For instance, at the time of this analysis, the cost of living in Charlotte, North Carolina was 28.6 percent lower than the cost of living in a city in Orange County, California.

Since the TSA is a federal agency, its salary structure is set by national standards and does not take into consideration the local employees cost of living. This directly results in higher tax-dollar expenditures than necessary per employee. Local civilian screening employees will do the same job at a cost based on the lower cost-of-living of locations throughout the United States. In July 2014, yet another tax increase was decreed by the government on airline fares from the previous $2.50 per ticket for a non-stop flight to $5 to meet the escalating cost of the TSA employees.

In 2015, in the approved House Appropriations Homeland Security Bill, the TSA was granted $4.6 billion for its operations at 450 United States commercial airports.[333] TSA employee entry-level salaries are higher than the national average for a high school diploma or less as a requirement to be hired. The United States' Congressional Budget Office (CBO) report "Comparing the Compensation of Federal and Private-Sector Employees," stated: "overall federal civilian workers with a high school diploma earned 21 percent more than similar workers in the private sector."[334]

Average Compensation for Federal and Private-Sector Employees, by Level of Educational Attainment

(2010 dollars per hour)

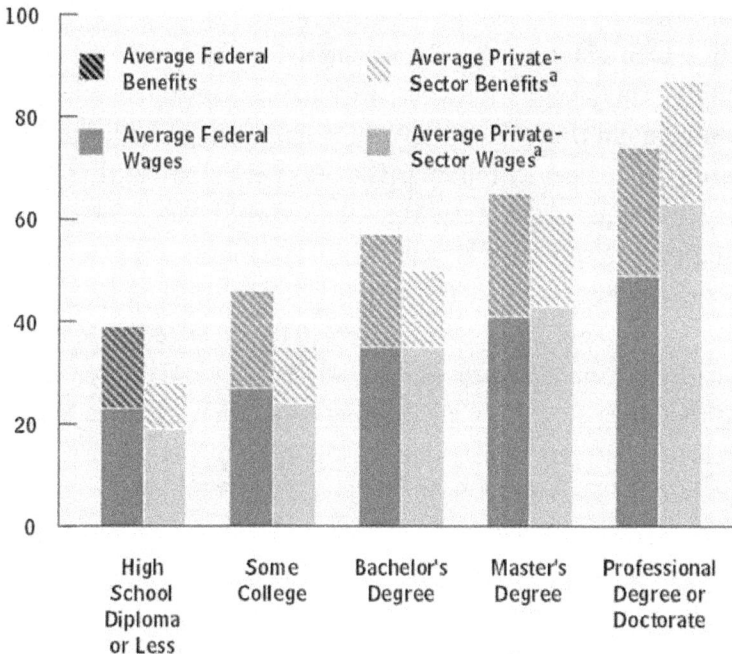

Source: Congressional Budget Office, 2012

Every airport has its busy, average, and slow months. In the past, the private screening companies had the luxury of bringing in temporary seasonal screeners to supplement a core staff during high volume travel months. But TSA allocation of screeners in airports is scheduled on an annual basis. Overstaffing is the result of the seasonal screening workload and is an inherent waste of taxpayers' money. Private screening companies with flexible hiring policies would save our nation's airports and the taxpayers a significant amount of money.

Because of this inefficient use of airport security funding, many airports are trying to move away from TSA screening. One of the largest airports to make this decision is Orlando Sanford International Airport. As reported by the *Miami Herald*, "One of America's busiest airports, Orlando Sanford International, has announced it will opt out of using TSA workers to screen passengers, a move which threatens the highly unpopular federal agency's role in other airports across the nation.[335]

The U.S. House of Representatives' House Transportation Committee conducted a study on privatization versus federal screening. The study found that private contractor screenings were more efficient, screening over 65 percent more passengers per employee than the TSA. The study estimated that taxpayers could save $1 billion over five years by using private screeners at just 35 of the nation's largest airports. To further exasperate the varied differences of opinion when it comes to the price tag of TSA, the TSA screeners have unionized under the AFL/CIO. Unionization has historically increased cost and created new regulations that are a drudge on any business operation.

In David Rittgers' Policy Analysis number 683 entitled Abolish the Department of Homeland Security, he states, "Congress should privatize airport screeners and pass the financial burden of passenger aviation security from the taxpayer to the flying public." Rittgers goes further and argues we should dismantle the entire Department of Homeland Security and to reunite its services and many of its components' to former governmental agencies that previously supplied its particular services. The foundation of Rittgers' argument is the duplication of services by DHS is an enormous waste of vital funding for our nation's security, and instead of fixing problems in existing federal agencies, the government instead created a new bureaucracy. Rittgers said if our airports re-privatized airport security, an estimated $3 billion in savings would occur.[336]

TSA whistleblower U.S. Federal Air Marshal Jeffrey Black directly linked the TSA's volatile work environment to its inability to keep air travelers safe. Black said the TSA concern for its appearance is more important than keeping passengers safe. Black went on to say the National Security Archives' Barbara Elias testified to Congress that TSA is an agency built on "dubious secrets" and is mired in secrecy [337]

RECOMMENDATIONS:

1. Eliminate TSA airport screening services and privatize the national airports' screening of passengers. I am not advocating returning to the private company pre-9/11 airport screening nomenclature. Jonathan Pierce in his paper, "TSA Airport Screeners: Private Contractors or Government Employees," argues for all airport screeners to be part of a public bureaucracy and not hired by private contractors. Pierce said airport screening companies before 9/11 did not provide the necessary oversight and regulations to secure our nation's airports. I argue the free markets will raise the bar for quality security companies who will compete to have their employees replace federal TSA screeners.

   Airport Law Enforcement Agency at each airport will select the private screening companies and will have a five-year period to assume screening operations, following these guidelines:

   * The designated airport law enforcement agency will select and supervise the private company security screening of employees.

- Private airport screener employee applicants must be U.S. citizens.
- The airport law enforcement agency will conduct background checks on all screening company employees.
- The airport police agency will provide on-scene screening lane law enforcement management and supervision of private screening companies in the screening lanes during all hours of operations.
- The private screening company will apply and must be granted the certification under the Support Anti-Terrorism by Fostering Effective Technologies (SAFETY) Act to conduct screening operations at an airport.
- Private screening companies will be required to provide a standard of competitive pay at or above the minimum wage and provide basic essential benefits to airport screeners with adjustment to the local area cost of living range.
- Funding for private screening and law enforcement cost increase will come from a portion of the DHS current per-passenger flight ticket fees from airlines and airports.

2. TSA will provide the following services to airports:
   - All regulatory procedures and policies for application to the specific airport's size, and individual airports' infrastructure and security needs.
   - Train and test all airports' private screening.
   - Administer The Federal Air Marshal Program.
   - Maintain the Threat Intelligence Advisories distribution for airports' law enforcement agencies.
   - Maintain the Airport Bomb Technician and Bomb Dog program in the nation's airports.

3. Eliminate the Screening of Passengers by Observations Techniques (SPOT) and Behavior Detection Officer (BDO) programs and utilize the $200 million spent annually on the SPOT program for improving security measures. The Government

Accountability Office stated the current program SPOT and BDO agent effectiveness in locating dangerous people in the airport terminal are "no better than chance." There were specific areas of concern that the GAO had about the TSA SPOT and BDO program:

* TSA cannot prove the programs are effective.
* SPOT and the BDO were used without proper scientific validation.
* SPOT/BDO did not have substantive performance measures to ensure uniformity. TSA has limited ways of evaluating the program's effectiveness.

4. Focus reassigned personnel to the needs of the international air cargo and international passenger screening and enforcement. The House of Representatives Bill H.R. 4698 Act cited as "Securing Aviation from Foreign Entry Points and Guarding Airports Through Enhanced Security Act of 2016," now requires the TSA to:

* Conduct a risk assessment of all last point of departure airports with nonstop flights to the United States.
* Create a plan to enhance collaboration with domestic and foreign partners to enhance security at foreign airports.
* Review their workforce in the Office of Global Strategies of the Administration to ascertain if they are assigned in a risk-base, intelligence-driven manner.
* Donate screening equipment to other countries who will not or cannot buy their own equipment, to safeguard non-stop flights from these countries into the U.S. Also, to create a plan to evacuate the sensitive security equipment in case of instability in that country.

The 2015 and 2016 New Aviation Security Acts have and will continue to engulf a TSA that is already overwhelmed. Many of the over 70 Acts passed by Congress come with the caveat; "Declares that no additional appropriations are authorized to carry out this Act," as stated in the Gerardo Hernandez Airport Security Act of 2015. The TSA employees and funding saved from the screening lanes focus will be on the threats from abroad and regulatory oversight of each airport for adherence to federal aviation security mandates.

CHAPTER 13

Airport Employee Federal Background Checks and Their Failures

———

"DHS (Department of Homeland Security) officials have
told us that job applicants in the fast-food industry typically
undergo a more robust background check than applicants for
a TWIC card, said Senator Mark Warner, referring to the
TSA-issued Transportation Worker Identity Credential."[338]

OUR AIRPORTS CONTINUE TO EXPAND by leaps and bounds with new airport terminals, runways, and a host of other infrastructure improvements. Demands from the public for more passenger flight selections and new destinations from their local airports spur our growth.[339] This accelerated growth increases the burden on an already overloaded airport security matrix that is falling behind in the security race to safeguard our aviation industry. One concern of aviation security is the accurate and thorough background checks of every employee who works at our nation's airports. America's aviation industry must have one of the strictest hiring guidelines in the nation. The industry is too valuable to America and the world economies, and for this reason, the best security measures are warranted.

In 2014, Los Angeles International Airport (LAX) was an example of an airport that allowed the expansion of its infrastructure that may have lessened some of its security capabilities. LAX has continuously expanded its operations and infrastructure since 9/11. In 2014, the airport had twenty individual construction projects ongoing with an average of over 60,000 contract workers a year at the airport. A large number of projects presented a huge contract worker credentialing problem to screen these temporary employees and issue them credentials that provide them access to restricted airport areas. Deputy Executive Director and Chief Information Officer at LAX, Dom Nessi told *Aviation Pros* during an interview that the over 20-year-old relic credentialing system is inefficient and inaccurate. "It required our credentialing staff to enter the same information on multiple screens, creating a good chance for inducing errors into the system," he explained that the software lacked internal business rules and editing capabilities.[340] In August of 2014, LAX launched its new software program that would eliminate many of the past ten years of credentialing problems.

The credentialing program at an airport consists of processing the employee security badge application, taking required fingerprints, and reviewing and managing background checks. The Federal Regulation 49 C.F.R. pt. 1542 Subpart C describes locations that airport workers must have clearances and be issued Secured Identification Display Area (SIDA) badges:

> "In general, secure areas of the airport include areas specified in an airport's security program (1) where air carriers enplane and deplane passengers, sort and load baggage, and any adjacent areas (secured areas), (2) in which appropriate identification must be worn (SIDAs), (3) that provide passengers access to boarding aircraft and to which access is general controlled through the screening of persons and property (sterile areas), and (4) that include aircraft movement areas, aircraft parking areas, loading ramps, and safety areas that are not separated by adequate security systems, measures, or procedures (air operations areas)."

Verifying that the "trusted" airport employee is not a criminal or terrorist is one of the most important components of a successful airport security plan. LAX airport's decade old credentialing system that has been "patched" together over the years and is an example of what has happened and may still be occurring in our nation's airports. A lesson learned from countries airport:

> "ISIS teen who killed priest passed background check for airport job. The bloodthirsty jihadist who executed a Catholic priest in France "easily" passed a background check to become an airport baggage handler. Abdel Malik Petitjean, 19, worked full time at Chambery Airport in the Sovoie region."[341]

AIRPORT SECURITY ENHANCEMENT AND OVERSIGHT ACT

Several major airport employees' security breaches from 2012 to 2014 spurred the U.S. Senate to pass the Airport Security Enhancement and Oversight Act in 2015. The House of Representatives received the Act, and in July 2016, the Senate Bill 2361 is still being debated in the House with a protracted fight concerning funding between the Democrats and Republicans.[342]

The Act once passed, will implement the F.B.I. "Rap Back" that:

> "Allows authorized agencies to receive notification of activity on individuals who hold positions of trust (e.g. school teachers, daycare workers) or who are under criminal justice supervision or investigation, thus eliminating the need for repeated background checks on a person from the same applicant agency. Prior to the deployment of Rap Back, the national criminal history background check system provided a one-time snapshot view of an individual's criminal history status. With Rap Back, authorized agencies can receive on-going status notifications of any criminal history reported to the FBI after the initial processing and

retention of criminal or civil transactions. By using fingerprint identification to identify persons arrested and prosecuted for crimes, Rap Back provides a nationwide notice to both criminal justice and noncriminal justice authorities regarding subsequent actions."[343]

The Act would also update unescorted contractors access rules and increase fines for airports whose employees lose five percent of the airport's total issued SIDA badges. The most important changes this Act would make are the airport employee 'vetting' process. The potential employee and current employees review will include the 'disqualifying criminal offenses' with parity to the Transportation Worker Identification Credential (TWIC) disqualifying criminal offenses.

An accurate and thorough background check credential program is essential to meet new employee hiring during airports expansion growth. Added measures will help, but there are additional steps the United States need to take to achieve these goals. In June 2017, the House of Representatives released a report that determined; "…that without a comprehensive background check for employees, TSA does not have the ability to screen for individuals who may "harbor ill-will" toward the United States, or have connections to individuals who do."

PRIVATE COMPANIES BACKGROUND CHECK FAILURES

In Washington D.C., in August 2014, I attended an investigators conference, and the FBI gave a briefing to the law enforcement group concerning Navy Shipyard Shooter Aaron Alexis. I watched the Navy Shipyard surveillance video where Alexis walked through the four-story building, using his shotgun to execute innocent people in their work cubicles and hallways. The police stopped Alexis hour-long rampage when they located him in the enormous complex, engaged him in a gun battle and killed him. Watching the innocent victim's fall, with the vivid blood flowing from their wounds turning their white shirts dark in the video seemed like a Hollywood movie, but was real as I watched people die on surveillance videos.

Could Alexis murderous acts have been prevented? It was discovered in the investigation afterward that there were red flags missed that should have ended his employment as a Navy contract worker with a secret clearance. In 2007, the contract company United States Investigative Services (USIS), completed a background investigation of Alexis.

Alexis first background check missed the crime he committed in Seattle Washington, where he became upset with a man and shot the man's car tires out with a Glock .45 handgun. Alexis told the arresting officer that he fired his gun in an anger-fueled "blackout." The Seattle Police misfiled the crime case with the Seattle Municipal Court when it should have gone to the City Attorney's Office. Alexis showed up at the court of jurisdiction, and the judge dropped the charges as neither court had the case on file.[344] Alexis failed to disclose his arrest for the crime and his history of bad credit in his background application used by the Department of Defense (DOD) to clear him for work in restricted areas. Because the background investigators failed to discover the arrest and credit issues, Alexis received a 'secret' security clearance that afforded him unscreened entry into the secure area of military bases as a civilian contractor.

In 2010, police arrested Alexis for firing a gun in Ft. Worth Texas into the ceiling of his apartment, narrowly missing his upstairs neighbor. Before firing the shot into the ceiling with a rifle, Alexis had earlier been in a shouting match with his upstairs neighbors, accusing them of making too much noise. Alexis criminal legal action in Texas and his previous crime in Seattle remained hidden to the DOD, and he kept his secret security clearance status. USIS said it was required to destroy records after some time, and it was unknown if they conducted the second required background check of Alexis.[345]

USIS was also required to conduct a second review of all background checks. An investigation by the U.S. Government discovered from 2008 to 2011, USIS failed to perform required secondary reviews in fifty percent of their background checks. This failure to conduct a secondary background review allowed Alexis bizarre behavior and criminal acts to remain hidden while he continued to hold his secret security clearance.

The United States House of Representatives Committee on Oversight and Government Reform released a report titled "Contracting Out Security Clearance Investigations: The Role of USIS and Allegations of Systemic Fraud." The report focused on the resigned, retired, or terminated 24 USIS executives who left due to allegations of a massive fraud by the company. The government's Office of Personnel Management (OPM) oversees 90 percent of background investigations, and in 2011 awarded USIS a five-year contract for fieldwork investigation and support services worth close to $3 billion. The OPM paid USIS by cases submitted, and the more cases USIS submitted to OPM, the more revenue it generated. The Department of Justice (DOJ) filed a civil complaint against USIS in 2014 for violating the False Claims Act and alleged the top USIS management devised a scheme of dumping incomplete background investigations reports to OPM. The DOJ stated in 2008 through 2012 that:

> "USIS management devised and executed a scheme to deliberately circumvent contractually-required quality reviews of completed background investigations in order to increase the company revenues and profits."[346]

But what was worst for USIS was the 2014 DOJ United States Complaint against USIS for "False Claims Act violation of Breach of Contract." The DOJ alleged in their complaint that more than 665,000 background investigations were not completed.[347]

On August 6, 2014, the U.S. Government placed a stop-work order on USIS due to a computer record outside security data breach that resulted in the theft of over twenty thousand government workers' personal and professional history by computer data thieves. The breach further destabilized and backlogged the government background checks to even greater numbers.

USIS at one time was the top company used by the Federal Government for over 45 percent of their background checks that included the TSA. USIS represents a particularly egregious example of failures in the government system of federal background checks that include our nation's aviation industry background checks.

DEPARTMENT OF HOMELAND SECURITY TSA BACKGROUND CHECK FAILURES

When TSA ramped up to meet the needs of taking over screening from private companies, their massive amount of background checks were not as substantial or detailed as they should be. Congressional Records reveal years of backlogged TSA background checks. The TSA's inability to conduct adequate background checks on TSA and airport employees is a security failure that brings doubts on the many programs of the TSA and the employees who run them.

News stories broke in 2013 that TSA allowed people with criminal records to obtain security badges before their background checks were completed, allowing them access to security-sensitive areas of airports. The TSA received requests from the airports to expedite the slow background check process, and TSA created the Aviation Channeling Services Provider (ASCP) in 2010 to increase the number of companies who would conduct background checks.

The TSA poor management and lack of oversight of the ASCP resulted in a lack of proper documentation and records delayed in the program until 2012. Once implemented, though, the airports reported numerous problems that directly affected many airports operations because airport employees could not be credentialed to access their work locations. The TSA did the unthinkable and during April through June 1, 2012, allowed airports to give badges to employees who had yet to have their background checks implemented. TSA gave the airports one option, if these authorized airport employees had not completed their background checks within 14 days, their credentials would be revoked.

The Office of the Inspector General (OIG) in reviewing the TSA programs discovered the TSA failed to follow up on their mandates to the airports. The OIG did not know which airports authorized employees without background checks to be issued badges to work in the high-security side of the airport. The OIG informed the TSA, who tried to remedy the failure of the major security breach. The TSA sent a survey to 446 airports asking them to "self-report" the employees who were given credentials without background checks. Only 290 of the 446 airports responded to the TSA. TSA does not have any data on the 156 remaining airports and the hundreds of unknown airport employees still working without background and criminal history checks. The OIG estimates that it will take years, and the TSA will still not end up with a full accounting of airport employees with criminal records in possession of security badges.[348]

The eight airports the U.S. Government Accountability Office (GAO) contacted for their official December 2011 report to Congress concerning the effectiveness of the TSA background checks, found the TSA was unable to manage and keep up with the workload. TSA has shouldered too much responsibility over the years with the hundreds of tasks it conducts. To continue to strain the TSA capacity to screen potential airport employees is not in the best interest of the nation's airports security. The GAO findings revealed that TSA could not "effectively and efficiently" conduct Security Assessments (SA) because the TSA has limited access, if any, of criminal records as the TSA requests, are classified as a noncriminal justice purpose requestor.[349]

In June 2015, it was discovered the TSA cleared 73 aviation employees, with possible connections to terrorism, to work in the high-security side of our nation's airports. The Inspector General of Homeland

Security, John Roth, conducted a review of the 900,000 aviation workers by having the FBI run the names through the TIDE database and discovered the major security breach.[350]

In July 2016, Congress passed the "FAA Extension, Safety, and Security Act of 2016" and directed the National Director of Intelligence to provide real-time access to TIDE by the TSA and any other terrorist-related categories. It is hard to understand why it took 15 years after 9/11 to authorize this clearance, as once implemented, this will improve the TSA ability to better their vetting for terrorist connections by airport employees who access the SIDA side of airports.

The TSA contracted private background screening agencies, such as USIS, perform background checks on employment application information and operate their search electronically to obtain the credit, criminal, employment, education/certificates, military and driving records of the airport applicant. The cost of the background check will range on average from $27 to $75 depending on the details of each background check. In some cases, the background checks are treated pro forma or in other words just as a formality by the employer and background investigation company.

EXAMINING MANAGEMENT PRACTICES AND MISCONDUCT AT TSA: PART II

John Roth is the Department of Homeland Security Inspector General. On May 12, 2016, Roth testified before the United States House of Representatives Committee on Oversight and Government Reform. In his report "Examining Management Practices and Misconduct at TSA: Part II," Roth said "in June of last year .....we found that TSA had less effective controls in place for ensuring aviation workers had:"

* Not committed crimes that would disqualify them from having unescorted access to secure airport areas.

- ✦ Lawful status and were authorized to work in the United States.
- ✦ Relied on airport operators to perform a criminal history and work authorization checks which had limited oversight over these commercial entities.

Further, Roth said TSA lacked "assurance that it properly vetted all credential applicants." The damning continued from the Inspector General who cited the TSA did not have the right edit checks to reject airport employee's applications when thousands of airports records used for vetting workers contained incomplete or inaccurate data. The inaccurate data consisted of errors like "an initial for a first name and missing social security numbers."

Fortunately, Roth said in the May 2016 report, "I am pleased to report that situation is now remedied." I for that matter am certainly pleased that in twelve months, the TSA has adequately remedied the vetting of airport employees. If so, time will tell, but in the previous 15 years, the TSA was making all of these vettings of employee's mistakes, how many airport employees are still working on the secured side of our nation's airports that should not be there now?

A TSA Job Applicant Personal Account

Barbara Peterson is the *Conde Nast Traveler Aviation* correspondent who conducted an investigation of the TSA by applying for a position as a TSA airport screener. Peterson said when she applied to TSA it took only a few minutes to fill out the online questionnaire and push the send button online. After an initial test, TSA notified Peterson that she would receive a background investigation. Peterson had listed six references, and she discovered the background company did not contact any of them. An interview with Patterson was next, and she said the interviewer was mechanical in nature and never deviated from the prescribed questions, no matter what answer she gave. Peterson was interviewed a second time by a privately contracted firm, which was paid $776 million for a 5-year contract to conduct interviews for TSA.

After the second interview, Peterson was directed to obtain a physical and was provided the clinic's name and location. Peterson completed the physical, but the background company called the next day and said the clinic forgot the "stamina" test. Peterson said TSA spends more than $50 million a year in disability payments due to on-the-job injuries, and this was an important part of the assessment process. The contract company representative on the phone told her she wouldn't have to go back to the clinic and asked if she was sitting down. Peterson sat down on the kitchen chair, and the phone interviewer said, "Now, lift your arm. Can you bend it?" She replied "Yes, " and that concluded the test. On the following Monday after the "stamina test," Peterson traveled to a hotel on the outskirts of the airport and was sworn in as a TSA screener.

THE COMPACT ACT, CREDENTIALING, AND THE CLEARINGHOUSE

A person who wishes to work at an airport starts by supplying his prospective employer their identification documents and background information. The airline, airport or airport affiliated company gives the information provided by the employee to the Transportation Security Clearinghouse (TSC). The TSC is a non-profit arm of the American Association of Airport Executives and serves as a channeling and credentialing background agency. Since 9/11, the TSC has taken lengthy background checks that sometimes ranged from 52 days to a mere couple of hours due to its primary use of a database of information and data gathering via the World Wide Web.[351] In essence, the security background checks for airport employment involves mostly, if not all, electronic processes and little human interaction.

The TSC provides the completed background check to the airport operator who then reviews it and passes it to the TSA. The TSA takes the employee information and runs the applicant through the database containing terrorist and immigration names, the FBI fingerprint check and the civilian only limited criminal history report. The TSA then provides their findings to the airport operator, who takes this profile report and determines the eligibility of the potential employee for work on the secured side of the airport.

A serious problem comes to light when you look below the surface of these whirlwind background checks. The TSA is limited when receiving FBI fingerprint and criminal history of airport applicants as explained by the National Crime Prevention and Privacy Compact Act of 1998.[352] This Compact allowed states to exchange criminal records for noncriminal justice purposes subject to the laws of individual states and their signing onto the Compact. The creation of the Compact Act occurred because each state has a variety of statutes and policies that prevent the sharing of criminal records for noncriminal justice purposes. Unfortunately, as of May 2015, only 30 states have ratified this agreement while merely ten others have signed a memorandum of understanding, and 16 states have taken no action to join the Compact. In essence, not all updated criminal history information in every state is provided to the FBI.

The Compact manages and shares a computer database system between the states and the federal government. This system allows the sharing of a person's criminal history for civil purposes authorized by state or federal law, i.e., employment and background checks for governmental licenses. Under the umbrella of the Compact, the states that are part of the Compact agree to maintain a current database of their initial arrests, disposition of cases, convictions and relevant criminal history with the FBI. The federal government and all members share this information for reasons agreed to in the Compact. The FBI provides a significant part of the infrastructure for the system and administers the federal data facilities.[353]

However, the good intentions of the Compact have yet to be fully implemented. The Congressional Accounting Office (GAO) report number GAO-12-60 stated:

"DOJ stated that the FBI remains concerned that readers [of the GAO report] must understand that the level of access afforded to TSA to FBI criminal history records information for Transportation Worker Security Threat Assessments is one prescribed by law and not merely an opinion of the FBI's. DHS stated that it recognizes that there are criminal records at the state level which TSA does not receive, and noted that its level of criminal history information access is equal to that of a private company doing an employment check on a new applicant."[354]

The local airports contract private background check companies who electronically channel the background information to the TSA so they can conduct civilian background checks required for individuals working in the secure areas of airports. Based on the failure of oversight of USIS and the fraud allegedly carried out by USIS, Congress recommended the creation of a system providing for the continuous evaluation or monitoring of federal personnel holding security clearances. The oversight would use the system to access critical information relevant to background check investigations, including arrest, court, financial records, and currency transactions, foreign travel, social media, and terrorist/criminal watch lists.

The elimination of the spider web of Federal and State regulations is a byproduct in the centralization of the FBI criminal history database. A serious gap remains in criminal history checks that include the 1978 legislation to streamline the criminal history record information with the Interstate Identification Index (III) project. The III System is an index that merges the criminal history files of the FBI with the state's files, but only the states that participate in the Compact Act can use the system.

The National Fingerprint File (NFF) is also a player in the Compact Act and is a database of fingerprints or other types of personal identification information of a person's criminal arrest for identification purposes of people in the III System. Again, states that have joined the Compact Act greatly enhance the criminal history checks by letting the FBI have access to their state's criminal history data. Without all states participating in the Compact Act, gaps remain that may allow an employee with a criminal arrest to work in an airport. Three steps that every state must take to ensure a complete criminal history database is accessible in every employee background check are:

1. States participate in the III.

   The state's centralized criminal history record repository agrees to make its III indexed records available in response to requests from federal and out-of-state criminal justice agencies for criminal justice purposes. The FBI maintains a duplicate record to meet the needs of federal, state, and local noncriminal justice agencies and private entities that use III information for authorized noncriminal justice purposes.

2. States ratify the Compact.

   States must make all unsealed CHRI available in response to authorized noncriminal justice requests. The Compact, when signed by a state or territory, supersedes any conflicting state laws, and thus allows for uniform criminal history record dissemination among states, while ensuring that each signatory state will participate in the NFF Program.

3. Compact States participate in the NFF Program.

   The NFF concept places the management and responsibility for the effective control, collection, maintenance, and dissemination of state criminal record files solely with the state. The NFF states respond to record requests for all authorized purposes, and the FBI ceases to maintain duplicate criminal records.[355]

A CASE EXAMPLE OF AN AIRPORT EMPLOYEE BACKGROUND CHECK FAILURE

An example of how an employee with the potential for becoming an insider threat can find his way into our nation's airports occurred at an airport in California. One of the airport police officers told the watch commander that he'd had a verbal altercation with a baggage handler a year earlier. The baggage handler, at that time, had been fired by the airline contract company and was at the airport to pick up his last paycheck. He had the lack of common sense to angrily insult a uniformed police officer as he was walking through the terminal, but he disappeared into a crowd before backup officers arrived to assist the officer. A violation of the law did not occur during the verbal altercation, but this former 'trusted' airport employee confrontation with a uniformed law enforcement officer was a concern at that time.

One year later, this same baggage handler was rehired by the same contract company and was back at work at the same airport as a cabin cleaner. The same officer who had reported the verbal altercation a year ago saw the former ramp worker going into the airport security door and notified the watch commander. A state law enforcement check revealed that during his year hiatus away from the airport jobs; he was arrested and convicted for possession of an explosive device. He was currently on three years' probation for the crime when the airport business hired him. The fact that this trusted airport employee was guilty of possession of an explosive device, and fired from a previous airport job should have prevented his new employment at the airport. His background check, or lack of, did not find his recent criminal activity, and he was rehired as a trusted employee to work inside an airplane in the highest security area of the airport.

This employee, like many contract employees, probably did not have a background check completed on him when he started his job at the airport. If anyone conducted a background check, it was a very limited or poorly conducted background check. Upon notification, the airport administration revoked his security badge, which restricted him from entering the secure area of the airport that led to his second termination. A correct background check would have prevented this problem from occurring.

How Good Are Private Background Checks?

Private successful businesses' everywhere have and will make mistakes during their years of operation. As any good business will, it recognizes the errors and corrects them to remain successful in their business ventures. The same errors in background checks are possible by private companies, whose range reaches from the employee applicant at a local food market to a fortune 500 company. Mistakes on the low end of the risk matrix will have an effect that is manageable. In a business with corporate secrets or homeland security at stake, errors on background checks must be caught with checks and balances and must be prevented to avoid a massive loss of trademark, data, breach of infrastructure security and potential loss of life in the event of an insider criminal or terrorist incident.

The Privacy Rights Clearinghouse is a private non-profit business whose central purpose is to safeguard individual's privacy rights. Beth Givens, Director of Privacy Rights Clearinghouse, presented insight into private company background checks' mistakes to the Federal Trade Commission on April 14, 2010. Givens cited her organization received complaints from citizens who stated the private companies' background checks had many mistakes. Some of the common errors by the variety of background check companies were:

- False information reported. An example provided was a background check company mixed one person's identifying information with that of another person.
- Impersonation by a family member. A family member stole another family member's identity, and the company could not solve the problem.

- An applicant was confused with a much younger man with a similar name but different race.
- Identity theft victim.[356]

NBC News technology correspondent, Bob Sullivan, interviewed CEO Rhonda Taylor of the background firm, Intellisense Corporation. Taylor said her background check company conducted tests on the U.S. databases used for background checks. Their findings revealed these database resources have a "41 percent error rate."[357]

A background check company in California called 'A Matter of Fact Employment Background Checks' is a leader in conducting background checks the right way. In today's expedited time schedules, the TSC completes an airport employee background check within hours. A Matter of Fact Background Check company stresses consideration in criminal checks of the cost versus risk is an important matter. As a law enforcement officer who has done extensive background checks, I cannot agree more. Private background companies have even purposely falsified backgrounds checks to expedite their workload and increase their profit margin. An example was when a Federal Court found the Argenbright Security Company guilty in 2000, for falsifying employee background investigations and job records. Argenbright paid $1.5 million in penalties.[358]

Fifteen years have passed since 9/11, yet the federal government is unable to work together with every state in the union to implement proactive employment background check policies to protect our airports from "insider threats." Five or more organizations are involved in looking at and clearing a single person in a background check as a prospective airport employee. Is there a better way of managing the security of the aviation industry with greater accuracy in conducting background checks at our nation's airports? The following is an airport employee's words in a blog expressing his concerns about ramp worker background checks reference the gang graffiti in an aircraft:

THE AIRPORT ACCESS CONTROL SECURITY IMPROVEMENT ACT OF 2015

In Chapter 8, I detailed the House of Representatives Bill H.R. 3102, titled "Airport Access Control Security Improvement Act of 2015." The Act directed the TSA to establish a program for airport badging offices to use the Federal Illegal Immigration Reform and Immigrant Responsibility Act of 1996, also known as 'E-Verify.' Congress would like to have all airports use E-Verify to determine if airport employees who work on the secure side of airports are even eligible to work in the United States. Many of the contract companies lower paid cabin cleaning and maintenance workers at my airport did not speak English, and I was hard pressed to believe that they were all legally allowed to work at my airport. There are excellent fraudulent worker identification papers and credentials available on the black market and in many inner cities, and people selling these identifications can be found hawking their wares on street corners. An increasing number of offshore identification counterfeiters in foreign countries are reaping big money by producing work papers and identifications for people within the U.S. Some of these countries even advertise on YouTube.

With many states granting illegal aliens the right to obtain state driver's licenses or similar documentation, it has become a quagmire of illegal aliens using real and fake identifications whose names, many now on legal identification, were not verified to be their true names. In 2013, California passed a state law that requires the DMV to issue a California driver's license to anyone who can satisfactorily establish California residency. Advocates for illegal aliens in 2013, warn the illegal alien community before they apply for a legitimate California license to contact an attorney if they previously used a false name to obtain a California driver licenses.[359]

The Twenty Eight States have taken no actions to stop companies within their borders from hiring illegal workers and currently do not mandate the use of E-Verify.[360] The Secretary of Transportation is directed by Congress to authorize each airport to have direct access to the E-Verify program. As of February 2017, it was believed President Trump would make enforcing E-Verify a requirement for all businesses.

"Employment screening is important in the hiring of airport workers, according to Nick Annan, ICE special agent in charge of Homeland Security investigations in Atlanta. Employees at the airport have "access to certain areas of the airport that the everyday traveler does not have," he said."[361]

RECOMMENDATIONS:

As the methods of background checks have evolved with technology, thorough background investigations of all airport employees must be implemented. Until every state is part of the 1998 Federal Compact, backgrounds will never be 100 percent accurate in regards to every state criminal history access of potential employees. All States must be a part of the compact and supply all criminal records to the central database for access to background checks.

1. Every airport employee thorough background check will be conducted by the individual airport's municipal law enforcement agency or a private background check company. Each background company completed employee check will be vetted by each specific airport law enforcement agency for accuracy.

Private civilian companies retained to perform contracted background checks by airport police agencies will incorporate all nationalized standards of background checks of airport employee applicants. The California-based 'A Matter of Fact Employment Background Check Company protocols are a good start. Another example of an intensive aviation employee background check process is the United Kingdom Procius Company. Here are some of their requirements:

* They must prove the applicant's whereabouts and activities every day for the past five years.
* A minimum of six certified references per worker, verified by the background investigation company.
* An average of 3 to 4 weeks allotted to each background check. (Most U.S. aviation employee's background checks average 4 to 6 hours.)
* The employer and the applicant share the cost of the background check

2. An increase in cost for law enforcement personnel to conduct background checks and the funding will be derived from additional fees paid by passengers to their carriers by these funding sources; TSA receives $2.50 up to a maximum of $5 per one-way trip from each passenger on flights originating in the United States. The Congressional Bipartisan Budget Act of 2013 allowed Congress to control the estimated $16.9 billion acquired each year from the passenger ticket 9/11 tax of $5.60 per round trip ticket. TSA is provided approximately $4.3 billion of the ticket tax for airport operations while Congress takes approximately $12 billion to pay down the federal budget deficit. A division of a percentage of the annual Congress and TSA $16.9 billion derived from the tax on passengers can be purposed and proportionally divided among the 446 airports. From the percentage of the $16.9 billion, the funding for law enforcement personnel who conduct background

checks is derived.[362] These funds will provide each airport the revenue to fund private company investigations background check costs. These designated fees would be equitably divided in proportion to the size of each airport's enplanement numbers with larger airports receiving a higher percentile while smaller airports received proportionally less. These fees would go directly to the local law enforcement airport agency bypassing airport governing authorities and be earmarked only for airport employee background checks. The U.S. airlines made $947 million in profit from baggage fees in the first quarter of 2016, which equates to a $100 million more than the first quarter of 2015.[363] In 2014, U.S. Airlines made a record profit of more than $6.5 Billion in baggage check fees and reservation change fees.[364] A percentage of the airlines and airports' baggage fees will pay their employees and their contract employee's local airport police agency pre-employment background checks cost. Prospective airport employee applicants shall pay a percentage of their background investigation cost.

3. The essential components of airport employee background checks must be standardized and agreed upon by all security agencies and airports. Key elements to consider when running a background check on a potential airport employee must include:

   * Identity Verification: Identity verification will be made as to citizenship, legally documented worker status, if not a U.S. citizen.

   * Employment History: This vital information includes the reasons for leaving past employers.

   * Applicant Neighbor Interviews: This quick and revealing step offers insight into an applicant's home life and residence verification. This step is essential to eliminating people who use others identity to obtain a job at our airports. An example of an airport employee using another person's identity was Nigerian illegal alien Bimbo Oyewole, who worked at Newark Airport for twenty years under the name Jerry

Thomas. Police suspected Oyewole in the killing of Jerry Thomas in Queens New York in 1992.[365]

* Personal References: Job applicant references from employers and personal acquaintances create a complete picture of the applicant. During the background, personal references should be asked to submit additional personal references that the applicant may know.

* Ten-Year Adult and Juvenile Criminal History: Mandatory checks of both adult and juvenile 10-year criminal history of potential airport employees. Knowing the possible juvenile criminal history and gang involvement of applicants is essential to the security of our aviation industry. An example of a 22-year-old applicant for an airport job would require him or her to submit their juvenile criminal history as a condition of employment.

4. Mandate all airports include the F.B.I. Rap Back System: Rap Back, authorized agencies can receive ongoing status notifications of any criminal history reported to the FBI after the initial processing and retention of criminal or civil transactions. By using fingerprint identification to identify persons arrested and prosecuted for crimes, Rap Back provides a nationwide notice to both criminal justice and noncriminal justice authorities regarding subsequent actions.[366]

Anything can happen to an airport worker while he is employed at an airport, even if his record has previously been clean. Severe financial problems, criminal arrests, and psychological breakdowns all can occur in an employee's life. While the federal mandate requires transportation workers to self-report when they are arrested or convicted of a disqualifying crime, it rarely happens.

5. The following criminal offenses are designated as grounds for employee disqualification under the Federal Aviation Administration Workers Program:

DISQUALIFYING CRIMINAL OFFENSES

Forgery of certificates, false marking of aircraft, and other aircraft registration violation (49 U.S.C. 46306); Interference with air navigation (49 U.S.C. 46308);

Improper transportation of a hazardous material (49 U.S.C. 46312);

Aircraft piracy in the special aircraft jurisdiction of the United States (49 U.S.C. 46502(a));

Interference with flight crew members or flight attendants (49 U.S.C. 46504);

Commission of certain crimes aboard aircraft in flight (49 U.S.C. 46506);

Carrying a weapon or explosive aboard aircraft (49 U.S.C. 46505);

Conveying false information and threats (49 U.S.C. 46507);

Aircraft piracy outside the special aircraft jurisdiction of the United States (49 U.S.C. 46502(b));

Lighting violations involving transportation of controlled substances (49 U.S.C. 46315);

Unlawful entry into an aircraft or airport area that serves air carriers or foreign air carriers contrary to established security requirements (49 U.S.C. 46314);

Destruction of an aircraft or aircraft facility (18 U.S.C. 32);

Murder;

Assault with intent to murder;

Espionage;

Sedition;

Kidnapping or hostage taking;

Treason;

Rape or aggravated sexual abuse;

Unlawful possession, use, sale, distribution, or manufacture of an explosive or weapon;

Extortion;

Armed or unarmed felony robbery;

Distribution of or intent to distribute, a controlled substance;

Felony arson;

Felony involving: A threat; Willful destruction of property; Importation or manufacture of a controlled substance; Burglary; Theft; Dishonesty, fraud, or misrepresentation; Possession or distribution of stolen property; Aggravated assault; Bribery; or Illegal possession of a controlled substance punishable by a maximum term of imprisonment of more than one year;

Violence at an airport serving international civil aviation (18 U.S.C. 37);

Embezzlement;

Perjury;

Robbery;

Crimes associated with terrorist activities;

Sabotage;

Assault with a deadly weapon;

Illegal use or possession of firearms or explosives;

Any violation of a U.S. immigration law;

Any violation of a Customs law or any other law administered or enforced by Customs involving narcotics or controlled substances, commercial fraud, currency or financial transactions, smuggling, failure to report, or failure to declare;

Airport security violations; or

Conspiracy or attempt to commit any of the offenses or acts referred to in paragraphs (a)(4)(i) through (a)(4) of this section;

Denial or suspension of the applicant's unescorted access authority to a Security Identification Display Area (SIDA) pursuant to regulations promulgated by the U.S. Federal Aviation Administration or other appropriate government agency; or

Inability of the applicant's employer or Customs to complete a meaningful background check or investigation of the applicant.

As of June 2016, the TSA's credentialing programs that disqualify applicants under the Aviation Workers Program from acquiring an airport-issued access badge are:

PERMANENT DISQUALIFYING CRIMINAL OFFENSES[367]

An applicant will be disqualified if he or she was convicted, pled guilty (Including 'no contest'), or found not guilty by reason of insanity for any of the following felonies regardless of when they occurred:

Espionage or conspiracy to commit espionage.

Sedition or conspiracy to commit sedition.

Treason or conspiracy to commit treason.

A federal crime of terrorism as defined in 18 U.S.C. 2332b (g), or comparable State law, or conspiracy to commit such crime.

A crime involving a TSI (Transportation Security Incident). Note: A transportation security incident is a security incident resulting in a significant loss of life, environmental damage, transportation system disruption, or economic disruption in a particular area, as defined in 46 U.S.C. 70101. The term "economic disruption" does not include a work stoppage or other employee-related action not related to terrorism and resulting from an employer-employee dispute.

Improper transportation of a hazardous material under 49 U.S.C. 5124 or a comparable state law.

Unlawful possession, use, sale, distribution, manufacture, purchase, receipt, transfer, shipping, transporting, import, export, storage of, or dealing in an explosive or explosive device. An explosive or explosive device includes an explosive or explosive material as defined in 18 U.S.C. 232(5), 841(c) through 841(f), and 844(j); and a destructive device, as defined in 18 U.S.C. 921(a)(4) and 26 U.S.C. 5845(f).

Murder.

Threat or maliciously conveying false information knowing the same to be false, concerning the deliverance, placement, or detonation of an explosive or other lethal device in or against a place of public use, a state or government facility, a public transportations system, or an infrastructure facility.

Violations of the Racketeer Influenced and Corrupt Organizations Act, 18 U.S.C. 1961, et seq., or a comparable State law, where one of the predicate acts found by a jury or admitted by the defendant, consists of one of the permanently disqualifying crimes.

Attempt to commit the crimes in items (1)-(4) of this section.

Conspiracy or attempt to commit the crimes in items (5)-(10) of this section

Interim Disqualifying Criminal Offenses

Conviction for one of the following felonies is disqualifying if the applicant was convicted, pled guilty (including 'no contest'), or found not guilty by reason of insanity within seven years of the date of the application; OR if the applicant was released from prison after conviction within five years of the date of the application.

Unlawful possession, use, sale, manufacture, purchase, distribution, receipt, transfer, shipping, transporting, delivery, import, export of, or dealing in a firearm or other weapon. A firearm or other weapon includes but is not limited to, firearms as defined in 18 U.S.C. 921(a)(3) or 26 U.S.C. 5 845(a), or items contained on the U.S. Munitions Import List at 27 CFR 447.21.

Extortion.

Dishonesty, fraud, or misrepresentation, including identity fraud and money laundering, where the money laundering is related to a crime listed in Parts A or B (except welfare fraud and passing bad checks).

Bribery.

Smuggling.

Immigration violations.

Distribution, possession w/ intent to distribute, or importation of a controlled substance.

Arson.

Kidnapping or hostage taking.

Rape or aggravated sexual abuse.

Assault with intent to kill.

Robbery.

Fraudulent entry into a seaport as described in 18 U.S.C. 1036, or comparable State law.

Violations of the Racketeer Influenced and Corrupt Organizations Act under 18 U.S.C. 1961, et seq., or a comparable state law, other than any permanently disqualifying offenses.

Voluntary manslaughter.

Conspiracy or attempt to commit crimes in this section.

CHAPTER 14

History Warned of 9/11; We Did Not Heed the Warnings

"The defense of U.S. airspace on 9/11 was not conducted in accord with preexisting training and protocols. It was improvised by civilians who had never handled a hijacked aircraft that attempted to disappear, and by a military unprepared for the transformation of commercial aircraft into weapons of mass destruction."

THE 9/11 COMMISSION REPORT

IN 1959, AN AIRLINER WITH 38 passengers and six crew members aboard was hijacked with one specific mission. That mission was to use the passenger aircraft to bomb government buildings and affect a coup on the current leadership of the country. The hijackers were not extremist zealots of any particular religion; rather they were sound, tactically trained Brazilian Air Force military men who planned a lethal attack on their own country's government.

On December 2, 1959, the military men commandeered the passenger aircraft and flew from Rio de Janeiro to Belem Brazil to prepare the aircraft for dropping bombs in a revolt against the government. The government stopped the coup before the hijackers could initiate their plan and the hijackers flew the plane to Buenos Aires in Argentina where they sought asylum.

Fifteen years before the Brazilian hijacking, the use of an airplane as a different type of weapon against a country occurred. The infamous Kamikaze operations by Japan were aircraft pilots willing to kill themselves in a flying bomb to destroy their enemies. The first Kamikaze attack took place in October 1944 and continued until the end of World War II. The number of men who killed themselves to kill their enemy totaled 2,800 Kamikaze attackers. These Japanese aviators killed 4,900 U.S. sailors and wounded more than 4,800 military personnel.

These are two of the ways aircraft were used as weapons in an attempt to bring about change in a country's government or attempt to win a war against a greater power. This first lesson given to us by history is clear. However, the next lessons were undoubtedly more explicit and direct.

Plots, Theories and Aviation Incidents that Foretold of 9/11

Many will say no one could have imagined that terrorist would kill themselves and others by flying passenger aircraft into America's iconic buildings. In a White House briefing on May 16, 2002, National Security Advisor Dr. Condoleezza Rice answered a reporter question on why they didn't predict 9/11 within the short nine months that President Bush was in office. Rice said; "Steve, I don't think anybody could have predicted that these people would take an airplane and slam it into the World Trade Center."[368] I agree with Rice; the new government was overwhelmed by an onslaught of government business to include the thousands of terrorist intelligence reports that the previous administration had attempted to handle during the past eight years of their administration.

Over the past six decades, I believe there are hundreds of individuals and groups to blame for 9/11. Individually or collectively, these people knew it was possible to enter an airliner's cockpit by force and take control of the airliner in midair. They should have pressed for implementation of preventative measures that would have stopped the four 9/11 passenger planes hijackings decades before the American tragedy. The following historical events, I feel, support my beliefs.

U.S. Army Ranger Dan Hill

U.S. Army Ranger Dan Hill attended officer training in 1969 and during the training received an assignment to pretend he was the leader of communist Russia and describe how he would launch a nuclear war against the United States. Hill writes and titles his paper "State of the Union" and describes how he would recruit a suicide pilot, fill a C-47 transport plane loaded with explosives and fly the plane into the Capitol Building during the State of the Union address by the President of the United States. Hill's plan detailed how the plane crash would kill virtually all of the U.S. Government leadership, and Soviet Russia would launch their ICBM's immediately following the attack. Hill submitted his paper, and the following Monday was summoned to a meeting with Major General John Carley, six other men in uniform and other government personnel wearing dark suits. They asked Hill how he came up with the ideas in his paper. Hill said he was an expert in "unconventional warfare," weapons and explosives. After some discussion, General Carley said: "We'd prefer you forget you ever did this."[369]

Popular Front for the Liberation of Palestine

Has a 9/11 type hijacking of multiple commercial passenger aircraft by a terrorist group, on the same day, ever occurred in the past? The answer is yes, on September 6, 1970, the Popular Front for the Liberation of Palestine (PFLP) simultaneously hijacked four commercial aircraft at the same time, two American, one Israeli and one Swiss passenger aircraft in mid-air on their way to New York. However, the comparison of four airliners hijacked at the same time between the PLFP and the 9/11 terrorist's acts bore even more remarkable similarities.

◆ The PFLP attempted and failed to hijack the Israeli airliner while the other three planes were being hijacked. The fourth hijacking failed after being stopped by an onboard Israeli passenger security guard. Similar to this failure, on 9/11, the hijacked Flight 93 was stopped by passengers.

◆ Three airports in the European Continent countries of Holland, Germany, and Switzerland, were used in the four 1970 hijackings, with 382 miles as the furthest distance between the European airports. In the four 9/11 hijackings, three specific airports were chosen as well in the states of Massachusetts, New Jersey, and Virginia, with 437 miles as the furthest distance between American airports.

◆ In the PFLP hijacking, two aircraft were hijacked from Amsterdam and in the 9/11 hijacking, two aircraft were hijacked from Boston.

The PFLP events of 1970 revealed coordinated quasi-military actions, by a terrorist group, could seize airborne passenger aircraft simultaneously in different parts of a land continent to fulfill their mission and objectives. Did history repeat itself with 9/11 with the exception of the outcome of the 1970 hijackings? Was the PFLP hijackings a forewarning of the 9/11 methodology?

A Passenger Jet Threat Against a Nuclear Facility

History provided an additional series of messages that warned passenger aircraft would be the object of a terrorist plan or criminal threat as suicide flying bombs. One message was the "most chilling" hijacking in U.S. history and resulted in President Nixon mandating passenger screening and their carry-on luggage. On November 10, 1972, a Southern Airways DC-9 was boarding passengers for a flight from Birmingham, Alabama to Memphis, Tennessee. Three men with criminal records, fleeing from authorities, hid guns and grenades under their raincoats and purchased tickets for the DC-9 flight. As the passenger aircraft became airborne, they broke into the cockpit and demanded $10 million in ransom while holding 31 passengers and crew hostage. The plane landed in Detroit, and the FBI offered them $500,000 in exchange for the hostages and plane. The hijackers refused the ransom amount, demanded the $10 million and made the pilot fly to Toronto, Canada. In Toronto, the airlines offered the hijackers $500,000, but they refused and demanded the full $10 million.

One of the hijackers had previously worked at the Oak Ridge Nuclear Research Center that was located 20 miles outside of Knoxville, Tennessee and ordered the pilot to fly there. The hijackers told the FBI; "This is the last chance, if we don't get what we want, we're going to bomb Oak Ridge." They ordered the pilot to fly circles over the Nuclear Center as they radioed the airlines they would fly the plane into the Oak Ridge Nuclear facility, killing them, the passengers, and the crew and spreading radioactive debris over the surrounding area. The airlines conceded and gave $2 million disguised as $10 million to the hijackers who then forced the pilots to fly the aircraft to Cuba.[370]

OPERATION PANDORA

In 1972, Samuel Byck had suffered from depression and had self-admitted himself into a psychiatric ward for treatment for two months. In 1974, Byck, still suffering from mental illness, believed President Nixon was oppressing the poor and decided to assassinate the sitting president of the United States. Byck stole a handgun and made an improvised bomb out of gasoline. He went to Baltimore/Washington Airport with plans to hijack a passenger jet and crash it into the White House to kill Nixon. Byck arrived at the airport and killed a police officer while storming aboard a Delta Airlines DC-9 passenger jet. He went inside the cockpit, locked the door, and shot the two pilots after they told him they could not move the aircraft because of blocked wheels. A police officer shot through the cockpit door wounding him. Byck then committed suicide by shooting himself. Byck had previously mailed to the news media, a tape recording of his plot: "Operation Pandora" that described in his words how he would kill Nixon.

FedEx Jet Suicide Mission into the Headquarters of FedEx

In 1994 a disgruntled FedEx employee, who was recently fired, planned revenge against the company by hijacking a FedEx plane. He intended to fly the commandeered jet into the company headquarters, killing the crew and likely hundreds of FedEx employees. Retaining his FedEx employee identification card after he was fired, he hitched a ride as a passenger on a FedEx cargo plane, and after takeoff, he attacked the pilot and co-pilot in the cockpit of the aircraft with a hammer. They fought back and captured the former FedEx employee. Their valiant fight for survival is reenacted in the Discovery Channel video; "Fed-Ex Flight 705-Fight for Your Life" on youtube.com.

The France Prelude to 9/11

In December 1994, the Islamic Mujahedeen wanted to establish an Islamic State in Algeria, and members of the terrorist group hijacked an Air France flight in Algeria. The terrorists told the crew and passengers they would all be safe and free once they arrived in Paris, France. The terrorists stated they wanted to hold a press conference in Paris to air their grievances, but their actual plan was to pilot the plane on a suicide mission into the symbol of France, the Paris Eiffel Tower. If not for a successful French Special Forces assault on the aircraft while refueling in Marseilles, France, the murder/suicide plan would have succeeded.

By 1994, these past aviation hijackings, their methods, and various goals were enough to educate the aviation security professionals that the hijacking and use of passenger or cargo jets as flying bombs by terrorist groups was a clear and present danger.

In 1994, one visionary and a lone voice in the wilderness did recognize the warning signs. This visionary was Marvin Cetron, who wrote a report to the U.S. Government where he detailed how terrorists could use passenger jets as weapons. Cetron even provided a scenario depicting how terrorists could fly a passenger jet by following the path of the Potomac River, turn left and crash into the White House or turn right to crash into the Pentagon. The Federal Government told Marvin Cetron that his 1994 study, called *'Terror 2000: The Future Face of Terrorism'* would not be discussed, and they would file the report away as confidential and not disclosed it to the public. Why did the U.S. government hide this report from an open debate? The government told Cetron his suggestion that terrorists could plan to use passenger jetliners as "guided bombs" to destroy major landmarks would propagate the idea among the world terrorists and hostile nations. The U.S. Government wanted any reference to a jetliner being used as a weapon to be redacted from the report.[371]

One would think if the U.S. Government were so frightened of the idea, they would take cautionary and preventative measures to stop Cetron's scenario from becoming a reality. We know the answer now, but these government officials were ignorant of history lessons when history repeatedly revealed these methods of terrorist attacks were already public record through actual past events.

That same year in 1994, the crazed pilot of a general aviation aircraft flew a private plane into the Whitehouse lawn-just short of the Whitehouse. This incident itself should have rattled the collective cages of President Clinton and the U.S. Government agencies to realize the 9/11 possibilities. I believe action could have been implemented under President Bill Clinton's oversight to reduce or eliminate the possibility of a 9/11 attack. The U.S. government in power in 1994 chose to disregard the potential reality of a 9/11 scenario. The stunning amount of evidence from 1959 to 1994 shouted the warning that 9/11 was possible, but even additional warnings were coming.

OPERATION BOJINKA

History gave us yet another chance to prevent 9/11 with the discovery in 1995 of a well-planned and rehearsed terrorist plot called Operation Bojinka. The Philippines police inadvertently discovered this plot when they responded to an apartment fire in Manila that January. At the apartment, they arrested Abdul Hakim Murad when they found pipe bombs, bomb-making manuals and a terrorist plan on a computer hard drive. The terrorist plan was titled 'Bojinka' which stood for 'explosion' and it detailed plans to blow up 12 passenger jets over the Pacific Ocean while they were flying to the cities of Honolulu, Los Angeles, San Francisco, and New York.

Ramzi Yousef was the mastermind of the 1991 World Trade Center, and in 1995 after his capture in Pakistan, it was determined that he also the mastermind of the plot to destroy eleven airliners in midair.[372] In the terrorist planning, their analysis determined the plot would result in more than 4,000 deaths in the multiple-plane attack. To prepare for this massive plan, the terrorists successfully completed a test run and bombing of a Philippine Airlines 747 jet. The bomb killed a businessman from Japan and wounded 10; and if not for a misplacement of the bomb away from the fuel tanks, all aboard would have perished. The police discovered documents in the terrorist apartment in the Philippines, and interrogations of the suspect revealed "a second wave" plot to fly passenger aircraft into American targets. The targets were the Bank of America Tower in Los Angeles, the World Trade Center, Pentagon, U.S. Capitol building, White House, CIA Headquarters and the Sears Tower in Chicago. The only reason cited by the terrorist as to why they did not attack American cities was their failure to recruit enough martyrs for all the flights.[373]

The cost of hardening cockpit doors, restricting any bladed weapon at the screening lanes, then, would have been pennies in cost when compared with the financial burden of 9/11. However, more importantly, the 3,000 souls lost forever would have been avoided. This was a failure of our government on a massive scale not to recognize, understand the strong possibility, and take measures to prevent a 9/11 style of terrorist attack based on decades of historical facts and Cetron detailed report.

What Types of Past Aviation Security Incidents Can Pose A Future 9/11?

Our airport perimeter fence lines are breached by vehicles and pedestrians on a monthly, if not weekly, basis across our country. These chronicled news media accounts were aired in the media from San Jose to Philadelphia. Yet, these incidents are placated by airport press information officers who state their airport fence security measures worked because they caught the person in the middle of the airfield. Are these decades of airport fence failures lessons from history that we continue to ignore? Are they a prelude to possible methods that may be used by terrorists in another 9/11?

General aviation small aircraft were used in separate attacks on the Bank of America building in Florida and two government buildings: the White House and an IRS building in Texas. Do these attacks bring a warning of what methods terrorist would use against our country's innocents? Our Homeland Security and agencies that protect our vital infrastructures, from city to federal, must step out of the "group think" trap that has failed to predict failed to see the possibilities and failed to take preventative measures against the 9/11 terrorist attacks.

The future success of our aviation industry's security will be the direct result of men and women, who strive to predict every imaginable threat and provide the protocols necessary to prevent their perceived threats to our aviation industry. These forward thinkers will convince airport administrators and their city, state and federal partners to strengthen the essential components of our airports' security requirements against both real and possible threats.

With today's unrestrained terrorist organizations in the world, aviation security professionals should consider what author Gavin De Becker instructs in his book, *The Gift of Fear:*

"While it might not be comfortable, we must face the possibilities. In order to be proactive, to cultivate plans for potential realities, sometimes we must allow our imaginations to take us to some dark and scary places.... if you cannot imagine it, you cannot predict it."[374]

A Summary of History Lessons That Foreshadowed and Warned of 9/11:

1945 - Japanese suicide pilots flew explosive-laden aircraft into American military targets.

1959 - A Brazilian passenger jet was hijacked to bomb government buildings.

1969 – U.S. Army Ranger Dan Hill's theory of a suicide piloted aircraft crashing into the Capitol Building was redacted by the military.

1970 - Four passenger jets were hijacked by the same terrorist group at the same time, mirroring the 9/11 terrorist attacks.

1972 - Criminals win concessions from the dominant world's superpower by threatening to commit suicide by flying a passenger jet into a nuclear facility.

1972 - Operation Pandora Box plot to fly a passenger jet into the White House to kill President Nixon.

1994 - Terrorists hijack a passenger plane to fly themselves, the aircraft crew, and passengers into the France Eiffel Tower.

1994 - A criminal attempted to hijack a jet cargo plane so he could fly it into his former employer Headquarters for revenge in a suicide-murder plot.

1994 - Marvin Cetron submits his report, *'Terror 2000: The Future Face of Terrorism'* that details how a terrorist can use passenger jets as a weapon and fly one into the Pentagon.

1994 - A suicide pilot crashes his private aircraft into the lawn of the Whitehouse.

1995 - The Bojinka Plot.

1996 – The Second Wave Plot of the Bojinka terrorists

CHAPTER 15

Conclusion

———————

"In ourselves, our safety must be sought. By our
own right hand, it must be wrought."

—WILLIAM WORDSWORTH

A TERRORIST HAS TO GET it right just once. Our Homeland Security, federal, state and local law enforcement have to get it right every single time. Our nation cannot fail even once if we are to keep you and your loved ones safe on the ground and in the skies. Yet, despite how dire the threats in this high stakes arena have been, security failures at our nation's airports continue to occur. Throughout U.S. airports, my fellow airport police officers have told me of their airports' security failures. In addition to these law enforcement accounts, the significant number of incidents in the news detailing security failures in our airports is overwhelming. Our aviation industry must always remember that America's worst terrorist attack was the result of the industry's acute lack of foresight, planning and a failure to heed history's lessons. Knowing what our nation's aviation security concerns are and failing to address them by learning from reoccurring lapses in our airport security is unacceptable.

The Islamic State of Iraq and the Levant (ISIL) Continuing Threat

In June 2014, the Al-Qaeda-linked ISIL overran Iraq's major city of Mosul and captured the city. ISIL quickly conquered most of the northern area of Iraq and Syria with cities such as Haditha and Sinjar captured as well. ISIL declared a long sought after Caliphate that spread over parts of Syria and Northern Iraq. This occurred due in part to the Syrian civil war where the last CIA estimate was more than 40,000 ISIL foreign fighters from 74 nations had gathered to fight the Syrian government in the vacuum left when U.S. troops were pulled out of Iraq.[375]

French journalist Nicolas Henin was held captive in Syria by ISIL with two Americans journalists. Henin was released in April 2013 and identified ISIL terrorist Mehdi Nemmouche, a Frenchman, as one of his captors. Henin said Nemmouche would nightly come into the hostage's cells and torture them until morning Islamic prayer time. Nemmouche later returned to France and killed a number of visitors to the Brussels Jewish Museum in June 2014.[376]

On Tuesday, March 22, 2016, ISIL-affiliated fighters attacked the Brussels Airport. The ISIL terrorists opened fire on the crowded airport terminal in front of the American Airlines ticket counter, and within minutes, the terrorists detonated explosive vests killing passengers and employees. Belgium authorities declared the level of unpreparedness was "shocking," regarding the lack of security.[377]

In 2016 through 2017, the United States, Russia, and several other countries increased the military attacks against the ISIL Caliphate in Syria and Northern Iraq. The increased military operations caused a dispersion of thousands of ISIL fighters from the current Caliphate location to areas unknown. FBI Director James Comey told the House of Representatives in July 2016 "Those thousands of fighters are going to go somewhere. Our job is to spot them and stop them before they come to the United States to harm innocent people."[378]

HOMEGROWN TERRORISTS LAST COMMENTS

Fox News show host Greta Van Susteren broke the news in September 2014, that ISIL terrorist fighter Abdirahmaan Muhumed had worked at the Minneapolis Airport. Muhumed left America, went to Syria and died in battle as a soldier for ISIL against the Syrian government. Muhumed was employed by Delta Airlines from 2001 to 2011 as a jet-fuel tanker driver and fueled the passenger aircraft. He also worked cleaning aircraft. Muhumed had unrestricted access to the security side where he entered unchecked and unscreened during his daily duties. [379]

The December 2015 report by Inquisitr News story, "ISIS In America: 2015 Map Shows Terrorist Threats in California, New York, Minnesota – Many Are Not Arab/Middle Eastern Men," reveals the extent of the problem we face.[380] America has more than 320 million citizens, and from this populace, the FBI has classified and continually monitors 1,000 hate groups. These groups' motives and covert actions often go undetected by authorities. The hundreds of terrorist plots discovered in the U.S. by authorities since 1995 leaves only the reality that many 'lone wolves' and terrorist groups are hidden and are waiting for the moment to act.

In May 2015, two men from Phoenix Arizona traveled to Garland, Texas where they died in a gun fight during their attack on a conference hosting exhibits that depicted the Prophet Mohammed in cartoons. Moments, before they attacked the police officers who were protecting the site, one of them tweeted on their Twitter website; "May Allah accept us as mujahideen." ISIL has claimed these two men were brothers in the Caliphate and were their soldiers.[381] Former CIA member, Michael Morell, said ISIL-inspired the deadly attack by the two men in Garland, Texas. Morell said; "But it's only a matter of time before the jihadist group is likely to be in a position to direct more sophisticated attacks on U.S. soil that could result in mass casualties. If we don't get ISIL under control, we're going to see that kind of attack."[382]

NBC News interviewed North Carolina-born Don Morgan about his attempt to join ISIL while in Beirut Lebanon in August 2014.[383] Morgan's history revealed he was a military school graduate, deputy sheriff, and body builder before he became a Muslim. Morgan swore his allegiance to ISIL leader Abu Bakral al-Baghadadi on June 29, 2014, but was arrested at JFK airport upon his return to the U.S. on an unrelated, 'convicted felon in possession of a firearm,' charge.

The threat by ISIL to America by homegrown terrorists elevates each day. On December 1, 2015, the news site 'The Hill' released a story titled "Analysis: US support for ISIL-Unprecedented." George Washington University conducted an analysis of 7,000 legal reports on 71 people who were arrested and affiliated with ISIL inside the United States. The director of the Universities program, Lorenzo Vidino, said; "What we do see in the United States is an unprecedented mobilization [Americans radicalized] that is bigger than any other mobilization we have seen since 9/11."[384] The Paris France ISIL attack two weeks before the release of the Hill's analysis provides a gloomy outlook for the safety of citizens in any state in America.

July 2014, a 25-year-old Garden Grove, California, man pled guilty to providing material support to a foreign terrorist group. Sinh Vinh Ngo Nguyen was arrested a few miles from my airport in Santa Ana, California while waiting for a bus to take him to Mexico. Nguyen had a passport with a false name. The investigation revealed Nguyen had a computer hard drive that contained 180 weapons training videos that he was going to take to Syria where he had previously fought, alongside terrorists, against the regime of Bashar al-Assad. He even noted on his Facebook page about his first kill of a Syrian soldier in previous combat. Terrorism is a growing threat to our Homeland and will remain one for decades to come.

"We have investigations of people in various stages of radicalizing in all 50 states. I have homegrown violent extremist investigations in every single state. ISIS, in particular, is putting out

a siren song with their slick propaganda through social media."
FBI Director James Comey[385]

On July 14, 2016, Homeland Security Secretary Jeh Johnson told the House Homeland Security subcommittee "I have a lot of things that keep me up at night, the prospect of homegrown violent extremists—another San Bernardino, another Orlando—is No. 1 on my list."[386] Other notable quotes concerning the threat to the U.S. are:

February 27, 2017, Iranian Revolutionary Guard Commander: "We have terror cells situated and ready to strike inside the U.S."

March 2, 2017, former CIA Deputy Director Michael Morell: "Al-Qaeda and ISIS often concentrate on attacking symbols of the modern world and airports are at the center of that target zone. So called lone wolf terrorists may not be as focused on the aviation system, but airports remain a prime target because they draw large numbers of people."

March 10, 2017: U.S. Homeland Secretary John Kelly: "The most significant threat is a terrorist attack, I think, in aviation. That seems to be their Stanley Cup playoff. They want to knock down airplanes, and they are trying every day to do it."

June 28, 2017, U.S. Homeland Secretary John Kelly: "Without ramped up airline security, terrorists will attack the weakest link."

August 15, 2017, Al Qaeda publishes a "Blueprint for Attacks on Key U.S. Transportation Systems."

LAST THOUGHTS ON OUR AIRPORTS PERIMETERS

The nation's airport managers and airport police chiefs know or should know of past security failures in Americas' airports. Aviation managers are aware of their airport's current vulnerabilities, the threats to airports described in this book and airport security failures daily news stories. What did the nation's airport management do year after year when vehicles drove through, or people climbed over perimeter fences at American airports across the country? Is there consistency in our airports' procedures to prevent these security threats before they drive or run onto the airfield or terminal and detonate a bomb? In my opinion, the answer is no.

An airport administrator and the airport watch commander at an airport in America were discussing a security breach at another airport.[387] The administrator told the watch commander not to worry about it and said; "It won't happen at our airport." This mindset is common throughout our nation's airports civilian administrations.

We cannot wait until the next 9/11 to get our house in order. The dangers are real and growing. American citizens must demand airports, communities and states reassess the security of the aviation industry and implement new ways to prevent future disasters at our airports or in the skies.

Scott Noll of the KHOU 11 News I-Team interviewed a Houston citizen concerning the July 2014 incident where a person climbed over the Houston Airport fence, stole a fully loaded fuel truck and drove it across an active runway. The citizen told the reporter "Unfortunately, we can't always predict everything crazy people will do. Sometimes we have to wait until they do those crazy things and then we have to react." [388] This type of statement from an uninformed citizen can be expected, but not by the professionals who are in charge of the safety of our airports and their passengers. This type of attitude and beliefs persist in the aviation industry groupthink.

Airports are obsessed with generating the largest profit their complex business model allows. We expect the airports and applaud them for successfully operating in the American free market way. However, this drive to be the largest or most beautiful airport in the state or nation is accomplished at some airports by skipping or delaying improving on their minimum-required Homeland Security compliant standards. Many airport managers expend the minimum required for security compliance and rarely more to strengthen their airport security above minimum standards. Generally speaking, many airport administration accountants will pull out the probability and risk management calculator and say, it won't happen at my airport, or the chances are slim and not worth the cost of security improvements to counter the threat in question. What happens if they are wrong, and a disaster occurs on their watch by the risk they decided to ignore? Under the Federal Aviation and Transportation Security Act, the 'Support Anti-Terrorism by Fostering Effective Technology (SAFETY) Act, airports, and their administrators are shielded from liability for deaths or destruction at their airports caused by terrorist acts if they are within FAA guidelines.[389]

On July 27, 2000, 22-year-old Aaron Commey pulled a Glock 9 mm handgun in the screening lanes at JFK airport and pointed it at a security screener. Commey ran through the screening lanes to National Airlines Flight 19 parked at the departure gate and ran aboard the Boeing 757. Commey held the crew and 143 passenger's hostage for several hours before releasing them and surrendering to the police and FBI.[390] During the next 14 years, Los Angeles, Toronto, Jamaica, Houston, and Seattle airports would suffer the same security breaches-some ending in the deaths of innocent people. What are we doing to prevent these screening lane incidents from happing again? Whoever said the definition of "insanity" is doing the same thing over and over again and expecting different results might have been describing decades of certain unchanging airport security protocols.

In March 2014, TSA completed a study on the Los Angeles International Airport assault on the passenger screening lanes. Their findings suggested that one armed police officer at screening lanes during high passenger volume time periods would be an appropriate measure to prevent any breach of security there. Many airports are open twenty-four hours, seven days a week and 52 weeks a year. I strongly recommend the airport screening lane armed police security must be maintained every day, all day, during high volume times, as well as during low passenger traffic periods. An incident could occur at any time, both inside and outside the terminal. A Band-Aid approach by the TSA, airports and police agencies tasked with protecting the American aviation industry is unacceptable.

Suicide bombers attacked Moscow, Brussels, and the Istanbul Airport Terminals through their open front doors. What has any airport done to prevent these types of attacks from walking into their terminal doors? Proactively, the Los Angeles International Airport Police Union endorsed the 'Checkpoint Safety Act of 2016' championed by Congressman Peter King and Dan Donovan in the House of Representatives. This new law, if passed, would require armed police officers stationed within 300 feet of airport checkpoints.[391] I feel the new proposed law is inadequate. If a police officer is 100 yards away from the screening lane, he will have a 10 to 12-second sprint to engage an active shooter in the screening lane if he is fast. The active shooter can empty a 30 round magazine in a semi-automatic rifle in 4 to 6 seconds. The math is not in our favor.

Last Thoughts on Airport Thefts

On the Budget Travel's Blog, the TSA responded to complaints of passengers who claim items were stolen from their bags with these statements, "When an item goes missing from a checked bag, it is often impossible to determine where the loss occurred given that checked bags pass through so many hands. We estimate that for every TSA employee that touches a bag, six to ten airline or airport employees and contractors touch the same bag out of view of passengers."[392]

By happenstance during my final research, I stumbled upon the 1994 General Accounting Office (GAO), Office of Special Investigations report, number B-256530. This report and investigation targeted pilfering of passenger luggage in the control of airlines at America's airports. This report supported the position that the reasons for and lack of solutions to airport pilfering has for decades been and continues to be a problem for the aviation industry.[393] The 1994 GAO investigators queried Los Angeles Airport and four other major international airports and found:

* Airport police authorities and other enforcement agencies have little information concerning pilfered baggage because the airlines attempt to settle passenger claims through restitution, and they do not routinely report passenger claims to the police.
* Airport police told the GAO that the airlines wanted to settle with the passengers without notifying the police to avoid adverse publicity.
* Airport police cited contract luggage handlers as the main suspects due to their low wages and lack of benefits.
* Targets of pilferage are expensive luggage, electronic equipment, and soft sided luggage.
* Items more frequently pilfered are cash, cameras, jewelry, and firearms.
* Pilferage methods consisted of:
  o Check-in handler identifies wealthy passengers and marks the bag for accomplices inside the airport.
  o Pilferage in the cargo bin of the aircraft consists of three baggage handlers: one on the ground as a lookout and the two inside build a wall of luggage to hide behind while they pilfer passenger luggage.
  o Baggage handlers divert passengers' luggage by removing the destination tags and retagging bags to a nearby airport where an accomplice picks up the diverted bag.
  o Baggage handlers avoid overt surveillance cameras and pilfer in other areas.
  o The airlines pressured the FAA from mandating that all individuals with unescorted access to sensitive areas of the airport have criminal history record checks be removed from the original proposal by the FAA and succeeded in doing so.

Since this damning, GAO Report in 1994, what progress been made in our nation's airports to stop employee thefts in an aviation wide standardized procedural and enforcement way? In my opinion, the theft problem continues to be pushed into the corner and is the elephant in the room. This elephant is symbolic of the obvious truth of the theft problem that remains unsolved by the aviation industry in a manner that would eliminate or greatly mitigate the problem finally. Passenger baggage thefts and pilfering have steadily persisted, and I feel it has grown worse. Eight years after the GAO report, in February 2002, police arrested a Los Angeles International Airport, (LAX), luggage theft and pilfering baggage handler ring for stealing from luggage. In September 2012, police arrested a LAX baggage handler criminal group of employees for stealing from passenger luggage. In March 2014, LAX police arrested a large group of approximately 25 LAX baggage handlers for stealing and pilfering passengers' luggage. In these 20 documented years, the evening news highlights the LAX criminal theft cases. It is with much certainty that there were many other luggage theft cases at LAX that did not make it to a news media during this period of time. What did LAX do to eliminate the problem and the news media negative publicity decade after decade? Only the airport directors and chiefs of police during these years at LAX can answer the questions.

LAX is not alone in its struggles against baggage theft and pilfering. The finger in the dike syndrome is probably in every airport in the nation. Nearly every airport has to deal with this problem to one extent or another. In the advent of technological advances and a forewarned airport management, will the aviation industry and security authorities continually fail to find new innovative ways to prevent the theft of passenger luggage or their contents? Will they write the crimes off as costs of doing business as many, retail businesses do? Alternatively, will a systemic change occur to eliminate the thefts and the accompanying glaring insider threat potential?

Aviation Will Always Attract Terrorism

"Rasmussen noted "a persistent effort by our terrorist
adversaries to target the aviation sector. While there's
much more I could say in a classified setting on this, I can
say here that both Al-Qaeda and IS remain focused on
defeating our defenses against aviation-related attacks."

*July 15, 2016, Office of the Director
of National Intelligence's
Counterterrorism Chief Nicolas Rasmussen[394]*

The terrorist group Al-Shabab press release in March 2016 in describing their bombing of a passenger airliner while it was in flight.

"While the operation did not bring down the plane as Allah had decreed, it struck terror in the hearts of the crusaders, demonstrating to the disbelievers that despite all their security measures and the strenuous efforts they make to conceal their presence, the Mujahideen can and will get to them."[395]

In one simple word used by Al-Shabab: 'terror,' lays the core reason why aviation has and will remain one of the most important tools to ISIL, al-Qaeda, Al-Shabab, Boko Haram, and the Russian Uighur-Bulgar Jamaat to name a few.

On Saturday, March 8, 2014, Malaysian Airlines flight MH370 with 239 souls on board went suddenly missing after takeoff. Day after day, leading into months, the entire world was captivated and watched 24/7 news coverage that offered theory after theory of where the airplane was and why. This missing passenger plane was not a terrorist event but serves as an example of the impact an aviation incident has in garnering the attention of the world. This passenger aircraft event prolonged exposure in the news media reveals how an aviation industry incident can provide a long-term propaganda platform to terrorist groups to promote their extreme ideology with aviation as their tool.

ALL MUST DEFEND THE HOMELAND

In August 2014, I flew to Washington D.C. to attend an investigators conference. During the connecting flights, with a layover in New York, I observed the passengers and was disheartened by what I saw. After nearly 14 years, 9/11 seemed to be a distant memory to those who travel on our airlines. During this trip, through two major international airports, I observed my fellow travelers enjoying themselves or being busy with their electronic devices conducting work or social networking pleasure while in transit. Today, more so than ever, the passenger is an integral part of airport security in our post 9/11 world. From the airport roadways to the boarding gates, the average citizen must focus on their surroundings. Passengers are essentially the tip of the spear in every airport security matrix in detecting suspicious behavior or an imminent threat. This is more important now than ever before, with porous national borders, the threat of terrorists from within and without is evident by terrorist watchlist subjects accessing the United States port of entries and our airports.[396]

If we do not learn from our airports' past security failures, we are doomed to suffer them again and again. If we think our airports are safe and think the terrorists will strike other soft targets, then we have returned to the mindset before 9/11 and have set ourselves up for another catastrophic aviation security failure. The collective security issues detailed in this book comprise warnings not only to America's airports and their regulatory agencies but also to each and every American. The warnings occur daily at different airports throughout our nation in incidents that compromise our airports' security defenses. These warnings resonate briefly then fade away like the frost on an early spring lawn as the sun rises. We hear it; we understand it, but then we become distracted by other matters. We shut it out and move on until the next incident blazes across television or the internet breaking news that instantly brings the reality of our future to our senses once again.

BIBLIOGRAPHY

Don Delillo "The Names," (New York: Vintage Books, A Division of Random House, Inc., 1989), pp. 254

Anthony Price: The Memory Trap, Harper Collins Publishers, 1989

Kenneth C. More; Aircraft and Airline Security, 2nd Edition, 1991, Chapter One, Page 13 Butterworth-Heinemann, a division of Reed Publishing (USA) Inc.

Martin Gill, Editor, "The Handbook of Security," Authors of Chapter 9 "Employee Theft & Staff Dishonesty;" pp. 203, Richard C. Hollinger and Jason L. Davis, Palgrave Macmillan, 2006

M. Felson, R. Boba, Crime & Everyday Life; Sage Publications, 2010

Scott T. Mueller, *The Empty Carousel A Consumer Guide to Checked and Carry-on Luggage*, Millkot Publishings Marketing, 2008

Taber, R. (n.d.). *The War of the Flea: Guerrilla Warfare Theory and Practice.*

R.C. Hollinger, J.L. Pavin, *Employee Theft and Staff Dishonesty*, in M. Gill (editor) The Handbook of Security, Basingstoke; Palgrave Macmillan, 2006

Gavin De Becker, *Gift of Fear*, Delta Publishing

George Thomas Kurian, "The AMA Dictionary of Business and Management, American Management Association, AMACOM, amacombooks.org

C. Pearce, J. Conger, *Shared Leadership, Reframing the Hows and Whys of Leadership*, Sage Publications 2002

SOURCES

The Federal Bureau of Investigation's

The Department of Homeland Security Office of the Inspector General

Government Accountability Office

The United States Department of Justice

Société Internationale de Télécommunications Aéronautiques, SITA

Government of Australia

City Council of San Jose: Airport Public Safety Level of Service, Office of the Auditor; October 2011

RAND Corporation

ABOUT THE AUTHOR

—■—

As a young deputy sheriff on the SWAT team, I rushed aboard a 737 passenger aircraft with an assault weapon and my ballistic vest. A metal plate insert covered my pounding heart. The regulation gas mask I wore was stifling and impeded my vision as I entered the airplane and stared down the sights of my weapon. Adrenaline pumped through my veins and coursed through me as I followed my team members. I was 31 years old, and the lives of many passengers were in our hands.

At the precise moment of entering the aircraft, six SWAT officers yelled simultaneously at the top of their voices, "Get down, get down, get down" to the occupants of the passenger jet as we searched for a target. Suddenly, the unrepentant hostage-takers rose from amid the screaming, frantic passengers. Microsecond analysis's whirled through each team member thoughts: shoot center mass or go for headshots, innocent passengers are down range at risk. As my mind raced, simultaneous automatic double and triple burst bullet explosions echoed through the metal, tubular aircraft body. Weapons fire erupted beside me and behind me. It was over in a matter of seconds.

The SWAT operation, thankfully, was only a training mission, but the emotions and thoughts I had were genuine. The actors posing as passengers and terrorists pushed our training to a new level. I reflected on the experience with my SWAT team members and the members of the FBI SWAT team during the debriefing. I knew if a real tactical military assault on a passenger aircraft jet were to happen, every airport security measure in place would have failed, and this worst-case scenario would have become a reality.

What inspires a law enforcement veteran of thirty-three years to write a book about his experiences as a watch commander in a commercial airport, a book that voices disagreement with many current security postures in our nation's airports? Did I have second thoughts about bringing this to my peer's and the public attention, about revealing what I feel is the dire state of our nation's airport security? I walked among the wreckage of an automobile that was shredded by 400 pounds of explosives at New Mexico Tech University. Seeing that wreckage from the car bomb revealed what 400 pounds of explosives, much less a 1000 or 5000 pounds, could do to the lobby of my airport terminal—and to the people inside. The explosive training and many other events in my career eliminated any doubt of not sharing my desire to see improvement in our aviation security industry.

My Sheriff's Department bomb squad sergeant and his investigator bomb technicians created a suicide bomber course as a necessary component of my department's Homeland Security training. It was mandatory that each officer assigned to the airport attend the course where the bomb squad techs spent two days teaching how suicide bombers think, look, prepare, and execute their attacks using inert suicide bomb vests and their components. Following our two-day in-class training, I spent a third day on the pistol range making split-second decisions and improving the shooting skills required to place accurate shots on the terrorist target silhouette area to stop a real terrorist from detonating his explosive suicide vest.

Airport police receive training in Homeland Security in many genres such as the Global Jihadi Threat, Emergency Response to Terrorist Incidents, Command Officer Response to Terrorism, and Prevention and Deterrence of Terrorist Acts, to name a few of the many Homeland Security curricula for law enforcement training in today's world.

With training and experience, the airport law enforcement officer's focus becomes very sharp, and he is intimately aware of the threats our nation's airports face. In the 2013 Los Angeles Airport screening lane attack, airport law enforcement knew what it took to neutralize a threat inside our airports. However, each incident like this brings an urgency to find solutions to prevent similar security breaches. I found many possible solutions after researching and writing executive summaries of intelligence reports and Homeland Security briefings. Coupled with my experiences and training, I advocated for a hardening of our nation's airports' security.

In my profession, it was difficult to write a book that presents pointed declarations of security failures throughout our countries airports. The airport managers and security professionals work hard to protect the public, but it's not enough. The issues and problems I present in this book are the results of systemic failures that grew throughout the history of our aviation industry and not of any failure of the dedicated men and women who serve in law enforcement. This book is a journal of what I have seen and learned. It is my greatest hope that it will serve as a tool to challenge the decision makers to institute the necessary changes that will make our nation's airports the safest in the world. As airport management and law enforcement add extensive security improvements to my airport, I can only stress that they accelerate their efforts for the greater good and safety of their constituents and serve as a model to other airports.

END NOTES

1. Don Delillo "The Names," (New York: Vintage Books, A Division of Random House, Inc., 1989), pp. 254

2. A.G. Lamplugh, British Aviation Insurance Group, London, 1930's, Dave English Great Aviation Quotes website, http://www.skygod. com/quotes/safety.html

3. Bill Gates, "Aviators: The Wright Brothers," Time Magazine; "The Century's Greatest 100 Minds," March 29, 1999

4. U.S. Travel Association Press Release, "U.S. Travel Praises Pistole, Congress for Handling of LAX Shooting," U.S. Travel Association President and CEO Roger Dow March 27, 2014, https://www. ustravel.org/news/press-releases/us-travel-praises-pistole-congress-handling-lax-shooting

5. Dr. Richard Stimson, "Worlds First Cargo Flight Creates New Paradigm of Transportation," The Wright Stories, http://wright-stories.com/worlds-first-cargo-flight-creates-new-paradigm-of -transportation/

6. Joe Richard Francis, "The 10 Longest Non-Stop Flights from New York," Hopper Blog, http://www.hopper.com/articles/854/ the-10-longest-non-stop-flights-from-new-york

7. Federal Aviation Administration, "FAA Aerospace Forecast, Fiscal Years 2016-2036," March 16, 2016

8. Federal Aviation Administration, "FAA Aerospace Forecast, Fiscal Years 2016-2036," March 16, 2016

9. Federal Aviation Administration, "The Economic Impact on Civil Aviation on the U.S. Economy," pp. 3, 4, 5, 15, June 2014, U.S. Department of Transportation, https://www.faa.gov/air_traffic/publications/media/2014-economic-impact-report.pdf

10. SelectUSA, Travel, Tourism & Hospitality Spotlight, 2017, https://www.selectusa.gov/travel-tourism-and-hospitality-industry-united-states

11. Gerald J. Arpey, "Appreciation," American Way American Airlines, April 15, 2009, http://hub.aa.com/en/aw/vantage-point-04-15-2009

12. Airports for the Future, "America's Airports, Where Job Creation Takes Off," http://airportsforthefuture.org/did-you-know/

13. John Wayne Airport, "Economic Impact Analysis," ocair.co/news-room, Updated 10/09/2012, http://www.ocair.com/newsroom/facts/economic_impact.pdf

14. National Intelligence Council, National Intelligence Estimate: The Terrorist Threat to the US Homeland, pp. 6, July 2007, http://news.findlaw.com/hdocs/docs/terrorism/nie71707terrorthreat-risk.pdf

15. Gabriel Weimann, YaleGlobal, June 4, 2009; War by Other Means: Econo-Jiahd; http://yaleglobal.yale.edu/content/econo-jihad

16. Emily Gersema, 'Attack on an airline or airport could cost the economy billions in losses,' February 9, 2017, USC News, http://news.usc.edu/116174/attack-on-an-airline-or-airport-could-cost-the-economy-billions-in-losses/

17. Muhammad Qasim, "On The Road To Khilafah," AZAN Magazine, Issue 1, pp. 14-15, March 2013, www.wrs.vcu.edu/ARTICLES/ JIHADISM/azan-magazine-issue-1.pdf

18. Gerald Dillingham, "Aviation Security, Vulnerabilities Still Exist in the Aviation Security System," Government Accountability Office Report # GAO/T-RCED/AIMD-00-142, pp. 2, April 6, 2000, http://www.gao.gov/assets/110/108370.pdf

19. Peter L. Bergen, "The Osama bin Laden I Know: An Oral History of al Qaeda's Leader," The Deuce Of Clubs Book Club, 2006, http:// www.deuceofclubs.com/books/219osama.htm

20. IntelCenter, al-Qaeda Arabian Peninsula's (AQAP) Qasim al-Rimi Video Indicator of Upcoming Attack Against Americans, "Message to the American Nation," June 2, 2013, http://intelcenter.com/ reports/AQAP-ThreatWarning-2Jun2013.html

21. Rand Corporation, "Near-Term Options for Improving Security at Los Angeles International Airport," Donald Stevens, Terry Schell, Thomas Hamilton, Richard Mesic, Michael Scott Brown, Edward Wei-Min Chan, Mel Eisman, Eric V. Larson, Marvin Schaffer, Bruce Newsome, John Gibson, Elwyn Harris, pp. 7, prepared for Los Angeles World Airports, 2004 http://trid.trb.org/view.aspx?id=795902

22. Maurice Tugwell, "Terrorism and Propaganda: Problem and Response," Conflict Quarterly, The Journal of Conflict Studies, The Gregg Centre For the Study of War and Society, pp. 5, http:// journals.hil.unb.ca/index.php/JCS/article/view/14713/15782

23. CNN Wire Staff, Hussein Saddique, Susan Candiotti, Julian Cummings, Nneji, "JFK bomb plot trial begins in New York," CNN

U.S. Edition, June 30, 2010, http://www.cnn.com/2010/US/06/30/new.york.jfk.bomb.plot.trial/

24. Emanuel Levy, "John Wayne: The Making of an American Icon," May 11, 2007, http://emanuellevy.com/comment/john-wayne-the-making-of-an-american-icon-3/

25. Tunde Balvanyos, Lester B. Lave, "The Economic Implications of Terrorist Attack on Commercial Aviation in the USA," Center for Risk and Economic Analysis of Terrorism Events (CREATE) under grant number EMW-2004-GR-0112, September 4, 2005, http://www.usc.edu/dept/create/assets/002/51831.pdf

26. R. Barry Johnston and Oana M. Nedelescu, "The Impact of Terrorism on Financial Markets," International Monetary Fund, IMF Working Paper WP/05/60, pp. 6-7, March 2005 http://www.imf.org/external/pubs/ft/wp/2005/wp0560.pdf

27. Susan Berfield, "Subway Chaos and the Man Who Saw It Coming," Bloomberg Businessweek Companies & Industries, October 31, 2012 http://www.businessweek.com/articles/2012-10-31/subway-chaos-and-the-man-who-saw-it-coming

28. Cletus C. Coughlin, Jeffrey P. Cohen, Sarosh R. Khan, "Aviation Security and Terrorism: A Review of the Economic Issues," pp. 10, The Federal Reserve Bank of St. Louis, September/October 2002, http://research.stlouisfed.org/publications/review/article/2339

29. Grace Bello, "Flight delays continue across US after LAX shooting," 4 WSMV-TV Nashville, November 2, 2013, http://www.wsmv.com/story/23859801/flight-delays-continue-across-us-after-lax-shooting

30. Jon Boone, "Heavy fighting at Karachi airport as militants and security forces clash," June 8, The Guardian, 2014, http://www.theguardian.com/world/2014/jun/08/karachi-airport-attacked-militants -pakistan

31. Michael Wynne, "Aviation: a crucial component of America's strength," Remarks to the Aero Club, Washington D.C., May 22, 2008, http:// www.af.mil/AboutUs/Speeches/Display/tabid/268/Article/143951/ aviation-a-crucial-component-of-americas-strength.aspx

32. Aerospace Industries Association, "NextGen: The Future of Flying," pp. 2, Mark Zandi, Chief Economist for Moody's Economy.com http://www.aia-aerospace.org/assets/brochure_aia_nextgen.pdf

33. Sheldon H. Jacobson, "Watching through the "I"s of aviation security," pp. 1, Springer Science Business Media, LLC 2011, Published online: June 23, 2011

34. Conor Gaffey, "Al-Shabab Looks to the Skies for Its Next Attack," Newsweek, March 1, 2016 http://www.newsweek.com/ al-shabaab-kenya-airlines-432018

35. Brent Smith, Ph.D., "A Look at Terrorist Behavior: How They Prepare, Where They Strike," National Institute of Justice, Office of Justice Programs, http://www.nij.gov/journals/260/pages/ terrorist-behavior.aspx

36. Kathleen Deloughery, Ryan D. King, Victor Asal, "Understanding Lone actor Terrorism: A Comparative Analysis with Violent Hate Crimes and Group based Terrorism," Report to the Resilient Systems Division, Science and Technology Directorate, U.S. Department of Homeland Security. College Park, MD: START, September 2013,

https://www.start.umd.edu/pubs/START_IUSSD_Understanding
LoneactorTerrorism_Sept2013.pdf

37. John Cornyn, U.S. Senator for Texas, News Releases, "Sen. Cornyn
    To President Obama: Recognize that Ft. Hood Attack Likely Act
    of Islamist Terrorism," November 17, 2009 http://www.cornyn.
    senate.gov/public/index.cfm?p=NewsReleases&ContentReco
    rd_id=7a857906-652d-44f8-b189-2f85d3ba921c

38. U.S. District Court, "Criminal Complaint U.S. versus Joshua
    Ryne Goldberg," September 10, 2015, https://www.scribd.com/
    doc/280138804/Bomb-plot-indictment

39. Patrick Frye, "ISIS IN AMERICA: 2015 map shows terrorist threats
    in California, New York, Minnesota – many are not Arab/Middle
    Eastern men," December 4, 2015, http://www.inquisitr.com/2609896/
    isis-in-america-2015-map-terrorist-threats-in-california-new-york-
    minnesota-not-arab-middle-eastern-men/

40. Jim Holt, 'Iranian Revolutionary Guards Commander Admits to
    Having Terror Cells Situated and Ready to Strike in U.S.,' February 26,
    2017, http://sgtreport.com/2017/02/iranian-revolutionary-guards-
    commander-admits-to-having-terror-cells-situated-and-ready-
    to-strike-in-us-video/

41. Kuwait News Agency, "IS, al-Qaeda target US aviation
    sector – US intelligence official," July 15, 2015, http://www.kuna.
    net.kw/ArticleDetails.aspx?id=2512228&Language=en

42. Criminal Complaint, United States District Court, United States
    of America v. Adam Dandach, Docket No. SA14-252M Violation of
    Title 18, United States Code, Section 1542 July 3 2014

43. Theresa Walker, "Hs ISIS reached O.C.? Arrest here intensifies questions," Orange County Register, August 30, 2014, http://www. ocregister.com/articles/dandach-633351-isis-orange.html

44. Mark Clayton, "Too much terrorism data? Connecting the dots may be getting harder," May 23, 2013, NBC News Investigations, first appeared on CSMonitor.com http://investigations.nbcnews.com/_ news/2013/05/23/18427431-too-much-terrorism-data-connecting the-dots-may-be-getting-harder

45. Transportation Security Administration, TSA.gov/travel/security-screening May 26, 2016

46. The FBI's Terrorist Watchlist Nomination Practices, U.S. Department of Justice, Office of the Inspector General, Audit Division, Audit Report 09-25 May 2009. http://www.justice.gov/oig/reports/ FBI/a0925/final.pdf

47. Karen Zeigler, Steven A. Camarota, "Immigrant Population Hits Record 42.1 Million in Second Quarter of 2015," August 2015, Center for Immigration Studies, http://cis.org/Immigrant-Population-Hits-Record-Second-Quarter-2015

48. The FBI's Terrorist Watchlist Nomination Practices, U.S. Department of Justice, Office of the Inspector General, Audit Division, Audit Report 09-25 May 2009, http://www.justice.gov/oig/ reports/FBI/a0925/final.pdf

49. CBS4 News Denver, "FBI Director: 'ISIS Using Online Tactics To Recruit Americans," August 21, 2014, http://denver.cbslocal. com/2014/08/21/fbi-director-isis-using-online-tactics-to-recruit-americans/

50. Alan Gathright, "19-year-old Arvada woman, Shannon Maureen Conley, charged with aiding ISIS terror group, FBI says," ABC 7News Denver, July 3, 2014, http://www.thedenverchannel.com/news/local-news/19-year-old-colorado-woman-shannon-mauree n-conley-charged-with-aiding-terrorist-group-fbi-says07022014

51. Raffi Khatchadourian, 'Azzam The American,' January 22, 2007, The New Yorker, http://www.newyorker.com/magazine/2007/01/22/ azzam-the-american

52. Jason Burke, "Adam Gadahn: California death metal fan who rose quickly in al-Qaida's ranks," April 23, 2015, The Guardian, http://www. theguardian.com/world/2015/apr/23/adam-gadahn-drone-strike-al -qaida

53. "Muslim Journeys | Item #109: The American Mosque 2011 Report", January 11, 2015 http://bridgingcultures.neh.gov/muslimjourneys/ items/show/109

54. "Muslim Journeys | Item #109: The American Mosque 2011 Report", January 11, 2015 http://bridgingcultures.neh.gov/muslimjourneys/ items/show/109

55. Robert Satloff, "Just Like Us! Really, Gallup says only 7 percent of the world's Muslims are political radicals. Yet 36 percent think the 9/11 attacks were in some way justified," The Weekly Standard Magazine online, May 12, 2008, http://www.weeklystandard.com/Content/Public/Articles/000/000/015/066chpzg. asp?page=2#

56. Gwladys Fouche, "Fewer than 100 Americans probed for fighting in Syria, Iraq: U.S. Attorney General," Reuters, July 8, 2014, http://www.reuters.com/article/2014/07/08/us-syria-crisis-usa-fighting -idUSKBN0FD19T20140708

57. Erick Stakelbeck, "ISIS in America: Radicalized in the Heartland," CBN News, October 27, 2014, http://www.cbn.com/cbnnews/us/2014/October/ISIS-in-America-Radicalized-in-the-Heartland/

58. James Meek & Lee Ferran, "L.A. Gang Members in Syria: Organized Crime, Terrorism 'Converge'," ABC News March 3, 2014, http://abcnews.go.com/Blotter/la-gang-members-syria-organized-crime-terrorism-converge/story?id=22757254

59. Robert Windrem, Pete Williams, "American Died in Suicide Bombing in Syria," March 28, 2014, NBC News, http://www.nbcnews.com/news/investigations/american-died-suicide-bombing-syria-u-s-officials-say-n116491

60. Proteus USA, "55 Trends Now Shaping the Future of Terrorism," Volume 1, Issue 2, February 2008, Shtulman, David, "The Terrorist Art of the Possible,"

61. Kenneth F. McKenzie, Jr., "The Rise of Asymmetric Threats: Priorities for Defense Planning,"The Institute for National Strategic Studies National Defense University, McNair Paper 62, Chapter 3, pp.75, http://kms2.isn.ethz.ch/serviceengine/Files/ESDP/101010/ichaptersection_singledocument/101f39d5-6580-4e66-a186-c840ee989772/en/Chap03.pdf

62. Gail Wesson, "Riverside: Two followers in terrorist plot are sentenced," The Press Enterprise, http://www.pe.com/articles/santana-762500-gojali-attorney.html

63. The Religion of Peace, "Islamic Terror Attacks on American Soil,' http://www.thereligionofpeace.com/pages/americanattacks.htm

64. LaFree, Gary, and Bianca Bersani, "Hot Spots of Terrorism and Other Crimes in the United States, 1970 to 2008," Final

Report to Human Factors/Behavioral Sciences Division, Science and Technology Directorate, U.S. Department of Homeland Security. College Park, MD: START, January 31, 2012, https://www.documentcloud.org/documents/288925-hot-spots-of-terrorism-and-other-crimes-in-the.html

65. Ben Shapiro, "8 Reasons to Close The Border Now, The Threat of Terrorism," Breitbart.com, July 8, 2014, http://www.breitbart.com/big-government/2014/07/08/8-reasons-to-close-the-border-now/

66. The Judicial Watch Blog, "Terrorist Wanted by FBI Crossed Back and Forth Into U.S. From Mexico," December 8, 2014, http://www.judicialwatch.org/blog/2014/12/al-qaeda-terrorist-wanted-fbi-crossed-back-forth-u-s-mexico/

67. United States Department of Justice, "North Carolina Man Charged with Conspiring to Provide Material Support to ISIL," August 4, 2016, National Security Division (NSD) USAO – Ohio, Northern

68. The Yucatan Times (Mexico) Report, "Hezbollah operative with U.S. citizenship arrested in Mexico," September 10, 2012, http://www.theyucatantimes.com/2012/09/hezbollah-suspected-terrorist-arrested-in-merida/

69. WSBTV Atlanta Channel 2 News; "Channel 2 Uncovers Proof Terrorists Crossed Mexican Border," November 2, 2010, http://www.wsbtv.com/news/news/channel-2-uncovers-proof-terrorists-crossed-mexica/nFDhw/

70. Allen West, 'Congressman says ISIS will use southern border to enter US: Muslim prayer rug found on Arizona border," Allen West.com, July 11, 2014, http://allenbwest.com/2014/07/

congressman-says-isis-will-use-southern-border-enter-us-muslim-prayer-rug-found-arizona-border/

71. By AFP, "Islamic State recruiting in Canada, local imam warns," The Telegraph, August 23, 2014, http://www.telegraph.co.uk/news/worldnews/northamerica/canada/11052667/Islamic-State-recruiting-in-Canada-local-imam-warns.html

72. Michael Pearson, Paul Vercammen, "LAX shooting suspect pleads not guilty," CNN U.S. Edition, December 26, 2013, http://www.cnn.com/2013/12/26/justice/lax-shooting-arraignment/

73. Wikipedia, "2002 Los Angeles International Airport Shooting," July 4, 2015, https://en.wikipedia.org/wiki/2002_Los_Angeles_International_Airport_shooting

74. Leah Barkoukis, "In New Video, ISIS Warns Paris-style Attack on US 'Isn't Far,'" March 9, 2016, http://townhall.com/tipsheet/leahbarkoukis/2016/03/09/englishspeaking-isis-jihadi-warns-america-they-will-be-attacked-very-soon-n2130917

75. Mark Hosenball, "U.S. has 55 daily encounters with "suspected terrorists." Reuters, May 16, 2012, http://www.reuters.com/article/2012/05/16/uk-usa-watchlists-idUSLNE84F00Z20120516

76. Grace Jean, "First New U.S. Airport Built Since 9/11 Gets Off the Ground," November 2005, National Defense Industrial Association, http://www.nationaldefensemagazine.org/archive/2005/November/Pages/First_New5524.aspx

77. Penny Jones, 'The Threat Within,' airport-technology.com, August 24, 2009, http://www.airport-technology.com/features/feature62043/

78. Perry A. Russel, Frederick W. Preston, "Airline Security After The Event, Unintended Consequences and Illusions," American Behavioral Scientist, Vol. 47, No. 11, July 2004, 2004 Sage Publications

79. Tom Murphy, "New U.S. airport designs specialize in 'security that you can't see,' June 3, 2008, The New York Times International Business, http://www.nytimes.com/2008/06/03/business/worldbusiness/03iht-terminal.4.13437493.html?_r=0

80. Tom Murphy, "New U.S. airport designs specialize in 'security that you can't see,' June 3, 2008, The New York Times International Business, http://www.nytimes.com/2008/06/03/business/worldbusiness/03iht-terminal.4.13437493.html?_r=0

81. Tom Dempsey, "Original KCI designer: New terminal could have dangerous possibilities," March 23, 2016, 41 KSHB Kansas City, http://www.kshb.com/news/local-news/original-kci-designer-new-terminal-could-attract-terrorists

82. Tom Dempsey, "Aviation Leaders: New terminal at KCI 'more convenient' than current design," April 12, 2016, 41 KSHB Kansas City, http://www.kshb.com/news/local-news/aviation-leaders-new-terminal-at-kci-more-convenient-than-current-design

83. Lyn Horsley, "Transportation Security Administration calls for KCI security changes," July 15, 2016, http://www.kansascity.com/news/politics-government/article89845862.html

84. Annika Smethurst, "Airport chiefs fear queues outside terminals are ripe for terror attack," Daily Telegraph, August 26, 2017, http://www.dailytelegraph.com.au/news/nsw/airport-chiefs-fear-

queues-outside-terminals-are-ripe-for-terror-attack/news-story/02f
eb4f19074efc646d8b9583873f4cc

85. Brian Michael Jenkins, "Aviation Security, After Four Decades, It's Time for a Fundamental Review," 2012

86. Brian Michael Jenkins, "Aviation Security, After Four Decades, It's Time for a Fundamental Review," 2012

87. University of Pennsylvania Law Review, Vol. 125:1134, 1977

88. Terry L. Schell, Brian G. Chow, Clifford Grammich, "Designing Airports for Security: An Analysis of Proposed Changes at LAX," RAND Corporation,

89. Aghahowa Enoma, Stephen Allen & Anthony Enoma (2009) Airport redesign for safety and security: Case studies of three Scottish airports, International Journal of Strategic Property Management, 13:2, 103-116

90. Penny Jones, Raffi Ron, "The Threat Within," August 24, 2009, Airport-technology.com http://www.airport-technology.com/features/feature62043/

91. Penny Jones, Raffi Ron, "The Threat Within," August 24, 2009, Airport-technology.comhttp://www.airport-technology.com/features/feature62043/

92. ACI Advisory Bulletin, "Landside Security," May 19, 2016

93. Aghahowa Enoma, Stephen Allen & Anthony Enoma (2009) Airport redesign for safety and security: Case studies of three Scottish

airports, International Journal of Strategic Property Management, 13:2, 103-116

94. ACI Advisory Bulletin, "Landside Security," May 19, 2016

95. ACI Advisory Bulletin, "Landside Security," May 19, 2016

96. ACI Advisory Bulletin, "Landside Security," May 19, 2016

97. Perry A. Russell, Frederick W. Preston, "Airline Security After The Event, Unintended Consequences and Illusions," American Behavioral Scientist, Vol. 47, No. 11, July 2004, 2004 Sage Publications

98. Perry A. Russell, Frederick W. Preston, "Airline Security After The Event, Unintended Consequences and Illusions," American Behavioral Scientist, Vol. 47, No. 11, July 2004, 2004 Sage Publications

99. Alan Black, "Managing The Aviation Insider Threat," Thesis; Naval Postgraduate School, December 2010, https://www.hsdl.org/?view&did=11539

100. Tome Curry, "Insider Threat To Aviation: More Than Terrorism," The Container, October 29, 2014, http://blogs.rollcall.com/the-container/insider-threat-to-aviation-more-than-terrorism/

101. William Watkinson, "Russian plane ash: 'Bomb in handbag' brought down MetroJet Russian passenger jet," January 29, 2016, http://www.ibtimes.co.uk/russian-plane-crash-bomb-handbag-brought-down-metrojet-russian-passenger-jet-1540915

102. Associated Press, "Somalia plane blast: airport worker 'handed device to bombing suspect', February 7, 2016, http://www.theguardian.com/world/2016/feb/08/somalia-plane-blast-airport-worker-handed-device-to-bombing-suspect

103. The Daily Mail.com, "French eject 70 terror suspect airport workers," November 2, 2006, http://www.dailymail.co.uk/news/article-414114/French-eject-70-terror-suspect-airportworkers

104. Rory Mulholland, "Seventy Paris airport workers have security passes revoked over extremism fears,' December 13, 2015, http://www.telegraph.co.uk/news/worldnews/europe/france/12048335/Seventy-Paris-airport-workers-have-security-passes-revoked-over-extremism-fears.html

105. Sullivan, Mike, "British Airways staff in second 'terror' arrest," The Sun, March 4, 2010, http://www.thesun.co.uk/sol/homepage/news/2877333/British-Airways-staff-in-second-terror-arrest.html

106. Steven Goff, "The Insider Threat to Airport Security," The National Interest Magazine, March 14, 2013, http://nationalinterest.org/commentary/the-insider-threat-airport-security-8217

107. The Local Germany, "Frankfurt man loses airport job over ISIS links," January 29, 2015, http://www.thelocal.de/20150129/frankfurt-airport-isis-terrorism-links-security

108. Steve Swann, "Rajib Karim: The terrorist inside British Airways," BBC News, February 28, 2011, http://www.bbc.com/news/uk-12573824

109. Bali Discovery Tours, "Indonesia Tightens Aviation Security," September 5, 2009, http://www.balidiscovery.com/messages/message.asp?Id=5473

110. CBC News Canada, "Large airports infiltrated by crime groups, RCMP report says," December 11, 2008, with files from the Associated Press, http://www.cbc.ca/news/canada/large-airports-infiltrated-by-crime-groups-rcmp-report-says-1.756216

111. Tom Lyden, "Insider Threat: Side-by-side with a future terrorist at MSP Airport," Myfox9.com, KMSP-TV/Minneapolis-St. Paul, November 26, 2014, http://www.myfoxtwincities.com/story/27399922/insider-threat-side-by-side-with-a-future-terrorist-at-msp-airport

112. 'America's Airports: The Threat From Within,' February 2017, HOUSE HOMELAND SECURITY COMMITTEE MAJORITY STAFF REPORT

113. Mike Pompeo, "FBI: Man spent months planning bomb plot at ICT," U.S. Congressman Mike Pompeo website, December 13, 2013, United States District Court For The District of Kansas, United States of America v. Terry L. Loewen Criminal Complaint Case Number: 13-M-6261 01-KMH, filed December 13, 2013, http://pompeo.house.gov/news/documentsingle.aspx?DocumentID=364598

114. Marty Griffin, "Dozens of TSA employees, Fired, Suspended For Illegal Gambling Ring At Pittsburg Int'l Airport" CBS Pittsburg KDKA2, September 19, 2013, http://pittsburgh.cbslocal.com/2013/09/19/dozens-of-tsa-employees-fired-suspended-for-illegal-gambling-ring-at-pittsburgh-intl-airport/

115. U.S. Department of Homeland Security, "Combating the Insider Threat," May 2, 2014, https://www.us-cert.gov/sites/default/files/publications/Combating%20the%20Insider%20Threat_0.pdf

116. http://en.wikipedia.org/wiki/Lufthansa_heist

117. N.J. Burkett, "5 Reputed Mobsters To Be Charged In Lufthansa Heist," Eyewitness News ABC 7 WABC-TV New York, January 23, 2014, http://7online.com/archive/9404377/

118. Scott Carmichael "JetBlue miserably fails TSA security test—ships random package for $100 Cash," Gadling Travel Blog, January 15, 2011, http://gadling.com/2011/01/15/jetblue-miserably-fails-tsa-security-test-ships-random-package/

119. Hillary Jackson, "Inside job: LAX cargo clerk key to suitcase drug smuggling ring?" July 15, 2015, mynewsla.com, http://mynewsla.com/crime/2015/07/15/former-lax-employee-arrested-for-alleged-role-in-drug-ring/

120. Associated Press, "Flight attendant and former Miss Jamaica World runner-up who 'fled LAX because she had two suitcases full of cocaine worth $3 million is arrested at JFK," March 23, 2016, http://www.dailymail.co.uk/news/article-3507041/Flight-attendant-ditched-heels-fled-LAX-security-nabbed.html

121. Jorge Milian, "Delta Airlines employee arrested at PBIA with $282,000 in backpack," March 28, 2016, http://www.palmbeachpost.com/news/news/crime-law/delta-air-lines-employee-arrested-at-pbia-with-282/nqtTd/

122. Mosi Secret, "New York Times, Baggage Handler Who Smuggled Cocaine in Planes Is Sentenced to Life," October 16, 2012, The New York Times, http://www.nytimes.com/2012/10/17/nyregion/jfk-baggage-handler-who-smuggled-cocaine-in-planes-gets-life-term.html?_r=0

123. Dennis Romero, "LAX Is Going Cocaine Crazy," April 5, 2016, LA Weekly, http://www.laweekly.com/news/lax-is-going-cocaine-crazy-6792077

124. Adolfo Flores, "TSA screener sentenced for role in drug smuggling operation at LAX," Los Angeles Times Newspaper, September 22, 2014, http://www.latimes.com/local/lanow/la-me-ln-tsa-screener-who-oversaw-drug-smuggling-operation-at-lax-sentenced-20140922-story.html

125. Adam Parris-Long, "Exclusive: Luton Airport Terror Cop Sacked for taking cocaine," March 28, 2016, Lutton News Herald & Post, http://www.lutontoday.co.uk/news/crime/exclusive-luton-airport-terror-cop-sacked-for-taking-cocaine-1-7288832

126. Robert F. Worth, "Defendants in drug ring and still behind in rent," New York Times, November 27, 2003, http://www.nytimes.com/2003/11/27/nyregion/defendants-in-drug-ring-and-still-behind-in-rent.html

127. Richard Esposito, Lee Ferran, ABC News; The Bourne Sentencing: Dirty Airline Employee Gets Life, October 2012

128. Mosi Secret, "New York Times, Baggage Handler Who Smuggled Cocaine in Planes Is Sentenced to Life," October 16, 2012, The New York Times, http://www.nytimes.com/2012/10/17/nyregion/

jfk-baggage-handler-who-smuggled-cocaine-in-planes-gets-life
-term.html?_r=0

129. Paul Thompson, "Baggage Handlers Arrested For Drug Trafficking in San Diego Sting," FlightClub Blog, March 18, 2014, http://flightclub. jalopnik.com/baggage-handlers-arrested-for-drug-trafficking-in-san-d-1546126260

130. Ashely Fantz, Holly Yen, Kevin Conlon, "DA: Guns smuggled on planes in Atlanta an 'egregious' security breach," CNN News, December 30, 2014, http://www.cnn.com/2014/12/23/us/delta-employee-gun-smuggling/

131. Mike Clary, "59 Workers Indicted in Drug Sting at Airport," Los Angeles Times, August 26, 1999, http://articles.latimes.com/1999/aug/26/news/mn-3814

132. FBI, "Two San Francisco International Airport Security Screeners Charged in Bribery and Drug Smuggling Scheme," San Francisco Division, March 6, 2015, Northern District of California, http://www.fbi.gov/sanfrancisco/press-releases/2015/two-san-francisco-international-airport-security-screeners-charged-in-bribery-and-drug-smuggling-scheme

133. U.S. Immigration and Customs Enforcement's News Release, "2 charged in drug smuggling scheme involving Philadelphia International Airport," ICE.gov, August 9, 2013, https://www.ice.gov/news/releases/2-charged-drug-smuggling-scheme-involving-philadelphia-international-airport

134. Airliners.net discussion forum, "Topic Redacted Airlines Gang Bin Graffiti," February 22, 2006, http://www.airliners.net/aviation-forums/general_aviation/read.main/2618098

135. Airliners.net; Forum on Alaskan Airlines Gangs; http://www.airliners.net/aviation-forums/general_aviation/read.main/2618098

136. Los Angeles World Airports, Patrol Services Section Office of Operations, http://www.lawa.org/AirportPolice/Operations.aspx?id=4607

137. Susan Bourette, "Gangs infiltrate Canada's airports," December 16, 2008, The Christian Science Monitor, http://www.csmonitor.com/World/2008/1216/p06s01-wogn.html

138. Bart Jansen, "Congested airport ramps risky before and after flights," USA TODAY, http://www.usatoday.com/story/news/nation/2014/12/17/airport-ramp-safety-airlines-iata-faa-osha-ntsb/18597565/

139. Wendy Fry, "Jet Fuel Driver Arrested After Driving Tanker While Drunk: Harbor Police," , NBC Channel 7 News, May 13, 2015, http://www.nbcsandiego.com/news/local/Jet-Fuel-Driver-Arrested-After-Driving-Tanker-While-Drunk-Harbor-Police-303676521.html

140. Emily Shapiro, "American Airlines Pilot Arrested After Failing Breathalyzer Test at Detroit Airport," March 26, 2016, ABC News, http://abcnews.go.com/US/american-airlines-pilot-arrested-failing-breathalyzer-test-detroit/story?id=37949289

141. Robert F. Worth, "Defendants in drug ring and still behind in rent," New York Times November 27, 2003, http://www.nytimes.com/2003/11/27/nyregion/defendants-in-drug-ring-and-still-behind-in-rent.html

142. WCBS 880 Exclusive, "Contractor Dies After Shooting Up Heroin With Woman At Newark Airport," March 6, 2016, CBS News New York, http://newyork.cbslocal.com/2016/03/06/newark-security-breach/

143. Mosi Secret, "In Bags at J.F.K., Handlers Found Niche for Crime," The New York Times, *December 9, 2011, Jo Graven McGinty contributed reporting, http://www.nytimes.com/2011/12/10/nyregion/cocaine-smuggling-case-shows-airline-baggage-handlers-misconduct.html? pagewanted=all*

144. GSG Computer Support Group, "Aviation Turbine Fuel, (Jet Fuel)," www.csgnetwork.com/jetfuel.html

145. Charles G. Slepian, "An Inside Examination of Airport Security," Foreseeable Risk Analysis Center, December 2, 2004. http://frac.com/security-negligence/2004/12/2/an-inside-examination-of-airport-security.html

146. Susan Ladika, "12/05 HR Magazine: Meth Madness," SHRM Society For Human Resource Management, December 1, 2005, University of Arkansas 'Drugs in the Workplace Methamphetamine Study' by Katherine Decker, http://www.shrm.org/publications/hrmagazine/editorialcontent/pages/1205cover.aspx

147. Fili Sagapoluele, "Update: Two plead guilty to drug charges in Honolulu," Samoan News, November 13, 2013, http://www.samoanews.com/node/78947

148. Kyle Iboshi, "Hundreds of TSA workers failed drug, alcohol tests, including 6 at PDX," April 5, 2017, KGW.com, http://www.kgw.com/

news/investigations/hundreds-of-tsa-workers-failed-drug-alcohol-tests-at-airports-across-us/428913091

149. Bruce R. Talbot, "General Population Drug Use Statistics," New Page 1, Drug Abuse Recognition Training, Use Statistics, http://drugrecognition.com/Use%20Statistics.htm

150. U.S. DEPARTMENT OF HEALTH AND HUMAN SERVICES Substance Abuse and Mental Health Services Administration Center for Behavioral Health Statistics and Quality, "Results from the 2013 National Survey on Drug Use and Health: Summary of National Findings, September 2014, http://www.samhsa.gov/data/

151. William Herrin interview

152. National Institute on Drug Abuse Info-Facts: Workplace Resources; Revised July 2008, http://www.drugabuse.gov/related-topics/drug-testing/drug-free-workplace-resources

153. Brian Watt and Erika Aguilar, "Despite years of security upgrades, LAX baggage theft remains a problem," March 27, 2014, KPCC 89.3 California Public Radio, http://www.scpr.org/news/2014/03/27/43097/despite-years-of-security-upgrades-airport-bagage/

154. Joe Yogerst, "Best and Worst Airlines for Lost Luggage," Travel & Leisure Magazine, February 2013, http://www.travelandleisure.com/articles/best-and-worst-airlines-for-lost-luggage

155. G.W.H. van Es, "Analysis of aircraft weight and balance related safety occurrences," National Aerospace Laboratory NLR, Report no. NLR-TP-2007-153, pp. 10, unclassified, based on a paper

presented at 19th annual European Aviation Safety Seminar (EASS) March 12-14, 2007 Amsterdam, the Netherlands, www. skybrary.aero/bookshelf/books/1149.pdf

156. Katie Johnston, "Union says Logan Airport companies broke law," The Boston Globe, June 8, 2013, http://www.bostonglobe. com/business/2013/06/07/union-files-unfair-labor-practice-complaints-against-logan-contractors/6NRZlW0l1Tp fQafa5vbnDL/story.html

157. Tim Gigelske, "Confessions Of...A Baggage Handler," September 2007, Budget Travel.com http://www.budgettravel.com/feature/ 0709_How_BaggageHandler,646/

158. Nerea Marteche Solans, Employee Theft From Passengers At U.S. Airports: An Environmental Criminology Perspective, January, 2013, Rutgers State University Dissertation submitted to the Graduate School for the degree of Doctor of Philosophy Graduate Program in Criminal Justice written under the direction of Dr. Ronald V. Clarke; C.P. Rosenbaum, T.L. Baumer, C.P. (1984) Combating retail theft: Programs and strategies, Boston, MA: Butterworth

159. Hollinger, R. D., & Clark, J. P. (1983), *Theft by employees*, Lexington, MA: Lexington Books

160. Marcus Felson, Rachel Boba, *Crime & Everyday Life*, pp. 20, 2010, Sage Publications

161. Charles G. Slepian, 'An Inside Examination of Airport Security,' Foreseeable Risk Analysis Center: December 2004. http://frac.com/ security-negligence/2004/12/2/an-inside-examination-of-airport-security.html

162. Press Release, June 2013, 25th Annual Retail Theft Survey; Jack L. Hayes International, Inc. Consultants in Asset Protection & Safety, http://hayesinternational.com/news/annual-retail-theft-survey/

163. Neal Trautman, "How & Why a Department or Jail Becomes Corrupt,"http://webcache.googleusercontent.com/search?q=cache: yqLVIo8p29IJ:alibi.com/media/docs/howto_corrupt. pdf+&cd=10&hl=en&ct=clnk&gl=us

164. Wesley Juhl, '3 baggage handlers facing charges after luggage thefts at McCarran airport,' February 8, 2017, Las Vegas Review-Journal, http://www.reviewjournal.com/crime/3-baggage-handlers-facing-charges-after-luggage-thefts-mccarran-airport

165. Airliners.net; Forum on Alaskan Airlines Gangs; http://www. airliners.net/aviation-forums/general_aviation/print.main?id= 2622264

166. Nunn, Lawrence and Great Britain, Police Research Group, "Crime investigation in a commercial environment : airports," Police Research Group, Home Office, [London], 1992

167. Martin Gill, Editor, "The Handbook of Security," Authors of Chapter 9 "Employee Theft & Staff Dishonesty;" pp. 203, Richard C. Hollinger and Jason L. Davis, Palgrave Macmillan, 2006

168. Jan Shury, David Vivian, Alistair Kuechel, Sian Nicholas, Mark Speed, "Crimes against retail and manufacturing premises: Findings from the 2002 Commercial Victimization Survey," pp. 2-3, Research, Development and Statistics Directorate, London, UK: Home Office.

169. Nunn, Lawrence and Great Britain, Police Research Group, "Crime investigation in a commercial environment : airports," Police Research Group, Home Office, [London], 1992

170. Nick Squires, "Italian airport baggage handlers caught stealing on camera," May 3, 2013, The Telegraph, http://www.telegraph.co.uk/news/worldnews/europe/italy/10036600/Italian-airport-baggage-handlers-caught-stealing-on-camera.html

171. CBS New York; "Exclusive The stunning JFK airport baggage scandal; 200 thefts per day, Sources: Baggage Handlers, Jetway Workers, Security All In On Ongoing Scam," Newyor.cbslocal.com, March 26, 2012, http://newyork.cbslocal.com/2012/03/26/exclusive-the-stunning-jfk-airport-baggage-scandal-200-thefts-per-day/

172. United States Department of Transportation Bureau of Transportation Statistics, Office of Airline Information Number 251 Part 234.6, Mishandled Baggage Reports, Issue Date: December 5, 2000, http://www.rita.dot.gov/bts/sites/rita.dot.gov.bts/files/subject_areas/airline_information/accounting_and_reporting_directives/number_251.html

173. SITA & Air Transport World, '2016 Air Transport Industry Insights, The Baggage Report, April 2016.

174. SITA, "Airline Bag Delivery Hits All-Time High," www.sita.aero March 26, 2014, http://www.sita.aero/content/Airline-bag-delivery-hits-all-time-high

175. U.S. Department of Transportation, '4th Quarter 2015 Airline Financial Data,' May 2, 2016

176. Scott T. Mueller, "The Truth And The Causes Behind Airline Mishandled Luggage Statistics," Author of 'The Empty Carousel,' March 3, 2011, http://theemptycarousel08.wordpress.com/2011/03/03/the-truth-and-the-causes-behind-airline-mishandled-luggage-statisitics/

177. Scott T. Mueller, "The Truth And The Causes Behind Airline Mishandled Luggage Statistics," Author of 'The Empty Carousel,' March 3, 2011, http://theemptycarousel08.wordpress.com/2011/03/03/the-truth-and-the-causes-behind-airline-mishandled-luggage-statisitics/

178. Scott T. Mueller, "The Truth And The Causes Behind Airline Mishandled Luggage Statistics," Author of 'The Empty Carousel,' March 3, 2011, http://theemptycarousel08.wordpress.com/2011/03/03/the-truth-and-the-causes-behind-airline-mishandled-luggage-statisitics/

179. Marcus Felson, Rachel Boba, *Crime & Everyday Life*, pp. 20, 2010, Sage Publications

180. Nerea Marteche Solans, "Employee Theft From Passengers At U.S. Airports: An Environmental Criminology Perspective," January, 2013, Rutgers State University Dissertation, pp. 155, submitted to the Graduate School for the degree of Doctor of Philosophy Graduate Program in Criminal Justice written under the direction of Dr. Ronald V. Clarke, Retrieved from http://dx.doi.org/doi:10.7282/T3W957WQ

181. Boyle, Matthew, "Laura Ingraham: Airport workers stole my baptismal cross!," The Daily Caller, July 18, 2011, http://dailycaller.com/2011/07/18/laura-ingraham-airport-workers-stole-my-baptismal-cross/

182. SITA Chief Executive Officer Francesco Vilante, "Baggage Report 2012,"

183. Wifredo A. Ferrer, U.S. Attorney, "Two Men Arrested In Connection With The Theft Of Gold Bars At Miami International Airport," United States Department of Justice Press Release Southern District of Florida, June 7, 2013 http://www.justice.gov/usao/fls/PressReleases/2013/130607-01.html

184. The Wall Street Journal, "When Sticky Fingers Handle Your Bags," December 17, 2009, http://www.wsj.com/articles/SB200014 24052748703581204574599953475913542

185. Scott McCartney, "Latest Airport Hassle: Carousel Crooks." The Wall Street Journal, December 18, 2009, http://www.wsj.com/news/articles/SB10001424052748703581204574599953475913542?mod=_newsreel_2

186. Erica Nochlin, "Police Arrest 4 adults, 2 children accused of stealing airport luggage," KATU News, January 7, 2013, KVAL.com, http://www.kval.com/news/local/Police-arrest-4-adults-2-children-accused-of-stealing-airport-luggage-185874802.html

187. Jeff Goldman, "Newark man with 40 prior arrests accused of stealing luggage at airport." The Star-Ledger, NJ.com, May 29, 2014, http://www.nj.com/essex/index.ssf/2014/05/newark_man_with_40_prior_arrests_accused_of_stealing_luggage_at_airport.html

188. Harriet Baskas, "Phoenix airport hikes security in baggage claim, Travelers concerned over Security after 1,000 bags lifted from carousels," Baskas; msnbc.com contributor/travel writer NBCNEWS.com, http://www.nbcnews.com/id/33833245/ns/

travel-travel_tips/t/phoenix-airport-hikes-security-baggage
-claim/#.VKbUeXs8p2A

189. Brian Maass, "DIA bag thief charged, suspected of stealing Peter Frampton's luggage," CBS4 TV, CBSDenver,
November 26, 2013, http://denver.cbslocal.com/2013/11/26/
dia-bag-thief-charged-suspected-of-stealing-peter-framptons
-luggage/

190. Brian Maass, "Bag Bandit strikes while CBS4 conducts interview on airport baggage thefts," CBS4 TV, CBSDenver,
November 27, 2013, http://denver.cbslocal.com/2013/11/27/
bag-bandit-strikes-while-cbs4-conducts-interview-on-airport-
baggage-thefts/

191. Bambi Vincent, "Bag Theft Epidemic at Atlanta Airport Carousel,"
Thief Hunters in Paradise Blog, September 25, 2012, http://bobarno.
com/thiefhunters/atlanta-airport-luggage-theft-at-baggage-claim/

192. Richard N. Velotta, " Delta running pilot program at McCarran
to curb baggage thefts," Vegasinc.com, December 24, 2013,
http://www.vegasinc.com/business/2013/dec/24/delta-running-
pilot-program-mccarran-curb-baggage-/

193. West Orlando News Online; "Orlando Airport to upgrade baggage claim area after luggage thefts," Westorlandonew.com,
September 20, 2012, http://westorlandonews.com/2012/09/20/
orlando-airport-to-upgrade-baggage-claim-area-after-luggage-
thefts/

194. BBC News, "Moscow bombing: Carnage at Russia's Domodedovo
airport," January 24, 2011, http://www.bbc.com/news/world-
europe-12268662

195. ASAC Meeting Minutes, Attachment C: Public Comment, NATIONAL ASSOCIATION OF AIRLINE PASSENGERS - A Review of the Final Report of the Aviation Security Advisory Committee's Working Group on Airport Access Control, November 20, 2015

196. Kirchenbaum, Alan, Michele Marini, Coen Van Gulijk, Sharon Lubasz, Carmit Rapaport, and Hinke Andriessen. "Airport Security: An Ethnographic Study," Journal of Air Transport Management, 18 (1). pp. 68-73. ISSN 0969-6997

197. Steven Goff, "The Insider Threat to Airport Security," The National Interest Magazine, March 14, 2013, http://nationalinterest.org/commentary/the-insider-threat-airport-security-8217

198. Amy Hollyfield, "SFO Pilot Exposes Airport Security Flaws," ABC7 News, December 22, 2010, http://abc7news.com/archive/7859952/

199. Frank, Thomas, USA Today; "TSA boosts checks on airport workers." March 28, 2007

200. Brian Summers, "For employees, LAX airport security is built on trust," October 19, 2013, Dailybreeze.com, http://www.dailybreeze.com/general-news/20131019/for-employees-lax-airport-security-is-built-on-trust

201. Richard Edwards, "Terrorist threat to airports over lax staff security," The Telegraph, July 22, 2008, http://www.telegraph.co.uk/news/uknews/2444844/Terrorist-threat-to-airports-over-lax-staff-security.html

202. BBC, "Terror manuals woman avoids jail," December 6, 2007, http://news.bbc.co.uk/2/hi/uk/7130495.stm

203. Becky Oliver, "Investigation: Airport Security," Fox 4 Investigation, Myfoxdfw.com, February 20, 2013, http://www.myfoxdfw.com/story/21290524/investigation-airport-security

204. Scott Friedman, "Airline, Airport Employees Caught abusing Security Badges," NBCDFW-News5, April 30, 2013, http://www.nbcdfw.com/investigations/Airline-Airport-Employees-Caught-Abusing-Security-Badges-205288061.html

205. The United States Attorney's Office Southern District of Texas Press Release, "Airport Employee Sent to Prison for Smuggling Heroin," June 24, 2013, http://www.justice.gov/usao/txs/1News/Releases/2013%20June/130624%20-%20Escober.html

206. U.S. Immigration and Customs Enforcement, "Former Houston airport employee sentenced to 9 years in prison for heroin smuggling," June 23, 2013, News Release Narcotics, http://www.ice.gov/news/releases/former-houston-airport-employee-sentenced-9-years-prison-heroin-smuggling

207. Mary Beth Quirk, "5 Airline Employees Accused of Smuggling Cash Through Boston Airport In Money Laundering Sting," Consumerist.com, May 30, 2014 http://consumerist.com/2014/05/30/5-airline-employees-accused-of-smuggling-cash-through-boston-airport-in-money-laundering-sting/

208. U.S. Attorney Michael Wheat, "Office of the United States Attorney Southern District of California, San Diego, California, March 17, 2014, http://www.justice.gov/usao/cas/press/2014/cas14-0317-airportBaggage.html

209. Jorge Milian, "Delta Airlines employee arrested at PBIA with $282,000 in backpack," March 28, 2016, Palm Beach Post, http://

www.palmbeachpost.com/news/news/crime-law/delta-air-lines-employee-arrested-at-pbia-with-282/nqtTd/

210. Staff Report, "FBI arrested Atlanta baggage handler for role in airport gunrunning," WJCL TV, Savannah Georgia, December 24, 2014, http://wjcl.com/2014/12/24/fbi-arrested-atlanta-baggage-handler-for-role-in-airport-gunrunning/

211. ASAC Meeting Minutes, Attachment C: Public Comment, NATIONAL ASSOCIATION OF AIRLINE PASSENGERS - A Review of the Final Report of the Aviation Security Advisory Committee's Working Group on Airport Access Control, November 20, 2015

212. Patricia Carlson, "U.S. Airports Scrutinized: Should You Re-Check Your Employees?" 2015, Active Screening a DBA for Priority Research Corporation, http://www.activescreening.com/u-s-airports-scrutinized-re-check-employees/

213. Charles G. Slepian, 'An Inside Examination of Airport Security,' Foreseeable Risk Analysis Center: December 2004. http://frac.com/security-negligence/2004/12/2/an-inside-examination-of-airport-security.html

214. Diane Ritchey, "Employee Screening Boosts Security at Miami Airport," July 1, 2015, Security Magazine, http://www.securitymagazine.com/articles/86470-employee-screening-boosts-security-at-miami-airport

215. Joe Douglas, "No daily security checks for many PDX employees," May 1, 2015, KATU Channel 2 News, http://www.katu.com/news/investigators/No-daily-security-checks-for-some-PDX-employees-301483461.html

216. Christopher Elliott, "Pilot who posted security flaw video online punished by the TSA," Elliott.org, December 23, 2010, http://elliott.org/blog/pilot-who-posted-security-flaw-video-online-is-punished-by-the-tsa/

217. Bill Keating, "Perimeter Security: Weakest Link in Airport Safety," Press Release, March 1, 2011, Office of Congressman Bill Keating, 9ᵗʰ District of Massachusetts, http://keating.house.gov/index.php?option=com_content&view=article&id=201:perimeter-security-weakest-link-in-airport-safety&catid=14:press-releases&Itemid=13

218. Martha Mendoza, Justin Pritchard, "AP Investigation Details Perimeter Breaches At US Airports," April 9, 2015, Associated Press, http://customwire.ap.org/dynamic/stories/U/US_AIRPORT_INTRUDERS_ABRIDGED?SITE=AP&SECTION=HOME&TEMPLATE=DEFAULT

219. William Herrin, Phoenix Police Department Interview.

220. David Sutta, "Good Jack…Bad Jack… Jesus Jack you're on the runway," NBC2 Crime Investigator Blog, September 14, 2006 http://nbc2crimebeat.blogspot.com/2006/09/good-jack-bad-jack-jesus-jack-youre-on.html

221. USA Today, "Man crashes through airport fence with officers in pursuit," August 8, 2006, http://usatoday30.usatoday.com/travel/flights/2006-08-10-runwaychase_x.htm

222. Pat Gillespie, "Driver cruises airport runway, Fort Myers man crashes airport gate, travels alongside departing jet," The Fort Myers News, August 9, 2006, archives.californiaaviation.org/airport/msg37983.html

223. Ginger D. Richardson, "Airport fences to get upgrade Reinforcing and upgrading Sky Harbor enclosures could cost $10 million," The Arizona Republic, Apr. 8, 2006, http://members.tripod.com/phoenix_copwatch/mud/police-news/cw2824.html

224. My foxalanta.com, "Security Breach at Sky Harbor Airport," November 15, 2012, http://www.myfoxatlanta.com/story/20114187/2012/11/16/security-breach-at-sky-harbor

225. Ray Sanchez, Ben Brumfield, "Inebriated man, cross-dressed man jump airport fences in Newark, Phoenix," CNN U.S., updated December 27, 2013, http://www.cnn.com/2013/12/26/us/new-jersey-airport-security-breach/

226. House Report 114-653 - Airport Perimeter and Access Control Security Act of 2016, July 1, 2016

227. Steve Lord, " Aviation Security, TSA Is Increasing Procurement and Deployment of Advance Imaging Technology, but Challenges to This Effort and Other Areas of Aviation Security Remain," Congressional Accounting Office Homeland Security and Justice Issues, Testimony Before the Subcommittee on Transportation Security and Infrastructure Protection, Committee on Homeland Security, House of Representatives, GAO-10-484T, pp. 4, www.gao.gov/new.items/d10484t.pdf

228. Airports for the Future, "America's Airports, Where Job Creation Takes Off," http://airportsforthefuture.org/did-you-know/

229. Palm Springs Police Interview by Bill Herrin

230. Channel 2 News Palm Springs Airport Shooting video, September 18, 2005 https://www.youtube.com/watch?v=RwYG9i7Vil8

231. Press-Enterprise, "Some Palm Springs Int'l Airport Precautions Can be for Naught," Source: Via Newsedge Corporation, AviationPros.com, http://www.aviationpros.com/news/10406101/some-palm-springs-intl-airport-precautions-can-be-for-naught

232. David H. Ready, "Approval of Plans and Specifications for Airport Perimeter Fence Improvements Phase II Project AIP, Grant No. 48," City of Palm Springs Council Staff Report. July 6, 2011, palmspringsca.gov/Modules/ShowDocument.aspx?documentid=18050

233. TSA, "Recommended Security Guidelines for Airport Planning, Design and Construction," Section Notice, pp. ii, May 2011, www.tsa.gov/airport_security_

234. FAA Airport Fence Wildlife Hazard Specifications: FAA 150/5370-10F. 30 September 2011.

235. TSA Recommended Security Guidelines for Airport Planning, Design and Construction, Revised 1 May 2011.

236. BJ Lutz; "O'Hare Least Secured in Nation, Says Former Security Boss, James Mauer says he was fired last year because he kept raising issues, pressing for more security," 5 NBC Chicago TV, March 3, 2011, http://www.nbcchicago.com/traffic/transit/ohare-security-86249327.html

237. Aaron Karp, 'Truck Rams into Southwest 737 at Omaha Airport Gate,' August 27, 2016 China Aviation Daily, http://www.chinaaviationdaily.com/news/55/55599.html

238. KHOU 11 News I-Team, "Trespasser jumps fence, steals truck with fuel from Hobby Airport," July 24, 2014, http://www.khou.com/story/news/investigations/2014/07/29/12673286/

239. Ronald Rokosz and Charles H Hash, "Changing the Mindset - Army Antiterrorism Force Protection," JFQ Joint Force Quarterly, Autumn/Winter 1997-1998

240. George B. Vold, Journal of Criminal Law and Criminology, Volume 35, Issue 5, Article 1, pp 300,305,307, 1945 Postwar Aviation and Crime

241. NBC 2 WBBH TV, "Foot chase ends on airport tarmac," February 10, 2008, http://www.nbc-2.com/story/10690612/foot-chase-ends-on-airport-tarmac

242. Katie Riordan, "Stranded Jet-Skier Unsuspectingly Breaches $100 Million Airport Security System" The Forum South and West, August 16, 2012, http://theforumnewsgroup.com/2012/08/16/stranded-jet-skier-unsuspectingly-breaches-100-million-airport-security-system/

243. Frederica Cade, "PRESS RELEASE: Kenneth Richard Mazik Charged for Disrupting Services at Philadelphia International Airport, Drove Car on Runway as Airplane Approached for Landing," U.S. Attorney's Office, Easter District of Pennsylvania, Frederica Cade's Blog, March 2, 2012

244. Tengri News TV, Eyewitness Kazakhstan, "Drunk driver shuts down Philadelphia Airport," March 2, 2012, http://en.tengrinews.kz/emergencies/Drunk-driver-shuts-down-Philadelphia-airport--8124/

245. Jelisa Castrodale, "San Jose's most recent security breach proof of American airports' perimeter security issues," April 25, 2015, USA Today Travel, https://usattravel.wordpress.com/2015/04/25/san-joses-most-recent-security-breach-proof-of-american-airports-perimeter-security-issues/

246. Gates L. Scott, "Illegal Usage of General Aviation/ Commercial Aircraft," PilotMag 2008, gateslscott.com, http:// www.gateslscott.com/gates-blog/illegal-usage-of-general-aviation-commercial-aircraft-pilotmag-2008

247. U.S. Attorney Sally Quillan Yates, "Drug Trafficker Sentenced For Distributing High-Grad Marijuana And Cocaine Throughout The United States," Press Release by the United States Northern District of Georgia, December 11, 2012 http://www.justice.gov/ usao/gan/press/2012/12-11-12.html

248. Gates L. Scott, "Illegal Usage of General Aviation/Commercial Aircraft," PilotMag 2008, gateslscott.com, http://www.gateslscott. com/gates-blog/illegal-usage-of-general-aviation-commercial-aircraft-pilotmag-2008

249. The TSA, "Security Guidelines for General Aviation Airport Operators and Users," Information Publication A-002, pp 9, September 11, 2013

250. Bill Roggio, "Suicide bomber kills 10 Afghan students, 2 U.S. Soldiers," The Long War Journal, A Project of the Foundation for Defense of Democracies, June 3,, 2013, http://www.longwarjournal.org/archives/2013/06/suicide_bomber_kills_78.php

251. Julia Love, "Security breach at Mineta San Jose International Airport," The San Jose Mercury News, November 24, 2014, http:// archives.californiaaviation.org/airport/msg53575.html

252. Jeffrey Goldberg, "Private Plane, Public Menace, Wealthy travelers routinely bypass the TSA by flying on private jets. How long until al-Qaeda does the same?," January 4, 2011, The Atlantic, http://www.theatlantic.com/magazine/archive/2011/01/private-plane-public-menace/308335/

253. Robert Wilonsky, 'Jesus' not 'Jihad': Man arrested at Love Field, now in federal custody, told police God had directed him' to airport; The Dallas Morning News, May 1, 2013, http://crimeblog.dallasnews.com/2013/05/jesus-not-jihad-man-arrested-at-love-field-now-in-federal-custody-told-police-god-had-directed-him-to-airport.html/

254. Jeremy Rogalski, General Aviation Security: Assessing Risks and the Road Ahead, Hearing of the Subcommittee on Transportation Security and Infrastructure Protection, Committee on Homeland Security House of Representatives, 111th Congress, July 15, 2009

255. General Aviation Security: Assessing Risks and the Road Ahead, Hearing of the Subcommittee on Transportation Security and Infrastructure Protection, Committee on Homeland Security House of Representatives, 111th Congress, July 15, 2009

256. C. Peter Chen, Tokko "Kamikaze" Special Attack Doctrine http://ww2db.com/other.php?other_id=18

257. WSAZ 3 News, Update: "Five Ashland residents charged in drug trafficking/organized crime ring," September 14, 2016

258. Wikipedia, "2002 Tampa plane crash," Last modified November 16, 2014 http://en.wikipedia.org/wiki/2002_Tampa_plane_crash Anomalies Unlimited http://www.anomalies-unlimited.com/Death/Bishop.html

259. Ron Roble, Undersecretary of the Treasury for Enforcement and Carl Meyer, Special Agent, United States Secret Service The White House Office of the Press Secretary: Press Briefing, Sept. 12, 1994, http://www.presidency.ucsb.edu/ws/?pid=59767

260. The Smoking Gun, "Plane Crash Suspects Diatribe, Posting rages at IRS, claims, I have had all I can stand," The Smoking Gun,

http://www.thesmokinggun.com/documents/crime/plane-crash-suspects-online-diatribe

261. Georgetown Municipal Airport, https://airport.georgetown.org/faq/

262. Amy Taxin, "Woman accused of flight school fraud, Associated Press, November 30, 2011, http://www.boston.com/news/nation/articles/2011/11/30/apnewsbreak_woman_accused_of_flight_school_fraud/

263. Representative Mike Rogers, A Majority Staff Report, "Rebuilding TSA Into A Smarter, Leaner Organization," Subcommittee on Transportation Security Committee on Homeland Security, 112th Congress, pp5, September 2012

264. Representative Mike Rogers, A Majority Staff Report, "Rebuilding TSA Into A Smarter, Leaner Organization," Subcommittee on Transportation Security Committee on Homeland Security, 112th Congress, pp5, September 2012

265. Ed Straker, Middle Eastern nationals currently in flight school 'not being properly vetted,' October 13, 2016

266. ASAC Meeting Minutes, July 28, 2016, https://www.tsa.gov/sites/default/files/asac_meeting_minutes_28jul2016-final.pdf

267. Alien Flight Student Program (AFSP), July 28, 2015, https://www.dhs.gov/sites/default/files/publications/privacy_pia_tsa%20alien%20flight%20student%20program_july%202014.pdf

268. Blain Tamari, "Jordanian Muslim student 'intentionally' crashes plane near major defense contractor," October 12, 2016

269. Andrew Russell, "Peterborough plane crash: Should there be more security at private airports?" Breaking Global News

270. Curt Epstein, Security More Important Than Ever at FBOs, March 16, 2016, http://www.ainonline.com/aviation-news/business-aviation/2016-03-16/security-more-important-ever-fbos

271. State of Maine Airport Managers Study Guide, The Maine Department of Transportation Office of Passenger Transportation, November 1, 2007

272. Matier & Ross, "Nephew up for SFO job despite disciplinary actions," August 25, 2013, SFGate, sister website of the San Francisco Chronicle Hearst-owned, http://www.sfgate.com/bayarea/matier-ross/article/Nephew-up-for-SFO-job-despite-disciplinary-actions-4760282.php

273. Risk Steering Committee, "DHS Risk Lexicon 2010 Edition," U.S. Department of Homeland Security, September 2010, http://www.dhs.gov/dhs-risk-lexicon

274. ASAC Meeting Minutes, Attachment C: Public Comment, NATIONAL ASSOCIATION OF AIRLINE PASSENGERS - A Review of the Final Report of the Aviation Security Advisory Committee's Working Group on Airport Access Control, November 20, 2015

275. Mary Douglas, Aaron Wildavsky, 'Risk and Culture: An Essay on the Selection of Technical and Environmental Dangers, Berkeley: University of California Press, 1982

276. ASAC Meeting Minutes, Attachment C: Public Comment, NATIONAL ASSOCIATION OF AIRLINE PASSENGERS - A Review of the Final Report of the Aviation Security Advisory

Committee's Working Group on Airport Access Control, November 20, 2015

277. Professor Dr. Wolfgang H. Thome, "Strike by Brussels airport police expose the soft underbelly of Europe's aviation security," April 2, 2016, eTN Global Travel Industry News, http://www.eturbonews.com/70018/strike-threats-brussels-airport-police-expose-soft-underbelly-eu

278. Dr. Marvin J. Cetron, and Davies Owen, "55 Trends Now Shaping the Future of Terrorism," Volume 1, Issue 2, Appendix A-2, The Forecasting International Incorporated, private think tank, produced a U.S. Government publication, February 2008, https://www.hsdl.org/?abstract&did=485366

279. Whelan, Chad & Palmer, Darren, "Responding to Terrorism through Networks at Sites of Critical Infrastructure: A Case Study of Australian Airport Security Networks," Paper presented to the Social Change in the 21st Century Conference, pp. 3, October 27, 2006, Queensland University of Technology, Carseldine, Brisbane, http://eprints.qut.edu.au/view/person/Whelan,_Chad.html

280. Committee on Oversight and Government Reform House of Representatives 112th Congress First Session, "TSA Oversight Part 2: Airport Perimeter Security," Serial# 112-75, pp 7, July 13, 2011

281. Committee on Oversight and Government Reform House of Representatives 112th Congress First Session, "TSA Oversight Part 2: Airport Perimeter Security," Serial# 112-75, pp 33-34, July 13, 2011

282. Rafi Ron, Statement by Rafi Ron," President of New-Age Security Solutions Inc., To The House Committee on Oversight and

Government Reforms Subcommittee on National Security, Homeland Defense and Foreign Operations, July 13, 2011

283. Robert W. Poole & Viggo Butler, "Improve Security: Hold airports accountable," pp 1, Cascade Policy Institute, October 2001

284. Andrew Park, Peter Burrows and bureau reports, "What You Don't KnowAboutDell,"BloombergBusinessWeekvMagazine:November 2, 2003, http://www.businessweek.com/stories/2003-11-02/what-you-dont-know-about-dell

285. C. Pearce, J. Conger: Shared Leadership, Reframing the How's and Whys of Leadership, pp xii, Sage Publications, 2002

286. C. Pearce, J. Conger, "Shared Leadership, Reframing the How's and Whys of Leadership," pp 6, Sage Publications, 2002

287. Nanette Monin, Ralph Bathurst, "Mary Follett on the Leadership of Everyman," Ephemera Articles, theory & politics in organization, pp 453, volume 8(4): 447-461

288. George Thomas Kurian, "The AMA Dictionary of Business and Management," pp 73

289. J. O'Toole, J. Galbraith, "When Two (or More) Heads are Better than One: The Promise and Pitfalls of Shared Leadership," E. E. Lawler III, Center for Effective Organizations, Marshall School of Business, University of Southern California, CEO Publication G 02-8 (417), Pp 5, 16, 18, March 2002

290. Sharon W. Erickson, City Auditor, Office of the Auditor; Report to the City Council of San Jose, "Airport Public Safety Level of

Service," Report 11-08, pp 31, October 12, 2011 http://www.sanjo-seca.gov/index.aspx?NID=307

291. Jelisa Castrodale, "San Jose's most recent security breach, proof of American airports' perimeter security issues," April 25, 2015, USA Today, http://roadwarriorvoices.com/2015/04/25/san-joses-most-recent-security-breach-proof-of-american-airports-perimeter-security-issues/

292. Sharon W. Erickson, City Auditor, Office of the Auditor; Report to the City Council of San Jose, "Airport Public Safety Level of Service," Report 11-08, pp 31, October 12, 2011 http://www.sanjo-seca.gov/index.aspx?NID=307

293. Matthew Bunn and Scott D. Sagan, A Worst Practices Guide to Insider Threats: Lessons from Past Mistakes (Cambridge, Mass.: American Academy of Arts and Sciences, 2014). Research Paper, pp. 10, https://www.amacad.org/content/publications/publication.aspx?i=1425

294. TSA, "Visible Intermodal Prevention and Response (VIPR) Office of Law Enforcement/Federal Air Marshal Service," www.TSA.gov

295. Covenant Services Worldwide LLC, "TSA hiring requirements," http://www.covenantsecurity.com

296. Representative Mike Rodgers Subcommittee on Transportation Security Committee on Homeland Security Majority Staff Report, "Rebuilding TSA into a Smarter, Leaner Organization," 112th Congress, September 2012

297. Susan O'Neill, "Security: Is job turnover high at the TSA?" Budget Travel http://www.budgettravel.com/blog/security-is-job-turnover-high-at-the-tsa,9687/

298. TSA Official Website, USAJOBS.gov, March 18, 2016 https://www.usajobs.gov/GetJob/ViewDetails/429751200/

299. WLOX ABC News, "MS TSA official charged in D'Ibervile stabbing," September 20, 2011, http://www.wlox.com/story/15503746/suspect-arrested-in-diberville-stabbing-death

300. Megan Chuchmach, Randy Kreider, Brian Ross, "Convicted TSA Officer Reveals Secrets of Thefts at Airports," September 28, 2012, ABC News, http://abcnews.go.com/Blotter/convicted-tsa-officer-reveals-secrets-thefts airports/story?id=17339513

301. TJ "Jerry" Orr, Aviation Director, Charlotte International Airport, Testimony on the TSA Oversight Part 2: Airport Perimeter Security Hearing before the Subcommittee on National Security, Homeland Defense and Foreign Threats, pp 5, July 8, 2011, http://oversight.house.gov/wp-content/uploads/2012/01/7-13-11_TJ_Orr_TSA_Testimony.pdf

302. Matthew Bunn, Scott D. Sagan, "A Worst Practices Guide to Insider Threats: Lessons from Past Mistakes," American Academy of Arts & Sciences, Research Paper, pp 10, 2014 https://www.amacad.org/content/publications/publication.aspx?i=1425

303. Alex Thomas, "Almost Half of All TSA Employees Commit Misconduct, New Report Says," July 18, 2016, Reason.com, http://reason.com/blog/2016/07/18/almost-half-of-all-tsa-employees-commit

304. Private Officer Breaking News, "Loaded guns allowed on planes after TSA screeners miss them." Privateofficerbreakingnews.blogspot.com, October 1, 2012, http://privateofficerbreakingnews.blogspot.com/2012/10/loaded-guns-allowed-on-planes-after-tsa.html

305. Thomas Frank, "Most fake bombs missed by screeners," USA Today, October 22, 2007, http://usatoday30.usatoday.com/news/nation/2007-10-17-airport-security_N.htm

306. Eric Bradner, Rene Marsh, Acting TSA director reassigned after screeners failed tests to detect explosives, weapons, June 2, 2015, http://www.cnn.com/2015/06/01/politics/tsa-failed-undercover-airport-screening-tests/

307. Bart Jansen, "TSA reacts to 'widespread' failures at Honolulu from 2010," USA Today, October 9, 2012, http://www.usatoday.com/story/todayinthesky/2012/10/09/tsa-honolulu-report/1623029/

308. Tamer El-Ghobashy, "Rape Suspect Carries Stun-Gun Past JFK Security," The Wall Street Journal, March 13, 2013, http://blogs.wsj.com/metropolis/2013/03/13/rape-suspect-carries-stun-gun-past-jfk-airport-security/

309. L.P. Phillips, "Former Dallas FBI Chief: Use TSA Security Breach As Training Video," July 25, 2016, ABC 6 Action News, http://6abc.com/travel/security-breach-caught-on-camera-at-texas-airport/1441821/

310. Francis Kerner, "And Now, a Word from Our Lawyers...," The TSA: Blog, Thursday, February 21, 2008, http://blog.tsa.gov/2008/02/and-now-word-from-our-lawyers.html

311. Common Sense: Wikipedia

312. Holly Millea, "Bradley Cooper plays an appealing rake in He's Just Not That Into You," Elle Magazine, ELLE Pop Culture, Celebrity Spotlight, December 11, 2008, http://www.elle.com/pop-culture/celebrities/high-infidelity-281841

313. Steve Strunsky, "TSA fires 4 screeners, suspends dozens in wake of probe at Newark Liberty airport," The Star-Ledger, NJ.com, March29, 2013, http://www.nj.com/news/index.ssf/2013/03/tsa_announces_dismissals_suspe.html

314. Flyertalk Blog, "9 Airport Screeners Removed From Newark After Failing Tests," Cited source: WNBC 4 News, October19,2004,http://www.flyertalk.com/forum/practical-travel-safety-security-issues/364660-9-airport-screeners-removed-newark-after-failing-tests.html

315. Ron Marsico, "TSA cracks down on screener sick time at Newark airport," March 13, 2005, The Newark (NJ) Star-Ledger, http://archives.californiaaviation.org/airport/msg34259.html

316. Ron Marsico, "Airport screeners fail to see most test bombs," The Seattle Times, October 28, 2006, http://seattletimes.com/html/traveloutdoors/2003327485_screeners28.html

317. CBS New York, "25 TSA Screeners at Newark Airport Being Fired; 19 Suspended," newyork.cbslocal.com, October 19, 2012, http://newyork.cbslocal.com/2012/10/19/44-tsa-workers-at-newark-airport-face-firing-or-suspension/

318. Megan Churchmach, Randy Kreider, Brian Ross, "Convicted TSA Officer Reveals Secrets of Thefts at Airports," NBC News, September 28, 2012, http://abcnews.go.com/Blotter/convicted-tsa-officer-reveals-secrets-thefts-airports/story?id=17339513

319. Megan Churchmach, Randy Kreider, Brian Ross, "Convicted TSA Officer Reveals Secrets of Thefts at Airports," NBC News, September 28, 2012, http://abcnews.go.com/Blotter/convicted-tsa-officer-reveals-secrets-thefts-airports/story?id=17339513

320. Megan Churchmach, Randy Kreider, Brian Ross, "Convicted TSA Officer Reveals Secrets of Thefts at Airports," NBC News, September 28, 2012, http://abcnews.go.com/Blotter/convicted-tsa-officer-reveals-secrets-thefts-airports/story?id=17339513

321. Megan Churchmach, Randy Kreider, Brian Ross, "Convicted TSA Officer Reveals Secrets of Thefts at Airports," NBC News, September 28, 2012, http://abcnews.go.com/Blotter/convicted-tsa-officer-reveals-secrets-thefts-airports/story?id=17339513

322. Jamie Goldberg, "Employee conduct making TSA's shattered public image even worse," Los Angeles Times, August 1, 2012, http://articles.latimes.com/2012/aug/01/news/la-pn-employee-conduct-making-tsas-shattered-public-image-even-worse-20120801

323. Victoria Kim, "TSA screeners allegedly let drug couriers through LAX for cash." Los Angeles Times, April 26, 2012, http://articles.latimes.com/2012/apr/26/local/la-me-tsa-screeners-20120426

324. Fr. Mark Hodges, "Homosexual TSA agent abused his job so he could grope 'attractive' men's genitals," Life Site News, May 12, 2015, https://www.lifesitenews.com/news/homosexual-tsa-agent-abused-his-job-so-he-could-grope-attractive-mens-genit

325. Pierce, Jonathan. "TSA Airport Screeners: Private Contractors or Government Employees" Paper presented at the annual meeting of the Northeastern Political Science Association, Omni Parker House, Boston, MA, Nov 13, 2008 http://citation.allacademic.com/meta/p_mla_apa_research_citation/2/7/6/0/2/pages276023/p276023-1.php

326. GovTrack.us, "S. 1447 (107th): Aviation and Transportation Security Act," September 21, 2001, Civic Impulse, LLC

327. Robert Poole, Bio, http://reason.org/staff/show/robert-poole.html

328. Robert W. Poole, Jr., "Airport Security: Time for a new model," Study 340 Reason, Foundation, January 2006, http://www.policy-archive.org/handle/10207/bitstreams/6021.pdf

329. Shon Agard, "Civilian Aviation Screening: A Time Series Analysis of Confiscated Firearms at Screening Checkpoints," (MS diss. Eastern Kentucky University 2012)

330. Shon Agard, "Civilian Aviation Screening: A Time-Series Analysis of Confiscated Firearms at Screening Checkpoints" (2012). Online Theses and Dissertations. Paper 60.

331. U.S. Travel Association in conjunction with the Blue Ribbon Panel for Aviation Security, "A Better Way, Building A World-Class System For Aviation Security," U.S. Travel Association, https://www.ustravel.org/government-affairs/blue-ribbon-panel

332. Subcommittee on National Security, Homeland Defense and Foreign Operations of the Committee on Oversight and Government Reform, "TSA Oversight Part 2: Airport Perimeter Security Hearing before the Subcommittee on National Security, Homeland Security," House of Representatives One Hundred Twelfth Congress First Session, July 13, 2011, http://www.gpo.gov/fdsys/pkg/CHRG-112hhrg71820/html/CHRG-112hhrg71820.htm

333. The U.S. House of Representatives Committee On Appropriations, Chairman Hal Rodgers, May 7, 2014 Press Release, http://appropria-tions.house.gov/news/documentsingle.aspx?DocumentID=381268

334. Congressional Budget Office Report: "Comparing the Compensation of Federal and Private Sector Employees," Summary Table VIII, January 30, 2012, https://www.cbo.gov/publication/42921

335. Paul Joseph Watson, "Major U.S. Airports to switch to private screeners," Inforwars.com March 14, 2012, the Miami Herald, http://www.infowars.com/major-us-airport-to-evict-tsa-screeners/

336. David Rittgers, "Policy Analysis No. 683, Abolish the Department of Homeland Security," CATO Institute, September 11, 2011

337. Annie Jacobsen; "Why 67,000 TSA Employees Left Their Jobs?" PJMedia.com http://pjmedia.com/blog/why_have_67000_tsa_employees_l/

338. Steve Watson, "Senator Blasts TSA: Fast Food Joints Do Better Employee Background Checks," May 1, 2014, Infowars.com, http://www.infowars.com/senator-blasts-tsa-fast-food-joints-do-better-employee-background-checks/

339. Hugo Martin, "Airlines fill planes to record capacity as demand continues to grow," Los Angeles Times, March 13, 2014, http://www.latimes.com/business/la-fi-mo-airlines-fill-planes-to-record-capacity-20140313-story.html

340. Ronnie Garrett, The Credentialing Challenge, Aviation Pros.com, August 13, 2014 http://www.aviationpros.com/article/11623254/the-credentialing-challenge

341. Yaron Steinbuch, "ISIS teen who killed priest passed background check for airport job," July 29, 2016, New York Post,

342. Timothy W. Drake and Patricia Doersch, "Short-Term FAA Reauthorization Likely Soon," June 20, 2016, https://www.lexology.com/library/detail.aspx?g=5d1070d9-93b6-4ec2-8158-739afc22461b

343. Federal Bureau of Investigation, 'Fingerprints & Other Biometrics,' June 26, 2016, https://www.fbi.gov/about-us/cjis/fingerprints_biometrics/ngi

344. Julia Dahl, "Why wasn't Aaron Alexis prosecuted for previous shooting incidents?" CBS News Crimesider, September 19, 2013; http://www.cbsnews.com/news/why-wasnt-aaron-alexis-prosecuted-for-previous-shooting-incidents/

345. Ed Morrissey, "Background check firm that OK'd Snowden cleared Navy Yard shooter," Hotair.com; September 20, 2013 http://hotair.com/archives/2013/09/20/background-check-firm-that-okd-snowden-cleared-navy-yard-shooter/

346. United States' Complaint, United States of America, Blake Percival vs. U.S. Investigative Services, United States District Court For The Middle District of Alabama Northern Division, Civil Action No. 11-CV-527-WKW, False Claims Act: Breach of Contract, pp 11, January 22, 2014, https://www.documentcloud.org/documents/1009281/usis-complaint.pdf.

347. United States' Complaint, United States of America, Blake Percival vs. U.S. Investigative Services, United States District Court For The Middle District of Alabama Northern Division, Civil Action No. 11-CV-527-WKW, False Claims Act: Breach of Contract, pp 16, January 22, 2014, https://www.documentcloud.org/documents/1009281/usis-complaint.pdf

348. Michael Tennant, "TSA Allowed People with Criminal Records to get Airport Security Badges," The New American Magazine, March 9, 2013, www.thenewamerican.com http://www.the-newamerican.com/usnews/crime/item/14729-tsa-allowed-people-with-criminal-records-to-get-airport-security-badges

349. Transportation Security-Actions Needed to Address Limitations in TSA's Transportation Worker Security Threat Assessments and Growing Workload, pp 28, Report to Congressional Committees, December 2011, GAO 12-60, United States Government Accountability Office.

350. Mark Weiner, "Katko leads reform effort after TSA clears 73 airport workers with terrorism ties," June 15, 2015, Syracuse News, http://www.syracuse.com/politics/index.ssf/2015/06/katko_leads_reform_effort_after_tsa_clears_73_airport_workers_with_terrorism_tie.html

351. Transportation Security Clearinghouse; Services: Aviation Overview, https://www.tsc-csc.com/aviation/index.cfm

352. FBI, The National Crime Prevention and Privacy Act of 1998, October 9, 1998

353. GAO: Transportation Security-Actions Needed to Address Limitations in TSA's\ Transportation Worker Security Threat Assessments and Growing Workload, pp 17, Report to Congressional Committees, December 2011, GAO12-60, United States Government Accountability Office.

354. Congressional Accountability Office; 'Transportation Security: Actions Needed to Address Limitations in TSA's Transportation

Worker Security Threat Assessments and Growing Workload,' pp 43, December 8, 2011, http://www.gao.gov/assets/590/586758.html

355. The National Crime Prevention and Privacy Compact "Frequently Asked Questions," May 2015

356. Beth Givens, Director Privacy Rights Clearinghouse; Privacy Roundtables-Comment, Project No. P095416, Submitted to the Federal Trade Commission April 14, 2014

357. Bob Sullivan, "Criminal background checks incomplete, How convicted felons can slip through safety net," Security on NBC News. com, April 12, 2005, http://www.nbcnews.com/id/7467732/ns/ technology_and_science-security/t/criminal-background-checks -incomplete/#.VMmrCi48p2A

358. Pierce, Jonathan. "TSA Airport Screeners: Private Contractors or Government Employees" Paper presented at the annual meeting of the Northeastern Political Science Association, Omni Parker House, Boston, MA, Nov 13, 2008 <Not Available>. 2014-11-30 http://citation.allacademic.com/meta/p276023_index.html

359. Lyttle Law Firm, "Immigrants Receive Warning About California Driver's Licenses," January 1, 2015, http://www. austinimmigrationlawyerblog.com/2015/01/immigrants- receive-warning-california-drivers-licenses.html

360. NumbersUSA, Map of States With E-Verify Laws, May 27, 2016, https://www.numbersusa.com/resource-article/everify-state-map

361. Kelly Yamanouchi, "ICE employee screening program" June 26, 2017, The Atlanta Journal-Constitution

362. Points Passport, 'What Is The Airline Security Fee?' September 19, 2015, http://pointspassport.co/what-is-the-airline-security-fee/

363. Airlines Economics, "US airlines flat on Q1 2015 but baggage revenue is up,' June 6, 2016 http://www.aviationnews-online.com/airline/us-airlines-flat-on-q1-2015-but-baggage-revenue-is-up/

364. Carly Ledbetter, 'U.S. Airlines Made More Than $6.5 Billion in Baggage And Reservation Fees in 2014,' May 15, 2015 http://www.huffingtonpost.com/2015/05/07/how-do-airlines-make-money_n_7232450.html

365. Fox News; "Longtime security supervisor arrested at NJ airport for using dead man's ID," May 14, 2012, http://www.foxnews.com/us/2012/05/14/longtime-security-supervisor-arrested-at-nj-airport-for-using-dead-man-id/

366. F.B.I., 'Fingerprints and other Biometrics,' June 26, 2013, https://www.fbi.gov/about-us/cjis/fingerprints_biometrics/ngi

367. Transportation Security Administration, 'Disqualifying Offenses," June 25, 2016, tsa.gov https://www.tsa.gov/disqualifying-offenses-factors

368. National Security Advisor Holds Press Briefing, The White House, President George W. Bush, Office of the Press Secretary, May 16, 2002. http://georgewbush-whitehouse.archives.gov/news/releases/2002/05/20020516-13.html

369. The Cannon Report, "Leaders V. Managers," September 8, 2014, Official Newsletter of the Michigan Company of Military Historians & Collectors.

370. Brendan I. Koerner, "We're going to bomb Oak Ridge: The hijacking that gave us airport security." June 19, 2013, Slate Magazine,

http://www.slate.com/articles/life/history/features/2013/sky-jacker_of_the_day/louis_moore_hijacked_a_plane_to_teach_the_city_of_detroit_a_lesson.html

371. History Commons, "Context of 1993-1994: Expert Panel Predicts Terrorists Will Use Planes as Weapons on Symbolic US Targets," http://www.historycommons.org/context.jsp?item=a93planesaswea pons&scale=1#a93planesasweapons

372. Los Angeles Times, "Terrorists plotted to blow up 11 U.S. jumbo jets," May 28, 1995 http://articles.baltimoresun.com/1995-05-28/news/1995148047_1_bojinka-philippines-plot

373. Paul Matt, "Complete 911 Timeline, The 1995 Bojinka Plot" History Commons, http://www.historycommons.org/timeline.jsp? warning_signs:_specific_cases=bojinka&timeline=compl ete_911_timeline

374. Gavin De Becker, "The Gift of Fear," (New York: Dell Publishing, 1997), pp. 194

375. Keith Ross, "How many fighters does ISIS have?" February 26, 2015, The Week, vocative, http://theweek.com/articles/540989/how-many-fighters-does-isis-have

376. Joel Gunter and agencies, "Iraq crisis: what is the Islamic State?" The Telegraph, June 11, 2014, http://www.telegraph.co.uk/news/world-news/middleeast/iraq/10891387/Iraq-crisis-what-is-the-Islamic-State.html

377. Josh Meyer, "Shocking Unpreparedness by Belgians: Ex-Official," March 22, 2016, NBC News, http://www.nbc-news.com/storyline/brussels-attacks/shocking-unpreparedness-belgians-ex-official-n543286

378. Kuwait News Agency, "IS, al-Qaeda target US aviation sector – US intelligence official," July 15, 2015, http://www.kuna.net.kw/ArticleDetails.aspx?id=2512228&Language=en

379. Greta Van Sustern, "American ISIS Fighter Worked At Minneapolis Airport for 10 Years," September 3, 2014, Fox News insider, the official blog of Fox News Channel as *seen On The Record, Fox News, September 3, 2014,* http://insider.foxnews.com/2014/09/03/american-isis-fighter-worked-minneapolis-airport-10-years

380. Patrick Frye, "ISIS In America: 2015 Map Shows Terrorist Threats In California, New York, Minnesota – Many Are Not Arab/Middle Eastern Men," December 15, 2015, Inquisitr, http://www.inquisitr.com/2609896/isis-in-america-2015-map-terrorist-threats-in-california-new-york-minnesota-not-arab-middle-eastern-men/

381. Eliott C. McLaughlin, "ISIS jihadi linked to Garland attack has long history of hacker," CNN News, May 7, 2015, http://www.cnn.com/2015/05/06/us/who-is-junaid-hussain-garland-texas-attack/

382. Susan Page, "CIA veteran Morell: ISIS' next test could be a 9/11-style attack," USA Today, May 11, 2015, http://www.usatoday.com/story/news/politics/2015/05/10/michael-morell-cia-the-great-war/27063655/

383. Richard Engel, James Novogrod, Michele Neubert, "Exclusive: American Extremist Reveals His Quest to Join ISIS", September 3, 2014, http://www.nbcnews.com/storyline/isis-terror/exclusive-american-extremist-reveals-his-quest-join-isis-n194796

384. Julian Hattem, "Analysis: US support for ISIS 'unprecedented'," December 1, 2015, thehill.com http://thehill.com/

policy/national-security/261597-unprecedented-support-f
or-isis-in-us-analysis-claims

385. Edwin Mora, "FBI Director: ISIS Tentacles Reach Into All 50 U.S. States," February 26, 2015, Breitbart, http://www.breitbart.com/big-government/2015/02/26/fbi-director-isis-tentacles-reach-into-all-50-u-s-states/

386. Nicole Duran, "DHS chief: 'Homegrown' terrorists, not foreigners, are his top worry," July 14, 2016, The Washington Examiner, http://www.washingtonexaminer.com/dhs-chief-homegrown-terrorists-not-foreigners-are-his-top-worry/article/2596484

387. William Herrin: Airport personnel statement to William Herrin

388. KHOU Staff, KHOU 11 News I-Team; "Trespasser jumps fence, steals truck with fuel from Houston Airport," July 18, 2014, http://www.khou.com/story/local/2014/12/18/12673286/

389. Raymond B. Biagini, Dana B. Pashkoff, Scott Gibbons, "Cincinnati/No. Kentucky International First to Obtain Federal Safety Act Coverage," pp 30-32 Airportmagazine.net, December 2011/January 2012 http://issuu.com/aaae/docs/airport-dec2011-jan2012

390. Dino Hazell, "Gunman Holds Crew, Passengers Hostage for Several Hours," Associated Press; Spartanburg Herald- Journal, July 29,2000 http://news.google.com/newspapers?nid=1876&dat=20000728&id=oj8fAAAAIBAJ&sjid=4M8EAAAAIBAJ&pg=6906,4872406

391. Stephanie Michaud, 'LAX cops demand armed officers at security,' July 14, 2016, http://mynewsla.com/crime/2016/07/14/lax-cops-demand-armed-officers-at-security/

392. Sean O'Neill, Budget Travel's Blog, "Theft from baggage: The TSA responds to our readers," The Budget Travel's Blog The latest travel news, vacation tips & advice, travel apps and more, May 2007, http://www.budgettravel.com/blog/theft-from-baggage-the-tsa-reponds-toour-readers,9834/

393. Richard C. Steiner, Director United States General Accounting Office, Office of Special Investigations, April 28, 1994, www.gao.gov/assets/90/83795.pdf

394. Kuwait News Agency, "IS, al-Qaeda target US aviation sector – US intelligence official," July 15, 2015, http://www.kuna.net.kw/ArticleDetails.aspx?id=2512228&Language=en

395. Conor Gaffey, "Al-Shabab Looks to the Skies for Its Next Attack," Newsweek, March 1, 2016, http://www.newsweek.com/al-shabaab-kenya-airlines-432018

396. Fox News, "Hands off' list? Senator questions whether DHS allowing those with terror ties into US," Published May 7, 2014, http://www.foxnews.com/politics/2014/05/08/hands-off-list/